THE POLITICAL ECONOMY
OF THE SOCIAL SCIENCES

GARLAND LIBRARY OF SOCIOLOGY
General Editor: Dan A. Chekki
(VOL. 19)

GARLAND REFERENCE LIBRARY
OF SOCIAL SCIENCE
(VOL. 699)

GARLAND LIBRARY OF SOCIOLOGY
General Editor: Dan A. Chekki

THE POLITICAL ECONOMY
OF THE SOCIAL SCIENCES

Frederick H. Gareau

GARLAND PUBLISHING, INC. • NEW YORK & LONDON
1991

Library of Congress Cataloging-in-Publication Data

Gareau, Frederick H. (Frederick Henry).
   The political economy of the social sciences / Frederick H.
Gareau.
      p. cm. —(Garland library of sociology ; vol. 19) (Garland
reference library of social science ; vol. 699)
   Includes bibliographical references and index.
   ISBN 0–8240–7267–7 (alk. paper)
   1. Social sciences—Research—Political aspects. I. Title.
II. Series. III. Series: Garland reference library of social
science ; v. 699.
H62.G254   1991
300'.72—dc20   91–4357
                                                          CIP

Printed on acid-free, 250-year-life paper
Manufactured in the United States of America

THIS WORK

IS DEDICATED TO

KASPER AND TO KARL, MY FATHER AND MY SON,

WHO WENT BEFORE ME, BUT WHO LEFT BEHIND A RICH MORAL

AND EMOTIONAL LEGACY AND TO EDNA, WHO REMAINS WITH ME,

A LOYAL AND INSPIRING PARTNER.

CONTENTS

TABLES

PREFACE OF THE GENERAL EDITOR

The social sciences as they are taught and practiced in each society are largely products of the complex sociocultural system. The sociology of sociology examines the significant role of sociocultural variables in the production and development of different types of knowledge about social phenomena. The importance of this intricate relationship has been more or less underestimated by a large majority of social scientists. Max Weber was very much concerned about the nature of scientific inquiry in the social sciences. He also discussed differences between the natural and social sciences and recognized that social forces are involved to a greater extent in the social sciences. Gunnar Myrdal argued that the social sciences in any country are part of a cultural system and cannot transcend the values and assumptions of this system.

This volume presents a panoramic comparative, historical, and critical view of the social sciences around the world. By adopting the political economy/structuralism perspective the author evaluates the salient features of social science and suggests that the contemporary social science enterprise is greatly influenced by government and elites. Professor Gareau rejects the dichotomy between the practioners of social and natural sciences and the rest of humanity and considers social scientists within the contours of society.

It is observed that during the past four decades the United States as dominant and political superpower and as the world's premier educator has had its major impact in disseminating American social science paradigms in the second and third worlds. It is argued that the governmental and other dominant elites discourage revolutionary paradigms and in general support the status quo. The prohibition of unwanted paradigms (e.g.) the non-Marxist in the Soviet Union and the Marxist in the United States) and the promotion and financing of preferred paradigms indicate how political elites and funding agencies control the nature and growth of the social sciences.

The multinational approach adopted by the author exposes the myth-laden social science as presented in "cook book" form and considers all paradigms as legitimate. The social sciences are considered as part of the knowledge industry subsidized by governments and influenced by them. According to the author, the economics of the social science industry favors the rich over the poor, the capitalized over the non-capitalized, and results in dependencies in international contexts.

Although many social scientists pride themselves on the international and universal character of their discipline and profession, it is noted that social science is a diverse and sectarian enterprise with several contemporary self-proclaimed orthodoxies. The American social science, as opposed to physics for example, tends to be nationalistic, ideological, ethnocentric and biased toward the white commonwealth and against the second and third worlds. The communication system of the American social science indicates a disporportionate percentage of the incoming channels to American social science are domestic rather than foreign. American social science journals have an ethnocentric bias both in the authorship and in the type of articles included. The empirical evidence presented by the author provides support to the nonscientific model of social science.

Because of America's dominant economic and political power in the global context, American social science has become world social science and the international reference models are the dominant American paradigms. The rich first world centers have established vertical relations not only with the poor and the underdeveloped third world peripheries but some semiperipheral affluent countries such as Canada have become recipients of American paradigms. However, in recent years, the third world has been revolting against first world domination. Gareau believes that the movement for the indigenization of social science in the third world, as exemplified by dependency theory, will reinforce the nonconsensual nonscientific nature of social science for the forseeable future.

The author observes an apparent contradiction between the nationalism/ethnocentrism and the internationalization of social science and raises the question: How can we resolve this apparent contradiction between third world indigenization and more open, universal social science? For Gareau this contradiction can be resolved if we perceive this nationalism/ethnocentrism as a necessary and transitory stage during which the third world countries regain their authenticity so as later voluntarily to cooperate internationally, on a horizontal basis. Of course, there is a possibility that his indigenization stage may be cut short at the nationalistic ethnocentric stage.

This volume takes its stand with the critical humanist brand of political economy and by looking outward to the social sciences around the world, it seeks to enhance our intellectual horizons. Professor Frederick Gareau, Florida State University, by providing a fairly comprehensive review of the evolution and contemporary state of multinational version of the social sciences, makes an important contribution to that as yet largely unwritten critical sociological history of the social sciences in the global context. It is a valuable book that should be of great interest to all committed and concerned social scientists.

DAN A. CHEKKI
University of Winnipeg

PREFACE

In 1989 Eastern Europe exploded in a series of revolutions whose far reaching consequences are daily becoming clearer. The manner in which the present volume interprets the consequences for social science of these revolutions and the previous changes in the Soviet Union which allowed these revolutions to take place reveals much about the approach to social science of this volume. In the broadest meaning of the term, this approach is external, not internal. This means that the social sciences are not seen essentially as intellectual exercises isolated from societal and elite influence. They are not treated as laissez-faire enterprises, in which the best generally rise to the top. The typical role of governmental elites is not portrayed merely as providing a favorable setting for the development of our disciplines, and then sitting back to let the "private sector" take over. Governmental and other elites take a much more active role in the development of our disciplines, forbidding some paradigms (the typical totalitarian/authoritarian technique) and encouraging others (the liberal approach, typical of elites in the free world). Both techniques have been used in Eastern Europe and the Soviet Union, with significant impacts upon our disciplines, as seen below in chapter VI.

The volume does to the social sciences what they do to others. It uses social science to analyze and to explain social science. This has been called the sociology of sociology, or more broadly the social science of social science. This last term is more descriptive here, because the volume employs a type of structuralism, which features several disciplines. The approach is best understood when contrasted with its opposite -- the one which assumes that social science proceeds by logic and the interpretations of research findings, in essential isolation from the social impacts which affect all other professions and other institutions. This latter approach divides humankind into two unequal groups -- the practitioners of science -- social and natural --

and the remainder of humankind. Scientists are privileged, the superpeople of modern times -- outside the grasp of societal forces and elite interests. The rest of humankind is seen as impacted by these forces and interests. The volume rejects this dichotomy, even when put in attenuated form. The latter sees societal forces acting only as a catalyst, which can encourage a discipline, but which does not encourage one paradigm over competing ones. The volume does not reduce social scientists to dependent variables, but they are put within the contours of society and human interest.

The volume does not pursue the issue of whether the natural sciences are, or to what extent they are, impacted by societal forces and elite interests. But it does draw a distinction between the natural sciences and social science. This is done in chapter IV. Over twenty studies are used there to generate data on the incoming communications system of American social science. This system is shown to be ethnocentric and biased toward English, the white commonwealth, and against the second and the third worlds. The communications of American physics is shown to be different, as are the characteristics usually imputed to science. The incoming communications of Western Europe, and even more so the third world, are disproportionally American. Thus social science communications greatly resemble global mass communications. This leads to the conclusion that both are impacted by the same forces. And the American system in both categories is privileged. The same unequal system which the third world complains about for mass communications applies to our disciplines as well.

Our external analysis of the social sciences starts with political economy, i.e. uses the insights from both politics and economics to shed light upon the subject matter. Our disciplines are first presented as economic enterprises (see chapter II). Historically, these enterprises were individualistic, but they underwent a process of capitalization and specialization in the nineteenth century to emerge as multinationals by the twentieth (see chapter III). The social sciences are part of the knowledge industry. They have reached the zenith of their development in the postwar United States, and they have accompanied this great superpower, as it has penetrated the free world politically, economically, and in many other ways as well. The immediate carrier of our disciplines has been education, and the postwar period witnessed the United States emerge as the world's premier educator. Education is controlled by governments even in the free world, and this control provides a channel through which dominant elites impact our disciplines. In chapter II we connect social science to politics and economics -- thus the political economy of social science. Other disciplines are not excluded from the analysis, the method is actually a form of structuralism.

The economic connection is interpreted to mean that the paradigms which are well financed have a competitive advantage over others, one not explained by intrinsic worth. The dominance of US favored paradigms in the postwar period can thus be explained more in terms of wealth, rather than in terms of intrinsic value. No doubt both factors have impact, but in enterprises of such low epistemic value, a competitive economic edge can be decisive. There are those who have argued that American dominant paradigms in the postwar period are becoming the international reference models, and this because of their superior intrinsic worth. This volume offers an alternate explanation. Moreover, the revolt of the third world against the first world includes the social sciences. The future thus seems to offer less consensus than is the case now. This revolt should be fueled and rationalized by paradigms at odds with the status quo, technocratic ones so in vogue in the United States. The fate of the social sciences at least for the immediate future thus promises to be less consensus, rather than the consensus enjoyed by natural science. Social science is not now in the process of maturing, becoming more like natural science. True, dogmatic Marxism has declined in Eastern Europe and the Soviet Union, but a less dogmatic Marxism still lives on, especially in the third world where its future seems especially bright.

In our view, the social sciences are generally tied to governmental and other dominant elites, and in general support the status quo. Reforms are countenanced, but revolutionary paradigms are discouraged. They are either forbidden, or they are discouraged, perhaps underfinanced while the status quo competition is favored. Eastern Europe and the Soviet Union provide obvious examples, but they do not exhaust the possibilities of this relationship. Our disciplines fared badly during the communist period in the second world, particularly during the long era of Stalinism. They often disappeared from academe, or they were reduced to the exegesis of Marxist texts -- at the expense of empirical investigation and analysis based upon it. Social science has a philosophical part, but also an analytic part based upon logic and observation. Second world social science neglected the latter component, as it promoted the positions and the policies of local elites. The critical aspects of Marxism were directed outside to undermine enemy regimes, but not inward to question local regimes or local politics. Sensitive areas and compromising data were off limits to research or were not published. With the Gorbachev regime, the social sciences have changed in the Soviet Union -- a development presented in chapter VI. In fact, they are now serving the interests of the new dispensation. The revolutions in Eastern Europe in 1989 should follow this general line as well -- to strengthen the position and the interests of the new elites.

Note that our interpretation above is not the standard one, what can be called the laissez faire interpretation. This latter view sees the social sciences as emerging and prospering in an environment of freedom, in which governmental and other elites provide a positive environment, but then withdraw to allow the practitioners to set their own course. The volume adopts the multinational version, which does not relegate governmental and other elites, even in the first world, to the sidelines -- to operate merely as catalysts for essentially autonomous disciplines. The exclusion of Marxism from academe for so many years after its founder's death cannot be adequately explained by this approach. Marxism was confined to the working class movement; much later it entered European academe; and even later the American university. The story is told in chapters III and V. We are not saying that the exclusion of non-Marxist paradigms from the educational institutions by Marxist regimes was a mere policy of revenge. Both exclusions reflect the interests and the policies of dominant elites. Furthermore, the history of Marxism and Marxist regimes does reveal two general ways of excluding or greatly weakening unwanted paradigms -- heavy handed prohibition or the more liberal way of promoting and financing preferred paradigms. Both methods were used in both exclusions, but the emphasis varied considerably. Heavy handed prohibition was the obvious method employed in Eastern Europe and the Soviet Union.

The relationship between our disciplines and freedom does not follow the laissez faire interpretation either. These disciplines have proved to be compatible with certain right wing totalitarian/authoritarian settings. True, they have not proved to be compatible with Nazism, the Cultural Revolution in China, and Stalinism and other brands of Communism. But social science flourished and even expanded in Fascist Italy (see chapter VII). Indeed, political science and sociology were institutionalized during the

Mussolini era. American functionalism was adopted during the later years of the Franco dictatorship, and American social science in general has been a prominent import by Latin American dictators, notably those in Brazil (see Chapter VIII). Nor have the social sciences always been on the side of the academic angels of humanism and progress. The case of social Darwinism is well known (see chapter III). Less well known is that social scientists were not in the forefront of the independence movement in India (chapter 8) nor in the Soviet reform movement associated with the name of Gorbachev (chapter VI).

The present volume seeks to strip the myths from the social sciences, and they are encrusted with myths, as is typical of all social institutions. At its best, social science -- especially the critical variety -- performs this valuable function. What is left after the completion of this process in the case of social science is a valuable, an alternate way of interpreting the social scene. In fact, social science offers several alternate ways of interpreting this scene. The present volume could prove especially useful in American academe, because it is a reaction to this setting. Typically, social scientists there present a larger than life portrait of the disciplines with the myths prominently attached and displayed. Criticism of the disciplines or of favored paradigms is often brushed aside as an attack upon "science" and, therefore, the criticism on its face is unacceptable. Such myths are easy to adopt if critical histories of the discipline are ignored or if the social science is presented in "cook book" form.

The last reference is to those books and courses on "how to do science", meaning actually "how to do social science", so popular in the United States. They mix together what the present volume concludes cannot be mixed together, i.e. social and natural science. They introduce the novice to the scientific method: how to define the problem, create a research design, conduct the research, and interpret the results "scientifically". Often their long range purpose is to prod the discipline on until it "matures", to become a "mature science". The present volume has been written to stand on its own, but also to act as the antithesis to confront these kinds of theses. Given the problematic nature of social science, the place of this volume can also be seen as complementary to the cook books on social science. Perhaps these later will improve the practice of social science. The fact that no social science has even matured does not warrant the judgment that none ever will, only the conclusion that such an event is improbable.

This preface ends in a "complementary" spirit -- with the volume paired off with the typical social science cook book to the benefit of the reader. Whereas the typical cook book presents one paradigm, the present volume provides four. Two of these are dogmatic or "scientific", and two are status quo (see chapter V). Two are humanistic, searching for insights rather than "scientific" laws; the other two look forward to radical change. In sociology, these four paradigms are functionalism, radical Marxism, humanist Marxism, and interpretive sociology. They are discussed in order in chapters V, VI, and VII. Each is sited in the area where it is dominant -- in order, in the United States, the second world, and the last two in Western Europe. All our paradigms are accepted as being legitimate. This contrasts with the typical cook book which sets forth rigid requirements for science -- paradigms which do not meet the restrictions are rejected as being "unscientific."

The typical cook book presents what is identified as functionalism in sociology or its equivalent in other disciplines. Those paradigms which do not measure up to the prescribed criteria (the other three presented above) are cast aside as being "unscientific." The present volume prides itself on being accepting and multi-paradigmatic, denying itself this power of excommunication. What may seem like rejection because of non-conformity to scientific criteria appears here as ethnocentrism and intolerance. The present volume also fancies itself as being international, in the spirit of natural science. Thus it presents an analysis of social science in the United States (chapter V), the second world (chapter VI), Western Europe (chapter VII), and the third world (chapter VIII). This contrasts with the American-centric focus of the typical social science cook book. The same disparity emerges in the stress upon history in the present volume. Its chapter III contrasts with the mere passing references to the history of social science found in the typical cook book.

The present volume is intended to produce an expanding, stretching experience -- not an intellectually confining and rigid one. It does this by looking outward to the social sciences around the world and by looking backward to the history of our disciplines. In no area is this outward reach more evident than in the study of third world social sciences. These disciplines are featured in the present volume to stretch and expand intellectual horizons, but for another reason as well. The third world revolt has its social science component, and this revolt should guarantee that world social science will not reach a consensus any time soon, even if the cold war is coming to an end.

Even before the events of 1989, the North/South conflict seemed of greater importance than the cold war. Any estimate of the future impact of this part of the world, the majority of humankind, upon our disciplines challenges the imagination. These third world countries with their diverse interests and often ancient cultures have only begun to put their mark upon our disciplines. The United States is now the world's social science superpower, but history is not at an end. Any estimate of the future course of the history of social science must take account of the majority of humankind.

I wish to thank Florene Ball, Mihali Krassacopoulos, and Mary Schneider for their help in putting the manuscript into shape for publication. Without their industry and competence, this volume would not have been possible. Appreciation is also due to Ali Kazangil, editor of the International Social Science Journal, and to Professor K. Ishwaran, Editor of the International Journal of Comparative Sociology, for their support and intellectual dialogue through the years. I also want to express my deep gratitude to Dona Herminia Marques Alves. Her prayers have been answered.

The Political Economy
of the Social Sciences

CHAPTER I

INTRODUCTION

The reader has the right to ask for justification for the appearance of this volume, the multinational version of social science. We respond with an example, the evaluation of a situation typical in American academe. The young professor asserts that "the literature" demonstrates "scientifically" that foreign aid and foreign investments increase the gross national product, in total or per capita, of the recipient nations. He does not assert, but he does imply, that this is to the benefit of these countries. Of course, he does not review all of the literature on the subject, but several sources are mentioned -- all written in English, all but one by Americans. All references are to scholarly journals, what this volume calls establishment publications, all published domestically. To prove his thesis, the professor concentrates upon a study by professors X and Y: 25 minutes of class time are devoted to elaborating upon the complicated (and boring) research design ingeniously constructed by X and Y. The design, so our professor assures us, is in accord with the latest canons of science, and a sprinkling of references to philosophers of science (Popper and Nagle) seemed to remove any doubt, at least on the part of the students, of the scientific authenticity of the study. They seemed awed by the performance (perhaps they are just bored).

The present volume which focuses on the nature of social science gives guidance on how to evaluate the performance of the young professor. His assertions are regular fare in American academe, and they must be confronted. Ours is no science cookbook, so it cannot help in evaluating the competence with which he applied the "scientific" approach which he used. Our focus is not the application of any single approach, but rather we reveal that there is a plurality of self-proclaimed scientific approaches. Our references to Popper are

1

critical: Sir Karl is made to compete with the ideological opposition. Our job is not so much to choose among the opposing ideologues, but rather to accept as legitimate and authentic opposing and conflicting social science (paradigms) sects. What Kuhn did for natural science viewed historically, we do for social science viewed contemporaneously. He did not reject as less than scientific the paradigms of the past, those which have been superceded by current ones. He accepted them as being scientific, since they were so considered by the scientists of the time. For Kuhn to have done otherwise would have been to write Whig history, to rewrite the past so as to conform to present ideas. For us it would mean to reject several contemporary social science paradigms as illegitimate. Instead, we accept, at least in principle, each of the conflicting contemporary social science paradigms as legitimate, i.e. as social science. Thus Kuhn tied science to paradigms, and each change in paradigm in a given discipline is considered to be a revolution. We tie the social sciences to their respective contemporary paradigms. Each period of a given science is tied to a paradigm, and the science of the time makes sense only within that framework. In our analysis, each contemporary paradigm is viewed in its own terms -- and each is likely to have its own philosophical basis. Kuhn's enlightenment came about when he stopped interpreting Aristotelian physics in modern terms, and when he interpreted it on its own terms.

Kuhn has modified his position downgrading the paradigm as a central focus in favor of the scientific community. But his former position suits us fine, since social science viewed at any given time is multi-paradigmatic whereas natural science is notoriously uni-paradigmatic. Moreover, we shift our analysis to the contemporary, rather than fixing upon the historical. This allows us to put our young professor's performance within the context of one of several competing contemporary paradigms. We, therefore, offer the insight of the comparativist -- the general moral being: do not take this one assertion of authenticity too seriously. There are many orthodoxies, and several claim the right not only to establish the canons of science, but to excommunicate practitioners who do not abide by these particular canons. Our approach is not unlike the comparativist in religion, a position which also draws support from Kuhn's formulation. Kuhn sees scientific paradigms as being founded on specific world views. A scientist trained in one, but forced to work in another, would be like a person socialized on one planet but forced to live on another.

Nothing would be familiar or "right" for this immigrant. Followers of contrary paradigms are often, but not always, followers of contrary ideologies -- their differences not subject to mediation by one kind of experimental evidence. The evidence is tied to the paradigm and makes sense only in relationship to its paradigm. Such is the case for gross national product and similar national accounting measures: they do not cut across paradigms. One would not be surprised that if challenged by contrary findings, say from a Marxist study, that our professor would deny the scientific character of the contrary study, insisting that it was ideological, outside the bounds of science. We are not saying that all contemporary social science paradigms are of equal value -- indeed, we have our favorites. We do insist, however, on recognizing their authenticity as legitimate social science. Our task is that of the sociologist of religion, to account for the subject matter in all its rich diversity, not to preserve the purity of the faith. In fact, this volume is a study in the social science of social science, one which uses the techniques of the disciplines better to understand the disciplines.

Chapters V, VI, VII, and VIII of this volume indicate that social science is a rich, diverse and sectarian enterprise with several contemporary self-proclaimed orthodoxies. We identify four major meta-paradigms there, two of which claim that they are scientific with the right to "excommunicate" the opposition as being "unscientific." Sectarianism becomes obvious when we view the enterprise from an international perspective and when we contrast disciplines on a national or regional basis. We do this in the chapters mentioned above. The claims of our young professor should experience a considerable deflation when forced into this comparative context. Chapter V will identify him as a functionalist, tied to the meta-paradigm dominant in the United States. His assertion is further clarified and diminished when we realize that national accounting measures such as gross national product have not attracted universal approval. Marxist countries use other measures, and third world scholars are becoming more and more dissatisfied with them. His implication that the recipient countries are better off with a higher gross national product is not that obvious. In fact, certain sectors of a society can have more income (as defined by the measure) with a lower gross national product, but with a more equal distribution of the product. A more basic criticism is that the measure at its roots is an ideological one which reflects a capitalist, a market mentality, perhaps even a masculine bias. The most trivial of all expenditures are given equal weight (proportional to their market prices) with the most basic necessities in this grossest of measures. The $35 haircut of the rich is given 35 times more weight than the $1 pound of beans which keeps a Chicano family alive. The $500 funeral of the dog of a Beverly Hills actor counts 500 times more than these beans. A mother's services at home do not count, but if she accepts outside employment as a manicurist (one can imagine a worse scenario), her salary does count, and the GNP thereby advances. The criterion is whether her services register in the market place. Such a measure is ideologically tied to the market. So close is the tie that shiny fingernails can take preference over the welfare of children. The Soviet counterpart is also ideological, rejecting services as part of its measure, and concentrating upon material production. This bias corrects for our fingernail example above, but excludes doctors' services as well. Both measures are ideological, biased one way or another, as are the sects of social science for which these measures do service.

The present chapter further deflates our young colleague's position by exposing the ambiguity of his use of the term "scientifically." We elaborate upon the concept science below. Here we merely highlight its two distinct meanings. The first is the restricted one, whose reference is natural science, and the second is the general one which refers to any organized discipline. The latter includes any serious organized study, no matter what methods are used, and no matter the subject matter. Natural science, social science, language, literary criticism, religion, philosophy, theology, and stamp collecting all fit this version of the term. In this latter sense, we can speak of the sciences of theology and religion, studies which among other things teach how to interpret the New Testament and set forth the principles for proving the existence of God. Too often, the functionalist (the positivist or those committed to naturalism or scientism) mix up the two meanings of the term, the resulting ambiguity used to buttress their argument. This is the case with our young professor. He asserted that the literature demonstrates "scientifically" that foreign aid and foreign investments increase the gross national product, and he assured his students that the study of X and Y followed the latest scientific criteria. References in the study to the work of Popper and Nagle, philosophers of science, further the impression that "scientifically" is used as an adverb to suggest the characteristic of natural science, not just those of some organized discipline. Our indictment would have been more persuasive had an argument ensued over contrary research findings of studies using competing paradigms. Such argument could have been initiated, for example, by a Latin American student who pointed to the research of a dependentista whose research tied foreign aid and foreign investment to foreign control and to the massive marginalization of the local populations. Our young colleague would then probably have responded by challenging the scientific credentials of dependency theory. This theory would have been downgraded to the status of an ideology, a variant of Marxism and, therefore, outside the circle of science. In this volume, we shall see that such excommunication is common, practiced not only by American functionalists, but also by their Kremlin counterparts. The fact that the process of excommunication is quite common takes the sharp edge from it. We argue that since no social science produces privileged knowledge with the epistemic value on a par with natural science, no social science is an authentic science. This is true of the claims of our young colleague, despite his assertive rhetoric. It is true for social science claims in general, obviously ours included as well.

Two additional remarks about the professor's assertions -- his reference to "the literature" and the fact that his supporting literature was only in English, and predominantly by Americans. Chapter IV of this volume analyzes, by reworking the findings of many studies, the communications system of American social science. The analysis finds it to be an inbred system, with mostly monolingual Americans communicating with each other. The system is congruent with world systems analysis and dependency theory, but not with an idealized version of the disciplines, in which foreign ideas are cherished side by side with domestic ones. American social scientists tend to be monolingual, along with their fellow countrymen. Here is one case of many in which social scientists duplicate the attributes of their respective societies. When our friend the professor asserts that "the literature" supports his thesis about the effects of foreign investments and foreign aid, chances are his reference is to the literature as it exists in the United States. Probably, he cannot with any fluency or comfort read a foreign language -- and so he is cut off from most of the world's social science journals. Chapter IV reveals that American social scientists read American literature, followed by that from the rest of the Anglo-Saxon world. Little is read from continental Europe and even less from the second and third worlds. The reading of a professor such as that of our friend is thus highly restricted and selective, not the inclusive fare suggested by an idealized view of international science. A further restriction on such reading is an ideological, sectarian one. Sectarians seldom lionize the works of the competition, for they feel uncomfortable if exposed too long to "erroneous" ideas. Our friend's view of "the literature" is probably much more restricted that the term suggests.

The Approach of This Volume

The above classroom vignette suggests the general tenor of this volume. Ours is an analysis of social science, an attempt at an interpretation, a view of social science. As this vignette sought to demonstrate, such theory has practical application -- indeed, the theory is necessary for an evaluation of the professor's performance. The vignette is not historical, but its epistemic value is in a sense greater since it is typical of much of American academe. We have witnessed the pattern unfold many times, and we would be less than honest if we did not grant at the outset that the image of such performances -- so smooth, so pat, so smug, so ethnocentric -- inspires our work. We contrast its ethnocentrism with our approach which we regard as being international. It also contrasts with natural science, one of whose cardinal principles we have been told is universalism. One of our tasks will be to explain how such smooth ethnocentrism can exist in disciplines, many of whose practitioners pride themselves on the international and universal character of their profession. We will find that social science is myth-ridden -- like other social institutions. When viewed from the outside, when viewed with the insights and with the measures and the instruments which social science uses on other institutions, we will see that it is supported by myths and by ideologies which are not all that obvious or persuasive to the outside observer. Such a myth encourages and provokes our young professor to use the term "scientifically" the way he does. When characterizing our disciplines as "ethnocentric," for example, we wish to avoid the notion that the term is meant to describe all aspects of them or that their situation is static. We argue that social situations are quite complicated, containing as they do contrary parts and that they are mobile rather than static.

We promise not to use our friend as a whipping boy throughout the volume, but he can stand a little more exposure. We view him as being an employee of the knowledge industry. As we point out in the following chapters, social science became a large scale industry, it industrialized in the latter part of the nineteenth century. This happened first either in Germany or in the United States, and it has burgeoned in the latter country since the end of World War II, and has spread to other countries. Although it can boast of ancient precedents, struggling and surviving on a small scale for a long time, social science assumed large proportions only within the last century, and especially since the end of World War II. The political economy of our disciplines is detailed in Chapter II, then history in Chapter III. This latter chapter III traces this history briefly from its ancient roots and what seem like its quaint beginnings as an individual enterprise to its expansion first at the hands of an Imperial Germany and the United States and then even more so with the American hegemony. The title of the volume provides two clues to our approach. The first is a reference to political economy. This suggests that the contemporary social science enterprise is greatly influenced by government, a point addressed below, but also by its cost. Creating new social science information or paradigms or disseminating old ones is a costly affair, and requires large capital investment in libraries, universities, and, for some paradigms, computers. Centers, thus capitalized, have an advantage over others. The capitalized enterprises require managers who scrounge around to get resources wherever they can, and the employees of the industries become dependent upon the capitalized enterprises.

Though significant, the above insight grows even more so when combined with others. Our approach includes insights from political economy, but also for the broader structural paradigm. The latter includes sociology, and we use insights from the sociology of sociology. An attribute of the knowledge industry is the separation which it witnesses between those who receive the information and those who pay for it. In the case of the social science enterprise, this is most easily seen in the case of education, a major component of the enterprise. Education is greatly subsidized by the government, even in capitalist countries which pay homage to market principles. We thus tie centers of the social sciences to their respective governments, the first step in our structural approach. This latter approach is suggested by the second part of the title of this volume, "the multinational version of the disciplines." The term has been borrowed from that used to describe the large business venture which carries on in many countries. The enterprise has been featured in dependency theory and world systems analysis, and we borrow the structures from these theories to analyze social science. These interdisciplinary structures which cross national frontiers play a central role in our analysis. We use them to help in accounting for the forms which our disciplines take and the nature of their communications networks. All this is too complicated to recount here, a task which has been reserved for Chapter II. Our approach is actually dualistic and non-reductionist. The structures we adopt interact with individual social scientists and their professional organizations such that a dialectic relationship ensues. Our young friend is not seen here as a mannequin or a puppet on a string. His performance is not just the result of outside forces far removed from his control. His performance is also his, and he is pictured here as able to impact the outside forces as well.

Forced to adjust to the world system, actually assigned a role within it, the social sciences look quite different then when treated in isolation. An additional advantage to our approach is that it recognizes the subordinate and the superordinate roles of the various centers of the disciplines. The present dominant role of the United States should become obvious, as well as the marginal roles of third world centers. This dominant role of the United States will be seen throughout the volume, and the communications network of its centers of social science are displayed in Chapter IV. It follows the same pattern as the communications network of the larger American society. This points to the interdisciplinary structures which we see as being associated with both sets of communications. In our approach, the economic is a starting point, a shorthand way or first step for arriving at the larger interdisciplinary structures. The insights from political economy thus start the process, and they cross and reinforce those from world systems analysis as well.

Our approach to social science is classified, in the most general terms, as an external one. This way of looking at social science contrasts with the internal approach which tends to isolate the enterprise, to analyze social science on its own terms and not in context. The internal approach sees the outer society at most merely as a catalyst, but not entering the disciplines as part of them. We said above that we tie the enterprise to structures, but that we do recognize the importance of the social science community as well. Ours is a kind of dualism, but we still come well within the confines of the external approach. A surprising phenomenon in social science literature is the popularity of the internal approach. Part of the reason is its support by Karl Popper, the positivist and naturalist philosopher of science.

He urges his followers to apply to the social sciences the same assumptions and methods which apply to physics. He distinguishes between the logic of science and the psychology of science. The former focuses inward upon the scientist's work, and Popper argues that our evaluation of science should focus there. The psychology of science refers to the personal characteristics of its practitioners, and they are essentially off limits to investigation. Such procedure seems legitimate (if confining) for physics, a mature science with one paradigm for each given area of research, a discipline which is blessed with the critical experiment. Experiments in this discipline seem actually "to force nature" to choose between alternatives -- at least there is a general consensus in the interpretation of research findings. Social science is deprived in this respect, and we thus argue for the investigation of the "psychology of the social sciences" -- better described in our case as structuralism or the social science of social science. Thus we initiated this chapter with assertions from a young, American professor -- both personal attributes which are part of the psychology of science. These attributes are important, since youth suggests an eager, recently socialized true believer. His nationality is also significant because the United States is the current social science superpower, and our hero shares its status: he is part of this as well.

Our approach to social science is critical, and it has much in common with that of Habermas, perhaps the most famous social scientist who operates under this banner. This German philosopher is famous for his differences with Popper. Habermas argues that positivism has revolutionized the position of philosophy with respect to the sciences. It has divorced epistemology from the perceiving and judging subject and reduced this study to the methodology or the philosophy of science.[1] It focuses attention upon what it assures us are the technical rules of the scientific method. It produces what we call "cookbooks" of science -- recipes on how to do science. But in doing this it turns away from the scientist as a human being or as a social being, the member of a professional group and also of a nation subject to its culture and government. We see this as a development congruent with technocracy, always eager to suppress what is human in favor of things and abstract rules. Perhaps this development can be justified for natural science, but it cuts off critical sources of information for social science.

Valuable as Habermas' work is in opening the door so that we can see the social scientist as a human being, we go to structuralism or to the field of the sociology of sociology to mark the characteristics of our approach. In order to suggest the broadest approach possible, we prefer structuralism, or to rename the sociology of sociology, the social science of social science. But we do not propose to quibble over names. We intend to picture the social scientist as a social being, made to cope with the structures described above. Some three decades ago, the observation was made that there existed a wealth of sociological studies of hobos, salesladies, thieves, and beggars, but a dearth of studies of social scientists. At first sight, this seems strange, for those committed to a field would seem to be eager to use the valuable insights it offers better to understand and to promote their own field. But this overlooks the probability that the findings of such studies might turn out to be more like disclosures, "slightly discomforting" to social science.[2] To subject social science disciplines to the scrutiny of social science analysis is the same as subjecting religion to the scrutiny of sociology. There is the real danger of desanctifying the saints, worse still of exposing the priests and bishops, and in general revealing that the enterprise is all too human. The ensuing scandal and pain must be balanced against the added insights which social science analysis offers for an understanding of itself.

Gouldner, often heralded as the founder of the sociology of sociology, argues that sociologists keep two sets of books, i.e. have two contrary methods of interpreting reality. One set is for themselves, the other is for the objects which they study. The method used on themselves is a purely rational one, free of the influence of culture and of the surrounding society.[3] In contrast, the objects are held to be shaped in many ways by culture and society. These subjects are seen as under the dominion of laws unknown to them and as perhaps apart from the intentions and the plans of the objects under analysis. But the typical sociologist fancies that practitioners are exempt from culture/society and that they can make purely rational professional decisions in accordance with technical standards. We take our cue from Gouldner, reject this dualism in approach which puts the social sciences aside as autonomous disciplines, and we subject their professional lives and their disciplines to the impact of culture and society. More accurately stated, we put them in the context of the same structures associated with politics, economics, culture, and education. Gouldner tells us that sociologists resist this integration, and we believe that this resistance is apparent not only for sociologists but for other social scientists as well. This volume has followed through with many studies to support assertions made or conclusions reached. The reader will find that this is true even in this chapter but even more so in Chapter IV where the communications system of our disciplines has been mapped by the use of several empirical studies. The danger in that chapter is one of overkill. And these studies are often desanctifying -- critical analyses which question and undermine the larger than life situations imagined to surround and to promote our disciplines. Our approach is critical, but we value the disciplines. We believe that they provide valuable explanations of social life.

Natural Science and Social Science

The studies "permitted" by the social science of social science will be put to good use in this section. They will perform the desanctifying function of debunking the supposed special virtues of social science which the positivist (the functionalist and the naturalist) imputes to this enterprise from a list of characteristics derived from the natural sciences. Chapter IV has been cast in this same vein. It uses a number of studies to demonstrate that the communications system of American social science resembles that of the larger society not that of natural science. The contrast between American physics and American psychology is dramatic. Certain of the characteristics usually applied to the mature natural sciences seem to fit, but we shall see below that their transfer to social science is not justified. Before turning to this problem, we face the question of definitions, and we examine a special problem of the research base for social science. Duverger's view of social science as the study of "men living in society"[4] seems reasonable. Cohen's view is similar. "The social sciences may be said to deal with the life of human beings in their group or associated life."[5] MacKenzie identifies them as those overlapping and academic disciplines which deal with human beings in their social context. They study the structure and the properties of human groups, and the ways in which individuals interact with each other and with their environment.[6] MacKenzie judged that this definition was not broad enough to accommodate psychology which he classified as a "human science." We include this discipline in our analysis and use the term "social science" to apply to it also. We note that the editor of the International Social Science Journal avoided the issue of definitions by listing the disciplines which were included in this work. Our listing serves a different purpose: to indicate which disciplines have played an especially important role in our analysis.

They are sociology, political science, economics, psychology, and international relations -- and to a lesser extent history and education. Countries selected for emphasis are the United States, the Soviet Union, Canada, West Germany, Italy, France, China, India, and Brazil. We believe that our sample is broad enough for us to assert that the portrait painted here refers to social science.

If our attitude toward social science definitions is indulgent, we insist that the word "science" be used in a narrow sense to mean natural science. We feel that confusion results when the term "science" is used indiscriminantly in place of the word "study," and we do not think it proper to refer to theology or to the social sciences as "science," nor to their findings as being "scientific." In fact, we prefer the label "social studies" to "social science," because the former name does not prejudice the identity and the nature of these disciplines. We employ the less desirable label less out of conviction than as a tribute to general usage. We realize that much of traditional usage does not support our position. The insistence on distinguishing is confined to Anglo-Saxon countries and then only in the last century.[7] Our case is based on "science" itself, i.e., on natural science -- one of whose critical traits is exactness. It is also based on common sense -- that words should convey exact meanings. One cannot use the same term to apply to disciplines whose traits are so different. Why not use the term "study," or "organized study," or "discipline" when referring to social science? Any of these terms would convey the meaning desired without suggesting those unique features which belong solely to natural science.

Certainly, natural science and social science have the common trait that both are disciplines carried on by human beings. Whether the laws of the mature disciplines are found in nature or whether they are human constructions is a problem we do not attempt to solve here. We are persuaded, however, that the "laws" of social science are human constructions and that they are intimately combined and intertwined with their creators. This is certainly more so the case for the social sciences than for natural science, because they are not only by human beings but about them as well. Natural science deals with things, animals, or parts of humans so dissected and arranged that social differences play no significant role. The enterprise social science impinges upon what a given social group treasures as being most important and even sacred -- the food supply, the economy, religion, the government, and the family. The information which it produces can affect the future of each of these. This information tends not to be undirected, objective, and castrated so as to be serviceable to all. Nor is its principal purpose knowledge for the survival of all as the functionalists would have us believe. It is ideological information which can serve the interest of one group over the other by favoring one over the other. Interest groups and governments thus attempt to influence the content of social science, and we recognize their success when we account for the causes of our disciplines.

Social sciences experience two crucial problems, both stemming from a common source. The common source is the division of human beings into social, competitive groups, each subject to its own culture and elites. Social scientists in each of these groups, influenced by the social norms and the dominant elites of the specific groups, study their own groups and others. The first problem is that the social scientists are influenced by their own social norms and dominant elites, and the second is that the social groups which are studied are different from each other because of their own specific local influence. The first problem was examined above; we now come to the second problem. The findings derived from research on one group are not necessarily transferable to the others. This is another way in which the social sciences differ from natural science. Social conditions and dominant elites vary from one domain to the other, whereas nature tends to be uniform. The natural scientist can with confidence do research on what is near at hand, realizing that his findings are transferable to other geographic areas. The social scientist has no such assurance. If he crosses a social or national boundary, he probably will have to leave his research findings behind. The dichotomy between social and natural science holds best in the case of physics, and not quite so well for biology, but it does hold in a greater or lesser way for all natural science.

The problem of the possible non-transferability of social science findings across social/political boundaries assumes proper proportions when we realize that the great majority of social scientists come from the first world, and so research has been disproportionately centered there. The anthropologist could be relied upon to mark this trend and to emphasize the narrow research base of the other social sciences, especially before his own research interests shifted to developed societies. Herskovits indicated that this concentration on Western cultures began quite naturally and "innocently." He argued that, like charity, the social sciences (other than anthropology) began at home, if only because of the convenience and the economy of working at things close at hand.[8] This natural tendency for using the home front as the area of research was reinforced by the fact that these disciplines arose as responses to the discrete practical problems existing in each country. And the social sciences (other than anthropology) for the most part have stayed at home. Herskovits continues: "the general principles advanced by them (the social sciences) have been based largely on the study of materials from a single country or, at most, a series of countries with similar historical backgrounds and bodies of tradition." Another anthropologist, Kluckhorn, reinforced this latter point some twenty years ago when he charged that contemporary sociology "deals almost wholly with Western societies" and that economics for the most part has devoted itself to the "analysis of a special case of economic activity -- Western European civilization".[9]

This bias is not solely in favor of the Western world over "primitive" societies or of first and second world countries over the third world, but it also has emerged among Western countries. Some twenty years ago Berelson and Steiner sought to collect findings from the "scientific" study of human behavior. They came up with some 1,045 of these, but granted that the number could have been one-fifth of, or five times greater, depending upon the stringency of the criteria used. What concerns us most at this juncture is the research source of these data, rather than the flexibility of the epistemology of "science." They granted alternately that, except for anthropological materials, a large proportion of the findings was based on data collected in the United States and that a good deal of their work was limited to Western culture and even to the American scene.[10] Morgan has asserted that the great bulk of the studies in the discipline of international relations has been done in the Western world, particularly in the United States.[11] We must admit that this imbalance has been modified in recent years, as the United States has promoted overseas research, but the imbalance has not been rectified.

Rather than multiplying sources which attest to this imbalance and bias in research, let us look at what effect this can have on the applicability or universality of social science findings. Can these findings, based as they are on research concentrated upon Western countries and societies or just upon a few of these countries and societies, be applied to the neglected countries and societies or to the world at large? The answer would be affirmative if the subject matter were physics. Przeworski and Teune identify two views which are relevant in answering this question for social science. The partisans of the first argue that social science statements can be true regardless of time and place. Those who hold to the second view deny this, insisting that the truth of such statements is relative to discrete social systems. If one accepts the second model, the answer to the original question is negative. We cannot in this view apply these findings to the neglected countries and societies or to the world at large. In this case, the findings from research in the first world cannot be universalized or applied to the third world.

But let us in order to complete our argument accept the first view and see what answer this leads us to give to our original question. Przeworski and Teune state that the first model demands a research strategy that has never been applied: random samples of the world's population, regardless of the social systems to which individuals or groups belong. Indeed, social scientists have not employed such random samples. By concentrating their research on developed countries or particular developed countries, they have provided the data base for partial and biased theories, not for universally applicable laws. This can be better illustrated by pretending, as the first model does, that national boundaries are no impediments to research, and that, therefore, conducting world-wide research is subject to the same rules as research carried on in one country, say the United States. Simon advises national pollsters in that country that if they want to measure a given characteristic of a population they must not ignore any part of that population.[12] Social science, viewed globally, has been doing this by essentially overlooking certain countries. Simon goes on to say (he is talking about the United States) that geography is no different in this respect from age or sex. "To sample only in the East, say, or only among Protestants would be erroneous." Simon adds that the laws of probability can be used to prevent geographical bias, if random samples are used. But we know that this has not been done, i.e., random samples of the world have not been used. Therefore, the research of social science has generally been "erroneous," whichever social science view we accept, provided that universally applicable laws are our goal, or the kind that natural science produces.

To produce the universal laws of physics, social scientists must adopt research designs of broader geographic dimensions than those of physics. They must act in a broader, more global manner just to match the universal character of physics, just to "break even" with it.

We seek to demonstrate in this volume, specifically in Chapter IV, that their conduct is the opposite, i.e. they tend to be more ethnocentric than their colleagues in physics. The reference there, however, is not to the geographic scope of research designs, but rather to interest in the work of colleagues. Our comments about the research domain of social science must both be interpreted to mean that the differences in disciplines are technical -- social sciences need only to broaden their research base, and they can become like natural science.

The naturalist (the functionalist) argues along these lines. Given the time and the effort, the social sciences will mature. Our view is that this also separates social from natural sciences and provides different world views, for social science, the chasms which Kuhn found dividing natural science historically. Such breaches cannot be healed by merely broadening research designs. They require structural, global changes. We return to this problem in the concluding chapter.

We must turn to the characteristics of science, what is indeed an idealization, but set forth by sociologists of science. We have chosen the works of Merton, Storer, and Cohen for this construction. Our major task will be to estimate to what extent social science measures up to the characterization. This is justified by the fact that functionalists (positivists) often refer to this idealization in order to describe the supposed behavior of social scientists. The rationale for such borrowing is that these disciplines are in some way natural science, or at least similar to it, so what is imputed to it can be imputed to the less mature disciplines as well. Merton finds four such characteristics -- sets of institutional imperatives, which make up the ethos of modern science.[13] They are universalism, communism, disinterestedness, and organized skepticism. In discussing universalism, Merton grants that deviations from the norm do occur, but he insists that they only presuppose the legitimacy of the norm. We interpret the norms as intended to refer in some general way to the behavior and attitudes of scientists, perhaps their modal behavior and attitudes. Our task is to see if these norms fit social science as well, admitting, as Merton does, that exceptions occur -- and even counter-currents.

Merton finds the universalism of science to be anchored deeply in the impersonal character of the enterprise. The norm mandates that truth claims be subjected to pre-established criteria consonant with previously confirmed knowledge. Acceptance of these claims is not to depend upon personal or social attributes -- race, nationality, class, or religion. Particularistic criteria are avoided, and ethnocentrism is incompatible with this norm. Merton presses this norm to include free access to scientific pursuits, and he draws a parallel between it and the norms of laissez-faire democracy. Storer refers to laissez-faire as well, but his assertion is that the scientific community probably approximates this ideal much more closely than the economic institutions of society ever did.[14] He argues that universalism in science is such that its practitioners learn a foreign language so that they can become aware of the contributions of foreign colleagues. Cohen concentrates upon the outputs of the enterprise, arguing that it produces abstract, universal laws.[15]

This general description does not fit well with social science. We have just attempted to demonstrate that social science does not have the research design to produce the universal laws which Cohen attributed to science in the last sentence of the last paragraph. True, social science recently has been broadening the geographic scope of its research base, but not enough to justify regarding its outputs as having universal application. We now turn to the first part of the last paragraph which asserts that truth claims are subjected to pre-established criteria "consonant with previously confirmed knowledge." A problem here is that social science has so little "confirmed knowledge," i.e., so little certainty, so little consensus on what truth claims have been confirmed. Cohen argues that certainty is a characteristic of science, a trait we return to soon along with a related trait consensus. The most general comment to be made about the previous paragraph, however, is that social science is hardly a universalist discipline; it is rather more an ethnocentric, nationalist one, which is divided up into inward looking ideological sects which tend to excommunicate each other from the field. It is not so much impersonal as it is elitist and ideological. It is more oligopolistic than laissez-faire, a point we make in the following chapter. Truth claims must be judged within the contours of given sects and ethnocentric groups, simply because no universal ones exist. This last statement must not be interpreted to mean that social science is not an international enterprise. Indeed it is, and there exists a communications system which crosses national boundaries. But this enterprise and this communications net are not subject to the principles of laissez-faire and perfect competition. The system is better seen as being oligopolistic, one that reflects international, interdisciplinary structures. The learning of foreign languages follows this same design, not the general principle of universalism enunciated by Storer. American social scientists remain remarkably monolingual, while other social scientists learn foreign languages. Both reflect the larger patterns of their societies. Social science reflects several different, and seemingly conflicting, tendencies which are described well by our structural approach.

Social science has great difficulty being reconciled with the other three institutional imperatives set forth by Merton as well. "Communism" refers to the common ownership of the science -- the enterprise is a community project, individual rights are severely limited. This institutional imperative must be modified to fit the fact that social science is divided into opposing sects, countries, and even regions. It is not a community enterprise; it is better described as a series of enterprises. Merton argues that "communism" induces the scientist to publish his findings, to share the wealth of the community, and that full and open communications is the rule. In a chapter below (Chapter IV) we trace the communications net of American social science, which we find to follow a structural pattern. The phrase "free and open communications" does not suggest the operations of the network. "Disinterestedness" is the tongue-twister which Merton uses to describe an enterprise virtually without fraud, chicanery, and irresponsible claims. The reason he gives for this idyllic state of affairs is the accountability of the scientist to his peers. They police the enterprise and prevent the abuse of expert authority or the creation of pseudo-sciences. We pass over the question of fraud and chicanery in social science to point to the difficulties of policing a multi-paradigmatic, ideological enterprise in which the police and the policed are from opposing, often warring, factions. The police function in these circumstances too often degenerates into the soldier's job of defending his faction against its enemies. The fourth institutional imperative, "organized skepticism" must be greatly modified if applied to the social sciences. Merton's scientists are skeptical, detached, and attentive only to logical criteria and empirical findings. Our social scientists also are attentive to these criteria, but they are persuaded by ideology and ethnocentrism as well.

The Ethnocentrism/Nationalism of Social Science

We next take up in some detail the ethnocentrism/nationalism of social science and its lack of consensus, a trait which we consider along with certainty. The operation of the social science community has been left to a subsequent chapter. Our first task is to deal with ethnocentrism/nationalism, which obviously is at odds with Merton's universalism, but which we believe can be reconciled with our approach. We see social sciences interacting as structures which have an international aspect -- and, consequently, the first world versions of these disciplines and their practitioners travel overseas, notably to the third world. They install the disciplines there, adoption more so than adaptation, and the nationalism/ethnocentric of the imported disciplines is that of the first world. It is only later than third world social scientists indigenize our disciplines, i.e., put their own national/ethnocentric marks on them. This process tends to occur according to structural logic. It plays a key role in the multinational version of social sciences, but we leave it for later in order to discuss a second caveat. It is true that some social sciences are less ethnocentric than others, obvious examples being transnational and transcultural disciplines; a list of comparative subdisciplines; and cultural anthropology. These studies are less ethnocentric, because they have deliberately set out to use as research objects humans other than nationals. They can remain ethnocentric in other ways, the social scientists can remain of the same nationality, culture, or civilization; and confine their communications to their peers. This obviously was the case for anthropology at its birth, for the first practitioners were the soldiers, the missionaries, and the administrators in the colonies.[16] And their output certainly reflected ethnocentric, European biases. Only recently have the objects of this research, the "natives" of the "backward" countries, become its practitioners, often with striking results. The third caveat is that some countries are more ethnocentric than others, the United States excelling in this area. We return to this question in the last chapter.

We cite only one author, and briefly at that, who thought that his discipline, in this case sociology, had to be interpreted on a national basis. It is Ayala who in his history of the discipline sociology argued that science looks for truth regardless of time and place, whereas sociology must be considered in a national context.[17] We turn next to a series of studies which attest to the ethnocentrism/nationalism of our disciplines. The first of these has been inspired by the ideas of Boulding who observed some time ago in an analysis meant for scholars in the discipline international relations that history and geography as presented in national schools is designed to give perspective, not truth, and that these disciplines are used by nation-

alists to present the world from the vantage point of the nation.[18]
The geography of the nation is given in detail, that of the remainder
of the world in outline. National history is emphasized, that of the rest
of the world is neglected or even falsified. In the spirit of the social
science of social science, we decided to apply a benign version of
Boulding's formulary to several accounts of the disciplines, mostly
American. Any imputation of deliberate falsification is avoided, and
the assumption is made that any excessive preoccupation with national
affairs over foreign ones be interpreted as evidence of unconscious
nationalism. Thus modified, the formulary was applied to the history
of the discipline international relations as found in some seven
American textbooks. The typical history, whether labelled this way or
not, was found to be confined to an account of the discipline in the
United States.[19] The typical account asserts that the discipline began
either just before or immediately after World War I, and it takes the
reader on safari to encounter a number of methodologies and
paradigms -- idealism, realism, behavioralism, and post-behavioralism.
The discipline is seen as first focusing on international law, diplomatic
history, and international organizations -- and with the behavioral
revolution -- on psychology, sociology, cybernetics, and statistics. The
typical account in fact records what happened in the United States, but
not in France, Germany, India, or the second and third worlds -- to
cite examples. It thus reveals unconsciously the nationalism in
Boulding's formulary of emphasizing national history and neglecting
that of the rest of the world. One could put it even stronger. The
history of the discipline in the United States is presented as though it
were the history of the discipline: national history becomes world
history.

We next apply this modified formulary to two American
works, one an essay by Waldo on political science and the other a
book by Schultz on psychology. The importance of the first can be
gauged by the fact that it served as the lead article of the six-volume
Handbook of Political Science. Of the 123 pages of the article (not
counting footnotes) 3½ were devoted to the discipline in foreign
countries and the remainder to the discipline in the United States.
The former was sandwiched between the discussion of things
American.[20] The American scholar referred to this foreign account
as a "horseback survey," but added that it "proved to be the most
vexing task imposed by the preparation of this essay." The same
technique applied to Schultz's book revealed that the American author

devoted 12½ pages to the contemporary situation in his country and only 2 pages to the contemporary scene in the remainder of the world.[21]

We continue with the application of Boulding's formulary, this time to the great men and to the best departments of political science. Our purpose is to determine if political scientists are influenced by nationalism in making such choices. If so, they violate the spirit of Merton's canon universalism. Men and institutions are central features of the ichnography of nationalism. A 1963 survey of the American Political Science Association asked respondents to name the political scientists who had made the most significant contribution prior to 1945 and after 1945.[22] The first eighteen of the latter group so designated were all American practitioners. Seventeen of the first eighteen of the former group were also American. The only foreigner on either list was a Britisher, Harold J. Laski, who ranked twelfth and a half (tied with an American) on the list for the earlier period.

No foreign political science department has made the ratings in any of the American studies which we have seen. This is true whether the study purports to judge the most prestigious or productive departments or the best graduate schools. A 1925 effort which tapped the opinions of 19 leading American political scientists named eleven American departments as being the eleven best.[23] Another in 1957, based this time on the opinions of the chairmen of 25 American departments, chose 15 American departments as being the 15 best.[24] The 1963 survey of Somit and Tannenhaus of the membership of the American Political Science Association resulted in the selection of the graduate program of 33 American universities as being the 33 best.[25] This time the respondents could write in universities other than the 33 American institutions already printed on the questionnaire. Therefore, foreign institutions could have been rated, if members of the sample were so disposed.

To understand the significance of these figures, the reader must keep in mind that these surveys were originally undertaken to identify the greatest contributors and the best departments and graduate programs in the discipline. Moreover, the original findings consisted of lists of individuals or institutions. We identified the nationalities of the names on the original lists and produced the nationality summaries exhibited above. Indeed, we are practicing the social science of social science by looking critically at how its practitioners ply their trade. The very fact that surveys of the American

Political Science Association are used for this purpose, and evidently accepted as such, are already indications of an unconscious nationalism. Those more conscious of this phenomenon would use, and demand, a more multinational group as judges. The findings would be labelled as the opinions of Americans, not those of the discipline as such. Unconsciously, the American discipline is assumed to be the world discipline.

The unanimous choice of American political science departments and the near unanimous choice of American scholars as the "great men" (no women were selected) of the discipline on its face betrays nationalism and the violation of the spirit of Merton's canon universalism. Fortunately, we have found comparable French studies, which no doubt betray some French bias, but which also corroborate our charge of American bias. The first study was a 1981 sample of political science professors which consisted of nine Parisian and ten provincial universities and seven "foreign" (non-French) members of the profession.[26] Respondents were asked to indicate in order five universities, French or foreign, which they would recommend for the third cycle (doctoral work) in political science. They were not to take account of residence as a criterion in their choice. French universities received 15 first choice selections and American institutions six. Of the 107 choices of any kind, however, 91 went to French institutions, eleven to the competition in America, and the remaining to Canada, Switzerland, and England.

The following year this journal published the findings of studies of the same type, but this time the methodology was spelled out.[27] The readership was assured that, although the samples making the judgments (almost all professors) were not in a statistical sense representative, considerable effort had been expended to make them so, i.e., between Paris and the interior, age groups, and academic sects. The respondents were told not to allow location to influence their choices. French institutions again were the overwhelming favorite with 12 choices for first place in experimental psychology, 13 in linguistics, and 13 in sociology. Of the choices of any kind, French institutions received all but 3. Similar samples in 1983 for political science and economics saw French institutions capturing the overwhelming number of first place positions and 160 of 174 choices of any kind.[28]

These findings attest to the nationalism of French and American social science when measured by institutional preference. What are considered to be the best institutions in the United States for social science are fortunate to be ranked at all by French social scientists. No foreign institution makes the ratings of American political scientists. One should recall that these opinions were found in two important social science centers and that the findings would probably be quite different if they reflected the opinions of social scientists in peripheral countries. This for the simple reason that the questionnaires dealt with the quality of institutions, and they are obviously better equipped in the first world. Secondly, third world scholars are subject to first world propaganda in general, and also that concerning universities. To tap third world nationalism we turn to a study of the Falklands/Malvinas war. The study was the work of the present writer and his wife and centered upon questionnaires answered at the 1982 tri-annual conference of the International Political Science Association and the quadri-annual gathering of the International Sociological Association, held respectively in Rio de Janeiro and Mexico City.[29] There were a total of 377 responses which could be used, all from social scientists (43 percent political scientists and 37.9 percent sociologists), mostly professors (77.7 percent); but researchers, other practitioners of these disciplines, and graduate students were also represented. Undergraduate students were excluded. A majority of the respondents (54.6 percent) had doctorates, a sizeable number masters (25.5 percent) and some the licenciado (14.6 percent). Indeed, this was an exercise in the social science of social science. The respondents were predominantly Latin American (107), North American (72), or Western European (96). Asia was sparsely represented, and the socialist bloc countries not at all. Delegates from this latter area (with the exception of Poland) declined to participate in the project. This is yet another reminder of the deep divisions which rack world social science. Several Soviet delegates took a copy of the questionnaire with them, but it obviously did not meet with their approval. They never returned it. One Soviet participant at the Rio conference did answer the questionnaire. We learned later that he defected to the West. We cherish his response as a momento, but it can hardly be regarded as representative of Soviet political science.

The ten substantive questions posed were designed to expose reactions to three related themes: (1) the ownership and the future of the Malvinas/Falklands; (2) the conflict itself; and (3) the implications of U.S. policy toward the conflict. Chi-square tests were run on the responses to the ten questions, broken down by nationality and region. Nine of the ten questions yielded significant divisions, with confidence levels higher than 95 percent. The second requirement posed above for nationalism was also fulfilled, e.g., the breakdown of the groups was biased in favor of the position of their respective governments and regions. The response of the British and the Argentine samples served as the extremes for issues which directly involved their governments and on which the latter pursued contrary policies. It was hypothesized beforehand that this general pattern would occur, and it did. Also hypothesized beforehand, and confirmed by the data, was the supposition that samples of social scientists from the United States and Western Europe would fall close to the British sample and that that of the rest of Latin America would locate close to the Argentine sample. When the United States and Argentina were in direct confrontation, their respective samples generally assumed the extreme positions, with those from the United Kingdom and Western Europe being close to that of the United States and that from the rest of Latin America close to the Argentine one.

The response to question five of the study, which asked the respondents to type the conflict, serves as our example. It highlights the importance of the findings of the study as well. The reader need not be reminded of the crucial role in science played by categories and typologies. Two of the three responses of one of the multiple-choice questions, namely "colonial" and "cold war," were taken from quantitative studies of conflicts by Haas and by Holsti. The third category, "territorial," was substituted for "non-cold war" and "other" found in the quantitative studies. The chi-square test run on the responses to this question, when broken down by major countries and regions, was found to be significant at the 100 percent confidence level. Eighty-three and three-tenths percent of the Argentine respondents chose "colonial" to classify the conflict, but only 9.5 percent of the British sample registered this choice. The sample of the remainder of Latin America was found to be in basic agreement with the Argentine assessment (61.3 percent), but not so the samples from North America and Western Europe. Only 36.1 percent of the former and 31.9 percent of the latter chose "colonial" to classify the conflict.

The findings of the study point to social science truth claims "contaminated" by ethnocentrism, by national and regional bias. These claims cannot be accepted at face value, as those of natural science. They invite the additional query: what is the nationality of the social scientists making the claims? This is a necessary and crucial question, and the answer to it provides another variable necessary for evaluating the outputs of social science. This is not a legitimate question for natural science, at least according to Merton who argues, as we have seen, that science processes truth claims without respect to nationality. Universalism is a trait of natural science. In contrast, the social sciences are so immersed in the local situation that it cannot be shaken off, and their truth claims reflect these factors. Social science truth claims thus represent outputs deficient in epistemic qualities. Argentine social science is free to claim as a "scientific fact" (actually as a "scientific" concept) that the "Malvinas" conflict and others like it are colonial and to turn out quantitative (or qualitative) studies based on this view. British social scientists have an equal right to classify "scientifically" this same "Falklands" conflict as a territorial one.

This study also helps confirm the assertion made below intended to account for the popularity of dependency theory in Latin America. This popularity is traced in part to the fact that the theory appeals to Latin American political beliefs and cultural dispositions by identifying the United States as the major center, and thus as the major controller and exploiter of the region. Most of the Latin American sample in the study (57.5 percent) identified as the reason for Haig's "peace mission" the attempt to establish an Anglo-American or a NATO base on the islands. This percentage was the highest in the study and contrasts with North American sample of only 13 percent, the lowest in the study. Furthermore, 65.3 percent of the Latin American sample saw the islands as possessing such a base in the future. Only 15.3 percent of the American sample chose this option. Again, the Latin American and the North American samples were on the opposite ends of the distribution. Like their fellow countrymen, Latin American social scientists have a deep distrust of the motives and actions of Washington. North American social sciences do not seem to share this view. The author never thought of asking the question about the possibility of establishing Anglo-American or NATO bases on the islands until he read the charge in Brazilian newspapers. The pre-testing of the project was done in Brazil, with only Latin Americans available as respondents. Perhaps this led to bias in some of the questions, at least this was the opinion of one irate British social scientist who refused to answer the questionnaire. No apology for the pre-testing is made here. It must be done some place.

The Uncertainty and Lack of Consensus of Social Science

We believe that enough has been said so that we can with some confidence classify social science in some respects as an inward looking, ethnocentric/ nationalistic enterprise. We must confess that this is really a tendency, and that its full realization can be blocked, as we shall see in our discussion in the succeeding chapter. We next turn to the certainty and the consensus of science and to the lack of these traits in the social sciences. These deficiencies on the part of the latter are really the other side of their division into ideological and ethnocentric groups. Better stated, the lack of consensus "allows" for the differences among the groups. And these differences highlight the uncertainty of our disciplines. If certainty reigned, as in natural science, then there would be consensus also. We believe that the two traits are related, and, therefore, we treat them together. One reason that the multinational approach bears witness to such a large measure of descensus (and disagreement) is that it has foresworn the right of excommunication. It has not, for example, argued that behaviorism in political science is "scientific" and that all other sects at odds with it are unscientific and thus not really social science. Such a process of pruning off heretical sects seemingly results in a more consensual enterprise and a more "agreeable" one.

We start our discussion with a comment by the leading experts of the Institute of Scientific Information on Social Science of the Soviet Academy of Sciences, who insisted on drawing the line between our disciplines and natural science. They argued that the scientific and technological information produced in the industrial countries (they produce most of it) is generally used by the rest of the world, "its form and content being the same for all".[30] Information on physics, chemistry, and technology is normally consumed in the form in which it is written. In contrast, socio-economic information varies significantly from country to country. Concepts in this area are not fixed; many terms are vague and neologisms are constantly introduced, making translation difficult. These Soviet scholars pointed to four characteristics which set social science information apart. It is less cumulative; more ideological; subject to cultural and social influence; and less amenable to mathematical formulation. In elaborating upon the first point, they asserted that it becomes obsolete more slowly and maintains its significance (but not its validity) longer. This is usually explained by the lack of the crucial experiment which would disconfirm what is false. This situation contrasts with physics, any textbook of which "can present quite thoroughly the most valuable findings of the last three centuries."

We continue to build the dichotomy science/social science with testimonials from the well placed -- social scientists and philosophers of science. The latter are first, and their purpose is to assert the settled, consensual, and the privileged position of science, and to defend it against other kinds of human effort. The social scientists testify to the uncertainty of their craft, and to the lack of consensus which haunts it. Ross argues that science, in contrast to art and philosophy, deals with resolvable problems: it is labor with the greatest chance of success. He assures us that a scientific conclusion "must be acceptable to everyone who understands the issues".[31] Kuhn has written: "It is precisely the abandonment of critical discourse that marks the transition to science".[32] During normal times (by far most of the time) Kuhn's scientist is reduced to a puzzle solver -- confronted with puzzles, not with choices among theories. If Ross and Kuhn stress prior acceptance of a theory as the main road to scientific consensus, Bronowski and Popper stress that this phenomenon is mediated by a process. Bronowski tells us that the sciences use the critical experiment in order "to force nature to decide between alternatives".[33] Popper agrees with this general line of reasoning, arguing that it is the continuous replication of experiments which results in "objective" statements, which can be translated here as consensual ones or monistic truth.[34] Popper is also strong in his affirmation of scientific consensus, illustrating it by describing the settled situation which awaits the scientist when he initiates a piece of research.

The following testimonies are to the lack of certitude and consensus in social science. This condition should be contrasted with that indicated above for natural science:

Malinowski on anthropology: it "is even now divided by many schools, tendencies, and partisan approaches. It is still in the fighting stage, engaged in the bellum omnium contra omnes . . .".[35]

Knute Wicksell on economics: "We cannot mention a single doctrine which is not flatly contradicted by the diametrically opposite view, also put forward as scientific truth by writers of good repute".[36]

Morgan on international relations: after having revealed that there is no generally accepted theory of integration, he added, "Once again international politics involves the study of something the nature of which is not exactly clear";[37]

Greenstein and Polsby on political science: "Early in his career, the fledgling political scientist learns that his discipline is ill-defined, amorphous, and heterogeneous".[38] This perception "will in no way be rebutted by this eight-volume handbook";

Nagel on psychology: "Indeed, unlike these sciences (physics and biology), psychology is marked by the existence of warring schools, which differ not only in their interpretations of newly gathered data -- disagreements on matters at the frontiers of research occur in all branches of science -- but are also at odds over the "proper" way of studying as well as interpreting phenomena that have long been subjects of investigation";[39]

Popper on psychology and sociology: those "often spurious sciences," that when compared with physics "are riddled with fashions, and with uncontrolled dogmas".[40]

We follow these testimonials with quantitative studies, what are usually called empirical studies. The evidence provided consists of surveys of social and natural scientists -- practitioners whose opinions should be worthwhile. The first of the two studies used here produced findings from a stratified sample of the professional personnel of 80 of the most prestigious graduate departments in the United States. Twenty such departments were selected from physics, chemistry, sociology, and political science. The respondents were asked to rank order seven disciplines on the degree to which they felt there is consensus on paradigms, i.e., on laws, theories, and methodology. The questionnaire stated that it was designed to test the "relative maturity" or "degree of development" of the seven fields. The respondents placed the natural sciences first -- in order physics, chemistry, and biology. The four social sciences were last. Economics was judged to enjoy the most consensus of the four, with psychology next, and political science and sociology last.[41] Unfortunately, the respondents merely rank ordered the responses, so that we cannot tell the degree to which they believed, for example, that sociology had obtained consensus contrasted with physics. But the results do support our insistence on separating natural from social science, in that the three disciplines of the former ranked first in consensus while the four social sciences were last.

A second survey on disciplinary consensus was conducted in Austria in 1973-1974. It sought to include all social science research units in that country, and it combined interviews of the heads of the units with written questionnaires for the staff. It yielded 624 responses. A series of questions were posed, designed to determine opinions on the degree of consensus which existed for eight social sciences. These questions asked for the degree of consensus with respect to such matters as the epistemological presuppositions of the fields; the most promising and most generally accepted theories, techniques, and methods used in the disciplines; and the findings that are generally accepted. The mean percentage for consensus was found to be 22.6. Those above the mean with their respective percentages were modern history (43.5), economics (33.7), business administration (28.8), and psychology (24.5). Those below the mean were sociology (17.1), pedagogy (14.9), political science (10.5), and urban and regional planning (7.4).[42] The mean of only 22.6 for the 8 disciplines points to an opinion in accord with ours that little consensus exists in social science. Knorr's study points to the presence of sectarianism in social science in another way. She found that opinions with respect to consensus varied more sharply among those using different methodologies than among those belonging to different disciplines. The partisans of dialectic methodologies saw the least consensus in their disciplines; partisans of formal mathematical models, the most; with those using empirical methods taking an intermediate position. Methodology is often used as the criteria for identifying social science sects. It is tempting to identify the dialectical method here with Marxism and the other two with some form of positivism or behaviorism. But the first could include conservatives of a Hegelian persuasion as well.

This evidence points to a social science cursed with uncertainty and lack of consensus among its members. Our disciplines are at odds with natural science in these respects, and social scientists should not attach the term "scientific" to their outputs, at least not without explaining that their use of the term does not imply the same epistemic value as the outputs of natural sense. The young professor introduced at the outset of this chapter violated the principle enunciated here. He used the term to suggest enhanced epistemic value of the studies he cited without clarifying the sense in which he used the word "scientifically." Melanson is so taken with the way that his fellow American political scientists misuse the term "science" that he would have them rename their outputs "vocational knowledge." He believes that these outputs lack reliability and other epistemic qualities. In his words, they are closer to empirical codification of value positions than to epistemically sound conclusions of reliable knowledge".[43] Their versatility is such that expert witnesses can be called before congressional committees with "scientific" information to buttress various and conflicting points of view. Melanson argues that his fellow American political scientists do not do enough in making the public aware of the epistemic limitations of their outputs. Part of the reason is self interest: to appear "scientific" in a science-loving society such as the United States is a professional subsidy. His suggestion has not been acted upon by his colleagues, nor by other American social science groups, as far as we are aware. Those committed to studying political science professionally should understand how difficult organizations find it to launch programs which would set back their interests, at least in the short run. We set forth in the next chapter our view of the operations of social science communities -- a view which makes it easy to understand why Melanson's suggestion has not been implemented.

Other Traits of the Multinational Approach

Like other human institutions, social science is myth-laden, a trait which the multinational approach will expose. We saw this above in the claim reputedly assumed by most sociologists that their professional power of reasoning is considered to be so finely tuned that they are not subject to the social structures which bind other human beings. We confess to some uneasiness and restlessness inhabiting such a professional environment. The feeling is the one which arises when asked: "You are a priest aren't you," an occurrence which happens to the author only in religious book stores in Brazil. We feel that a neophyte to the profession, when told how social science communities operate, might be reminded of the lives of the saints as portrayed by a nun of long ago in the fourth grade. We face the social science community in the next chapter, and we give the details of the social science myth in the third chapter. The latter is a construction which involves time periods and thus it may be classified as "historical." It pictures a given discipline as evolving from a "pre-scientific" period to a higher level when it becomes a social science. The heart of the myth is the third step, the future when the discipline will mature, really take off, and take on the attributes of the natural sciences. The fact that this has never happened to a single social science seems not to have dimmed the popularity of the myth. It is an open-ended construction, so that it cannot be disconfirmed. When called to account, the myth makers explain that more time is necessary for its realization. The fact that maturity has not been realized does not prevent the upholders of the myth from using the name of science to increase the epistemic appearance of their current work or to excommunicate heretical sects. The myth helps to provide self-identification for social science -- thus reference to it belongs in this introductory chapter. The myth holds that social science is an enterprise suspended between the natural sciences and non-science, but closer to the former and already even before maturity sharing some of their characteristics. The myth is not shared by all social scientists. Those not involved are the interpretive sociologists and their allies in other disciplines, humanistic Marxists, and Kremlin Marxists. The last mentioned brag that their sect is already a science.

Koch's criticism of the myth helps to highlight its characteristics, and our approach is in basic agreement with this criticism. He argues that the assertion that his specialty, psychology, will mature has been disconfirmed. Quite correctly he points to the discipline as the central one in social science, at least in the United States. It has provided the "methodological marching orders" for other disciplines, and it has tended to serve as the foundation discipline, an enterprise which is saturated with the imagery of science. But the reality of the discipline is quite different. No knowledge accrues in the discipline, one generation wipes out the false information created by its predecessors: "the hard knowledge that accrues in one generation typically disenfranchises the theoretical fictions of the previous one".[44] Koch points to the fact that the American Psychological Association alone has 25,000 members and that the federal government subsidized social science research to the tune of $326 millions in 1967. Despite such modern expenditures (much of this on psychology), hundreds of theoretical formulations, thousands of research studies, psychology has not matured. There is still, for example, no wide agreement, even at the crassest descriptive level, on the empirical conditions under which learning takes place. He would disassociate the term "science" from his discipline and call it "psychological studies." This discipline has not earned the right to use a term which conjures up the imagery of natural science. Koch argues that the empirical record of psychology requires us to conclude that the Millian dream at least for it has been disconfirmed. His reference is to the assertion by John Stuart Mill in 1843 that the backward state of the moral sciences (read psychology) can only be remedied by applying to them the methods of the physical sciences. The British philosopher assured his readers that if this were done, then there would be general consensus "for all who have attended to the proof." In our terms, maturity would be reached, for we use consensus as a central gauge for measuring the existence of science.

Koch would thus destroy a central myth of much of social science (the functionalists and the Kremlin Marxists) by disassociating from natural science. He argues that it is not now scientific, nor is it likely to become so. The multinational version agrees with these assertions. He destroyed the maturity myth by attaching a time limit to it, a limit which he argues has now been passed. The experiment is over, and psychology has failed the test. His approach could readily be applied to social science in general; indeed, his recurrent allusions to the general enterprise suggest his receptivity to this expansion. We have our own idea of the future of social science, the parallel with Koch is there in that we see continuing uncertainty and lack of consensus, at least for the immediate future. But our analysis is more consciously dynamic and internationally oriented than that of Koch. The structures to which we bind the disciplines are not only interdisciplinary with a foreign and a domestic side, but they are dynamic, tied to the past and of course to the present, but evolving into an emerging future. Thus Chapter III traces briefly the history of our disciplines from their small beginnings in classical Greece (here we essentially ignore non-Western sources) to their emergence approaching large scale ventures in Imperial Germany and in the United States, flowering into full scale multinational enterprises in the latter country. These enterprises are analyzed in Chapter II, and the American communications network in social science with the outside world in Chapter IV. The United States has become the social science superpower, and its version of the disciplines has been the favorite one exported to that part of the world, alternately called the "free world" or the "American empire." This export has followed our interdisciplinary structures, whose presence is best detected by the economic dimension. Thus the importance of political economy to our analysis.

But we do not let the matter rest there: the United States serves as the head of the free world and as the premier social science superpower. First of all, we recognize that this position has been contested by the USSR and its allies, causing the discipline of international relations to describe the international system as a bipolar one. We recognize this division by giving second world social science its own chapter, number VI. There the reader can readily see that the chasm which separates the dominant paradigms of the United States and those of the Soviet Union is such as to prevent the consensus as set forth in the social science myth. This dream could have been put to rest with the success of the Russian Revolution, which put the resources of the Russian state at the service of a paradigm so much at odds with the ascendant ones in the first world. Friedricks has interpreted this matter in a contrary fashion, observing similarities, at least for his discipline sociology, between Soviet Marxism and functionalism, the dominant American sect for that discipline.[45] He sees the sects converging, a phenomenon which would be a significant step toward achieving the Millian consensus, at least in sociology. His conclusion is based more upon his assessment of the similarities between the two social science sects than upon the "consent" of the belligerents involved. It is as though he forced detente, more accurately stated, integration, upon the contestants.

The third world plays no role in Friedrick's futurology, an omission which we do not duplicate. Chapter VIII is devoted to social science in that portion of the world which houses most of the globe's humans, but at present a minority of its social scientists. But a portion of this world and its social scientists are in open revolt against the first world, and our structural approach helps put the matter in perspective. The revolt is an historic development -- a series of battles waged to liberate a majority of mankind from an imposed dominion, starting with Portuguese expansion and the great discoveries. Like our structures the revolt has been many faceted -- first political independence, spreading to the economic, culture, communications, education, and social science. Structuralism bids us to see these categories as parts of a whole, although the revolts took place sequentially. These revolts promise to be every bit as fundamental as the Russian Revolution, some might think more so. This latter viewpoint is the more persuasive since the events of Eastern Europe in 1989. Marx was a Westerner, and his materialism is easily recognizable in the West and certainly in social science. His atheism is alive and prosperous, and well practiced -- if not often acknowledged in capitalist countries, and his equation of religion with opium directly parallels the functionalist equation of it with social control. This is not to deny that Marxism has been enemy number one in the capitalist world. The third world revolt is likely to result in the mixture of social science with ideology extracted from Islam, Hinduism, and other non-Western ideologies and religions hardly recognizable to the present Western oriented discipline. An example is Varma's condemnation of Parsons' functionalist sociology on the grounds of its support for capitalism, but more to the point, because its reflection of life is that of urban American life, not Indian life. Its emphasis upon voluntarism reflects American ideology, not the most important Indian philosophical schools which accept the determinism of the Karma.[46] The Indian scholar found this same ethnocentric quality in the goal-oriented behavior and the hedonism of Parsons' model. Such examples as these are bound to multiply as the third world comes into its own and arranges social science to fit its vision of the world. Further uncertainty and growing descensus should result, and the Millian dream should be pushed farther from realization. Perhaps sometime in the distant future cooperation on the basis of equality will be possible, a prospect examined in the last chapter.

It should be obvious by now that the multinational version of social science has many facets. It is critical as we have seen, yet accepting as we shall see. It hopes to expose and to analyze social science myths, and to explode them. But it is not an enemy of our disciplines, but rather a supporter of them. This support extends to their use in order to understand themselves. What greater compliment to pay them than to regard their employment as useful, even essential, for self-understanding? To do otherwise is to be condemned to a folk version of them. The use of structural analysis and of the social science of social science can deflate myths and help better to understand the subject matter. Our approach is accepting in that in principle it regards as social science all applicants. Included are Fascist social science regarded here as authentic, as well as social Darwinism, Marxism, the communist brand -- as well as the more standard conservative types. We show below that political science and sociology were institutionalized in Italy during the time of Mussolini, and that social Darwinism was widespread in the United States a century ago. Burgess, the "father" of American political science, was a notorious racist. We do not excommunicate such sects or heroes, whether they are contemporaneous or historical, on the grounds that they do not measure up to our ideology or mythology. Of course, the sects must have an analytical side to them, not merely an ideological one. But their analytical categories can be grounded in race or ethnic groups, as was the case with Burgess' political science. We disagree completely with his notion that blacks and Italians are inferior to Anglo-Saxons and those of German stock, but we do not deny that he was a political scientist for that reason, and he appears to have earned the title "father" for this discipline in the United States.

Our accepting approach parallels the historiography which Kuhn has applied to natural science. When he first entered the field, he found that it was the natural scientists themselves who dominated it. He soon realized also that their historical approach was flawed, an approach called Whig history. They wrote history in terms of the present. When findings and ideas, historically regarded as being scientific, but which currently appear more like errors or myths, were encountered, they were discarded or ignored. Kuhn chose to follow the recognized canons of historiography, i.e. to interpret the past on its own terms. This led him to accept as legitimate natural science that was so regarded in the past, even if today such ideas and findings appear to be errors or myths. This accepting approach required him to tie natural science to the paradigm. When viewed historically, natural science makes sense only in terms of the then existing paradigms. Thus Aristotelian physics makes sense only on its own terms, not in terms of modern physics. In these latter terms it appears quaint and riddled with errors and myths. It was a small step from Kuhn's acceptance of the paramount importance of the paradigm to his assertion that science progresses by revolutions, not by accretion.

We adopt Kuhn's approach, but we use it for contemporary, not merely for historical, analysis. When viewed historically, the natural sciences parallel social science view contemporaneously -- both are multi-paradigm enterprises. Of course, there exist no generally accepted contemporary social science paradigms, consensual standards, deviations from which one can accuse of being errors or myths. In social science the place of the consensual standard is taken by the various paradigms in a given discipline. The adherents of each can usually be relied upon to defend it and to denounce the competition. We do not participate in such denunciations. Rather we accept all contemporary social science paradigms as being legitimate, not allowing ourselves the privilege of excommunicating paradigms which do not agree with our favorites. This is the same accepting approach which characterizes Kuhn's historiography of natural science. We are also playing the role of social scientist, our unique situation being that social science is both the method used and the object of our studies. For us to excommunicate paradigms would be equivalent to the refusal on the part of a sociologist of religion to analyze some religions on the grounds that they are not orthodox. The result of our "accepting" approach is to consider all paradigms as legitimate, and we must in principle account for them all.

Another insight which arises from Kuhn's analysis is his assertion that the historical paradigms of natural science are discontinuous. The content of a given discipline makes little sense when viewed ahistorically, outside the jurisdiction of its respective paradigm. Furthermore, paradigms are discontinuous constructions. The deep divisions among them are not trivial; they cannot be washed away, or wished away, with the application of a little logic or common sense. Kuhn puts it this way: professional communities, reeling from a scientific revolution, have the feeling that they have been "suddenly transported to another planet where familiar objects are seen in a different light and are joined by unfamiliar ones as well".[47] What were ducks in the discipline before the revolution become rabbits afterwards. We put it somewhat differently. Social science is an ideological enterprise bound to many factors besides logic, and communications across paradigms is difficult. The ideological nature of the enterprise is emphasized in Chapter V, and in the ensuring three chapters as well. Social science communications are the subject of Chapter IV. We do not wish to leave the impression that such a chasm divides all paradigms, but it does divide many.

The multinational version of social science has several other facets. We have already referred to its historic side. It pictures social sciences as arising from humble beginnings in classical Greece, flowering in Europe and the United States in the last century, and emerging in the postwar period to assume the proportions of a multinational enterprise. Stamped with the American brand, our disciplines spread along with the American postwar extension, with the "American empire." But this imperium, formerly facing the Soviet challenge, now faces a greater one, this time from the third world. The present, never stationary and always evolving, is passing over to an emerging future. This future, at least the immediate future, promises not to fulfill the Millian dream -- the emergence of consensual, mature disciplines, but rather an even less consensual one. The multinational version betrays other facets -- characteristics which fit and complement the studies and other characteristics divulged above. Our disciplines are not presented here as the creators of objective, detached, and disemboweled information, available to all on the same terms. Their purpose is not necessarily as the functionalist argues: essentially to improve our chances of survival. Finally, the multinational version is international, insisting that our disciplines be made to live in the world, with each center of the disciplines assigned its peculiar role. Developing this now would be to overstep the jurisdiction of this chapter and would impinge upon what belongs to the following one. There we meet the disciplines presented from the points of view of political economy and interdisciplinary structures.

NOTES

1. Jurgen Habermas, Knowledge and Human Interest (Boston: Beacon Press, 1971), 73.

2. Elisabeth T. Crawford and Albert O. Biderman, eds., Social Scientists and International Affairs: A Case for Sociology of Social Science (New York: John Wiley and Son Inc., 1969), 14.

3. Alvin W. Gouldner, The Coming Crisis of Western Sociology (New York: Basic Books, 1970), 54.

4. Maurice Durverger, An Introduction to the Social Sciences: With Special Reference to Their Method (New York: Praeger, 1961), 11.

5. Morris Raphael Cohen, Reason and Nature: An Essay on the Meaning of the Scientific Method (New York: Free Press, 1953), 314.

6. W.J.M. Mackenzie, Politics and Social Science (Baltimore: Penguin, 1969), 1, 2.

7. Fritz Machlup, Knowledge: Its Creation, Distribution, and Economic Significance, Vol. 1, Knowledge and Knowledge Production (Princeton: Princeton University Press, 1980), 65.

8. Melville J. Herskowitz, Man and His Works, The Science of Cultural Anthropology (New York: Alfred Knopf, 1960), 5.

9. Richard Kluckhorn, Collected Essays of Clyde Kluckhorn: Culture and Behavior (New York: Free Press, 1962), 7, 12.

10. Bernard Berelson and Gary A. Steiner, Human Behavior: An Inventory of Scientific Findings (New York: Harcourt, Brace and World, 1964), 8.

11.   Patrick M. Morgan, Theories and Approaches to International Politics: What are We to Think? (Palo Alto: Page Fichlin, 1975), 71.

12.   Julian L. Simon, Basic Research Methods in Social Science: The Art of Empirical Investigation, (New York: Random House, 1969), 139.

13.   Robert K. Merton, The Sociology of Science: Theoretical and Empirical Investigations (Chicago: The University of Chicago Press, 1973), 270.

14.   Norman W. Storer, "The Internationality of Science and the Nationality of Scientists," International Social Science Journal, 22 (1970), 80-93.

15.   Cohen, 99.

16.   Louis-Vincent Thomas, "A Etnologia Mistificacoes Desmistificacoes", A Filosofia Das Ciencias Sociais, (Rio De Janeiro: Zahar, 1974), 127.

17.   Francisco Ayala, Tratado De Sociologia, Vol. 1, Historia de la Sociologia. (Buenos Aires: Editoria Losada, 1947), 32-33.

18.   Kenneth E. Boulding, "National Images and International System", ed. James E. Rosenau, International Politics and Foreign Policy: A Reader in Research and Theory (New York: Free Press, 1969), 424.

19.   Frederick H. Gareau, "The Discipline International Relations: A Multinational Perspective", The Journal of Politics, 43, (1981): 779.

20.   Dwight Waldo, "Political Science: Tradition, Discipline, Profession, Science, Enterprise", ed. Fred I. Greenstein and Nelson W. Polsby, Handbook of Political Science, Vol. 1, Political Science: Scope and Method (Massachusetts: Addison-Wesley, 1975), 1-130.

21.   Duane P. Schultz, A History of Modern Psychology (New York: Academic Press, 1969).

22.   Albert Somit and Joseph Tannenhaus, The Development of American Political Science: From Burgess to Behavioralism, (Boston: Allyn and Bacon, 1967), 65-67.

23.   Ibid., 32-34.

24.   John S. Robey, "Political Science Departments: Reputation Versus Productivity", Political Science (Spring, 1979), 202.

25.   Somit and Tannenhaus, 34.

26.   Le Monde de l'Education, (1981), 12,16,17.

27.   Ibid., (1982), 68-75.

28.   Ibid., (July-August, 1983).

29.   Frederick H. Gareau and Edna C. Gareau, "Are Social Scientists Biased Nationally? An Analysis of Data From the Falklands/Malvinas Conflict," The International Social Science Journal 27 (1986), 475-485. See also Frederick H. Gareau, "The Multinational Version of Social Science," Current Sociology, 33 (1985), 55-59.

30.   V.A. Vinogradov et al., "Toward An International Information System", International Social Science Journal, 33 (1981), 10-49.

31.   Stephen David Ross, The Scientific Process, (The Hague: Martinus Nijhoff, 1971), 124.

32.   Thomas S. Kuhn, The Essential Tension: Selected Studies in Scientific Tradition and Change (Chicago: University of Chicago Press, 1977), 273.

33.   Jacob Bronowski, "The Logic of the Mind", ed. William R. Coulson and Carl Rogers, Man and the Science of Man (Columbus: Merrill, 1968), 38.

34. Karl R. Popper, The Logic of Scientific Discovery (New York: Basic Books, 1959), 44.

35. Bronislaw Malinowski, A Scientific Theory of Culture and Other Essays (New York: Oxford University Press, 1961), 212-213.

36. Gunnar Myrdal, The Political Element in the Development of Economic Theory (New York: Simon and Schuster, 1969), XIV.

37. Patrick M. Morgan, Theories and Approaches to International Politics: What Are We to Think? (Palo Alto: Page Fichlin, 1975), 211.

38. Fred I. Greenstein and Nelson W. Polsby, V.

39. Ernest Nagel, "Psychology and the Philosophy of Science", ed. Benjamin B. Wolman, Scientific Psychology: Principles and Approaches (New York: Basic Books, 1965), 25.

40. Karl R. Popper, "Normal Science and Its Dangers", ed. I. Lakatos and A. Musgrove, Criticism and the Growth of Knowledge (London: Cambridge University Press, 1970), 57-58.

41. Janice Lodahl and Gerald Gordon, "The Structure of Scientific Fields and the Functioning of University Graduate Departments", American Sociological Review, 37 (1972), 57-60.

42. Karin D. Knorr, "The Nature of Scientific Consensus and the Case of Social Sciences", International Journal of Sociology, 7 (1978) 113-145.

43. Philip H. Melanson, Political Science and Political Knowledge (Washington: Public Affairs Press, 1975), 107.

44. Sigmund Koch, "Reflections on the State of Psychology", Social Research, 38, (1971), 687.

45.   Robert W. Friedricks, A Sociology of Sociology (New York: The Free Press, 1970), 286-287.

46.   V.P. Varma, "Talcott Parsons and the Behavioral Sciences", The Indian Journal of Political Science, 13 (1981), 2.

47.   Thomas S. Kuhn, The Structure of Scientific Revolutions (Chicago: University of Chicago Press, 1970), 111.

CHAPTER II

POLITICAL ECONOMY, STRUCTURALISM, AND THE SOCIAL SCIENCE COMMUNITY

This chapter is devoted to the major methods which we use to analyze social science. But since different methods unearth different characteristics, it is tied also to these latter, and, in that sense, it continues on, as the last chapter, to present characteristics of the multinational version of the social sciences. Our two major methods are to treat the disciplines from the standpoint of political economy and structurally according to the canons of world systems analysis. Our first step along this path is to identify the social sciences as part of the knowledge industry. In 1967 they employed between 100,000 and 150,000 (depending on the definition of social science) just in the United States.[1] They have become big business, and this is demonstrated by looking at their economic side, at their costs. Social science outputs are expensive to produce and to distribute, and the enterprise in its developed form is a highly capitalized and specialized one. This is the case particularly if the decision is made to produce new knowledge, not just to distribute knowledge produced elsewhere. The economics of the social science industry favors the rich over the poor, the capitalized over the non-capitalized, and it results in dependencies. This theme runs through the volume, and the inequality and the dependency are exposed when the centers which have carry on relations with the centers which have not. Their modal relationship is a vertical, dependent one with the more capitalized gaining advantage - - profiting more than and probably to the disadvantage, of the less capitalized. Viewed from the economic aspect, social sciences tend to be oligopolies, with the same consequences which obtain in what are traditionally classified as economic enterprises. Here the multinational approach takes exception to Storer's assertion that social science is a

<u>laissez-faire</u> enterprise, in which ability almost always rises to the top. Our approach contains no principle which prohibits such a happy result, but it insists that the wealthy and the capitalized are those who tend to make it to the summit.

Having linked our disciplines to economics, we next tie them to the political. Thus our approach is political economy. This second link is easy, even without help from world systems analysis, since this segment of the knowledge industry is subsidized by governments and influenced by them. The political economic connection leads naturally to a third step, linkage to the structures of world systems analysis. These structures are international and multi-disciplinary, the last characteristic providing broad ramifications for our analysis. Our disciplines are thereby connected not only to the political and to the economic (already accomplished by political economy), but also to the cultural, communications, and education. Education, in practice, is very close to the social sciences. These structures are not intended as independent variables -- elites/classes serve better in this capacity. It is they that "lurk" behind the structures. These structures are the stable and recurrent patterns which result from the past struggles of these classes/ elites.[2]   They are used here as interdisciplinary connectors, which put social science in a broad context. Cardoso and Faletto nominate the economic as the surest guidepost for the discovery of these multidisciplinary structures, even though it is not an infallible one. Only the economic determinist thinks that it is. We shall follow the cue set forth by Cardoso and Faletto using the economic, but skeptically for what it is worth. We shall also be very attentive to education. World systems analysis has its own list of characteristics which we discuss below. Not the least of them is its international focus, a foremost characteristic of this volume as well. The first step in our analysis is to put social science within the contours of the "knowledge industry," a step bound to raise eyebrows. When a president of a university declared that his institution was part of the industry which produced knowledge, he received the inevitable rejoinders from the humanistically inclined, who would protect the virtue of the university against the onslaught of the materialist.[3] Such high minded readers are assured that our approach is a dualistic, non-reductionist one, which has made room for virtue, voluntarism, and a measure of freedom for social science practitioners.

We have made room in this chapter for a brief section on social science communities. Though the focus of the volume is multinational, we recognize that these national institutions play a role in the evolution of social science. Our presentation of these institutions is congruent with the analysis found in the remainder of the volume -- critical, rather than idealized. Also congruent is that their service to our disciplines finds a place in the analysis as well.

The Social Science Enterprise

Even a hard-nosed humanist will admit that the social sciences produce and exchange (and even store) knowledge and that these activities often result in certain costs and incomes. One need not be a materialist to recognize this fact, and this recognition does not require that we deny the existence of the intellectual side of social science. We point to this duality, this coexistence, not merely to assuage the feelings of the humanist, but because both sides of the enterprise are necessary to account for the various forms the social sciences take and the roads which they travel. Nonetheless, let us illustrate the kind of conclusion to which our analysis can lead. The world's largest producers of social science journals in order are the United States, France, the United Kingdom, Italy, West Germany, Japan, India, the Soviet Union, Brazil, and Holland. These top ten produce 52.4 percent of the total.[4] We argue that the relative size of the national professional social science journal industry is a reasonable index of the relative size and importance of the national social science enterprise. In fact, the concentration is greater than the above figures suggest, since they refer to number of titles, not to circulation. An examination of this list of countries reveals that it includes many of the world's leading economic powers -- the correlation between these two characteristics is striking. This correlation is by no means perfect, some countries obviously being out of order. But a relationship obviously exists, an important insight from political economy. This discipline also offers an insight to explain the US postwar position as the world's greatest social science power. Political economy offers this insight when the discipline is tied to the structures of world systems analysis. The insight is offered as competition to the standard explanation that US social science paradigms spread far and wide in the postwar period to achieve a status close to international reference models because of their innate qualities. The insight is that the spread of US paradigms was parallel to US dominance in the economic, military, political, cultural, communications, and educational spheres.

Our immediate task, step one, is to stake out the economic aspects of social science, i.e. to see how it can be fitted out as part of the knowledge industry. We do this by comparing its component parts with the generic ones of the knowledge industry. Machlup has identified six of the latter, five of which can be matched to components of social science. Along with this match up, we consider the theory of human capital for the light which it can shed on our analysis. The reader can take comfort in the fact that our assigned task is not so much to stretch out, so as to analyze, the social sciences on the wrack of economic theory, but rather to make general points which further our analysis. We envisage our role as not that of the expert, meticulous economist, but more as the social scientist who analyzes social science.

Five of the six generic components of the knowledge industry identified by Machlup can be matched up with corresponding parts of social science. These five generic components are education, research and development, media of communication, information services, and information machines.[5] Machlup identifies education as probably the most important component, but his version of it includes institutions beyond those of interest to us. We use education as that structure which is the closest to social science, and so it has special relevance for our analysis. So far as that structure is concerned, we concentrate upon universities and institutes which produce and distribute most social science knowledge. Primary and secondary schools are ignored, they do distribute, even if they seldom create, social science knowledge. As we learn below, however, it is hard to maintain the distinction between production and distribution in the knowledge industry. A notion of the costs and, therefore, the economic aspect of schools is suggested by such estimates as state expenditures for education, earnings foregone by students of working age, tuition and book payments, and subsidies and grants to students. This list is meant only to be suggestive; it is by no means complete.

Education results in more productive human beings, in our case scholars able to produce and distribute social science. This leads to the attempt to assess the results of the outputs of education, usually described by the theory of human capital. Our discussion of this theory should not be interpreted to mean that we have forgotten that education, actually access to it, is used to maintain class structures. The gate keepers of education are usually the gate keepers of class structure. Education in this interpretation is not so much a way of increasing capital goods as a means of maintaining a given class structure. In a sense, the theory of human capital applies to the education of humans what is usually applied to inanimate objects as they become more able to produce objects. Actually, the analogy seems closer to improving land values, i.e. educated labor is like improved land in that by means of an investment it becomes more productive. It is harder to speak of "unimproved" human beings than unimproved land, and much of the improvement via education in a human being may go for consumption, not production. The better educated may become more cultured, thereby listening to classical music rather than "wasting" their time on television -- the switch not really increasing production. Such conceptual ambiguities need not concern us, the important point is that educating social scientists represents an expense, and the result can be a capital asset when none existed before or an improved capital asset. Knowledge acquired by them creates their status or improves their performance as social scientists, and these scholars are part of a social science infrastructure. Education is typically paid for, and regulated by, government, thus the link of social science to politics and to political economy, subjects treated below.

It is difficult to estimate the mean educational level of social scientists, especially if we insist upon a global view. For want of a better source, we use a sample of 377 social scientists collected at two world congresses held in 1982 -- that of the International Sociological Association and that of the International Political Science Association. The sample includes 48 nationalities, but since both congresses were held in Latin America (Rio de Janeiro and Mexico City), that region is well represented, the only one so represented from the third world. The other region with a sizeable number of delegates was Western Europe. The United States, of course, had a substantial share. A large percentage of the conferees had the doctorate (54.6 percent), many had a master's (25.5 percent), and 14.6 percent had the licenciado.[6] Such credentials represent a large investment in economic resources, but the capital thus amassed is deemed necessary for the operation of the social science enterprise.

The doctorate was created as a research degree, so that those who hold it would be trained to generate new knowledge and not just act as conveyor belts for the transmission of knowledge created by others. This degree along with the graduate programs which spawn it was transferred after the Civil War from Germany to the United States, where it produces much of the knowledge for this "post-industrial" society. This discussion leads to the second generic component of the knowledge industry identified by Machlup, and also to the notion of varying levels of social science and degrees of capitalization of sections of the social science enterprise. This second generic component is research and development, usually referred to in the social sciences simply as research. This means the generation of "socially new knowledge," in our case the creation of new social science information not known by anyone before. Knowledge is a special kind of "product," more ethereal than most, and, therefore, it requires a distinctive way of being viewed. Knowledge can be defined as anything which is known by someone. Its production refers to any activity by which a person learns of something which the person in question did not know before.[7] This definition includes under production the exchange of knowledge from a knower to one not having known. Exchange is thus counted as production, because the exchange of this ethereal product enhances the share of knowledge of the receiver. Moreover, this is done without prejudice to the original product and often without prejudice to its original owner. It is not like the exchange of most products, in which case the stock of goods of the seller is diminished. This characteristic has economic consequences to which we return below. Now we remark that Machlup uses the term "socially new knowledge" to designate knowledge previously unknown to anyone.

"Socially new" social science information can conceivably be produced by chance and by anyone, but the probability of this occurring at present is remote. Much more likely is its creation by social science professionals, probably with doctorates, those who are paid for the time spent on research and with adequate language backgrounds. The probability of success is greatly enhanced if our subjects are part of a developed, highly capitalized social science infrastructure. Until the nineteenth century, social science was a product of the leisure classes. In that century it was industrialized/ specialized, a development which first occurred in Germany and the United States. This development was marked in the latter country by the founding of specialized social science organizations and by a change in the structure and the philosophy of the American university away from training based upon a liberal, general education.[8] The new infrastructure involved many capital resources and professional services -- a minimum might be access to specialized library facilities, typing assistance, a fine personal library, and, depending upon the kind of research, access to a computer. All of these conditions entail expenses, thus again pointing to the economic aspects and the capitalization of social science. The result of creating "socially new" knowledge is an enhancement of the productivity of a given social science facility. The facility no longer serves merely as a distributor of knowledge passing on this commodity which originates elsewhere, to those who were unaware of it. Now it produces "socially new" social science information. It has added another "product" to its line. Those facilities which have added this research capability, which are so capitalized, and which do well at research are the most prestigious in their field. Countries which house such facilities are the rich centers to which poor, peripheral countries send their students to be trained. Typically, such centers hire the most prestigious professors, who receive much better salaries than their less well known colleagues.

The three last generic parts of the knowledge industry, identified by Machlup, are also related to the degree of capitalization of a social science enterprise, and thus also to the value and to the quantity of its outputs. The generic parts are media of communications, information services, and information machines. The respective examples from social science are social science journals and relevant books; libraries and information services such as the Rand Corporation; and copiers, typewriters, and now the computer and the word processor. Perhaps the most important means of communication for social science is the professional journal. It represents the crucial network by which the members of a social science communicate with each other. These networks are typically national, as are the journals which service them. Such nationalism is modified by dependency relations and by some real regional cooperation. There is at the regional level, for example, a common political science journal for Scandinavia. Members of national social science associations write articles for mutual consideration, and the journals provide information about the profession usually in a given country. We have noted above that the countries with the largest number of these journals tend to be the richest nations.

Advanced nations in social science tend to be the big book publishers and tend to have the famous, comprehensive libraries. Leopold von Ranke, the famous German nineteenth century historian, had a personal library of 20,000 volumes. In the present age of specialization ,the scholar depends more upon institutional libraries. Thirty-four industrialized countries with only 30 percent of the world's population produce 81 percent of the world's book titles.[9] Those who have had intercultural experience in the matter of books and libraries can vouch for the dichotomy which describes the situation in a social science rich and a social science poor situation. The author has studied in Washington DC, and, therefore, had access to the Library of Congress, and he has studied in the interior of Brazil in a small city where the library was minimal. The Library of Congress is reputed to be the largest in the United States, and its sources are, indeed, impressive except that too often they are checked out to members of Congress, or what is more probable, to the staffs of the members. The library in the interior of Brazil was not adequate for any serious scholarship or research. The facilities for social science found in Rio de Janeiro and Brasilia are better, but not comparable to a middle ranked university in the United States. An anthropologist in Brazil advised that the best place to carry on research on some aspects of Brazilian anthropology is the United States, and an Indian historian we know regularly goes to London to do research on India. A dramatic aspect of our experience at a university in the interior of Brazil was the general lack of books among the students. They came to class without books, I believe because they did not have any. The professor's request that each student buy a dictionary and a grammar was honored by few students. This seemed like a reasonable request, because the course was on the Portuguese language.

That the social science enterprise has an economic aspect should be evident by now. We need not belabor the point by emphasizing the importance of secretarial help, nor shall we sing the praises of the word processor. But these are support facilities for our enterprise, part of its infrastructure. The information service industries are the most obvious parts of the knowledge industry. They sell knowledge for a price. The most obvious individual entrepreneurs in the industry are those who do the same, but for their personal accounts. Some of these in the United States serve as itinerant scholars, doing a stint with a university, then the government, only to switch to an information service industry, or to a regular commercial enterprise. The computer adds another dimension to the infrastructure of the social sciences; it tends to make the enterprise more capital intensive. It seems only natural that social science in the United States should be computer driven, because this reflects a trait of the larger society. The effect of quantification is more mechanization, more capital is needed, and social science knowledge thus becomes that much more capital intensive, if not more expensive. This puts the poor centers of the enterprise at an increased disadvantage. They not only lack library facilities -- now they lack a computer capacity as well. They are doubly disadvantaged, just as the rich countries are doubly advantaged.

We have glossed over several of the traits of the knowledge industry, because we judge that they have little relevance to our analysis of social science. But three have particular importance to this analysis. The first is the trend toward the expansion of the industry. No doubt there are numerous reasons for this -- one of which is that knowledge is power and influence. To control the kind of social science used locally is to have an impact on the state of local ideology -- and thus to have local power and influence. But we concentrate upon the economics of the impulse for expansion. Important in this respect is the fact that knowledge can be duplicated seemingly endlessly, without prejudice to the original findings. The same knowledge which produces one airplane can produce others, just as the same social science paradigm which guides one research design can guide others. Repetitions do no injury to the original, nor do they diminish the original stock. This leaves aside the question of the cost of producing the original or the cost of distributing it from its origin to others for subsequent application. This means that the social science enterprise, or at least parts of it, are a high fixed cost undertaking, with low variable costs. In this kind of undertaking, the expenditures are relatively great for those costs which do not vary with the amount produced (fixed costs), whereas the costs for those expenditures which do vary with the amount produced (variable costs) are relatively modest. An example is the one given above, the paradigm, or we could use the production of a book or a professional journal. Fixed costs can be relatively high -- the usual overhead, but also typesetting and secretarial expense. The cost for producing additional copies of the book or journal can be relatively modest -- e.g. the cost of paper, the ink, as examples. A relatively large number of copies would have to be sold just to break even, after which profits are forthcoming. This phenomenon of a break even point is present in every undertaking -- thus the pressure is on and the premium goes to sales volume. In high fixed costs undertakings, however, this trend is accentuated. The drive for greater sales volume also tends to lead to higher concentration in the social science enterprise.

The pressure is on the knowledge industry to increase its sales of products and services, so as to enhance profits (if a private enterprise) or to reduce unit costs (a guide for public enterprise). Academic books are advertised in the appropriate media, and free "desk copies" are given to professors so as to increase adoptions and expand sales. College campuses play host to "representatives" of book companies. Better dressed than the average student, they look like the college administrator, but they are usually more agreeable. They smile more often, and they bring news from New York. This is the soft sell, the best face of capitalism.   Book companies have become multinationals, "pushed" overseas by the search for profits or for survival. Empty college classrooms at night in residential institutions testify to the failure of college administrators fully to succeed in applying economic logic to their affairs. The book business seems more amenable to this logic. Universities should be run like the steel or glass industries, continuous production with three shifts.   The human factor interferes with such a fanciful idea -- students prefer to sleep or to do other things at night. More feasible are the attempts to increase summer enrollment, the adoption of the trimester system, or the increase in class size. These attempts, if successful, tend to lower unit costs by spreading the fixed costs over a larger volume.   This analysis must be modified also by the realization that most universities are public supported, and so the economic calculus can be attenuated by other considerations.

The economics of the knowledge industry applicable to our disciplines thus tends to push the social science enterprise toward expansion. Textbooks, written in the rich centers of social science, are exported to the poorer centers.   This has not meant that the most prestigious universities have expanded to look like IBM, but they usually have found the space to include room for students from the colonies, and more recently, room for students from the third world. Social science information from the rich countries thus has penetrated colonies and poorer countries. This penetration is partly the result of the push of the economic -- paradigms, once produced, can be reproduced without damage to the original creation. Social science has become a highly capitalized enterprise in the developed world; it has penetrated the developing countries; and this penetration has caused dependence and ultimately has been at the expense of the penetrated. This last charge is the hardest to prove, and in order to tell our whole story we must go beyond economics to political economy and even further to the structures of world systems analysis.

The tendency toward expansion of the capitalized part of the social science industry pushes it toward penetration of the less capitalized, and this results in the dependence of the latter upon the part with the more developed facilities. We count dependence as the second major characteristic of the knowledge industry of particular relevance to our study. We have already alluded to this phenomenon when viewed internationally, but it has a domestic side as well. The experts who emerge from this greater capitalized situation depend upon more expensive resources which they cannot afford. Usually the resources are provided by a university which in turn generally depends upon the government for such financing. In the case of the United States, private funds defray much of the expense. The funds obtain their finances from private business, the big corporations. This leads to the third major characteristic.

The third major characteristic of the knowledge industry full of significance for the social sciences is its close connection with governmental and other dominant elites. This is true for much of the social science enterprise, not just in socialist countries, but in capitalist ones as well. It is true for most of the school system even in capitalist countries, but not for most of the book industry in those countries. Many universities are state owned and controlled, and the government subsidizes much of the research. Social science knowledge in the United States and in most countries is produced by government bureaucrats, usually they take the form of professors, and various methods have been devised to cushion the control of their professional lives. This governmental connection, however, exists, and knowledge of it makes easier the conceptual transition from the social sciences as part of the knowledge industry to political economy and to the world systems analysis of our disciplines. Political economy would have us look at a subject, social science in our case, with insights from both the disciplines economics and politics. An insight from the former, as we have seen, is social science as a fixed cost industry, an enterprise driven toward expansion by the logic of economic efficiency or profit. An insight from the latter is social science as a means by which elites stay in power or conquer power. The fate of Marx and Marxism illustrates this point. Everyone knows that Marx lost his university position in Imperial Germany; that system would not aid and abet such a revolutionary thinker. We also realize that to be a Marxist is the necessary, or at least the smart, thing to be in the Soviet Union and similar countries. Moreover, the social sciences had a hard time of it during the time of Stalin and until recently in China. But how does one explain the virtual absence of Marxism in "free world" universities long after the death of its founder? Part of the explanation is internal to the disciplines; the other part is external, i.e. ideological and political. Even today, Marxists in American universities still tend to be the covert, closet type. Political economy suggests the reason for what otherwise might appear to be an unexplained bizarre tale of Marxist social science. If social science were merely an intellectual exercise or even one with an economic component, but no political one, the dichotomous distribution indicated above could hardly be explained. Are we to believe that isolated individuals or groups just come together, but in two opposing dichotomous groups, without political and ideological nudging or pressure? Political economy features the latter, thus making this "bizarre tale" more understandable. We are not saying that social scientists are always obedient state bureaucrats. Sometimes they get out of hand and oppose dominant elites. The complications of this admission will be considered in the ensuing chapter.

Structuralism and World Systems Analysis

We use political economy, not as a terminal step, but rather as an introduction. It is a beginning, the first crack in the door which allows expansion to a broader multidisciplinary structural analysis. We have already referred to the sociology of sociology and to the social science of social science, approaches close to structuralism. A major difference is that our structures are not merely interdisciplinary, they are also international. They include the political, the economic, culture, education, communications, and social science. But they have an overseas as well as a domestic focus. The United States is introduced here to the reader as the undisputed leader of the "free" world (the capitalist world) and as the superpower of social science -- this introduction without benefit of historical background. The author seriously considered delaying this discussion of world systems analysis and this introduction until after the historical account. Then the reader would appreciate better how the United States rose to the top, and the significance of her being there. Further consideration led to the conclusion that the prior reading of the historical account would aid in understanding world systems analysis, but that the converse is true as well. So the present order was decided upon: world systems analysis now and the historical account in the following chapter. Those who prefer the contrary order are invited to read Chapter III first and then to return here. The discussion of world systems analysis below starts with an exposition of the theory, and is followed by its application first to colonies, then to the third and the first worlds.

Cardoso and Faletto would have us analyze social life in terms of relatively stable global structures.[10] The structures do eventually change over time, and the authors name their approach historical/structural. The area of interest of these scholars is Latin America, and they find that the structures there result from asymmetrical dependent relations which cause exploitation; the structures are the stable results of the class struggle, and they are more intermediate variables than independent ones. Their paradigm centers upon these structures, which have interrelated domestic and foreign components. The Latin American scholars insist that each dependent relationship, each concrete set of structures, must be individually analyzed. No standard set of detailed conclusions can be inferred from the structure and imposed upon every dependency relationship. They insist that domestic elites have a role to play, and the impact of the different categories of structures can vary with each given case. Their paradigm was "invented" to analyze the situation existing in their region, and they insist that their approach does not necessarily apply, for example, to the socialist countries. We apply it there, but with some modifications.

We quote these two Latin American authors because we are in general agreement with them. Their non-dogmatic attitude is appealing, as is their emphasis upon the particular. In our own case, we must grant that social science does not always support the status quo. Nonetheless, we shall apply a modified dependency theory to the former socialist countries of Eastern Europe, at least to the social science of the region as it existed until 1989. We like the non-reductionism of Cardoso and Faletto; they do not, for example, reduce global structures to economics. But they do argue that the key to, the golden thread for finding, the structures is the economic -- it is located at the top of the hierarchy of the components of these structures. If not the inevitable cause, economics thus seems to be the usual companion. We do not accept this assertion as a necessary one. It should ring true in the case of the United States, because her postwar expansion, even if a many splendored thing, economics has been most

obvious. Another point of disagreement, actually a point of modification by way of expansion, is that our approach is world systems
analysis, not dependent bilateralism. The two approaches have most
things in common, but one focuses upon the relationship between two
countries, center and periphery, whereas world systems analysis has the
entire world as its domain.

The next two items on the agenda are the continuation of the
elaboration of the distinctive features of the global structures already
partially described and the larger task of a detailed discussion of the
world systems analysis of social science. We rely to a considerable
extent upon the work of Galtung's analysis of what he calls
"imperialism." Global structures are a many faceted phenomena.
Galtung identifies the categories they present as the economic, the
political, the military, communications, the social, and the cultural.[11]
We add to this list education and, of course, social science, which is
very closely tied to education. Galtung does not give priority or any
special status to the economic, arguing that the interaction patterns
which we see as producing global structures can arise from any
discipline on his list, and any combination of them is possible. We
agree with him, but we still are on the lookout for the economic,
because it usually plays a featured role in human affairs. He offers
three examples to counterpose against the Marxist grant of primacy to
the economic and against any view that the list must always be
complete. The first is the Chinese complaint against the Soviet Union
of "social imperialism," a complaint we are advised to take quite
literally. The Chinese complaint was that the Soviet Union was trying
to force its social system upon the Asian nation. The complaint was
not economic exploitation, and it was lodged after Chinese processed
materials had been accorded increasingly better access to Soviet
markets. Indeed, the Soviets seem to give favored economic treatment
to many of their "clients," for example, those in Eastern Europe receive
higher than world prices for their products. Galtung argues that
Eastern European countries have been culturally penetrated by the
West, despite their military and political subservience to the Soviets.
The third example is the Japanese who have penetrated many
countries economically, but they have had little cultural impact. One
obstacle is their language, which presents a formidable barrier to
cultural penetration. In contrast, American cultural and social science
penetration have had a much easier time of it as the inheritors of a
language spread far and wide by the British empire.

We embrace structural analysis, but with some caution, on the lookout for modifications and amplifications. Our embrace is qualified, but not a mere flirtation, more a serious affair. The same is true of our acceptance of world systems analysis, a concept which features structures. We are attracted because this kind of analysis is holistic, the notion being used here in the double sense that social science cannot be understood unless many disciplines are included and unless the content goes beyond the domestic to include the global as well. We must stress, therefore, that the structures used in our analysis are interdisciplinary and global -- consisting of many disciplines and of the domestic and the foreign as well. Such a setting is seen as being interrelated -- with the components in a package impacting each other in a dialectic fashion, but the main independent variables are classes/elites. The classes/elites are domestic, but the strength of foreign ones must be reckoned with, particularly in the case of the third world. We see the global structures as helping to fashion social science, as subsidiary causes but the latter "fights back" and takes its turn as actor to impact the structures and the classes/elites as well. Behind the structures are the classes/elites, the result of whose struggle results in the structures. Especially noticeable in the shorter run, the social sciences have a measure of influence -- they have a visible and significant intellectual component.

In this view, there exists a multitude of social elements, these are linked by a plurality of relationships, and the relationships are integrated into patterned structures.[12] These structures are not substances, they are arrangements or organizations of components, and the properties and regularities of the components are derived from their positions within the comprehensive networks, the structures. This approach does not deny the importance and the role of the human being, nor the substance of the individual. But social objects are very different from a simple sum of individuals -- seen as singularistic, unconnected atoms. We see the individual and the group as social agents because of a role imposed by enduring socially structured relations. The power of social agents results from social structures which shape human action, not from the social agents as individuals. The black was a slave and the white a slave owner, not because of the physical characteristics of these races, but because of specific social structures. The same is true of student and teacher, worker and capitalist. The structure is incarnate in the products and in the practices of the relevant group -- it is not otherwise witnessable.[13]

Since structures do not exist independently of activities, they are not simply reproduced, but they are also transformed. To talk about a structure is a static idealization of a process which is going on in individuals. The structure is enduring, yet evolving and changing.

The variables treated in our analysis not only interact with each other, but they do this in such a patterned manner that each is assigned a role in the system. After all, structures refer to persistent behavioral and attitudinal patterns to the point that roles can be assigned to the actors. The roles can be seen as being assigned exclusively in a capitalist setting, or other systems may be given this power as well. We see this role granting power in a broad context -- the Soviet system being included as well. We argue that the systems existing in global social science and in most national systems is elitist, closer to what the economist calls oligopoly than to perfect competition. The situation in most third world countries is best described as dependency, and roles there are assigned according to the principles of dependent capitalism. Certainly, egalitarian systems with perfect competition must reign someplace in social science, but this pattern is not the norm, certainly not when viewed from a world perspective.

The process by which this elitism and stratification is preserved and fortified, once it has been established, can be shown by analogy with economic exchange between the center (the developed) and the peripheral (the underdeveloped). With some modification, this process can also describe how elitism and stratification are initiated as well. Let us assume that the center developed country has already devoted the resources to, and has had the time to augment, its social science infrastructure. It has the necessary personnel -- social scientists and secretaries, universities, institutes, and other educational facilities, the libraries, the available books and journals, the paradigms, and computers if they are necessary. This infrastructure, as we have seen, is very much related to economics. Our setting will be international, but a similar process takes place within countries as well. Harvard or the Sorbonne can serve as center institutions having relations with less prestigious, peripheral ones in the same nation. Galtung shows the unequal internal benefits which arise when an undeveloped country exchanges its unprocessed crude oil for the tractors of a developed country. Note that his assumption is that both sides benefit from the exchange, an insight which agrees with the great insight of classical economics of the mutual benefit of exchange.

Galtung's criticism is only that the benefits are unequally distributed. Our view is less charitable, also harder to prove. It is that at least part of the dependent country suffers as a result of the transaction. Galtung's emphasis is not upon the impact of the imported item, but rather upon the domestic effects of the production of the item exported. The exchange is crude petroleum, almost pure nature, exchanged for a tractor, almost pure culture.[14] In his illustration, the oil deposit is near the ocean, the tanker which transports the petroleum is foreign, and the oil derricks and their crews are imported. He maintains that the transaction can be visualized such that the positive internal effects in the underdeveloped nation are practically nil; and those in the developed country are far-reaching. Our advice for improving this illustration would be to substitute for the tractor a Rolls Royce or air conditioners for the Sheik's harem. This would also nullify the possible developmental impact of the use of the imported tractor. In any case, there is a marked distinction to be made between the internal development impact of the production of crude oil as set forth here and the internal impact of the production of a finished product whether tractors, a Rolls Royce, or air conditioners.

The transaction need not contribute at all to the developmental infrastructure of the underdeveloped country -- luxurious transportation and a cooler harem are marginal to this goal. But these developments increase the pleasure of certain elites. The same for taking oil out of the ground under the circumstances cited above. Not so for manufacturing finished products. This latter requires and reinforces and strengthens infrastructures in many subject areas. Included are industrial technology, research, universities, etc. The effects are cumulative, and the leading developed countries serve as centers to several peripheral countries. The raw materials from underdeveloped countries support and complement the industrialization of their trading partner. The social science model parallels this economic one. The foreign students from underdeveloped countries, for example, study in a developed country with an advanced social science infrastructure. The latter has the necessary educational system, the professors, the books, the professional journals, the libraries, the paradigms, and the research findings. The students' minds serve as the focus, the stuff around which human capital is centered. Such capital will be created with the transfer of the local knowledge of the paradigms and the research findings. Such a process requires the social infrastructure, the capital goods already existing in the center.

In the economic exchange model set forth by Galtung, the undeveloped, peripheral country exports unprocessed petroleum under circumstances which do not add to its productive capacity. But the gross national product is increased. The social science parallel is the graduate student who goes home to collect raw information or data to be processed, using the physical social science infrastructure and the paradigms of the developed country. Or a professor from the center country, using these same productive factors, collects and processes information and data from the periphery. This information and these data fuel the center's social science infrastructure in ways not much different from the way imported oil fuels its industry. The impact upon the developed country is discussed below. The importance of such imports for the center country is the more significant when we realize that this country plays the same dominant role for many peripheries. It thus draws on raw data and information from many peripheral sources and builds up a stock of knowledge from many of them -- processed by its infrastructure and according to its own paradigms. Soon the center becomes the depository for readily available, "processed" knowledge about many peripheries. It can even surpass a peripheral country in social science knowledge about itself. Certainly, the center will become more important than the neighbors of the peripheral countries. It, therefore, becomes a knowledge center, a place stocked with this kind of knowledge -- the stock in the form of, and bearing the brand name of, center paradigms. The center has the infrastructure to run off many copies of its paradigms and research findings. The fact that the knowledge industry is often a high fixed cost industry promotes the elitism and the stratification of the enterprise. This is the case for the book industry and for professional journals, and thus they lean in the same direction. For obvious reasons, the peripheries of social science tend to communicate each with its respective center, not with each other -- a pattern discernible also in general patterns of communications. This pattern for social science is verified in Chapter IV.

The Impact of Social Science Imports upon Third World Countries
        The social science exchange between center and periphery takes other forms as well, but note that the relationship continues to be vertical. This is the case when the book publishing company or the

professional journal in the center uses its productive capacity to publish using center paradigms and research findings, the latter being generated locally or in foreign lands. The product is then transferred to the receiving country to the readers of such literature. Another mode of transmission is through the professional visits of social scientists -- they transfer paradigms and research findings much as professors do to the students who attend the center university. In fact, they most probable are professors, but their general role is that of an expert who goes to underdeveloped areas to help the locals install or develop our disciplines. The generic term given to describe the process is often "technical assistance," a term which we regard as inappropriate for social science. We restrict this term to the transfer of natural science and its application, technology, and exclude social science which is disqualified because of its heavy layer of internal ideology and philosophy. To accept natural science knowledge is not without a political side. But social science is much more political because of the contrary ideology of the various paradigms existing within the same discipline. The ideology is part and parcel of a social science paradigm, woven into its fabric and basic assumptions. The "technical" does not suggest these latter truths.

These latter assertions are pertinent to our view of the impact of social science exchange upon the developing countries. This impact cannot properly be interpreted as the simple development of its human capital, a kind of straightforward technical assistance which improves the social science capability of developing countries. This would be close to the mark if social science knowledge were what functionalists claim it is, a kind of objective, disemboweled information which serves the general purpose of survival. But we insist upon putting social science in the context of its proper structure, the latter providing a crucial clue as to the kind of social science transferred and whose interests are served by the transfer. And now we can return to Galtung's exchange above of tractors for raw petroleum. His conclusion was that the exportation of this petroleum would not aid development, not necessarily a correct conclusion. The analogy with social science is not a perfect one, and we reach a different conclusion. We have to admit that the social science transactions noted above can aid the development of the social science infrastructure of the developing country. This exchange can improve the human capital of this country, the personnel so trained can, and will probably, serve as transmission belts to carry home the paradigms and supporting data which they learned at the center. They may even maintain personal contacts with the center, join social science communities there, or subscribe to its professional journals. The insight from structuralism is that the kind of social science learned is related to these structures, intertwined with and supportive of them. If the structures involved are those of dependent capitalism (most likely the case), then the social science learned will probably rationalize this kind of relationship. The relationship is probable, not absolute, but well within the parameters usually assumed by the social science enterprise.

To understand whether these social science exchanges benefit the developing country, we must dig further into the matter and continue to build our analogy. Galtung speaks of a bridgehead, the center in the periphery, and of the crucial role which it plays in his structural analysis. The center in the periphery, usually identified as the local elites in a relationship of dependent capitalism, is linked to the center, and its interests are in a general sense those of the center. Sometimes these elites are irreverently referred to as the "clients" of the center. The Norwegian scholar finds a strong coupling, a harmonious relationship between the elites in both areas. This closeness, in fact, can be exaggerated, or even break down. Inequality exists in the center and in the periphery, but in the latter, at least, in situations of dependent capitalism, inequality assumes the proportions of an abyss. In fact, the center in the periphery enjoys a standard of living and a pattern of consumption very much like that in the center. Indeed, the luxury products consumed in the center in the periphery tend to be either imported from the center or produced locally by multinationals from the center. Galtung argues that it is incorrect to see the "clients" of the center as a traditional bourgeoisie -- they are often political elites trained in the center and even intellectuals "whose souls remain in the metropolitan university at which they got their degrees".[15] The tie to the center extends to the internalization of its values, including its expression in the metropolitan's language. Galtung offers as a clear expression of dependence the social science penetration of Latin America, Africa, and Asia. It is to the interest of the center that capitalist economics and other supporting disciplines be prevalent in the periphery. Another point full of significance for our analysis is the charge that the local needs which require satisfaction from the center are those of the clients and not those of the masses.

The social science exchange introduced earlier in our analysis need not benefit the peripheral nation. Indeed our analysis suggests that this question cannot be answered in this form -- with the nation reified. It suggests that this exchange benefits the clients of the center -- the social science imported tends to be the type which does this and which, of course, benefits the client social scientists as well. They tend to become the most prestigious social scientists in the local country, their status stemming from the general esteem in which the center is held and/or from the fact that they have attended a developed central university. Dependency theory points to the probability of multiple local elites, which can be grouped into two opposing currents, one national, and perhaps also radical, the other international. By extension and analogy, we see two general local social science groups. The clients are the "internationalists" who are tied to the center, and the nationalists are more inward bound, "ethnocentric", but more authentic. The social science exchange with the center thus tends to divide the local social science enterprise. Furthermore, the communications of the clients tends to be with the center, not with fellow national groups nor with national groups in other peripheral countries. "Pan-movements" in third world countries are thus set back. The national fragmentation also interferes with the development of a national social science capability. The social scientists of the "international" segment tend to interact with the center, and they remain inferior to it and dependent upon it. They tend to be cut off from their fellow nationalists. Thus Indian social scientists did not play a large role in the decolonization movement. Social scientists from similarly situated peripheral countries, despite common problems, tend not to communicate with each other, nor to present a united front against the center countries. This becomes clear in chapter VIII, our chapter on the third world. They tend to be divided nationally and regionally. Peripheral social science thus tends to be divided -- the usual condition for social science, but with an additional species of cleavage.

The conclusion that social science does not develop under the circumstances outlined above is not warranted. It develops, but the process is not a repetition of the pattern followed by the developed countries. They developed their versions of the disciplines in response to their problems (i.e. those of their dominant classes) and in accord with their own ideologies, or if they imported foreign products, by now they have had opportunity to indigenize them. Third world countries have not had this opportunity. The exceptions are noted in Chapter VIII. Their situation parallels that arising from the importation and the use of a foreign technology for production. Multinational corporations use in peripheral countries the technologies which they develop in and for the center, where the relative cost of labor and capital is quite unique. For its circumstances, a capital intensive technology is the one indicated. But the multinational typically uses this same technology in a third world situation where a labor intensive technology would be warranted. The result is that fewer workers are hired than if a more relevant local technology were used -- thus more unemployment exists or fewer jobs are created in industry. Technology here serves as an analogy for a social science paradigm -- both are patterns for production, one of a part of the knowledge industry, the other for what are more obviously economic goods.

The countries which develop a social science infrastructure under conditions of dependency will follow a path different from that followed where our disciplines originated. This is a way of applying to social science what the dependentista applies to economic development in general. The United Kingdom originated the industrial revolution under conditions set by itself, more accurately stated, according to the dictates of its own conditions and those of its own elites. They were instrumental in its origin and development. The same situation obtained for the emergence of social science. Economics emerged as a social science in Britain or France (there is no general agreement on which), but on the terms set by local conditions and influenced by local elites. This is not the case for the introduction and the development of social science in dependent areas, at least for the more "dynamic" paradigms which are the very ones which are imported. They are not local products, more impositions from the outside, more or less maladapted to local conditions and ideologies. They are in accord with the ideology of the central elites, and they serve their interests and those of the local clients, but not those of local nationalists and radicals. Shils writes in his general article on the sociology of center and periphery that elites are never completely integrated into a system. This is particularly the case as we move from the center to the periphery; attachment there to the central value system is attenuated.[16] The farther one moves territorially from the geographic center of the system, the less likely central authority will be appreciated. A dependency system is unstable -- the social science imported from the center is likely to be opposed by some nationalist and radical social scientists. It turns out that social science has a nationalist side -- given time, the drive for indigenization is likely to be strong and probably successful. It also has a radical side which can be victorious as well.

This above interpretation differs from the traditional one offered by Storer. He does grant that a favorable government attitude is necessary if science is to flourish, but his recommendation for implementing this is similar to that of laissez-faire business for the success of capitalism. The government is asked to set up a favorable framework and climate, and then leave science alone. Indeed, he characterizes the scientific community as an individualistic enterprise which "probably approximates the ideal of laissez-faire, much more closely than the economic institutions of society ever did".[17]   Its members seem to ignore all those influences we described in our discussion of structures, including nationalism, in their unwavering dedication to the truth. The scientists operate by rules different from the rest of society, a larger than life ethic and environment, with one "fault" -- a craving for professional recognition from their colleagues. A nation reaches the take-off stage in scientific development when it has a "critical mass" of scientists, to be sure well equipped, but sufficient in size and competence to provide its own feedback without being dependent upon this from abroad. This critical mass cannot be determined by any hard and fast rule, because the standards for each scientist are individual and discrete.

We delay until the end of the chapter the discussion of the social science community from a domestic perspective. Our discussion there, as here, is critical. We admit exploitation at the domestic level, just as we see its presence when social science infrastructures are developed under conditions of global dependency. Our perspective at this juncture is international.   Obviously, the local clients (internationalists) gain from social science imports, but this is at the expense of the nationalists and radicals. The additional cleavage in social science is hardly an advantage to the dependent country. The left views dependent social sciences as a method of control, by foreign capital and by local capital. They are a way by which an exploiting capitalism helps to keep control. But exploitation can be viewed from a cultural perspective as well. This is the viewpoint of Mazrui, an African scholar who has specifically repudiated Marxism because, after all, it is Western. He has equated the Western university transplanted to Africa with the multinational, a vehicle of Western cultural and economic exploitation. Although he has not focused specifically upon our disciplines, his discussion of the university includes them as well.

Mazrui's experience was with British universities, but he argues that
their relations with their African subsidiaries were less intimate than
French and Belgian relations with their African universities. The
relationship was one of cultural dependence, and Mazrui sees the
impact as paralleling that of the multinational corporation. The
African scholar speaks from personal experience of the tie between
Makerere College in Uganda and the University of London. Makerere
originated as a branch of the British institution, which determined
entrance requirements, appointed the faculty, and controlled syllabi
and examinations. He tells the story of the deletions by the "home
office" of two of the three questions on Marx on the draft examination
which he, as the local professor, had written. Mazrui had alerted his
students to the importance which he attached to Marxism, but
university rules forbade him to explain to the students after the test
that it was the London "home office," not he, that had deleted two of
the three questions on Marxism. The university authorities in London
originally had objected to Marxism being included on the syllabus on
the grounds that Marx was not a political philosopher, but they
explained the deletion of the two questions on Marxism from the test
as a printing error.[18]   Mazrui remarks that the links between the
African and the European universities greatly impacted the curriculum
of the former. There was an indifference to African languages, and
the core of the classics as taught in West Africa was Greek, Latin, and
the history of Greece. Mazrui deplores the injury which this inflicted
on African culture. Note that such complaints can easily be made by
third world conservatives and nationalists. African dance was ignored,
and African intellectuals acquiesced in this slight to African culture.
Here the behavior of the African intellectual parallels that of the black
bourgeoisie who at first seemed to accept everything which was
European and thus "civilized" and to denigrate everything which was
indigenous and thus "uncivilized." Mazrui ties the Western imposition
of its educational system upon Africa to the economic needs of the
colonial power, to produce appropriate local manpower and to provide
a local market for its products. To do this, Western values had to be
propagated, and the university helped in this endeavor. Mazrui sees
the university as a potential emancipator as well, an institution whereby
Africa can fight back and gain its own authenticity. This is a dual
judgment with which we agree. Social science can act as emancipator
as well.

The relevant point about the above relationship is that African universities obtained their kind of social science from their respective metropoles. The paradigms came along in the intellectual baggage as European type universities, almost without modification, were transplanted to Africa and to other colonial areas as well. As we shall see below, this happened in Asia and in colonies in general. This importation has by now been opposed on political grounds -- the implantation opposed as a way of justifying imperialism. Another objection has been that local cultures have thereby been damaged, an argument often made by local nationalists and even conservatives. It is easy to conclude that harm was inflicted upon Africa with this import, even if some benefit accrued as well.

Bipolarity and the Challenge to It

Our discussion above is more dependency theory than world systems analysis. Fortunately, the two greatly overlap, a crucial feature of both being the structures featured above. To convert to world systems analysis we need do little more than refocus the discussion from the bilateral to the multilateral and to identify the new actors thus exposed and their roles. Instead of center and periphery, we now have several actors, and the vertical relations must be adjusted accordingly. Since the system described here is that obtaining in the postwar period, we start with the United States at the top of the heap, the "top dog." How she got to the summit is a theme of the following chapter. There we give the history of this ascent; here our emphasis is more theoretical. Her geographic domain is the "free world" or the "American empire," each appellation having obvious ideological overtones. This domain consists of Western Europe, Japan, the great bulk of the third world, and some states classifiable more readily by enumeration than by geographic region -- Israel, South Africa, Australia, and New Zealand. Eastern Europe should be added as well, at least this is the process at work at this writing. What all these states have in common is ties to world capitalism and freedom from Soviet domination. The reader no doubt remembers that national social science situations are assumed here to be related to general structural relations.

It is not too much to say that each vertical relation in the system has its own special traits, as each state has its own particular class structure, and this structure relates to foreign ones in distinctive ways as well. Nonetheless, some generalizations about these vertical relations are warranted. The closest ones are colonial, with metropolitan impositions being so obvious and so thorough. These ties generally have endured after political independence, only now they are often combined with those with the United States. A crucial insight from world systems analysis is that colonialism is not a necessary condition for the formation of these relations -- they are a general feature of contemporary capitalism. Vertical relations can be dualistic, as they often involve the United States sharing the role of center with another state. A state can serve as a center for peripheral countries, and it can in turn serve as peripheral to a center. This is the case for Japan and for several Western European countries, especially those which had colonies. They remain centers to the colonies, but are peripheral to the United States. Their vertical status was so apparent in the immediate postwar period, but their position has improved since then.

The predominant position of the United States in the immediate postwar period was so evident -- she was or soon became the superpower militarily, politically, economically, and culturally -- and from the standpoint of communications, education, and social science. Her educational system spread with her general extension, and her dominant paradigms were copied by foreign students who attended her institutions of higher learning, and they were disseminated in the lectures of her itinerant professors on safari abroad. Her superpower status in social science was related to her status as the world's premier educator. In the late nineteenth and early twentieth century, 90 percent of all students who studied abroad did so in France and Great Britain. But this situation witnessed a dramatic reversal in the post-World War II period, a turn of events particularly evident at the onset of the period. In 1963, even after the recovery of Western Europe and the Soviet entrance into the field, the United States was hosting almost 40 percent of the students studying abroad -- almost three times as many as France, her nearest rival.[19] Most of these students came from third world countries, but a substantial number were nationals of such developed countries as Canada, the United Kingdom, and Japan. Dominant American social science paradigms became part of the intellectual baggage of these sojourning students, and these paradigms returned to the homeland with them. The same transfer occurred as the United States poured millions of dollars into foreign educational systems after the war, "helping to remold the educational systems of perhaps seventy-five countries in the American pattern".[20] The remolding process involved visiting professors, equipment, books, reading lists, syllabi, and American social science.

The US dominance in social science was misinterpreted by many as a major step in the fulfillment of the Millian dream. This was an easy mistake for the American establishment to make, given the ethnocentric propensity to equate world affairs with American affairs, to equate happenings in its "village" with those of the world. But this village was so powerful, so eminent in social science, all possible competitors having been burned out by the war. Even a scholar of the calibre of Friedricks equated American sociology with world sociology. A countercurrent to this ethnocentrism was the great expansion of the disciplines international relations and comparative government, necessary to service the emerging "empire" and to explain US policies in the proper way. An essential ethnocentrism was preserved, for if the field of research was typically foreign, the paradigms used in the analysis were typically domestic.

The structures elaborated above have application to United States relations with Western Europe and Japan, not merely to third world countries. They fit better in the immediate postwar period than now after the recovery of these areas. Chapter IV analyses the social science communications of the United States with other centers of the discipline. Western European countries fit in the same general subordinate position as the third world, but this subordination is attenuated. These countries always had their own social science traditions to fall back upon. Indeed, they were never fully eclipsed by imports from the United States. The early postwar period was designated "bipolarity" by the discipline international relations to designate a postwar distribution of power divided between two poles, one held by the United States, the other by the Soviet Union. Each superpower completely overwhelmed its allies, who were, indeed, clients. But these relations moderated as the postwar period evolved. The blocs became less cohesive, and the discipline international relations invented such concepts as "diffuse bloc system" to describe the looser situation. Both powers have declined in relative power, the Soviets more dramatically than the United States. A similar loosening of the ties of social science occurred in the first world during the Vietnam War. The second part of the sixties witnessed the emergence of dependency theory in Latin America, a self-conscious invention intended to fight against all forms of first world domination, including that arising from our disciplines.

"Bipolarity" in one sense describes the essential relations between first world and second world social science. The establishment on each side excommunicated the other side. Both are accused of creating paradigms which rationalize their respective systems. The multinational version accepts both accusations as being generally accurate, from its perspective similarities between the blocs are more apparent than differences. These themes will be explored at greater length in the chapters which follow. "Bipolarity" should not be interpreted to mean that the two halves of the world were equal either in power or geographic extension. The disparity became even greater in 1989. The social sciences in the Soviet Union were in eclipse during the Stalin years. We believe that the more controversial ones existed more as servants of the government than as university subjects. Since Stalin's death, our disciplines have done better, but the government keeps close tabs on them. There is less freedom there for the practitioners, less room for dissent than in the first world. Certainly, the Soviet bloc as a bloc has experienced dissonance as the postwar period progressed. Bipolarity never meant a complete lack of relations between the blocs, and the first world weighed heavier on the second than the converse. Polish sociology never did completely sever its relations with the West. A clear sign of the dissonance in Soviet bloc social science has been the fate of Chinese social science. Since the arrest of the Gang of Four, it has followed the same trajectory as the larger society. Now Chinese students study social science in the West, especially in the United States. Immediately after the revolution, they studied in the Soviet Union. It is not clear what impact this new dispensation will have on Chinese Marxism, but the impact should be substantial. Even greater should be the impact of recent events in Eastern Europe.

A last word before we leave this subject. The reader should not conclude from the above discussion that we have written off the third world revolt as a minor cause of dissonance. We continue to believe that it is a revolutionary development which will destroy any attainment of the Millian dream in the near future. This is a theme of the last chapter. The reader is invited to go on to the next chapter where, among other things, we will put in historical perspective what we assumed here -- US dominance in social science.

The Social Science Community

The same vertical relationships and dependency which we witnessed above viewed from the international level are noticeable when viewed nationally as well. The same hope for liberation also exists at the lower level. And now we turn to the national level, specifically to the social science community. If the United States dominates global social science, Paris dominates the disciplines in France. This reminds us that our analysis of the social science community must be congruent with the rest of our analysis. The present level of analysis is national, as are most social science communities. The extant regional and international ones are of less importance. We must guard against exaggerating the power of these national institutions. They serve mostly as the dependent variable -- they implement decisions taken elsewhere, by persons whose livelihood and careers are dependent upon power brokers outside their jurisdiction. Our presentation of the socialization process in this section, for example, should not be taken to mean that the form which it assumes is determined by social science communities.

Our discussion above about the ostracism of Marxism deliberately focused upon universities, not upon the social science community, because real political/economic power resides more with them. It is their managers who receive resources from governments and foundations, allocate these resources, and chose to hire and fire personnel whether Marxists or non-Marxists. True, these managers are not free agents, but the social science community is even further removed from the levers of power. It is mainly honorific, or it registers important decisions taken elsewhere. Nonetheless, the social science community merits a place in our analysis. The honors it grants can effect the careers of members, and its decisions may be implemented by others. Its location here, in a chapter on methodology, helps to put it in proper focus. The term can be used in at least two senses: in a broad sense as the community of the social scientists, no matter where their activities occur or under whose leadership and direction. Or the term can be used in a narrow sense to designate the activities solely of an organization as such. We use the term in both senses, but the emphasis is upon the broader construction. The context will indicate to the reader which sense is appropriate. The social science community is a logical companion of the specialization of the social sciences. It is not a labor union -- it does not negotiate salaries nor engage in strikes. Nor does it hire and fire and carry on entrepreneurial functions. The literature which we have seen places it alongside the professional organizations of natural science. This connection befits the predominant middle class membership of such organizations -- the members picturing themselves as professionals, as "scientists" seeking the truth, not as "workers" as the word is commonly used. The leadership does look to the interests of the organizations, but activities are bounded by "professional" restraints. We indicated above that the trend (some would say "mania") for specialization and the concomitant founding of the specialized social science organization in large numbers was initiated in the United States in the last part of the nineteenth century. Obviously, it has not gone as far in some countries as it has in this superpower. We attended a congress of Latin American sociology only to find that a political scientist (Theotonio dos Santos) presided over it. The "mania" for specialization in American social science parallels that of the university, and that of the greater society. This trend has not gone so far in other settings, but the general direction is toward greater specialization.

A major function of the social science organization is communications. The earliest natural science organizations arose in Italy in the seventeenth century, and communications at first took the form of personal contact and letter writing. By now, the professional journal has become dominant, a trend also true for the social sciences. A crucial feature of such professional institutions, if for natural or for social science, is the encouragement given the practitioners. Seen in the best light, practitioners are no longer lonely pilgrims, but rather they become part of a common effort wherein colleagues offer mutual encouragement to each other. Bernal points out that this institutionalization results in a certain amount of pomp and pedantry, but more importantly the societies "become in effect a jury for science".[21] This means, in our case, that social science institutions become in effect "sovereign": they become the judges and the juries in their own cases. At least in the countries we know of, institutionalization is simple and there is no outside authority, no board of examiners, to determine if the organization and its work meet the standards of social science. Indeed, American political scientists have argued that the Soviet Association of Political Science (SAPS) is not really what its name implies, and that it has been set up by the Soviet government for propaganda purposes and actually to impede the development of political science in the Soviet Union. Social science organizations are notoriously national or local, enjoying a kind of local or national self-government. Thus SAPS is free to make its own claims, as are the American Political Science Association, and American political scientists in general. International associations of social scientists are weak and meet infrequently, and the centers of power (such as they are) are national. The fact that the membership of the national organizations of physicists in the United States and in the Soviet Union, for example, are nationals of their respective countries has no relevance to the fact that the same condition obtains for their political science organizations. The "juries" in the first case apply one internationally recognized "law"; while in the second, decisions are made by the use of divergent ideologies of social science sects, and thus the verdict depends upon which jury has jurisdiction. The assertion that decisions are made by scientific communities can have quite different meanings for social and for natural science.

Melanson identifies the primary goal of professional organizations, including social science communities, as the establishment of patterns of social integration and differentiation favorable to the professional self-interest of the group.[22] He goes on to say that the chief means used by a profession to promote its goals are control over entry; its definition of the service it renders society; and the allocation of rewards and punishments to the membership. Entry for nominal members may be easy, i.e., perhaps involving the mere payment of a fee, but this does not concern us here. That for serious members is another matter, and usually involves a university degree with a major in the social science involved. The intellectual requirements can be demanding, and they can vary from university to university, and they do from country to country. A crucial factor in the professional socialization process is the matter of sects and ideologies. The graduate student will usually find some choice here among the professors in his department. He usually can "attach himself" to a major professor with a compatible ideology. The system in many ways is feudal, but the client often has a choice of his patron. This choice can be easily exaggerated, especially if we view the matter from the standpoint of the social science of social science. The student's option will be restricted by what is available locally, and these dominant trends suggest the limitation. The student will naturally be influenced by the general socialization process of his own locality. The content of his professional socialization process can differ dramatically from the United States as contrasted with continental Western Europe, China, or the Soviet Union. There is no general agreement on the place of philosophy, foreign languages, statistics, and mathematics in the process. Our initiates, no matter where socialized, will probably learn that allegiance to the ascendant ideology or to that of their major professor, or at least no outward signs of defiance of it, serves as a lubricant in gaining entrance to the upper echelons of the discipline. Most of them will not need to be reminded of this, because by the time of their graduation they will have internalized the ascendant social science ideology. Those upward bound professionally in the United States are advised to attach themselves to an important name already on the grant trail, do his bidding, and hopefully find room on the trail for themselves, with help from their patron.

Socialization which results in allegiance to contrary ideologies makes later social science communications difficult. The situation is different for the natural sciences, including the rights of passage for initiates, as set forth by Kuhn. He speaks of the "scientific community" as it exists in the world of natural science, and he presents it without national or regional boundaries, obviously intending that it encompass the scientists of a discipline throughout the world. The members are "bound together by common elements in their education and apprenticeship" and see themselves as pursuing a set of shared goals.[23] To a remarkable extent, they read the same literature and draw similar conclusions from it. They enjoy relative fullness of communications with each other and relative unanimity in judging professional matters. Little wonder that their communications are so easy, despite national and cultural boundaries.

The second means used by a social science organization to promote its goals is suggested by the definition it gives of its role in society, its assertion of the service it renders the particular society in which it is located. This definition results from pressure from many factors, including all those presented in this essay which account for the forms which social science assumes. Melanson argues that in technologically advanced societies professional groups usually define their service in terms of science. Here the factors culture and self-interest would seem to be predominant. Public acceptance of this claim certainly enhances the prestige of a discipline in such societies, but also among the modern, science-loving social strata in third world countries. Melanson alleges that the discipline has a crucial stake in cultivating a highly regarded public image, and it will usually cast itself in the most prestigious and idealized role. The social science myth, self-interest, and the local culture all come together to suggest that the discipline be described as a type of science.

The third method set forth by Melanson by which professional organizations achieve their goals is the allocation of rewards and punishments to the membership and the determination of its status. In actuality, these rewards and punishments are honorific -- more substantial ones come from the university, often based on these honors. This is crucial for the practitioner's professional self-image and as a means by which the organization preserves its authority over the members as well as the position and the interests of the leadership. These assertions raise the fundamental question of the modus operandi of social science organizations. We have already put them in the context of structures, the outward pressures which shape them. Now we look at their inward governance. By all accounts, they are stratified and elitist -- a characteristic they share with universities and with the older natural science organizations. Both kinds of disciplines are elitist and stratified, whether viewed from the standpoint of the prestige of university departments, professional journals, or the "great men" in a field. Certainly, the university has done its part to mold and to maintain this structure. Graduate schools typically have a feudal structure, with the position of the student often ameliorated by the personal democratic characteristics and the benign paternalism of the faculty involved. The only issue is whether the elitism and the stratification of social science is reined in and restrained by the existence of a consensual meritocracy, as seems to be the case for natural science. Polanyi attributed a highly aristocratic structure to natural science, arguing that even those scientists with the appropriate degrees cannot get a hearing if they wish to protest against the work of a leading scientist.[24] Natural science, in this view, is an oligarchy, dominated by a small number of scientists who dominate a scientific community. But this type of governance is by no means arbitrary, for it has consensual rules for deciding merit. The right to intervene in a debate is earned by positive achievement in the field. Severe and prompt retribution awaits those who publish spurious research findings and consensus on what is spurious is attainable. If natural science is an oligarchy, it is a constitutional oligarchy. This is not the case for social science, as we shall see below.

Lemert finds that the patron-cluster system is still a force in French sociology, even if its importance is diminishing. It has been criticized for its creation of closed shops, for its restrictions on diversity and inventiveness, and for the personal distance which it puts between masters and apprentices.[25]   Lemert finds that the system first emerged with the original Durkheimians, perhaps necessary then because of the paucity of practitioners of the discipline. At present, however, the system is decentralizing, and some sociologists work independently of the clusters. A critical feature of the system is the arrangement which the patrons often establish with a publishing house, whereby they control a special series of books. Another feature is the control which the media have on the visibility of published works. The emerging scholar, unaffiliated with a patron, has a difficult time publishing. Lemert argues that to be well connected is a great advantage in other systems, such as the American, but it works differently in the French one -- it seems to be more important.

Rex would generalize the patron-client system to cover social science in general, although his frame of reference is sociology. He views his construction as an ideal type, one which is as worthy of a hearing as the idealistic one of Shils, the more so because ideal types are more useful if contraposed as opposite pairs.[26] We view the matter differently, arguing that the predominance of evidence (found in other chapters) supports our point of view. We believe that the other ideal type describes a smaller part of reality. Rex finds the patron-client system in operation in natural science, encouraged by the feudal structure of universities. These latter institutions encourage practitioners to be "ritualist," rather than to be innovative -- to abandon the goal of scientific discovery in order to be meticulous about method. The methods of the ritualist are impeccable, and he searches around for a highly placed protector, a highly placed "baron" with whom he can establish a direct personal link. Rex transforms this same relationship and system to the social sciences, with his examples coming from sociology. The sociologist proves himself by ritualistic adherence to research techniques, by showing that he can undertake typical pieces of work of a scientific kind. Innovative work in sociology can be politically more threatening than in natural science, and it is avoided in favor of technique. The social science practitioner also attaches himself to a protector, a highly placed professor, preferably one with a large measure of political influence. Rex finds that the projects that receive financing by government and the foundations do not transcend ideological limits. Thus the patron-client system and the institutionalization of social science are likely to work in support of the basic status quo.

Constitutionalism is much less probable in social science governance than in that of natural science, with sectarianism rather than consensus the prevailing undercurrent. Melanson's conclusions with respect to the repute system of American political science have direct relevance to our discussion. He finds that this repute system is shakier than that of natural science, based as it is more on the subjective judgments and myths of peers and less on technical, firmly grounded knowledge. Rarely can political science use reliable laws or theorems to evaluate scholarly worth, and peer group perceptions must be relied upon to determine which scholars, works, and methodologies can legitimately claim "scientific" status. In such a milieu, prestige "accrues to those who seek, achieve, approximate, or imitate science".[27] Melanson offers as a contrast the situation of the atomic physicist. His repute system is the equivalent of the constitutionalism referred to above, as his discipline is the consensual meritocracy also cited above. His repute system is encumbered by the refined nature of his field's knowledge and by its epistemological standards and procedures. He is not as free to engage in wildcat speculation, nor to substitute salesmanship for scholarship.

A basic deficiency of the above analysis is that it is all of one piece: it provides no space for those mavericks in a social science community who challenge the establishment. Such space was provided in our discussion of social science from a global perspective. We noted there the existence of strains of radicalism and nationalism. In contrast, the discussion of the national community until now has focused upon dominant sects and it has shielded them from adverse events. The latter have been used by several authors to help account for shifts in the popularity of competing paradigms. We have been told that the rejection of the North American development paradigms in favor of dependency theory was facilitated by Castro's success in Cuba. Indeed, this phenomenon helped to radicalize Latin American social scientists. The rejection of North American social science by practitioners from Brazil has been linked to the acceptance of a nationalist development paradigm by that country. But such events need not be external to the world of paradigms itself. Thus the spread of Keynesian economics has been related to the failure of the neo-classical brand to explain the depression, just as its eclipse followed its deficiency as an explanatory device. The same internal cause has been given for the birth of dependency theory. Its predecessor, North

American development theory, reputedly did not explain the situation in Latin America.

These explanatory deficiencies and adverse events have been referred to and expanded upon in the following chapters. Here we add another factor -- the role of the social scientist. Of course, we reject Mannheim's thesis that the practitioner stands outside the class struggle, in a detached domain where objectivity seems to reign. The practitioner of this volume is too much the dependent bureaucrat to inhabit this domain. But this is not the whole story, for institutional devices have been put in place to insulate from control of the dominant elites. The practitioner is certainly generally freer than most bureaucrats, public or private -- at least his job is more secure, even if the ladder to higher position is a conformist one. Rush and his associates speak of the contrary ways that social scientists are treated in the literature and their contrary position in actuality.[28] They reject the notion that the social scientist is merely a part of the new professional - managerial class or a member of the petite bourgeoisie, whose role is to rationalize capitalism. This position is a contradictory one -- featuring dependency upon wages without owning the means of production -- yet the practitioner retains a high degree of control over his own work whether teaching or research. Rationalization of the status quo may be the mode, but alienation and radicalism do result as well.

Concluding Remarks
        The basic task of this chapter was to lay out the method by which we analyze social science. We chose an external one. External here means that the disciplines are not seen as isolated, merely intellectual exercises, but rather as activities very much interacting with local culture and elites and even with foreign elites. They are much more imbedded in the local milieu than is natural science. We name our approach "multinational," a term meant to conjure up a vision of the situation created by the multinational corporation. The chapter linked our disciplines first to economics and then to politics -- political economy serving as a first step toward the broader structures of world systems analysis. The disciplines were put in the context of the knowledge industry, in an economic setting, which was seen to be a political one as well, and still later they were placed into a multi-disciplinary one. The advantage here is that all of the social sciences are put at our disposal; this is the social science of social science. Our

disciplines can thus be viewed in a multidisciplinary setting, with education emerging as their closest companion. This setting is also multinational, foreign as well as domestic influences are acknowledged. The approach is humanistic in the sense that although external causes are admitted, the disciplines have an internal side as well. Social scientists are not reduced to ciphers: they also affect the state of their disciplines.

Our model is world systems analysis, of the same genre as dependency theory, but it goes beyond bilateralism to attempt to structure the world of the social sciences. It sees social science relations as following the global pattern of other subjects and transactions, often their trajectory is vertical, notably between the first and the third worlds. This latter relationship is presented here, but its full significance becomes obvious only when we call to mind the third world revolt against first world domination. The revolt is multidisciplinary, with the social sciences being included. The last section of the chapter dealt with the social science community; that generally national institution which plays a role in the evolution of our disciplines. It fits into this chapter, because it is part of the knowledge industry, featuring the same elitism and vertical relations which are the traits of our disciplines when viewed transnationally.

This chapter gave evidence to illustrate the economic side of our disciplines -- this side suggests an advantage for the well-heeled and the highly capitalized. Those centers not so situated are likely to suffer from dependency and vertical relations. Social science was revealed to be a high fixed cost industry -- the economic impulse is thus for expansion. This same impulse is fueled by ideology -- elites trying to push those sects which favor their interests. Social science knowledge was seen as being a special kind of product -- distribution being equivalent to production. The production of socially new social science knowledge, however, is most noteworthy, because its production tends to be concentrated in the most capitalized and most prestigious institutions. The transition from the economic to the political was facilitated by references to education. Governmental elites take a strong interest in education and thus greatly impact our disciplines.

The structures used in this volume are humanistic phenomena. They are arrangements, not substances. They reside in human beings, not in strange out of the way places. Structuralism offers the key insight that the power of social agents results from structures, not from the personal attributes of individuals. We drew a parallel above between the situation in social science and Galtung's contrast between the production of tractors in first world countries and that of crude oil in the third world. The latter provides the raw social information, and the former provide the paradigms and the capitalized social science infrastructures for processing the raw data. In this way, the first world becomes rich in knowledge, of course about itself, but also about third world countries. They might become better sources of information than their dependent, peripheral countries even about the situation in the latter. But the information is likely to take the slant -- follow the dominant paradigm -- of the central country. Herein lies the influence and the basis for charges of exploitation. Herein also lies the attraction of central countries -- they are rich in information, because they are rich in the means to produce it.

In our view, central connections do not prevent the development of social science. Rather they tend to deform it -- to produce a type of it in accord with the interests of foreign elites. Domestic social science elites, those tied to the center, also benefit. The nationalists or national radicals do not, and they can be relied upon to strive for indigenization -- to change paradigms better to suit local conditions and their own interests. Our continuing reference to dominant social science sects does not mean that we do not recognize that a given social science community is likely to be split into numerous sects. Furthermore, the dominance of one or the other can shift over time in response to new events and circumstances. Furthermore, we intend our approach to be more humanistic than deterministic. The structures presented here and the classes/elites behind them should not be visualized as being in absolute control, producing or representing laws in the sense of natural science. What is produced here are insights into a process, in which social scientists themselves have a significant role to play. Evidence which tends to confirm the validity of our structures is found in chapter IV. In that chapter they predict the nature of American social science communications.

NOTES

1. David A. Goshin, "Social Science Communications in the United States", International Social Science Journal, 26 (1974), 509-516.

2. Fernando Henrique Cardoso and Enzo Faletto, Dependencia e Desenvolvimento na America Latina (Rio De Janeiro: Zahar, 1979), 14.

3. Fritz Machlup, Knowledge: Its Creation, Distribution, and Economic Significance, Vol. 1, Knowledge and Knowledge Production (Princeton: Princeton University Press, 1980), xxiv.

4. Maurice Line and Stephen Roberts, "The Size, Growth, and Composition of Social Science Literature", International Social Science Journal, 28, (1976), 122-159.

5. Machlup, 232-233.

6. Frederick H. Gareau and Edna C. Gareau, "Are Social Scientists Biased Nationally? An Analysis of Data from the Falklands/Malvinas Conflict", The International Social Science Journal 38 (1986), 476.

7. Machlup, 7.

8. Edward T. Silva and Sheila A. Slaughter, Serving Power: The Making of the Academic Social Science Expert, (Westport, Conn.: Greenwood Press, 1984), 69-70.

9. Robert F. Arnove, "Comparative Education and World Systems Analysis," Comparative Education Review 24 (1980), 57.

10.   Fernando H. Cardoso and Enzo Faletto, "Repensado Dependencia e Desenvolvimento no America Latina" in Fernando Cardoso et al., Economia e Movementos Sociais na America Latina, (Sao Paulo: Brasilense, 1985), 15.

11.   Johan Galtung, The True Worlds: A Transnational Perspective, (New York: Free Press, 1980), 128.

12.   Piotr Sztompka, Sociological Dilemmas. Toward a Dialectic Paradigm (New York: Harcourt, Brace, Jovanovich, 1979), 307.

13.   Peter T. Manicas, A History and Philosophy of the Social Sciences, (New York: Basil Blackwell, 1987), 272.

14.   Galtung, 115.

15.   Ibid. 120.

16.   Edward Shils, The Logic of Personal Knowledge: Essays Presented to Michael Polanyi on His Seventieth Birthday, 11th March 1961. (London: Routledge & Kegan Paul, 1961), 124.

17.   Norman W. Storer, "The Internationality of Science and the Nationality of Scientists," International Social Science Journal, 22, (1970), 93.

18.   Ali Mazrui, "The African University as a Multinational Corporation: Problems of Penetration and Dependency," Harvard Education Review, 45 (1975), 195.

19.   Marshall R. Singer, Weak States in a World of Powers: The Dynamics of International Relations, (New York: Free Press, 1972), 162, 163.

20.   Ibid., 171.

21.   J.D. Bernal, Science in History, The Social Sciences: Conclusion, 4 (Cambridge, MIT Press, 1971), 457.

22.   Philip H. Melanson, Political Science and Political Knowledge, (Public Affairs Press, Washington DC), 1975, 13. For what follows see also Frederick H. Gareau, "The Multinational Version of Social Science," Current Sociology, 33 (1985), 72-76.

23.   Thomas S. Kuhn, "Second Thoughts on Paradigms," in Frederick Suppe (ed.) The Structure of Scientific Theories, (Urbana, University of Illinois Press, 1974), 461.

24.   Bertrand De Jouvenel, "The Republic of Science," in The Logic of Personal of Personal Knowledge: Essays Presented to Michael Polanyi on His Seventieth Birthday, (London, Kegan Paul, 1961), 132-133.

25.   Charles Lemert, "Literary Politics and the Champ of French Sociology," Theory and Society, 10 (1981), 655-656.

26.   John A. Rex, "The Spread of the Pathology of Natural Science to the Social Sciences," The Sociological Review, 16 (1970): 148.

27.   Melanson, Political Science, 97.

28.   G.B. Rush, W. Christensen, and J. Malcolmson, "Lament for a Notion: the Development of Social Science in Canada", Review of Canadian Sociology and Anthropology, 18, (1981): 523.

CHAPTER III

AN HISTORICAL INTERPRETATION OF SOCIAL SCIENCE

This chapter must not be seen as a fill-in, an attempt to honor some commitment to an a priori notion that nothing is complete without an account of its past. Rather its task is central to our analysis, necessary to give a correct perspective to our disciplines. For example, we learn below that social science has been racist. True, this is an occasional occurrence, but it is part of the historical record, and a serious social scientist should be aware of this unsavory fact. On the other hand, the idea that social science offers an alternate explanation, based to some extent on logic and sound conclusions, is re-enforced here. The explanation is alternate to religion and tradition, among other possibilities. Our perspective of social science must strive to escape ethnocentrism, and the surest paths which escape this trap are history and geography. The geography of our discipline is displayed later, here we concentrate upon history. Two aspects are investigated - - the record as it actually unfolded, and the myths which surround this unfolding. We terminate the chapter with an account of the myth. We can only give a brief account of the historical record, and such strict picking and choosing lends itself to the interpretive account given here. Our emphasis is upon the modern period -- Comte, Spencer, social Darwinism, and American dominance. We believe that our interpretation is a reasonable one, but certainly not the only one. The discussion of myths is necessary, because our disciplines are myth-ridden, and their major myth has been woven together with an historical account. History is also central to the multinational approach, because it insists upon viewing the subjects not in iron clad, static categories, but in movement and evolution. In this chapter, we shall trace the climb of the United States to the summit of the social sciences, a fact which we assumed in the last chapter. We shall insist, as we did before, that her dominance be viewed as being transitory. Her position has been challenged by the second world and more recently, and more importantly, by the third.

We ask the reader to keep in mind for ready reference two basic theses offered as the thread to make sense of the historical account of our disciplines, a minimalist position and a maximalist one. This distinction is the historical equivalent of Gouldner's charge that his fellow sociologists keep two sets of books -- one for themselves, the other for the humans who are the objects of their study. The first set exempts sociologists in their professional lives from the grip of society/culture -- whereas the rest of mankind is alleged to be bound by the rules of society/culture. The historical parallel to this is the establishment of a special place for our disciplines -- divorced from many of the effects generally experienced in the flow of history. This is the minimalist position. In this view, a more rational period of history, for example, acts as a catalyst in promoting our disciplines, but historical events other than the general rationalizing trend do not enter into the disciplines. Historical trends and events are mere catalysts, acting to encourage or to discourage social science. The other view, the maximalist one, is that society has a much heavier grip upon our subjects; this approach is the one applied here.

The minimalist approach can easily be related to the social science myth. The myth posits for each discipline a "pre-scientific" period. For example, Schumpeter found the beginnings of this period for economics, and thus the beginnings of this discipline as well, in classical Greek philosophy especially in the work of Aristotle.[1] The German scholar paid homage to the classical contribution, but ultimately disparaged it as having "presented an exceedingly poor and above all 'pre-scientific' picture of economics." The myth sees the transition from this pre-scientific to the "scientific" period as being accomplished by two conditions. The first of these is the emergence of an autonomous, separate field of study, and the second is the use of the "scientific method" in studying the subject matter. The first condition can arise from the invention of a new discipline where none existed before or from the formation of a new one by the breaking off of the new from a pre-existing one. Economics represents an example of the first case, and Schumpeter gives credit to the Physiocrats for presiding over the birth of this discipline. Their circular flow represented the formation of an autonomous and separate field. Haney helps us with this second point. He envisages the pre-scientific period of economics as one in which the discipline was mingled with religious and ethical doctrines.[2] Hostile religious concepts held mankind's attention, at the expense of thinking in terms of cause and effect. The Physiocrats lead the way to the scientific breakthrough by their attempt to formulate a body of positive principles separate from morals, politics, and jurisprudence. What was started by these French innovators reached fruition in the Wealth of Nations. In it, the discipline became associated with a body of causal explanations of phenomena.

No matter that the circular flow of the Physiocrats had a short lifespan, and that Adam Smith rejected it and oriented the discipline in a quite different direction. Despite this, economics left behind for good its pre-scientific period, and entered the scientific one, i.e. became a social science and remains one until today. Similarly, Wundt established experimental psychology as a science.[3] It turns out that the "scientific" method he used to make the metamorphosis was self-observation or introspection, with the subject reporting his reaction to a stimulus administered by the researcher. This method has long since been repudiated as being unscientific, at least in the United States. But psychology entered its scientific phase at that time, and remains there even to this day.

The above discussion of part of the social science myth merits some comment. The change in social science paradigms over time does not contradict Kuhn's view of the evolution of natural science by changes in paradigms -- his famous revolutions. Each presents a contrary world view -- certainly the shift from the dominance of the Physiocrats to that of the classicists was no greater than this. The real importance of this part of the myth is that it establishes the self identity of the discipline. The change from the studying of the subject matter in a scattered and "unscientific" manner, often as part of religion, to the shift to a structured approach and to the "scientific" method creates a social science. The links which the discipline forges with universities and institutes, the formation of social science organizations, and the capitalization of the enterprise are separate issues, usually later ones. The enterprise, at least in the past, started small. It was typically the work of the few elites. Only later did it expand, institutionalize, and capitalize. The metamorphosis from the pre-scientific to the scientific creates one of our disciplines and locates it in a half way house between natural science and non-science. We object to the misuse of the term "science," unless one specifically adds that the term is used to mean merely an organized field of study, and perhaps, in addition, one which uses logic and human experience in the procedures to discover the truth. But to go on with our account, those who hold to this view (the myth-makers) divide vocational knowledge (that produced at present by professionals) into three kinds: (1) natural science, (2) social science, and (3) non-science. Examples of non-science are literary criticism, the humanities, and religion (taught from the standpoint of the believers themselves). Those who subscribe to the myth argue that the first two use the "scientific" method, even if the epistemic value of social science does not match that of natural science, not yet. Often the myth makers use the terms "science" and "scientific" to suggest the superior epistemic value of their findings over those of the non-scientific disciplines or over those of the competition in their own field. We initiated this volume with such a hypothetical example. The last step in the myth is maturity, the golden age in the future when social science matures, i.e. becomes like natural science. The coming of the golden age of maturity is set forth with varying degrees of insistence and certitude -- faith here being in direct confrontation with the empirical evidence. The historic record indicates that the maturity of a social science has never occurred. The equivalent of maturity for the discipline history is to tell the story of the past as it actually happened, or for those who emphasize facts, to lay out the actual facts of the past. We return to the problem of the maturity of this discipline below.

For our purposes, the history of Western social science will be divided into the following periods. We deal with most of the crucial events which occurred in these periods at some length in this chapter, but others are slighted or only mentioned. The four periods are the following:

1.   Early beginnings: classical Greece and the Middle Ages. We deal only with the former.

2.   Early developments in Europe from the Italian Renaissance and the Great Discoveries and merchant capitalism to the French and the industrial revolutions.

3.   The development of our paradigms in Europe from the industrial revolution, the French revolution, and industrial capitalism to the last third of the nineteenth century. Emphasis here is on Adam Smith, Comte, Spencer, and Marxism.

4.   American dominance and the challenge to it, from
the last third of the nineteenth century to the present.
The Americanization and specialization
(industrialization) of the disciplines, and the
widespread export of dominant American paradigms
after World War II. The challenges are from the
Soviet Union and, more recently, from the third
world.

Early Beginnings: Classical Greece, the Middle Ages
For those who insist on going back to the "very beginning," the
starting point for considering the history of social science is usually
given as classical Greece. All human knowledge before this time is
pictured as being bunched together in what appears today in our
specialized society to be an untidy amorphous conglomerate. Included
are what today are called natural science, social science, religion, and
philosophy including values. Social and natural sciences are seen as
peeling off one at a time from the conglomerate into specialized
disciplines whose analysis becomes secular, based upon logic and
research findings and not upon custom and religion, i.e. the
interference of God or gods. There is a difference here in
interpretation between those designated above as the minimalists, who
think social science is a technical, purely scientific matter, and those
who believe that a discipline includes in addition an ideology, perhaps
even a religious component (the maximalists). Those on both sides of
the argument agree that a given social science has an analytic part --
a mundane process outside the "interference" of custom or God, a
sphere amenable to human logic and to the interpretation of research
findings. This is, of course, the significant contribution of social
science to human thought and human action. Not to produce pure
knowledge, but to produce alternate explanations, which are based to
some extent on logic and human experience.
This volume insists that we recognize the role of the third
world in contemporary social science, and so we add the following.
When Indian social scientists go back to the "very beginning," chances
are this will not be to ancient Greece. Dube finds that his India has
a long indigenous "tradition of reflection and writing on man and
society".[4] Completed in the second and third century AD, Manu's
Dharmashastra outlined a comprehensive normative structure of
society. Kautilya's Arthashastra (324-296 BC) is better known in the

West, and it has been compared to Machiavelli's The Prince. It contains insights into international affairs, as well as the expression of the need to gather information on different parts of India and on different segments of its population -- in the interests of administration. The Kama Sutra (300-400 AD) is also well known in the West, mainly we suspect because of its comprehensive explication of sexual techniques. But it also shifted focus away from the art of love and sex to offer vivid glimpses of society as it existed at that time. Western sociology was "implanted" in India without any reference to this indigenous tradition, but it exists today, a possible source of strength and inspiration for India in its struggle to craft a more authentic, indigenous social science.

Barraclough puts us on notice that the Orient has not been unhistorical, and he finds the roots of historiography there to be the same as in the West. In the remote past, the affiliation of history in both regions was with local cults and gods who had to be placated. Broadly speaking, its social purpose was the socialization of the populace and political control. At a later stage, this purpose became even more obvious as history was given over to the acts of kings, who were regarded as gods or near gods, "and history became a form of propaganda in which the great deeds of kings were sung by priests and musicians".[5]   Classical Chinese history has been characterized as history written by bureaucrats for bureaucrats, i.e., to support the ruling dynasty and to perpetuate the prevalent social order. The official chronicles of medieval France and England had a similar object, and sixteenth century English historiography served the interests of the Tudor dynasty. The nineteenth century saw the attempt to present objective, scientific history, but often such attempts were found to be compatible with the interests of dominant local groups. Marxism was excluded from academe until quite recently, but it provided a means to challenge the status quo. It has been taken up by the third world as a weapon against the first. The third world has learned much from European historiography, but it has also suffered from Eurocentric history. The question of indigenization will be taken up in the final section of this chapter.

Both the minimalists (the myth makers) and the maximalists agree that social science has grown and flourished in periods of rationalization and secularization -- more so than in other historical periods. But differences remain. The myth-makers are looking for pure knowledge, something close to that produced by natural science.

So they see social science as absorbing less of the surrounding culture and not reflecting the interests of domestic groups. These periods of rationalization and secularization serve for them merely or mostly as lubricant or encouragement to accept a given discipline, but it remains separate from them. Both approaches agree that the trend toward secularization in Western history has aided the development of social science. This is due to the fact that much of Western history featured domination by a clergy intolerant of secular explanations, and thus against social science. Secularization has meant the decline in their power and the acceptance of the secular logic which is part of social science. But this does not mean that social science is necessarily against religion, the clergy, or even the status quo. Functionalism in the United States and Soviet Marxism, each in its own way, supports the status quo. Social Darwinism helped to rationalize a burgeoning capitalism in the United States. We discuss below sociology in Quebec, which originally featured Catholic ideology. At present, theologists of liberation in Latin America use critical Marxism as a way of expressing the evils of dependent capitalism, so that the kingdom of God in this world can be established. To be sure, the materialism and atheism of Marxism is not accepted, but the Marxist indictment of capitalism is considered invaluable for promoting what is thought of as a system in accord with Catholic ethics. What the historical record shows is that social science provides a secular, logical interpretation of events, often an alternative to religious or traditional interpretations. But the two can be combined, one serving as the logic of the paradigm, the other as its ideology.

In the typical history of our disciplines, a number of events and periods in Western history are graded by whether they encouraged or discouraged the foundation and the growth of our disciplines. Classical Greece is singled out as the period when reason was first given a central place in explaining human affairs. The use of reason and natural causes are found in the histories of Herodotus and Thucydides, and each has been designated as the father of history. The first has given us a fascinating account of the Persian Wars, and the second a very readable analysis of the follow-up conflict fought between the winners of the first conflict. The ambitious and expanding Athens led its allies to defeat in a struggle against Sparta and its allies. Of the two accounts, that of Thucydides better meets the criteria of the historian's craft. Herodotus often mixed his account of events with the will of the gods. His history thus very much resembles the literature of the times: as in Greek tragedies, the gods strike down the powerful. The mighty Persian warlords met this fate. He traveled widely and collected materials on the social customs of different peoples -- thus suggesting to some that he was the founder also of anthropology or sociology. The credentials of Herodotus as the first historian rest to a great extent on his conceiving the idea of investigating and recording an event of monumental importance. Thucydides' historiography has a better claim of being "scientific," because his account of the Peloponnesian Wars leaves no room for the intervention of the gods. This is profane history. He looked critically upon his sources -- again making a lasting contribution to the legacy of his discipline. Thucydides often explained events in terms of power politics, thus providing some support for his parentage for this kind of explanation as well. He has the further distinction of having participated in the conflict as a general, before being relieved of his command.

There is much consensus that classical Greece deserves credit for its worldly and rational explanations, but little for the thesis that it sired many social sciences. Thus Seligman's assertion that she created four of them is not widely accepted. Of the four, politics is probably the most interesting candidate (besides history which already has been discussed)[6] Aristotle is said to have studied 158 constitutions, sufficient to provide a strong empirical base for the discipline. Our interest is whetted by the fact that the literature we have seen on this discipline speaks of the nineteenth century emergence of "American political science," a strange name for a discipline which has international pretensions. We discuss its emergence below. The Middle Ages in most accounts of social science is the dark ages. Hearshaw's view of the period is all too typical. He found its contribution to be religious and ethical, not in the area of knowledge creation. This because "medieval man was entombed, and his spirit wandered ghostlike amid sepulchral superstitions".[7] We see this period as having a bright side as well, but limitations of space bid us to proceed to the next period.

Early Development in Europe from the Italian Renaissance to the Industrial Revolution

This is the period which includes the Italian Renaissance, the great discoveries, and the contributions of Galileo and Newton. It represents humanism, the spirit of rationalism, and thus a period when our disciplines would be expected to prosper. The period also witnessed the absolute state, slavery on a scale probably never witnessed before, and the plundering of nearly all, and the extinction of many, Indian tribes. Conservatives tend to stress the rational spirit of the time, leftists the immoral acts of a burgeoning merchant capitalism. It is a period when the rising class of bankers and merchants was allied with the sovereign in what has been called the "mercantilist compromise."[8] It was only later when they became strong that these groups called for laissez faire. Capitalism thus developed with the help of a strong state and on a scale which involved foreign trade and other foreign transactions.

The Italian Renaissance is cast in a different light from that of the Middle Ages. It represented humanism, a challenge to church authority, and a return to pagan Rome for inspiration. The writings of Machiavelli exhibited all of these traits, and his The Prince could with some justification be considered as the first book (at least in the West) on the discipline of international relations. The American version of the emergence of this discipline manages to overlook this famous work in favor of its own nationals.[9] This is another instance of the nationalism which tends to characterize the history of our disciplines. The Prince is the bible of realism. Politics is a struggle for power, and a prince who does not heed the power calculus will be condemned to frustration, failure, and even worse. He must be strong like the lion and deceptive like the fox. Machiavelli was telling it like it was -- at least how he learned it was when he practiced diplomacy for his native Tuscany. His justification for deception, the strangulation of political rivals, the use of religion for political ends -- all these things made his words a favorite of diplomats. It was said that even though The Prince was put on the index by the church, it could be found under the pillows of the leading statesmen of Europe. Machiavelli was an immoralist, but not a hypocrite, and he does describe one aspect of international relations.

Other events which stimulated and impacted the growth of the social sciences were the Copernican Revolution, the great discoveries, and the founding of modern physics. The work of Copernicus undermined the geocentric view of the universe, one of the crucial supports for the medieval world view. Mankind was downgraded, from being the favorite of God to living on an ordinary planet. Like other planets, it went around the sun. The fate of Galileo at the hands of a bigoted church is welcome news for those science lovers who would transfer the halos from the medieval saints to modern scientists. Newtonian physics became an inspiration, an end toward which the social sciences could strive. The myth makers went farther and argued, not only that the social sciences should go in this direction, but that they would, and that they would arrive there some day to become mature sciences. Physics impacted international relations in a more immediate way. The balance of power adopted physics as its symbolism and its model, the symbol of this paradigm being the apothecary's scale which operates on the basis of the laws of gravity. For every action there is an opposite and equal reaction. Any rupture in the equilibrium of power in a geographical area will, over time, be met by countervailing power, and equilibrium will be re-established. The actions of states thus were equated with those of inanimate forces in a paradigm which called for the recurring reinstitution of the status quo. The paradigm took little account of ideology or domestic politics in an era in which politics was the preserve of the upper classes. The paradigm corresponded to a period of domination by these classes, in which its members had more in common with each than with the lesser breeds in their respective countries. The balance of power not only explained European statescraft, but it justified it and promoted the status quo. The more so since it regarded itself as scientific, with many references to Newtonian physics. This made its arguments more persuasive. It is characteristic of social science to have both an analytical and an ideological side. This paradigm easily lends itself to the structural analysis of this volume.

The great discoveries are usually presented in the literature as part of the internationalization of the West; its inward focus was changed to an outward one. They helped to put the Weltanschauung of the Middle Ages to rest. This is actually only part of the story. The great discoveries resulted ultimately in the material "unification" of the world, better stated, in its conquest by the West. Slavery reached huge proportions, as Africans were brutalized and made to work as slaves in those parts of the new world where their labor could be used profitably. Indians also served as slaves; too often they were exterminated because of their unprofitability as slaves. The conquerors brought their culture and their educational systems with them. Ultimately the social sciences were implanted as well, either as a result of formal colonialism, or the informal type. The colonized are by now in open revolt against the West, their revolt including our subjects as well. Slavery was not the only brutality inflicted upon the peoples of the non-Western world. And the worms have turned, and they are now telling their side of the story, a history often at odds with the

Western version. It is no accident that world systems analysis begins with the great discoveries, when the potential reach of the structures assumed worldwide proportions. The great discoveries thus represent much more than a lesson in internationalism for the West.

At the outset of this section, the idea was set forth that the Physiocrats were the midwives who aided the discipline economics enter its scientific stage. There is no general agreement on this point. Drucker, for example, designates French cameralists and mercantilists as the midwives and sets the birthdate in the first half of the seventeenth century.[10] This scholar argues that they were the first to treat economics as an autonomous subject. Others give this credit to Adam Smith. This dispute over a birthdate is characteristic of a discipline which is truly one of dissension. Laski found this dissension existing among the mercantilists themselves, but he attributed to them four grand principles which they generally espoused. They insisted on the value to a nation of possessing a large horde of precious metals, and they preferred foreign over domestic trade and manufacturing over raw material production. And finally they approved of state action to accomplish these goals. Laski finds that prosperity did seem to correlate with these principles, at least in the first part of the seventeenth century.

The Development of the Paradigms in Europe from the Industrial Revolution to the Third Quarter of the Nineteenth Century

Adam Smith's Wealth of Nations was in many respects an attack upon mercantilism. His work was taken up by the emerging industrial bourgeoisie as a way of increasing their own prerogatives. His view of value was quite at odds with that of the mercantilists, and he espoused methodological individualism and a laissez-faire policy of noninterference by the government in economic affairs. His was essentially a benign view of economic affairs; the common good arises if everyone pursues selfish interests. The economy was seen as a self-regulating system. Smith and his followers focused upon microeconomics and stressed the supply side of the system and the labor theory of value. Here was a paradigm which obviously was valuable to certain elites, one which they used in their rise to the top. The Smithian attack upon mercantilism raised many fundamental issues which have not been resolved to this day. In fact, disagreement increased and academic temperatures have risen with the emergence of Marxism, a subject referred to in this section. Subjects of central interest in this section include positivism and social Darwinism as well. The section includes what has to be one of the most fertile periods for our subjects, the period of their emergence as organized, specialized studies using the "scientific" method, i.e., some type of logic for their production of vocational knowledge. The period referred to is the 19th century, a century which witnessed, if we confine our remarks to sociology, the appearance of the work of Comte, Durkheim, Spencer, and Marx. The minimalists point to the industrial revolution of this epoch and to the increasing rationalism which it represented and promoted. Natural science and its application, technology, came to the fore and became part of this rationalization and industrialization. Moreover, problems resulted from these developments, for example, the growing urbanization. Minimalists tell us that our disciplines arose also to provide rational, "scientific" solutions to urban problems and any others for that matter. The maximalist position (also that of the multinational version) sees structures and the classes behind them as important in accounting for social science. Mercantilism obviously tended to serve one elite's interests, and classical economics served that of another. These classes did not so much invent the paradigms, as to promote the one which was partial to their own interests. Classical economics continued on after Adam Smith, and it received strong support from social Darwinism. Marxism provided a strong challenge to these points of view and to the interests which they served, but it was excluded from academe during the period under review.

As the nineteenth century progressed, the major adversary of social scientists was certainly not God. More and more, it became obvious that theirs was a civil war; their major foes were each other. By this time, God was not dead as an explanatory device, but he had been seriously wounded, at least in Western Europe. The ideological element became more evident in our disciplines as the social Darwinist belittled the positivist, and both were attacked by the Marxists. Social science not only suffers from the fact that its findings are not cumulative, but also from the fact that arguments seem interminable and assertions are never put to rest. Every argument and every assertion seems to survive, regardless of how it fits the evidence. The fit and the unfit appear to have equal survival potential. The result is that arguments and assertions are cumulative, not truth claims.

We have been impressed by the extent to which the ideas of the dominant paradigms in the first world reflect those of Auguste Comte. The latter's ideas are collectively referred to as positivism, and they deserve inclusion even in a brief account of the history of social science. The French philosopher is often referred to as the father of sociology. Positivism has been characterized as representing and reflecting the victorious bourgeoisie after the French Revolution.[11] This class had supreme confidence in science, technology, and industrialization, and its members were quite confident that they would lead humanity to a higher stage of development. Comte believed in progress, but he insisted that it be combined with order. Change without order spells anarchy, order without change leads to decay. No revolutionary, he did accept gradual change, but with order and stability. He expressed many generous sentiments, those associated with the enlightenment, and his approach lacks the naked brutality of social Darwinism. The role of science is to explain and predict, but also to act as the servant of the community. Social scientists are not meant to be merely intellectuals: they are social engineers as well. Industry is seen as being peaceful. Comte's three stages of humanity are quite similar to the social science myth set forth in this chapter. He admitted that sociology is more complicated than physics, but it too can be made a science, even if it may have to develop its own version of the scientific method. In his later years Comte turned to religion, but it was his own creation, the religion of humanity. It had priests and ceremonies, its outward model being the Catholic Church, but it was dedicated to the service of mankind. Most modern social scientists would find this quaint, if not Gothic and barbaric. They express their generous sentiments in a less ritualized and ostentatious manner.

Many of Comte's ideas can be traced to the enlightenment, but a more obvious and immediate source was Saint-Simon. Comte served as his secretary and collaborator until the two were separated by a serious quarrel. Saint-Simon lead a less contemplative life than his younger colleague, serving both in the American and the French revolutions. He was a great friend of natural science, and he believed that its method could and should be applied to social affairs. Perhaps he is best known for his plan for peace. He advocated rule by scientists and industrialists, the latter group in his view included workers. He believed that these groups would serve the interests of society and bring peace to Europe. Government would become administration and promote the real interests of society. Saint-Simon obviously did not believe in the class struggle. His plan is often offered as a forerunner of the modern theory of functionalism, a theory used to explain the current European Economic Community. Ernst Haas has proposed such a theory in which technicians from European businesses and governments collaborate with labor representatives to serve the common good by increasing production and by promoting European integration.

In Comte's view, the sciences subsume observed facts under general laws, and positive knowledge is restricted to observed facts and to the coordinating and descriptive laws of phenomena.[12] Only that which can stand up to empirical testing can count as knowledge. The formulation of general laws enables mankind to explain and to predict. Comte found it useless to look for primary or final causes, and he had little patience with those who doubted the existence of physical objects external to the mind. On the other hand, he did grant that the application of the scientific method could vary from discipline to discipline. He classified the following disciplines in the order in which they have entered, or would enter, the positivist (scientific) stage: astronomy, physics, chemistry, biology, and sociology. The disciplines go through three stages -- but these stages can overlap. Each represents a distinctive way in which truth claims are established and each corresponds to a period of European history. These stages are the theological, the metaphysical, and the positive. The disciplines reach the last stage, the desirable stage, at different historic epochs. The beginning of the nineteenth century witnessed biology enter this stage, but the study of society still rested in the land of theology and, even more so, in that of metaphysics.

We next describe these three stages through which mankind supposedly passes, and we ask the reader to compare them with what we refer to below as the social science myth. The first is the theological, the period in which mankind seeks the ultimate causes of events and finds them in animism or the wills of a plurality of super-human beings or in one such deity. In the age of animism, man endows things with wills and passions, and things act accordingly. As time goes on, the animating forces imminent in the objects are projected externally in the form of a plurality of gods, and later in the form of one god. In the second stage, cause is attributed to metaphysical abstractions, such as ether or vital principles. This second stage is reached when an all inclusive nature takes the place of a deity. In his analysis of the possibility of political science, Comte argued that these stages could be lumped together so far as analysis or method is concerned. Detectable in either the first or the second stage is a preponderance of imagination over observation and a search for absolute ideas.[13] Arbitrary and indefinite activity is found in this stage, rather than the regularity resulting from invariable natural laws. Comte put political science in these two overlapping stages, and he argued that its situation parallels alchemy, astrology, and cure-alls as contrasted with chemistry, astronomy, and medicine. The third stage is the positive one, that of a mature scientific outlook. The focus is upon observed facts, the regular occurrence of which is explained by a scientific law. This knowledge is real, certain, and useful -- and it allows prediction.[14] Positive knowledge is knowledge of the world. It does not lend itself to theological and metaphysical speculation, which positivism holds to be a waste of time in any case. The question of the existence of God is in this category.

Comte associated each of his three stages with a distinct form of social organization. The theological he put with a belief in absolute authority, the diving right of kings, and a militaristic order. Authority comes from above, and the warrior class is dominant. The ancient world and the Middle Ages represent this stage, whereas the metaphysical stage corresponds to the enlightenment. In this later stage, belief in abstract rights and popular sovereignty came to the fore, and the reign of law was instituted. The third stage corresponds to industrial society. Economic life and its problems become the major preoccupation, and a scientific elite arises to organize it in a rational way. Industrial society is a peaceful society, organized for production, and for the serving of the common good. But for its proper development a new science is required, namely sociology. This later "science" presupposes, and is the culmination of the existence of the other sciences, and it represents the special contribution of the positive era to man's intellectual advance. Under the unifying influence of science and industry, social instincts tend to take the form of the love of humanity in general. It is not that no industrial nation has gone to war. What Comte claims is that as industrial society grows to maturity and as society is more and more directed by a scientific elite, a peaceful society will result as differences are settled by rational discussion. One is reminded of Saint-Simon's utopian scheme for peace.

A reading of Comte gives the impression that his legacy lives on -- particularly in contemporary American social science. The same generous sentiments about science, the same faith in science and in industrialization, in order and in progress, in the evolution of knowledge from natural to social science, the same assurance that capitalism is peaceful, and, together with science, will lead to a new world order. All this seems current, contemporary, the grist of those on the cutting edges of the disciplines. Two aspects of positivism would find less support in contemporary American social science. The first is Comte's faith, not in democracy, but in paternalistic government, in government according to the principles formulated by the positivistic elites. Comte would have this elite lay down the principles by which the government would be run. This helps explain why positivism became so popular among the Brazilian military, for example, which has little commitment to popular rule. Another divergence is Comte's establishment of a religion of humanity, complete with catechism, liturgy, priests, and temples. It was modeled after the Catholic Church, but it was dedicated not to God, but to the service of humanity. The common good was extolled, not individual interests. Positivism itself divided over this, the "religious" issue, with the orthodox wing supporting the church of humanity and the heterodox dissenting. Positivism became an export item, particularly to Latin America, and in that region, particularly to Brazil, Mexico, and Chile. Positivists played an important role in the abolition of slavery in Brazil and in the establishment of the first republic there. Their slogan "order and progress" can be seen today emblazoned on the flag of that country.

Social Darwinism and Herbert Spencer

"After Comte, Herbert Spencer was undoubtedly the scholar chiefly responsible for the foundation of sociology during the nineteenth century".[15] These two men stimulated the growth of the subject in Europe and in the United States. Spencer's influence was enormous, even if today his works stay unread or are of interest chiefly to historians. His influence extended to Durkheim who followed through with some of his ideas -- chiefly his evolutionism and the division of labor. The early American sociologists acknowledged their debt to him, as did Radcliffe-Brown in his development of structural functionalism. Systems analysis is in his debt, as well as the industrialists of the time. His support of <u>laissez-faire</u> provided "scientific" support for policies of direct interest to them. Spencer serves here as our chief representative of social Darwinism, other scholars will be used to round out the discussion.

We next discuss social Darwinism, to be followed by Marxism. We do not explicate the latter in this section, but rather discuss its exclusion from academe. This "ism" was effectively barred from academia during the nineteenth century, and it was academic social science which helped keep it out. The academics provided "scientific" explanations which exposed its ideological underpinnings. Positivism, social Darwinism, Marxism -- each provided an alterative, "scientific," but often contradictory, explanation of social affairs. These explanations were alternate to each other, but also to any notion of God as cause. Each of the three giants of social science discussed in this section had rid himself of any such notion, and each could be classified as either agnostic or atheist. Marxism was distinctive in that it lent itself to revolutionary change, the other two were tilted toward the status quo which was being established in the West. Positivism posited rationality, man the thinker. Social Darwinism was scientific also, but it insisted on seeing humankind as animal, or putting him/her back in the cave or jungle. By emphasizing the worst in analyzing humankind, social Darwinism often justified what is the worst in him/her. By insisting that it was scientific, it put this stamp upon brutality. Low wages, miserable conditions for the poor, imperialism, racism, ethnic discrimination, and war -- nothing seemed too base to fall outside the parameters of its justification. After all, nature proceeds this way, by eliminating failures -- and those who survive, by this very fact, are the fittest and also the torch bearers of future progress. It is not too much to say that of the two status quo paradigms, positivism supported liberalism, gradual change; whereas social Darwinism was the favorite paradigm of the conservatives and reactionaries. By the nineteenth century the minimalist view of the history of social science was exposed as being deficient. The social sciences were not providing anything like pure analysis. True, the major social scientists had agreed to dethrone God, only to fall out with each other. Certainly by the nineteenth century, it was obvious that social science comes in many flavors, one to satisfy almost any ideology. The only way that the fiction of the minimalist school could be maintained was by using the rite of excommunication, i.e., denying that competing paradigms are legitimate social science.

Darwinism completed the destruction of the old order, at least for those who are modern in the West. Copernicus and Galileo had contributed to the process by demonstrating that the earth moves around the sun, but Darwin completed it by showing that mankind arose naturally from the animal kingdom, a process which did not require special creation. Darwin explained the process quite simply, by the principle of natural selection. More individual plants and animals are born than can possibly survive -- the numbers press upon the limited means of subsistence. The forms which emerge within each species are not identical, some inter-species variations always occur. Those plants and animals whose characteristics are most useful in adapting to the environment have the greatest chance to survive, and to transmit their favorable variations to subsequent generations through inheritance. Favorable ones are preserved, and unfavorable ones destroyed. In Darwin's view, the gradual accumulation over a long period of time results in a progressive divergence from the original species and the emergence of a new one.[16] Later the theory was changed; mutations or drastic variations were substituted for the progressive slight changes. The process which came down from Darwin involved variation, adaptation, and inheritance. But the vision of nature which he set forth was a universal battlefield. Adaptability was at a premium, famine and death were the norm. The higher forms were produced at the cost of the lives and misery of endless numbers of lesser individuals.

Darwin himself restricted his activities to biology. It was Spencer who emerged as the great systemitizer, the generalist who walked -- actually ran -- across fields, publishing in biology, psychology, and sociology, serving as the general propagandist for evolution. Spencer cannot properly be called a Darwinist, because his version of evolution took form before Darwinism emerged, and he drew heavily upon Lamarck's view of the inheritance of acquired characteristics. Darwinism should be seen, not as the initial source, but as the culmination of evolutionary thinking. Of special interest to us is that Darwin had read Malthus on population in 1838, twenty-one years before he published his On the Origin of Species. We have been assured that the discipline economics was little affected by social Darwinism. The probable reason is that this discipline had no need for this current of pessimism and conservatism, for it had its own Malthus. He had already done for classical economics what social Darwinism was to do for sociology. Any increase in wages would simply increase the supply of labor (for the lower classes were breeders), thus bringing down wage rates. In the Malthusian analysis, the poor were responsible for their own miserable conditions of life -- their breeding habits insured their misery. Spencer had the idiosyncracies which we allow for genius. Although he had only three months of formal schooling (actually, he was tutored at home), his book on biology was accepted as a text at Oxford, another on psychology was used at Harvard. He was not your everyday cheerful extrovert. A bachelor, a hypochondriac, and a dyspeptic, he habitually carried earmuffs which he would put on when the conversation bored him, and so retire to his own thoughts. Needless to say he was a very productive scholar.

Spencer was, if nothing else, a scientist and a synthesizer, the man of the huge generalization. He believed in the unity of the sciences, not only in the Comtian sense of the scientific method for all disciplines, but also in the sense that the basic scientific processes are the same in all realms. He accepted the basic unity of the world and the laws which govern it. He attempted to combine in one system of generalization the ideas of evolution and those of thermodynamics. We are not concerned here with the latter, but we deem it significant to point out that Spencer believed that a science of sociology was possible.[17] He, of course, included this discipline in his general scheme, and he made it subject to the law of evolution. His assertion that sociology could become a science was challenged at the time, notably by historians. He counterattacked, disdainfully asserting that their works related to sociology much as heaps of random stones and bricks compare to a standing building. Not only were the historians' facts scattered promiscuously in unrelated heaps, but they were the wrong facts. So often what historians presented was trivial, for example, the lives of kings. What should be of concern was the natural history of society. Historians questioned his work, arguing that it violated the concept of free will. Spencer was an unequivocal determinist -- arguing that free will and the science of mankind are contradictory concepts. Despite disclaimers, Spencer appears to have been a materialist. He argued that the deepest truths we can reach are simply statements of the widest experience of the relations of matter, motion, and force.[18] His laws, when stripped to their essentials, were expressions of physical laws. He saw evolution as being equivalent to the conservation of energy. As we saw above, he rejected the great men thesis for explaining history. Moreover, he was fond of saying that society is a growth, not a manufacture. Institutions did not arise because of rational choice -- conditions, not intentions, are determinant. Likewise, the values and the attitudes of a society reflect that society and do not determine it. His penchant for generalizing led him to suggest to Galton how to conduct research on fingerprints. Galton explained that the fingers of unborn children had been dissected to ascertain their earliest stages. Spencer remarked that this was the wrong way to proceed. The proper way was to consider functions first and then work back to the facts. One cannot conclude from this that Spencer ignored sociological facts. In fact, his Descriptive Sociology comes to 17 volumes, which are jammed full of facts. He hired others to collect the material to be presented in categories which he had determined beforehand.

Spencer saw evolution as being a process of change from a state of relatively indefinite, incoherent homogeneity to a state of relatively definite, coherent heterogeneity. The process involved the advance from the simple to the complex, through a process of successive differentiation and specialization. This process has now been accepted in biology, but Spencer meant it to apply to sociology as well, to its political, religious, and economic organizations. This process also involves integration, i.e., the mutual interdependence of the structurally differentiated parts and the coordination of their functions. He coined the term "superorganic" which later was used interchangeably with the term "culture." But this was not Spencer's intent. For him, it meant something beyond the purely biological, and it referred to the behavior of bees, wasps, and the beavers, as well as mankind. He did not regard the differences between the behavior of mankind and that of the social animals to be sufficient to merit a separate category. The origins of what we call today social life thus seem to have been in the animal world. Spencer found the answer on how societies first emerged in the works of Malthus. The pressure of population growth compelled people to enter into the social state, made social institutions indispensable, and developed social feelings.[19] The emergence of the social institution, however, did not see the end of the struggle for existence, but rather its transference from the level of personal relations to that of inter-group relations. Conflict then became the habitual activity of society, but it is directed to the outside. Social cooperation becomes manifest on the inside, initiated by joint defense and offense. The emergence of society means the beginning of the social division of labor and class structure, which results from a gradual differentiation of tasks within a society forced into military action. The societies maintain the struggle as do societal institutions, and only those survive which can adapt. In this view, a society is not an accidental assemblage of institutions and beliefs. If its structural parts are not adjusted to each other or to the environment, it will not survive. It will be destroyed by the competition.

The habitual conflict of society leads to the militarization of the society, which in turn results in the formation of larger groups and in their integration.[20] The process widens the area in which an increasingly large proportion of the population is habitually at peace and industrially employed. This opens the door to peace, one chief beneficent end to which Spencerian evolution leads, the formation of peaceful societies. But their attainment is tied to the evolution of societies, a subject in Spencer's analysis made to be as complicated as it is ambiguous. He provided both a classification and a typology of societies, as well as an assertion of the supposed relationship between them. The classification divided societies by their complexity: from the simple to the compound, the doubly compound, and finally the trebly compound. The typology was more a dichotomy, featuring at one pole the militant society with its warrior masters and worker slaves, its economic base being in landed property. At the other pole was industrial society, peaceful, decentralized, pursuing individual ends, and respect for the rights of others. The classification was offered as a framework for collecting and arranging data, the typology an interpretive device and one which expressed Spencer's ideology. Logically, there should have been a close relationship between the two schemes. The more complex should be the most industrialized and the most peaceful. Spencer did, in fact, speak of the inevitable demilitarization of societies, but he also mentioned highly advanced militant societies (Russia and Germany), and he deplored the militarization (the "rebarbarization") of England with its imperial expansion.[21] He named as militant societies ancient Egypt, Sparta, Peru, and Russia. He offered as their opposite Athens, the Hanseatic towns, the Netherlands, North America, and England. The examples given allow the observer to see how tenuous his distinction is. Shades of gray more so than a black/white dichotomy distinguish the war policies of these two sets of polities.

But such niceties did not deter Spencer, the ideologue, a term which must be added to the long list which suggests his accomplishments and the tenure of his message. He assured us that evolution will not go on forever in the direction of increasing heterogeneity. Organisms must decay and die, but not society. It will reach a state of permanent equilibrium, "in the establishment of the greatest perfection and the most competent happiness".[22]   Individual and group struggle was necessary in the past to produce higher types of mankind and the growth and development of society. True, untold suffering resulted, but without it the world would still be inhabited by feeble types hiding in caves and eating wild berries. Modern capitalism represented for Spencer the industrial, peaceful type of society. One is reminded of Comte's stage of positivism or of Marx's period of communism. But Spencer did not believe that competition had atrophied in modern industrial society. Indeed, it was a necessary ingredient for industrial progress. While industrial order introduced cooperation, it was limited. Spencer was stubbornly against state action and, more so, against the socialist system. This system would be more akin to the military than to the industrial state, and he denigrated it as "the coming slavery." He ridiculed the idea that there should be no suffering and that society is to blame for what exists. Individuals were responsible for their own suffering, and human pain should be allowed to run its course so as to produce its chastening effect.

William Graham Sumner, a Spencerian and a professor of political science and sociology at Yale, argued that millionaires are a product of natural selection, just like the great statesmen, scientists, or military leaders.[23] What does it matter if they are idle or have silly personal ideas? It is because they are thus selected that wealth -- their own and that entrusted to them -- aggregates in their hands. Let them make a mistake, and the money will disappear from their hands. They live in luxury, but they are a good bargain for society. Sumner answered the question which he says is often put to sociology: does the sociologist want to kill off "certain classes of troublesome and burdensome persons?" He took the moral high ground by responding in the negative, but he added that it would be better for society had they not been born, and no pain to them. Sir Francis Galton, a cousin of Darwin and founder of the eugenics movement, took up the same general problem -- but his purpose was to excuse the extinction of an inferior race. He asserted that "it may be somewhat brutally argued" that when competition exists, someone must yield, and there will on the whole be no more unhappiness if the inferior yield to the superior or if victor and vanquished are reversed.[24]   He then drew a distinction between the extinction of a race and that of the individual, and he elaborated upon the theme of how race extinction could be accomplished smoothly by such things as late marriage among the inferiors. In another book, Galton went through the whole dreary exercise of race analysis -- all this after having referred to Darwin's law of natural selection. The negro race was, of course, deficient when compared to the Anglo-Saxon race, and the native Australian even more so. He argued that the number of half-witted American negroes is very high, and he found that Africans make many "childish, stupid, and simpleton-like" mistakes even on their own turf. He had visited Africa and witnessed this personally. The ablest races for which history bears record are the ancient Greek, and of these the ablest was the Athenian. Athens "built up a magnificent breed of human animals."

The temptation is to multiple examples, so as to nail down the intimate connection in social science between its analysis and its ideology. We promise not to multiply, but simply to add, and then only one more example, early British anthropology in Africa. That it was a form of social Darwinism will become apparent. Porter observes that one could have expected that the knowledge amassed by early anthropologists would have led to an appreciation of African culture. But the early anthropologists were surprisingly unhelpful, despite the fact that by the nineteenth century their study had become better organized and more "scientific." He claimed that the discipline in the early part of that century came under the influence of the biologists and after 1860 evolutionary anthropology became dominant, but the latter only reinforced the trend already set.[25] The biologists sought to examine, to classify, and to arrange the whole order of nature in a rational pattern. Human races were deployed in a hierarchical fashion, with the caucasian at the top and the negro at the bottom, just above the monkeys. Evolutionary anthropology modified, but in a general way, reinforced this pattern. One single scale of civilization was posited, with Western Europe at its summit. Cultural differences among contemporary societies were ascribed to different stages of the same essential process. Insofar as cultures diverged from that of nineteenth century England, so much the worse for them. They were relegated to the lower part of the scale. Much information about Africa emerged from these scholarly efforts, but it was cast in an Anglocentric and an often intolerant framework. African culture could not be appreciated for itself; it always travelled second class. British anthropology held onto this pejorative framework until well into the twentieth century, when functionalism and cultural relativism essentially displaced evolutionary anthropology. We will see below in Chapter V that the tradition of bad-mouthing other cultures continues on in cultural deficiency models. Black and Chicano social science in the United States make this charge against establishment disciplines.

Marxism

This section could be dramatized on television by three chairs in a college classroom. One would be occupied by Comte; the second by Spencer with his earmuffs at the ready, prepared to block out disagreeing and, therefore, disagreeable arguments; and the third would be empty. Marx himself had been sent packing from Germany, France, and Belgium, and he was forced to live most of his life as an exile in England. Marxism fared little better, at least in academe. The remainder of this section will be concerned with the empty chair, mainly as it has appeared in American classrooms. Our explication of Marxism as a paradigm has been preserved for later. The empty chair symbolizes successful excommunication, the professed right of dominant paradigms to exclude the competition. Each of the three paradigms referred to in this section considered itself to be scientific. Thus each had the right to excommunicate, i.e., to speak to the competition authoritatively, and vertically from science to non-science. The unorthodox conclusions and their paradigms become "unscientific," and the holders of such views have an empty chair to plead their case. The Russian Revolution resulted in a warm welcome for Marxism, but only in the Soviet Union. The occupants of the other chairs lost their seats. By then these represented all bourgeois social science, not just social Darwinism and positivism. This turn of events was not so much revenge as the exercise of the right of excommunication, and our structural analysis puts it in different terms. By now, Marxism has become more respectable and more widespread in the West, but its history gives useful insights into the nature of social science. Part of the reason for the acceptance of Marxism in the West is that a sect of it, Marxism humanism, a less doctrinaire sect, has emerged. Part of the reason is thus internal to our disciplines, but we insist on the structural reasons as well.

Duverger pointed to the immediate acceptance of Comte's work by sociologists in the late nineteenth and early twentieth centuries. "In contrast the contribution of Marx was neglected in scientific circles for a long time because of its political context".[26]

Marx's direct "scientific" influence hardly developed until the middle of the twentieth century, although a certain diffuse influence was perceptible well before this. The assessment of Bernal, a Marxist himself, is quite similar. He asserted that it has taken more than a hundred years for Marxism to penetrate the "official social sciences." The reason he gave was that the Marxist picture of the class struggle was so foreign to academic thought and so unlikely to appeal to the powers controlling universities.[27] Bernal went on to say that even in his time where Marxism is taught in "free" and "democratic" countries it is taught by anti-Marxists. Whatever the truth of this statement at the time, it cannot now be taken as the rule. He likened the contribution of Marx and Engels in social science to that of Galileo and Darwin in natural science. Bourgeois social sciences are nothing more than an intellectual camouflage for capitalism. These sentiments are typically Marxist, and they can easily lead (in a Marxist academe) to empty capitalist chairs.

Barraclough documents the same long-standing exclusion of Marxism from academic history, until recent times. This despite the spread of Marxist doctrines among European socialist parties in the latter part of the nineteenth century. Marx was not even mentioned in the standard survey of nineteenth century historiography which G.P. Gooch published in 1913.[28] Barraclough attributes this to "the hatred and fear of communism." In any case, most countries virtually excluded Marxists and socialists from their university faculties. France was the exception. In Germany and England, professional historians usually ignored the subject or even misrepresented it. The Russian Revolution required academic historians to take account of it, but the account was "essentially hostile, conditioned by ideological rather than scientific or scholarly considerations." The great depression again brought historians face to face with Marxism, although the majority remained hostile. Marxism became important in China in the 1920's and elsewhere in Asia. We return to this subject in the last section of this chapter.

Bottomore notes that Marx's ideas received little academic attention during his lifetime, the most receptive academic area being Russia.[29] Marxism did become the social theory debated most in European working class circles and in the German Social Democratic Party. This author notes the later impact which Marxism had on the development of Austrian sociology and upon individual German sociologists, notably Max Weber. Our view is less euphoric than his, an attitude which we document below with the case of American sociology. A point to be made in our general discussion is that three of the most prominent Marxists of the interwar period, Lukacs, Korsch, and Gramsci all denied that Marxism is a social science. Later, Korsch changed his mind. The "fault" for the separation of Marxism and academic social science thus seems to be bilateral. Moreover, under Stalin social science in the Soviet Union was severely restricted. Despite a common interest in explaining society, academic sociology and Marxism generally segregated themselves from each other, at least until recently. One of several reasons given by Szacki is the one stressed in this volume.[30]   Sociology was a bourgeois discipline which sought at most to reform capitalism. Marx sought to abolish it. Bottomore notes a revival of Marxist thinking in the social sciences in the last two decades.

We next turn to three studies of Marxism as it relates to American sociology. Admittedly, Marxism has a harder time of it in the United States than in most other first world countries. Given the importance of the United States in social science, however, whatever happens there is of general interest. Gurney examined American sociology in its formative years from 1895 to 1920, specifically the books of seven early presidents of the American Sociological Association, the relevant 25 volumes of <u>The American Journal of Sociology</u>, and the <u>Publications of the American Sociological Society</u>. References to Marx, Marxism, and socialism were analyzed. The first finding was that Marx, Marxism, and socialism were generally simply ignored. Thus the material left to analyze "is actually a very small part of the work of early American sociologists".[31]   Indeed, the Marxist chair was left essentially empty. Gurney divided the references which were made to the subject matter into three categories: positive, indifferent, and negative. There were so few in the first two categories as to defy sub-classification. Only two indifferent comments were found. One author (Small) responded favorably to socialism at times, but references to Marx and Marxism were generally unfavorable. He charged that Marx and Marxism were scientifically inadequate, one of the six general categories of negative responses used in the analysis. Ward regarded Marx as a politician, not a scientist, and thus not a sociologist. Sumner rejected socialism (he did not mention Marxism), because it failed to realize that the social order was fixed by natural law. Here is a case of social Darwinism speaking to a vastly different paradigm and excommunicating it from the world of science.

Gurney's typology of the negative reactions of early American sociologists contained five other categories. These charges were that Marxism or socialism were in error because of their mechanism and determinism; their emphasis on the class struggle; their failure to take account of the psychological realm; and because they were a threat to individualism and to private property. The charges included dogmatism and rigidity, and overemphasis upon economics, the single factor, and the class struggle. Ward maintained high hopes for the middle class, and Giddings deplored working class movements insisting that any attempt to improve the lot of the working class would upset natural development. Ellwood argued that emphasis should be put upon the psychological, and he found Marxism incompatible with modern psychology. Gurney concluded that these objections, in sum, are ideological, i.e., they reflect the prescriptions of a capitalist society. Certainly, the emphasis upon the common good, individualism, and private property reflect the ideology of this system. The other aspects of their objections also fit into the ideology. In the next section of this chapter we return to the relationship between early American social science and the burgeoning industrialization of the time.

We now turn to another study of American sociology, but of a later period. Sallach grants that by the time of his writing (the early 1970's) Marx had made his appearance in American textbooks on sociology. But Sallach rejects the consoling assertion that this historic "oversight" has now been corrected, and that sociology has now earned its reputation as an unrestricted marketplace of ideas. His complaint is that to study a tradition seriously one must not stop with reading its founder and neglect subsequent writers within the tradition, and this is what American sociology has done to Marxism. If subsequent materials within the tradition are ignored, the whole tradition can be depicted as out of date and decreasingly relevant. Parsons seems to do just that by placing Marx in a phase of development which has long since passed. Sallach has no bone to pick with this if taken literally. His complaint is that the same conclusion, at least by implication, is applied to the Marxist tradition as well. He argues that no other tradition has been subjected to such criteria. No theoretical tradition is expected to be relevant in the modern era apart from its subsequent development and modification.

Sallach examined eight popular American sociology texts and readers in search of twenty prominent Marxists who were subsequent to Marx. Six of the books had been published in the 1960's, two in

1970. The twenty Marxists included some well known scholars Althusser, Deutscher, Gramsci, Habermas, Korsch, Lenin, Lukacs, Luxemburg, Mao, Sweezy, and Trotsky. Not one reference to any of the twenty scholars was found.[32] A case of a completely empty chair, an oddity in social science whose research seldom finds absolutes. The exclusions seem odd, in view of the authors which American sociology accepts. For example, Georg Lukacs has been excluded, but his mentors (Simmel and Weber) are included as well as his student (Mannheim). This, despite the similarity between Ideology and Utopia and Lukacs' earlier work History and Class Consciousness. Sallach goes on to suggest that by excluding post-Marx Marxist debate, establishment sociology has cut itself off from vigorous and generally fertile debate, not spared itself from monolithic dogmatism and endless exegetic discussions (as the rationalizers for exclusion maintain). His conclusion is that the thorough exclusion of Marxist scholars from American sociology shows that establishment sociology has been cast in political and ideological terms.

The third study, this one appeared in 1979, heralds the arrival of the Marxist in American sociology. The empty chair has been filled, but it has been relegated to the back of the American classroom. Hechter points to the founding of Marxist journals, Marxist graduate programs, and an occasional article on a Marxist theme in a mainstream sociology journal.[33] And the Marxist professor has made his appearance in the classroom. Hechter argues that Marxism has always been considered in the United States to be a foreign import, part of the unwanted baggage of European immigrants. It has no institutional base in the new world, and to be a Marxist in this setting is to renounce any hope of gaining power in most institutions, including the academic world. Few Marxists have senior appointments in elite universities, and these few are not treated well. Certainly, structural analysts who see elites behind the structures have no problem in believing the beleaguered status of these infiltrators. The present author has witnessed this infiltration, always admiring how its perpetrators disguise their ideology by using a thousand names to describe it, but never the forbidden term "Marxism." Their exercise in deception and double talk is necessary for academic survival in the local milieu, and this necessity again highlights the political and ideological nature of our disciplines. The mirror image of the American Marxist is found in those countries where Marxism is the official ideology. To be a Marxist there, or at least to appear to be one, is the pragmatic thing to do. These two images should be viewed as polar ones. Other situations also exist, somewhere between these opposites, shades of gray, not just black or white.

American Dominance and the Challenge to It

This section is in part a continuation of the last in the sense that it helps to explain the process by which Marxism was excluded for so long from American academic social science. But this is only part of a busy section which recounts the tremendous expansion, the capitalization, the specialization, and the indigenization of the disciplines in the United States. It has been alleged that it was in the United States where the patterns of specialization and capitalization for capitalist social science were set. The success of the Russian Revolution made certain that this pattern would by no means be universal. In fact, this fact put the resources of what had been the Russian Empire at the services of a contrary and outcast paradigm. Moreover, the widespread distribution of the dominant American paradigm would have to await the early post World War II period. Before this, the dominant British and French paradigms held firm, each nurtured and protected by its own imperial power. Nazism resulted in the dispersal of many German social scientists, but Italy fared better. Most professors there took the required oath of loyalty to Il Duce, and social science seems to have expanded and prospered under the new dispensation.

The historic key to the present state of social science rests, of all places, in the policies of Prussia. It was the Prussian state which tied the university and natural science together, social science came along in the common package, but this union was passed on to a conquered Germany and then was adopted in the United States. This connection with the university converted the scientist and his younger colleague, the social scientist, from an amateur into a professional. The new professional became more and more specialized, thus requiring more and more specialized capital equipment with which to carry on his profession. The need for more capital goods was met to some extent, of course, by the government through its funding of school systems, but also directly, and now we are referring to the United States, through the foundations funded by the rising industrial bourgeoisie. We need not scurry around looking for evidence to see if it took interest in our disciplines. Its interest was in the open. Silva and Slaughter use exchange theory in their attempt to show that mainline American social science accepted the "tainted money" from the robber barons in exchange for the acceptance of their essential ideological position. This sounds too much like conscious exchange to us, a variation of economic theory -- but it is generally compatible with our structural approach. Mainline social science defended the interests of the dominant classes, even if most of those involved believed that they were being objective or scientific. Another event of signal importance in this section is the "Americanization" of the disciplines. This term can have at least two meanings. One is that American social science has become world social science -- the international references models are the dominant American paradigms. We reject this assertion if taken literally, since in a literal since there are no international reference models. It is true, however, that the American dominant models are the most widespread ones. A second meaning of "Americanization" is the process by which foreign imported paradigms are modified and adapted better to fit American ideas, conditions, and the interests of her elites. This is a special case of indigenization, a process which plays a large role in our analysis. We develop the notion Americanization in the sense of indigenization in this section, and refer to it in the sense of its catholicity as well.

Law, theology, and the classics were the most important college subjects taught in colonial America and on into the eighteen hundreds. This is true with the modification that law was first learned in law offices as a practical subject before it became a college subject. History and philosophy were added as well, and the social sciences often were offered in conjunction with (mixed with) other subjects, or the same professors taught more than one social science or a social science as well as his regular courses. The colleges had often been established for religious reasons, and the historic battle between God and social science, a feature of the old world, was refought in the new world as well, and with the same victor. The American Social Science Association (ASSA) was formed in 1865, the year which witnessed the end of the Civil War. It was an association of the well-born, a self-selected socio-economic elite centered in New England, mostly around Boston.[34] The fathers of this elite were professors, clergy, and businessmen, and ASSA supported free trade, hard currency, and, of course, capitalism. Its members rendered service by giving advice on social problems to American society. That this society needed advice (but not necessarily from ASSA) is indicated by the fact that half the years between 1875 and 1921 were depression years. The organization had been modeled after a British counterpart (the National Association for the Promotion of Social Science), and ASSA members valued a general, liberal education. The period immediately after the Civil War thus witnessed some growth in American social science, but little in the way of its specialization. Moreover, social scientists often were not professionals tied to institutions of higher learning.

Crucial for the development of our disciplines was what happened in Prussia, later in Germany, i.e., the university system founded there. Germany in the words of Manicas "industrialized" science, and she did it by tying it to the university.[35] Chairs, seminars, and institutes were established mainly for the natural sciences, but social science received the spin-off from this. Initially the product of the leisure classes, who were scattered in Europe without substantial outside resources, natural science was given a home in the universities, a furnished home, one with the necessary equipment and structure. It was tied to industry as well. Natural science was prized both for the pure knowledge which it produces, but also for the technology which aided greatly in making Germany a great industrial power. The industrialization of science was thus tied to a positivist perspective, a technocratic, instrumental one. The industrialization of science paid off, most noticeably in chemistry. German social science served as the tail of the dog, but it fared better with the added nourishment and resources.

In the period 1820 to 1920 nearly 9,000 Americans attended German universities. Before 1870, the majority were enrolled in natural science and medicine, but by 1878 this majority had turned to social science and to the liberal arts. The literature indicates that American students seemed to revel in the greater choices, the seminars, the emphasis on research, the all around greater freedom, and the quality of the product offered. This contrasted with the then typical American college whose major mission seemed to be to train preachers. The itinerant scholars recognized how backward their country was, and they brought back the strong urge to effect these improvements at home. Note that we are not saying that the American social science of the time was unaffected by the discipline in England and France. In fact, the French physiocrats seemed to be the most important influence in economics, and Spencer and Comte retained influence in sociology and anthropology. The latter two were the most often cited in early American sociology texts.[36] The lasting German influences were more structural, capable of being summarized by reference to the founding of universities rather than colleges and the awarding of the Ph.D. This, of course, involved the greater capitalization of the university and the resulting greater dependence of social scientists upon the providers of capital. If before they were independent craftsmen, now they became professionals, but essentially dependent ones. Their equivocal position was outlined in the previous chapter. A few figures and instances are instructive in suggesting the evolution of our disciplines in the United States. She constructed her first psychology laboratory sometime in the 1870's , by 1904 there were 48 of them there. By 1917 the United States had a larger stock of psychologists than the combined total for England, France, and Germany. The first graduate program in the social sciences was Columbia's School of Political Science, founded in 1880 by the German trained John W. Burgess. We return to the work of this notorious racist, the "father of American political science". The world's first sociology department was founded at Chicago University. Several specialized professional organizations were launched at the time. They contrast with the generalized American Social Science Association. The list of the disciplines along with the respective dates of the founding of their specialized associations follows: history (1884), economics (1892), psychology (1892), sociology (1893), and political science (1903). Specialized journals in these fields were launched as well. The university population along with its graduate complement increased dramatically by 1930, way beyond anything Europe had ever seen, to respectively 1,053,000 and 47,300. The numbers again skyrocketed after World War II, when the impact of the GI Bill of Rights was felt.

Social science had an easier time penetrating the American university than its European counterpart. In Europe the professorate was, indeed, a mandarin class, representatives of the ancien regime, influential in the highest circles of government in Germany and France.[37] This professorate resisted the upstart intruders: its actions are congruent with those we impute to social scientists as well. Turf battles are a common occurrence in academe. But the situation in the United States was different. It is true that the new social sciences faced challenge from clergymen, lawyers, and local merchants, but aid was successfully enlisted from the rising industrial classes: the Vanderbilts, the Harrimans, the Goulds, the Rockefellers, the Carnegies, and the Morgans. Their dominance seemed assured by the North's victory in the Civil War. The American society of the time can be seen as divided into three sections: (1) the plantation society of the rural South, originally founded upon slavery; (2) the industrial capitalism of the northeast; and (3) the family agricultural system of the West.[38] The plantocracy was at first dominant, but it was challenged by the creation of the Republican party in 1854 and by the victory of the latter in the election of 1860. The victory of the North in the Civil War prevented the southern secession, and provided the background for postwar industrial expansion. This included a protective tariff and the encouragement of immigration which provided the labor force for the new industries. More and more, these <u>nouveau</u> <u>riches</u> were put on the boards of directors of universities, and the academic manager begged money from their "charitable" foundations. Thorstein Veblen, who had such trouble himself maintaining employment in the system, complained that the rulers of American universities changed from the clergy to government and businessmen, the latter really meaning business rule.

Silva and Slaughter see the new specialists, as indicated in the emergent specialized social science organizations, accept resources from the rising industrial elites in exchange for producing information in accord with the elites' interests. The universities produced what they chose to call certified knowledge, what is in any case specialized vocational knowledge. This knowledge was presented as being technical, even objective and privileged, and it was used to battle Marxists and other radicals, and upon occasion also against the far right. The struggle against the far left was more consistent, as American social science generally cut out a liberal ideological swath for itself. The key go-between in this exchange was the university manager, who set out to provide professional housing and capital facilities for all sorts of experts to produce ideologically acceptable certified knowledge. To do this, the managers needed to finance the operation -- the salaries, the specialized libraries, professional schools, special institutes and graduate schools, the secretarial help, time off from teaching -- the whole panorama of payments for capital goods and current expenses. The managers replaced the broad classical curriculum of the generalist with the elective and specialized system of the expert.[39] The latter became even more dependent upon the system. Those who do well within the system -- those of ability who do not stray ideologically and who cultivate the right people, i.e., the managers -- receive quite comfortable salaries. The more successful become academic entrepreneurs, and circulate about from the university to government, then perhaps to business or to a foundation, or even set up their own consulting firms and produce and sell information as capitalists themselves.

By discussing these "academic guns for hire" we are getting ahead of our story. Silva and Slaughter discuss the "tainted money" debate which arose over whether moneys from the notorious robber baron Russell Sage should be accepted by social scientists. All of the nine leaders in the American Economic Association whose views were made known expressed the view that such "tainted money" should be accepted, and following this in 1908 the American Economics Association elected the head of the Russell Sage Foundation to its third presidency. At first glance, the use of exchange theory to explain the essential establishment orientation of American social science seems blatant, too explicit, too rational, too much like a business deal or open prostitution. It is much easier to accept if we realize that social science is myth-ridden and that the acceptance of "tainted money" was cast in a quite different light by the participants, money donated by philanthropic industrialists in the interests of discovering the objective truth. Structural analysis would generally expect the social science of an industrial system such as that of the United States in the post Civil War period to correspond to the interests of the dominant elites, but this approach makes no charge of an explicit business deal or of academic prostitution.

We next turn to the Americanization of the social sciences. The term can mean the indigenization of our disciplines or their attaining a dominant position. American dominance so far as specialization of the disciplines was concerned arose early. Manicas states that the present essential specialization, its institutionalization, occurred in the United States. The extension of American paradigms overseas awaited the creation of the United States "empire" after World War II. Then dominant American paradigms became the world's favorite import models.

Americanization in the sense of indigenization means the conversion of foreign paradigms to fit American conditions, or the jettisoning of them in favor of home grown ones. The term domestication has been used by others for the former process, and indigenization saved for the latter, but we subsume both processes under one heading. Our first example is political science, which was introduced at Columbia University by John W. Burgess. He and others had studied Staateswissenschaft under Droysen and brought it back to the United States with them. Staateswissenschaft was a comparative paradigm, historically, institutionally, and constitutionally centered, with great emphasis upon the state as a sovereign and as a moral force. The undisputed leader of the movement to institutionalize political science in the United States was Burgess. He had studied the subject in Berlin, Leipzig, and Gottingen, and he gathered around himself at Columbia a faculty composed almost entirely of the German educated. In his words, the system of graduate study he fashioned at Columbia had been modeled after that of the Imperial University of Strassbourg and the Ecole Libre des Sciences Politiques in Paris.[40] Emphasis was put upon research, publications, and the training of professors; and the focus was placed upon historical, legal, and constitutional methodologies. In his own publications, Burgess tried to reconcile the German notion of the sovereign state with the traditional American commitment to popular sovereignty and liberty. He did not counterpoise the two; rather, he made the state the guarantor of liberty. But the requisites for such a happy marriage only occurred under certain conditions, traceable to the psychology of the race or ethnic group involved. Thus Burgess became a notorious racist. Let the record show that the first graduate program introduced in the United States (at Columbia in political science) was by a racist. We insist on stating this because a well known book on the history of American political science, one used to socialize American graduate students, fails to do this. Rather Burgess is praised as being the father of American political science and as "among the truly great figures in its history".[41] He is presented as part of the movement which made American political science more scientific. This minimalist approach resembles an official, expurgated church history, with all the naughty parts taken out. It is to the credit of American political science that it did not continue along racist lines.

Burgess found the key to the reconciliation of state sovereignty and individual liberty in the racial psychology of people. Actually, it was the Teutonic race which Burgess thought was most successful at this reconciliation. The other races of modern Europe -- the Greek, Latin, Celtic, or Slav -- had failed at this, although the Greek and Latin at one time had been successful. In recent times the Latin races have recklessly killed the ruling class, the most intelligent part of their peoples, while the Teutons have preserved this class and constantly improved their political systems. The Teutonic nations have been entrusted "in the general economy of history, with the mission of conducting the political civilization of the modern world".[42] (Burgess, 1891: 44). This conviction led Burgess to countenance the suppression of the political rights of non-Teutonic elements of a given society, colonialism by Teutonic peoples, and the expulsion of non-Teutons from given territories. He even warned against "weak sentimentality" which might prevent the implementation of his policies. He specifically denied that either Asian, African, or "Mohammedan" people have been able to reconcile government with liberty. He upgraded North America as being Teuton, and thus within the charmed circle, but South America suffered from having a majority consisting of Indians, Negroes, and Mestizos.[43] The exception to this was Argentina, "the light and the hope of South America;" this because of its solidly white population.

The social science myth would have us believe, and this is its fragile side, that the German import Staatswissenschaft represented but a step in the direction of a more scientific political science paradigm. It was more scientific than what preceded it, and less so than what followed it. Moreover, the claim (more fragility here) is that this results from logical causes, essentially internal to the social science, except that the external plays the role of a catalyst effecting the paradigm, but it does not become a part of it. The myth takes natural science as its model and applies it to social science. The multinational approach is quite different. Staatswissenschaft had a strong state as a central feature, a characteristic compatible with the interests and the purposes of the Prussian elite, intent upon unifying Germany by force. The paradigm was easily made compatible with German traditions as well. But it was not compatible with the political tradition of the United States. Fries sees the confrontation as one between "the sovereign state of German political science -- absolute and self-limiting; on the other, stood the sovereign citizen of American politics".[44] The former gave way, as the latter asserted itself. Crick argues that the face off was with pragmatism and the progressive movement,[45] and his ideas are closer to our structural approach. The political tradition of the individual was certainly compatible with the interests of the rising American industrial classes, especially since in the myth which was created the large corporation was equated with the individual. The process of the Americanization of political science went beyond paradigms. Nearly half of those who made up the American political science establishment in 1904 had studied abroad, a figure which had fallen to less than one-third in 1914.[46] Of the 18 new members of the executive committee of the American Political Science Association added between 1915 and 1920, only three had studied abroad. In 1906 both the <u>Political Science Quarterly</u> and the <u>American Political Science Review</u> had reviewed 25 books written in foreign languages. By 1920 the number had fallen respectively to four and three. By 1911 the most popular course in the discipline was American government; before this it had been comparative government/general political science.

Wilhelm Wundt's claim to the fatherhood of experimental psychology is based in large measure upon his establishment of a laboratory in Leipzig. He attracted many American students, most of whom returned home to establish their own laboratories.[47] Wundt has the distinction of having published 53,735 pages of material, an average output of 2.2 pages per day from 1853 to 1920. His claim to distinction, however, is his experimental method. His approach was rule-laden, even if it was introspective, featuring self-observation. In this approach, the investigator applies a stimulus to a sense organ and asks the subject to report on the sensation produced. He set forth explicit rules for the use of introspection in his laboratory, and arduous training was required to apply it. This method, of course, was quite different from that of the latter day behaviorist, as was his general view of the discipline. Germans in general saw the discipline as being tied to philosophy. Moreover, he and his colleagues focused exclusively upon the generalized normal adult mind of the human, not upon the psychology of individual differences. This latter focus came from that part of British psychology which had been inspired by Sir Francis Galton, Darwin's half cousin.[48] The Americans were the spiritual cousins of this. The Americans made psychology into the "science of behavior" and thus made it a socially useful discipline. Boring has concluded that by 1900 American psychology had taken form. Its physical body had been inherited from German experimentalism, but its mind was Darwinian. Thorndike brought animals into the laboratory, and testing was introduced by Galton and Pearson. But it was the Americans who have made so much of testing. Psychological testing has become an industry, and psychology itself has become the queen of American social science.

The "Americanization" of economics is still a different story. Prior to 1880 the Americans followed the traditions of the classical British or the French physiocrats, more so the latter than the former.[49] The returning German scholars proved to be too "radical," the German economic style of the time being more state centric and interventionist. Some difficulty was encountered in reconciling the views of the two groups, but the reconciliation was effected, and the American Economics Associated was successfully launched. Silva and Slaughter recount the plight of three economists involved in the formation of the American Economics Association, who stepped over the permissible line by openly criticizing capital's domination of labor. They were Henry Carter Adams, Richard T. Ely, and Edward Alsworthy. "Each was sharply disciplined by his university managers for utterances ignoring the vested interests of sponsors and trustees".[50] We do not go into the details of the cases but these cases should remind us again of the last section, which attested to the exclusion of Marxism from American academe in the period under consideration. The exclusion often went beyond Marxism, to include other radicals and those not so radical as well.

The Social Science Myth

We return in the next chapter to American predominance in social science, the emphasis there shifting to communications. Our focus in this section is upon the social science myth. The minimalist view of history and Comte's third stage of mankind (positivism), both sketched above, parallel the myth's vision of the future. The first part of the myth, also sketched above, saw our disciplines evolve from the pre-scientific to arrive at the scientific stage, at which time they became social sciences. The myth would have us believe that the future offers maturity, a condition similar to that enjoyed by natural science. The multinational version sees matters differently. The immediate future is woven together with the third world revolt and the inevitable mounting disagreement, rather than the consensus associated with natural science. This revolt and our view of the future has been saved for a subsequent chapter. We use the discipline history as our usual standard for examples and comparison in this section. Perhaps it is appropriate for this role, especially considering the strong movement in the postwar period to heal the breach between this discipline and the social sciences (the "other" social sciences). We learned in the first chapter that the four major traits of natural science are universalism, communism, disinterestedness, and organized skepticism. A scientific history presumably would possess such traits, but maturity for history is expressed below in terms of its outputs.

When we last made reference to the myth, our disciplines had been so organized and their methods so improved that they had become social sciences, an epistemic step above non-science, but not yet on a par with mature science. Before turning to the stage maturity, we make these preliminary comments by way of exceptions to the myth. The first exception consists of those scholars who take their discipline "lightly." They are referred to in Chapter VII as adherents of humanistic or Western Marxism, and of interpretive sociology and kindred paradigms from other disciplines. To them, the term "science" in social science means "study," and they never expect our disciplines to go much beyond increasing our understanding of society and its problems, and certainly never to become a science in the sense in which we use the term. Secondly, Chinese social science does not fit into the general mold forged below. It draws a line between knowledge acquired in the struggle for production, and thus related to nature. This corresponds to natural science. This contrasts with knowledge acquired in social relations, the equivalent of social science. But the latter includes literature, the fine arts, and the humanities.[51] The discussion below proceeds despite these exceptions.

We consider only three general forms of the social science myth -- but other forms exist. One of the three considered is Marxism (but not Chinese or humanistic/Western Marxism); the other two, non-Marxist. The three have one element in common: the assumption that method determines the degree to which a discipline is a science. Interestingly, our example from history has the opposite emphasis, the focus on outputs. Method, however, is the usual focal point, the element stressed, and some practitioners seem at first brush to be indifferent to outputs as a measure of scientific status. We save until later our argument that this emphasis is misplaced. We are not saying that the myths are generally unconcerned with social science output, only that they often do not focus on it in judging scientific status. But the more thoughtful are concerned with output in making this judgment, as we indicated in the first chapter.

The Soviet Marxist myth is quite simple in that it sees a social science arising in a one-step process by the application of dialectic materialism (historical materialism), plus other techniques specific to a given discipline, to that study of social affairs. It appears to be somewhat of an exaggeration to call this a myth, because of its brevity and its lack of an historical part. The scientific basis of such studies "is the theory of historical materialism and the method of materialistic

dialectics constituting the living soul of Marxism".[53]   True, a given
discipline requires more than this. Thus Osipov and Rutkevich have
asserted that Soviet sociology includes in addition to dialectic
materialism a series of partial or middle range theories and "pieces of
concrete sociological research which are carried out on the basis of
theory and provide certain empirical results".[54] But when dialectic
materialism has once been put in place, "science" results -- and this
brand of science is already mature. Soviet Marxism does not have the
equivalent of the Millian imperative. Simply stated, this sect does not
feel the need for it. Thus Osipov and Yovchuk quoted Merton to the
effect that sociology was at the same level as natural science had been in
the seventeenth century and that it might not be ready for an Einstein
since it had not as yet found its Kepler. The Soviet authors argued that
this comment applied to sociology in Western Europe and the United
States, but not to "Marxist scientific sociology." The latter has been
tested for 125 years "and has been proved by the entire process of
historical development." Sanakoyev argued, in effect, that "the Soviet
science of international relations" is a mature science. It was initiated
by Lenin, and for the first time in history the discipline became "a
special branch of scientific knowledge".[55] The Soviet professor went on
to describe and to praise a publication of the Soviet Ministry of Foreign
Affairs which he argued is based on the discipline founded by Lenin.
He asserted that it provides "highly scientific" research on current world
problems and on Soviet diplomacy.

          The two non-Marxist myths, described below, see social
science as reaching maturity only after having gone through a
preliminary phase of apprenticeship as a proto or immature science.
Since no social science has ever passed on to the mature phase, all of
them are in the preliminary stage. In this view, therefore, a social
science is necessarily a proto or immature science. This status does not
make non-Marxist myths less functional or less inspirational, rather it
seems to induce practitioners to work even harder, so as to become the
Newton or the Einstein of their discipline by discovering the method
which will lead it to maturity.

          We next turn to what we call the short form of the non-Marxist
social science myth. It is in its essentials compatible with the longer
form, and it seems to be more popular with contemporary American
social science. A problem is that it is not explicitly stated, it lies
dormant and mixed in with the rest of the text. The observer must
extract it from the source in which it is found, and it thus might

appear somewhat of an exaggeration to call it a myth. It is certainly a myth in the making, perhaps a proto myth. Thus the volume of Reynolds, which serves as the first of two examples of this phenomenon, was intended as a way of improving the method of social science by applying to it the lessons of the philosophy of science. The work would introduce the reader to theory construction and to theory testing "in empirically based social science".[55] Reynolds has been persuaded that progress has already been made in social science by the growing body of its literature which meets all the criteria of scientific knowledge, and much of the extant literature could be put in this form. He was aware of problems inherent in developing a scientific body of knowledge on social and human phenomena, and he declared that "social scientists are not yet 'ideal' scientists." But neither did he find them to be more vague or more biased than physical or biological scientists. These upbeat remarks can be interpreted to mean that social science is in its preliminary phase. Furthermore, Reynolds identified the major impediments which prevent it from transferring to maturity. They are ambiguity in formulating statements and ignorance of the structure of scientific writing. His book was designed to help remove these impediments. He registered his belief that "scientific knowledge related to social and human phenomena" is possible, i.e., that the maturity of social science is possible, because of the increasing scientific awareness of social scientists, the successes they have already made, and the unacceptability of alternatives. Reynolds obviously believes in the "autonomy" of social science and that it is essentially an intellectual undertaking.

The short form of the non-Marxist myth, together with the same upbeat remarks, can also be found in, or extracted from, Popper's The Poverty of Historicism. It is used here even though Popper is not a practicing social scientist, because of its popularity among, and its great impact upon, those who are practitioners. Like Reynolds, Popper finds that social science has made some progress, but he sees less of it than Reynolds. The success has been registered in economics, and some measure of it in psychology.[56] This assertion can refer to the present intermediate phase of our disciplines, that of proto or immature science. Popper put the blame for not having achieved more on the widespread use of the historicist method. Those who use this method assume that historical prediction is the principal aim of the social sciences and argue that this aim can be achieved by discovering patterns or trends in history. His book was intended to expose the weakness of this approach and to set forth the methods used by physics. He divided all social science into the pro-naturalistic school and the anti-naturalistic school, the former favoring the application of the methods of physics to the enterprise and the latter opposing it. Popper himself comes down heavy on the pro-naturalist side and, of course, he puts historicism in the opposite camp.

Popper's view of the future of social science is the more interesting in that much of his book is dedicated to the proposition that historical prediction is not possible. Indeed, his view of the future of social science is cast within the limits of this assertion, but just barely, for it lies near the outer edge of these limits. He introduced his book with the allegation that in antiquity during the epoch of Plato and Aristotle "the science of society" seemed to be more advanced than "the science of nature." We judge the use of the term "the science of society" to be ambiguous, since no such discipline has ever existed. For the term "science" to be used in this sense it must be first emptied of all the specialized meaning which Popper has helped to give the term. Popper continued his account, stating that with Galileo and Newton physics attained success beyond expectation, far surpassing "the other sciences." And since the time of Pasteur, whom he identifies as the Galileo of biology, the biological sciences have been almost equally successful. His historical sketch ended with this sentence: "But the social sciences do not as yet seem to have found their Galileo." The clear implication is that they will, i.e., that this type of "science," the third in his chain of such studies, will follow in the footsteps of the biological and natural sciences and reach maturity. The phrase "as yet" clearly implies that this will occur, and Popper comes dangerously close to historicism so far as the future of the social sciences is concerned. Curiously, Sir Karl makes these assertions in the introduction to a volume which denies the ability of the social scientists to make historical predictions and which attributes their backward state to the attempt to do so.

The full force of the non-Marxist myth is delivered by the long form. As befits a myth, it is cast in story or historical form, and it features the ambiguity shown above in Popper's work. It posits for each discipline a period of maturity when the particular social science under review will become like the natural sciences. We sketched their attributes in the first chapter, but operationalized the period of maturity as one of consensus. The reader will recall that these traits are universalism, communism, disinterestedness, and organized skepticism. We promised that in this section our examples would come from history. We made the promise despite the well known fact that many historians consider themselves to be engaged in a craft or in a form of humanities. Others disagree, arguing that their enterprise is on a different track, like much of the rest of the social sciences. Cardoso is one of the latter: he alleges that history is a "science in construction," i.e., that its attainment of the scientific method is not yet complete, adequate to analyze the subject matter.[57] And he believes that it will complete the process. Lord Acton was, if anything, more optimistic. He identified history as a "progressive science," and averred that even though the time for ultimate or definitive history might not have arrived, it was just around the corner. Since the European archives had just then been opened, all information was within reach, and every problem had "become capable of solution".[58] Maturity for this discipline is seen as the ability, through the possession of the right method, to write definitive or ultimate history. It would accomplish what von Ranke said was the purpose of history: to tell "what actually happened." Fustel Coulanges put it this way: "It is not I who speak, but history which speaks through me." Note that maturity here concentrates on telling the correct "story," on providing a narrative in accord with reality. The emphasis is upon outputs, but these are achieved by employing the equivalent of the privileged, objective, scientific laws sought by other social sciences, through the use of scientific methodology. As noted above, not every historian has put faith in this myth. Perhaps Dilthey was the most famous of those who rejected it and who insisted on making a sharp distinction between history and science.

It would take some effort to exaggerate the significance of the social science myth. The first part of it does have some factual, historic referents -- after all the disciplines since their founding have become better organized and explanations based to some extent on logic and human experience have been provided. The other part of the myth, however, future maturity, is pure aspiration. But the significance of the myth is not its facticity, but its service as part of so many paradigms. It is a large part of their ideology, and it does no less than to establish the professional identity of the craft and of the practitioner, as well as to trace the future of the enterprise. For this reason we discuss it here in an early chapter, and not save it for the end of the volume. It identifies the practitioner as a social scientist, the appellation puts the practitioner closer to the scientist than to the non-scientist -- and in science loving societies this is a plus for the ego and sometimes for the pocketbook as well. The largest slice of the academic pie customarily goes to natural science. If one cannot be there for this feast, one can at least hope to get a share before the humanities and other non-sciences are made to do with leftovers. Moreover, it makes a difference whether one thinks that he is a theologian or a scholar engaged in humanities or literature, or whether one belongs to the world of science or near science. A different set of values goes with this identity. Ideally, one is expected to be intelligent and logical -- not necessarily humble or "good." The last two attributes characteristically are for nuns and monks, but Comte argued that the science of society would benefit society in ways that traditional religion could not. This part of positivism has been absorbed by much of social science. The term "myth" is merited by this set of beliefs, because of their inspirational and affective qualities for insiders, and because of their obvious epistemic poverty to the outsider. As befits a myth, it is so formulated so as to be disprovable, "unkikable" to use a word made popular by Popper. No time limit has been set for maturity, so if maturity is not reached by a given date, the time can be extended. The only limit to these extensions is the credulity of the faithful.

The social science myth is an essential part of the ideologies which serve many social science sects. It is embedded in them and intertwined with them. It serves the sect and those associated with it. It helps to identify and to legitimize at both these levels. We do not say that it legitimizes at the level of the discipline, because when combined with the ideology of a given sect, the resulting ideology can be used to delegitimize rival sects. Legitimization and delegitimization of the multiparadigmatic social sciences is at the sectarian level, whereas these processes occur at the disciplinarian level for natural science. All of this is not to say that social science is bad or sub-standard, only that it is all too human (like other non-scientific enterprises) and very social. Our disciplines do use logic and human experience as their guides, not just myths and ideology. A myth which overstates the use of the former is deceiving, but it can also encourage their use. Deviations can be condemned by pointing to their discordance with the myth. One is reminded of the American Declaration of Independence, written by a slave owner for a country which maintained slavery for 80 some years after its independence. The word which comes to mind is "hypocrisy," but the declaration became a handy propaganda weapon during the civil rights movement.

Brief Summary and Conclusions

This concludes our history of social science, a dimension which we regard as essential for an understanding of our disciplines. They should be seen, not as the prisoners of static categories, but in full evolution. The present hegemony of the United States should be viewed as a transitory stage, as the inheritor of European dominance to give way to other centers of power. This chapter gave a brief account of the American rise to pre-eminence, her borrowing from Germany, her capitalization and specialization of the disciplines, and their Americanization. The university curriculum was changed from one producing generalists to one featuring specialists, including social scientists. The emerging industrial class in the post Civil War period supported the social sciences -- and the latter lent their authority in the battle against radicalism. Our contention above is that this is better explained by structural analysis than by exchange theory. Our approach in this chapter, as in others, is external, so that the history of the disciplines follows closely what happens in the outside world. Our approach is that of the maximalist, not the minimalist. The stress here was modern history -- Comte, Spencer, social Darwinism, and the American rise to dominance. Much of what Comte stood for seems current, his positivism preserved in modern American social science. This extends to the social science myth, very close to the third stage, Comte's age of positivism. Spencer lives on in functionalism, and social Darwinism has not been completely put to rest. Its spirit pervades the economics of the establishment.

Our narrative provides vital information, helping us to sort out the characteristics of our disciplines. The discussion of social Darwinism and the related Spencerian sociology helps to desanctify the disciplines. They are not invariably on the side of progress and humanism. These paradigms justified the oppression of the poor, war, and all sorts of barbarities. John W. Burgess, the "father" of American political science, was pictured in this chapter as a racist, not as one link in an ever more scientific discipline. Early British anthropology was influenced by biology and by an evolutionary paradigm. In both cases, mankind was graded in a hierarchical scheme with the Caucasian and the European at the top and the black at the bottom. It is not that knowledge was not generated in this milieu, but the ideology in which the information came justified British colonialism. Both Comte and Spencer justified the emerging industrial system, maintaining that industrial capitalism promoted peace. Galton and Graham could advocate the extinction of inferior groups by "kind" measures such as late marriage, not the killing of people. The exclusion of Marxism from American academe for so long raises basic issues as to the nature of social science, and this chapter marks the inception of the secular war between Marxism and the more traditional paradigms. The war continues as Marxist regimes in power restrict our disciplines.

The above account was not meant to impugn the social sciences, but rather to put them in proper perspective. We intend this perspective to be unvarnished, without the shiny false gloss of myth. We presented, "exposed" a better term, the social science myth -- its place is in this chapter because ideally it is cast in an historic context. Indeed, it is a myth, lacking empirical, logical roots. Political economy/structuralism reveals that social scientists are all too human, not a breed apart. The chapter reveals also that their disciplines provide a real service to mankind, a logical explanation of human events based upon humankind's record. The explanation can be twisted in many directions -- the false ones singled out above are not the only ones. The explanations can be fashioned so as to promote human welfare as well. This chapter demonstrates that our disciplines come in many ideologies, just as humanity does. The social sciences provide useful explanations different from the purely theological, ideological or traditional, in that they use reason and secular experience in their explanations. These added ingredients produce alternate explanations which certainly justify the existence of our disciplines.

This chapter promotes the structural approach to our disciplines. It certainly makes the point that social science is an ideological enterprise, and that it is available for use by elites to promote their own interests. An emerging industrial class in the post Civil War period seems to have done just this. This class set up foundations to patronize the social sciences, and it exerted great influence upon the American university. And the social science outputs of academe generally were in accord with these class interests -- liberal perhaps, often conservative, but very rarely radical. Social Darwinism and Spencer's approach promoted the interests of this emerging class, and they became part of the academic landscape. Comte argued that an industrial society was a peaceful society. The universities even changed their generalist curriculum to one more in accord with the new industrial dispensation. Academic social science often claimed to be scientific. What better legitimization to use in its arguments against working class radicalism. The latter presented a danger to the emerging industrial class, as European immigrants were welcomed to man the industries of the Northeast. Marxism was effectively excluded from American academe until very recently, an exclusion easily explained by our structural analysis. No doubt, there were internal reasons as well, and a shift in the latter help explain its later acceptance. Some decline in American Marxism can be expected from the recent events in Eastern Europe and the Soviet Union.

These three last chapters in the broadest sense have been elaborating upon the characteristics of social science. The upcoming chapter continues within this general framework, but it deals specifically with the communications net of American social science. This subject is construed, so as to test whether these communications follow the pattern of natural science or that of the larger American society. The chapter is thus a litmus, designed to test if American social science is really scientific, or if it better fits into our political economy/structural analysis. The chapter is highly empirical/quantitative, and thus it should be persuasive to some brands of social science.

NOTES

1.   Joseph Schumpeter, Economic Doctrines and Method: An Historical Sketch, (New York: Oxford University Press, 1954), 11.

2.   Lewis H. Haney, History of Economic Thought, (New York: Macmillan, 1949), 907.

3.   Duane P. Schultz, A History of Modern Psychology, (New York: Academic Press, 1969), 41.

4.   S.C. Dube, "India," Social Science in Asia 4, (Paris: UNESCO, 1980): 53.

5.   Geoffrey Barraclough, "History" chapter III, 324, Main Trends of Research in the Social and Human Sciences, Part II, Vol. 1, Jacques Havet (ed.) (Paris: Mouton/UNESCO, 1978), 324.

6.   Edwin R. Seligman, "What are the Social Sciences," Encyclopedia of the Social Sciences, 1 (New York: Macmillan, 1957): 3, 4,.

7.   F.J. Hearnshaw, "Renaissance and Reformation", Encyclopedia of the Social Sciences (New York: Macmillan, 1957), 1, 86.

8.   Michel Beaud, Historia De Capitalismo de 1500 Aos Nossos Dias, (Sao Paulo: Brasiliense, 1987), 62.

9.   Frederick H. Gareau, "The Discipline International Relations: A Multinational Perspective," The Journal of Politics, 43, (1981): 789-790.

10.   Peter Drucker, Toward the Next Economics, and Other Essays, (New York: Harper & Row, 1981)., 6.

11.   Encyclopedia Mirador, "Positivisco" 17 (Rio de Janeiro: Mirador, 1976), 9230.

12.   Frederick Copleston, A History of Philosophy, 9, (Garden City: Image Books, 1977) 96.

13.   Stanislav Andreski (Ed.), The Essential Comte: Selected From Cours de Philosophie Positive, (New York: Barnes & Noble, 1974), 139.

14.   Copleston, 99.

15.   Stanislav Andreski (Ed.), Herbert Spencer: Structure, Function and Evolution, (London: Joseph, 1971), 1.

16.   Richard Hofstadter, "The Impact of Darwinism," Chapters in Western Civilization, (New York: Columbia University Press, 1948), 126.

17.   Robert L. Carneiro (Ed.), The Evolution of Society: Selections From Herbert Spencer's Principles of Sociology, (Chicago: University of Chicago Press, 1967), XXIV.

18.   Ibid., XXXV.

19.   Jerzy Szacki, History of Sociological Thought, (Westport, Conn: Greenwood Press, 1979), 219.

20.   Franklin Henry Giddings, Studies in the Theory of Human Society, (New York: The Macmillan Company, 1922), 114.

21.   Szacki, 224.

22.   Hofstadter, 130.

23.   Graham Sumner, Social Darwinism: Selected Essays of William Graham Sumner, (Englewood Cliffs: Prentice Hall, 1963), 157.

24.   Francis Galton, Inquiries Into Human Faculty and Its
        Development, (London: Dent, 1919), 201.

25.   Bernard Porter, Critics of Empire: Radical Attitudes to
        Colonialism (London: Macmillan, 1968), 30.

26.   Maurice Duverger, An Introduction to the Social Sciences:
        With Special Reference to Their Method, (New York: Praeger,
        1961), 18.

27.   J.D. Bernal, Science in History, the Social Sciences:
        Conclusion, 4, (Cambridge, MIT Press, 1971), 1071-1072.

28.   Geoffrey Barraclough, "History" Chapter III, Main Trends of
        Research in the Social and Human Sciences, Part II, 1 Jacques
        Havet (Ed.), (Paris: Mouton/UNESCO, 1978), 248.

29.   Tom Bottomore, Sociology and Socialism, (London:
        Harvester, 1984), 41.

30.   Szacki, 375.

31.   Patrick J. Gurney, "Historical Origins of Ideological Denial:
        The Case of Marx in American Sociology," The American
        Sociologist, 16, August (1981), 197.

32.   David L. Sallach, "What is Sociological Theory", The
        American Sociologist, 8, (1973), 136.

33.   Michael Hechter, "Notes on Marxism and Sociology in the
        USA," Theory and Society, 3 (1979), 378.

34.   Edward T. Silva and Sheila A. Slaughter, Serving Power: The
        Making of the Academic Social Science Expert, (Westport,
        Conn.: Greenwood Press, 1984), 42.

35.   Peter T. Manicas, A History and Philosophy of the Social
        Sciences, (New York: Basil Blackwell, 1987), 200.

36.   Roscoe C. Hinkle, Founding Theory of American Sociology, (Boston: Routledge & Kegan Paul, 1980), 50-51.

37.   Manicas, 209.

38.   Beaud, 159.

39.   Silva and Slaughter, 71.

40.   Sylvia D. Fried, "Staatstheorie and the New American Science of Politics", Journal of the History of Ideas, 3 (1973), 395.

41.   Albert Somit and Joseph Tanenhaus, The Development of American Political Science: From Burgess to Behavioralism, (Boston, Allyn and Bacon, 1967), 3.

42.   John W. Burgess, Political Science and Comparative Constitutional Law (Boston: Genin and Co., 1891), 1, 44.

43.   John W. Burgess, The Reconciliation of Government with Liberty (N.Y.: Scribner's, 1915), 339.

44.   Fries, 404.

45.   Bernard Crick, The American Science of Politics: Its Origins and Conditions, (Berkeley: University of California Press, 1959), 95.

46.   Somit and Tanenhaus, 61.

47.   Schultz, 45.

48.   Manicas, 234.

49.   Ibid., 221.

50.   Silva and Slaughter, 88.

51.   F. Braybrooke, "Recent Development in Chinese Social Science," China Quarterly, 79 (1979), 594.

52.   G. Osipov and M. Yovchuk, "Some Principles of Theory. Problems and Methods of Research in Sociology in the USSR," American Sociological Review, 38, (1963), 620. For what follows see also Frederick H. Gareau, "The Multinational Version of Social Science," Current Sociology, 33 (1985), 35-39.

53.   G.Y. Osipov and M.N. Rutkevich, "Sociology in the USSR, 1965-1975," Current Sociology, 26, (1978), 1.

54.   S.H. Sanakoyev, "A New Yearbook on Soviet Foreign Policy and Diplomacy," International Affairs, 10 (1983), 92.

55.   Paul D. Reynolds, A Primer in Theory Construction, (Indianapolis: Bobbs-Merrill, 1971), vii.

56.   Karl R. Popper, The Poverty of Historicism, (New York: Harper and Row, 1961), 1-2.

57.   Ciro Cardoso, Uma Introducao A Historia, (Sao Paulo: Brsasiliense, 1988), 49.

58.   Barraclough, 235.

CHAPTER IV

THE COMMUNICATIONS SYSTEM OF US SOCIAL SCIENCE

In this chapter we describe the communications system of US social science, and in so doing, shed light upon the communications of our disciplines in many other settings as well. It is fitting that this chapter, a highly empirical one, based upon more than 20 quantitative studies, should follow an historical one whose purpose was to prevent a frozen, mummified view of the state of the disciplines. We believe that the empirical and the dialectic can be made to be compatible. If the latter argues that social matters are in constant process, the former is necessary at least for identifying the general location and slant, if not the general nature, of the process. We have argued above that structural analysis is successful in reconciling disciplines which often reveal that they are ethnocentric with the fact that they travel across national boundaries. Their demeanor is assumed to be the same as other "products" referred to by the inter disciplinary/international structures. We test this similarity in this chapter, more specifically the test is between the foreign communications network of US social science and that of the communications network of the larger American society. We find the two to be congruent, thus helping to justify our structural analysis.

We first set forth a definition, the uses, and the significance of communications for natural science and social science. This is followed by our scheme for obtaining and using the pattern of US social science communications better to understand our disciplines. Kaplan and Storer define scientific communications as the exchange of information and ideas among scientists in their professional roles.[1] It includes publications, facilities, institutional arrangements, and customs which effect the transmission of messages. It is distinguished from everyday communications in that it refers to a particular body of codified knowledge. In the case of social science, there is a multiplicity of codes, not necessarily compatible with each other. Kaplan and Storer argue that full and open communications of scientific results have always been a hallmark of science, a remark which in this age of massive military sponsored research and development is subject to qualification. They argue, moreover, that without communications science could not provide a cumulative record of its "certified" knowledge, and they doubt that without this resource science would survive as a viable system. This record constitutes a point of reference for each scientist, providing a foundation from which he can make his own contribution. Other functions of these communications include answers to specific questions, keeping up with the field, getting a grasp on a new field, the verification of information already acquired, and critical feedback for a given scientist's work. The general thrust of the above assertions apply to social science communities as well, but just how far one can go with this transfer is a major problem which this chapter hopefully will help solve. One can see already that a difficulty does arise with respect to the concept "certified" knowledge. But our focus is more upon "full and open" communications, more specifically cultural bias and the presence of feedback.

The logic of our research follows this simple pattern. We use communications literature to reveal the contours of the foreign communications of American society, and this becomes our point of reference for comparing and judging the communications net of the American social sciences. The incoming network of these disciplines is built upon the empirical studies already cited, so to a lesser extent is the outgoing network. The status of this latter is also exposed by qualitative studies and statements. Our purpose in this chapter is not solely to justify the use of structures as a research tool or even merely to characterize the US social science communications net. We aim at using the results to help in characterizing the disciplines themselves, i.e. for indicating whether they are scientific or not. Our findings are corroborative of chapter I which found that they are not. There is considerable justification in the literature for making the broad claims for communications found in the present chapter. Wiener did this when he argued that a society can only be understood through the study of its communications.[2] Tooze explains that such study has been used to measure the traits of the international system.[3] Deutsch marked off communities and nationalities in this fashion. He argued that the primary basis for nationality is the complementarity of communication habits.[4] Moreover, nationalities can be separated from each other by this method, and a common culture promotes communications.

The Scientific Versus the Non-Scientific Model

Two general propositions in the above narrative are of interest to our analysis: the assertion that patterns of communications reveal much about their respective systems and the claim that a common culture facilitates communications. The first proposition is the soul of our project: a scientific pattern of communications will be held to undergird a scientific enterprise, a non-scientific pattern a non-scientific one. And we will construct below two models of communications -- a scientific one and a non-scientific one. The first will correspond to natural science and the other to American society, and in general, to our structural approach. The second proposition mentioned above has been assigned a large role in our approach, but we have had to modify it, to "shrink" it, to suit our purposes. Our focus centers on a different level of analysis, and so we have substituted the values of small professional groups for the culture of larger and much more variegated societies. In fact, we visualize a community of natural scientists as one which operates professionally on the basis of its own values without substantive interference from the larger cultures from which the membership is drawn, the very cultures which divide other communities. As Ben-David argues, the scientific community is effectively insulated from the outside society, so effectively that the characteristics of the various societies in which the scientists live can for many intents and purposes be disregarded.[5] They are also effectively insulated for many intents and purposes from our structures. What scientists do professionally and the way in which they do it are determined to a great extent by their own work traditions. The reader will recall that already in the first chapter we alleged that social science is affected by culture and dominant elites, and in the second chapter we put our disciplines in the context of political economy and structures. In this chapter, we will marshall evidence to justify what we said and did there. In the original Kuhnian perspective, it was the paradigm (now Kuhn would say the scientific community) which acts like, or provides, a common language and a common culture, deciding which questions are legitimate and establishing norms of conduct and criteria of evaluation. The younger scientists are socialized into the community, while the mature scientists uphold its norms and pass them on to the next generation. Ben-David uses physics as the example of the science which is the same in the USSR as elsewhere, despite what he calls the totalistic intellectual claims of communism. He points to the fact that Lysenkoism was a singular and a specific disease which singled out genetics, and not an overall Stalinist malignancy which attacked all of Soviet science.

Kuhn's approach is congruent with this general assessment, and his comments also help us to construct the scientific model. He points to the elements which unite scientific communities. He finds these communities bound together by common elements in their education and apprenticeship and by a set of shared goals.[6] Such communities are characterized by relative fullness of communications within the group and relative unanimity of judgment in professional matters. To a remarkable extent, the group reads the same publications and draws similar conclusions from them. Since Kuhn believes in the internationalism of science, the group within which the "relative fullness of communications" takes place is international in scope. This characterization is similar to Merton's universalism already set forth in the first chapter. It asks us to believe that the truth claims of science are judged by impersonal criteria and conversely that particularistic ones are not used. In this view, science is part of a detached intellectual world, firmly rooted in the realm of abstract symbols with universal application, and ignorant of national boundaries. In elaborating upon the Mertonian notion of universalism, Storer argues that "first of all" the scientist feels the need to develop competence in one or more foreign languages "to understand the contributions of his foreign colleagues".[7]

The first model, the scientific one, reflects this trait universalism, and it sees interaction as free of particularistic biases. Actually, the data used in our analysis is able to test for national, linguistic, and political/ ideological bias, not bias motivated by race, religion, or class. Both incoming and outgoing channels will be put to test, but most data focus on the former, i.e. those received by American social science. We have found an empirical way of judging the relative importance of the various national social science centers, and we shall use this measure to see if US incoming channels correlate in a general way with the relative importance of the national centers involved. Another comparison -- a better one -- is American physics, and we shall use its pattern of communications as the standard of science. The first model assumes that these correlations will hold both when contrasting domestic with foreign channels and also when comparing all the foreign channels. Of crucial importance is the domestic/ foreign ratio, because it will serve as a measure of nationalism. Another crucial test will be whether the Soviet bloc receives its "appropriate" share of channels. This will serve as our prime measure of ideological/political bias. Fortunately, some of our data indicate the language of the incoming channels. The first model assumes that a reasonable number of these will be foreign language publications and that American social scientists have taken the time and made the effort to develop language skills, so as to understand the contributions of their foreign colleagues.

The second model is a non-science, particularistic, inward-oriented one, reflecting national, political/ideological, and linguistic bias. It corresponds in a general way to the structural model used in this essay, and it applies to the communications system of the larger American society. It assumes that the non-science community is not insulated from outside culture/society/elites or the global structures and that this community is not a consensual one. The model reserves an inordinate number of incoming social science channels for fellow Americans, friendly Western nations, and those in the English language. This model assumes that the values of the larger culture/society/elites or the global structures affect American social scientists to the extent that their communications will take place mainly with colleagues whose larger cultures/societies are similar. This latter statement applies to incoming American communications, not to incoming ones in peripheral countries. Social scientists in those countries are in a different position. This model reflects national, regional, and linguistic biases, responding in the same manner as other non-scientific enterprises and their communications nets.

The non-science model can be expressed either in cultural terms or in structural ones. And it will be of extreme interest to us to determine which approach triumphs when we force them to confront our data. The cultural thesis was set forth above by Deutsch in this statement that a common culture facilitates communications, and we set forth our version of structural analysis in Chapter II. The cultural and the structural explanations can account for the pattern of social science messages received by the United States, but not for that formed by outgoing messages. The cultural explanation would expect a greater outflow of messages to go to those countries which are culturally similar to the United States. The structuralist does not see things this way -- the pattern should follow the structures regardless of the similarity or the dissimilarity of the receiving culture with that of the United States. We test the two explanations below by focusing upon Japan, Korea, India, and Quebec -- areas with which the United States has little in common culturally, but with which it carries on a high level of social science transactions. The cultural and the structural explanations agree on one crucial, salient point, which constitutes the basis of the non-science model. Both expect the great bulk of messages received to be domestic in origin -- a result of an ethnocentric American culture or, in the case of structuralism, perhaps for other reasons. Closer to a structural explanation is the finding of Rosenberg that the US general communications system is the largest in the world -- a position which "effectively excludes foreign material".[8] The inward directed focus is so pronounced that almost no room is left for imports. Similar is the remark that the great bulk of the foreign transactions of the United States is with the United Kingdom, the rest of the countries of the European Community, and Canada.[9] This incoming pattern receives support from the cultural model as well, the outgoing pattern is better explained by structuralism. Incoming channels should be biased heavily in favor of the United Kingdom, because of cultural and linguistic similarities with the United States. In this model, the great bulk of incoming channels should be in English -- social scientists thus betraying the monolingualism of American society. This societal trait was the subject of the report of a presidential commission on the state of foreign languages in the United States. The commission concluded that "Americans' incompetence in foreign languages is nothing short of scandalous, and it is becoming worse".[10] It granted that English had become a major international language, but argued that on innumerable occasions it cannot be counted on for direct communications. American social scientists would thus seem to have to put forth a special effort to learn foreign languages, and thus to be really interested in the contributions of their foreign colleagues. They would have to rise above the general monolingualism of their fellow countrymen, to break ranks with the others who inhabit their culture.

The other Mertonian traits cannot be directly tested by our data, but they help indirectly by suggesting either the first or the second model. These remaining Mertonian traits are more compatible with the first model than they are with the second. Moreover, after we have made our choice between models, other evidence will be called forth to cast further light upon the existence of these remaining traits. Merton defines the "communism" of science as its common ownership, at the expense of the equity of the individual scientist. Our models are more group oriented. Nonetheless, this trait is more in line with the first model than with the second particularist one. The latter model suggests cliques and sectarian ownership of outputs, rather than the communal and common ownership which is closer to the first model.

The remaining two Mertonian traits suggest the first model as well. Disinterestedness results in the virtual absence of fraud, spurious claims, and attempts to create pseudo-sciences. This trait is grounded in the public and testable nature of science and in the accountability of the scientist to his peers. But if social scientific communities are particularistic and impacted by such factors as nationalism and culture, as the second model suggests their transactions to be, then the tests and the peers who do the testing presumably will be similarly influenced. This does not imply the existence of fraud, nor the conscious or actual creation of pseudo sciences. But it could mean that social science communities are nationally and culturally biased and that they characterize their rivals as making spurious claims and as practicing pseudo science. Such characterization is quite compatible with the second model. The final trait imputed to science by Merton is organized skepticism. It mandates the temporary suspension of judgment, detached scrutiny, and the use of empirical and logical criteria. It runs parallel with the first model, and it is obviously at odds with the second. The latter pictures nationalism and cultural affinity as major forces which drive the social science enterprise, and these would likely be at the expense of empirical and logical criteria and might well foreclose the temporary suspension of judgment and the detached scrutiny referred to above.

The scientific model pictures the members of the scientific community as engaged in open and full communications. These members obviously are eager to learn from each other. Therefore, they not only talk -- they also listen. This is communications with feedback -- it is dialogue. The Brazilian educator Paulo Freire makes much of the distinction between education which involves genuine dialogue and education without it. The latter he calls the banker's approach to education, or traditional education. We equate the former with our scientific model, and the banker's/traditional approach with the non-scientific model. Freire denied that genuine dialogue can be reduced to the act of one person's depositing ideas with another, to a simple presentation of ideas to be consumed by an audience.[11] He sees the traditional approach as an act of depositing, in which the students are the depositories and the teacher is the depositor. The teacher issues communiques, which the students patiently accept, file, and store like bank deposits. Students are reduced to passive collectors and catalogers of things received from their betters. In contrast to this, our first general model assumes a lively dialogue, with give and take and feedback. The second model posits the above process described by Freire, a depositing system, a one-way monologue with US social scientists depositing ideas abroad, but accepting few in return. The same basic patterns are visible at the international level of general communications, and the Third World has been loud in its condemnation. We will speak below of the "unrelenting one-way traffic" of communications from the West to the Third World, with no commensurate return flow. The second non-scientific model will assume that this is a characteristic of US social science communications as well, i.e., a volume of messages sent to the "free world" (more than the Third World) with little counter flow.

A few additional comments before we put our models to the test. The present study purports to represent social science in general, our sample being broadly based to include sociology, political science, international relations, and psychology. Education is also included. The rare enterprise that is science is illustrated by the Mertonian traits detailed above, and by physics. By incorporating, or at least reflecting these traits, our first model attests to the uniqueness of the scientific enterprise, while the second one is the natural "normal" one of the non-scientific, i.e., the usual pattern for the great bulk of human activity. The reader is advised that what follows is super-factual and empirical, not the most entertaining reading. The reader is warned to be braced for this, but to be encouraged that this is the only chapter of this kind.

The Test of the Models on Incoming Communications

Our principal effort in this section is to choose between the two alternate science and non/science models detailed above, the choice being dictated by a large and diverse quantity of empirical data. The data of this section are directed solely at revealing patterns of incoming channels of American social science. Outgoing channels are outside their jurisdiction and are reserved for the upcoming section. The nature of the outflow will consequently be decided, much of the evidence being more traditional. The data on incoming channels rely upon 24 studies of social science, all except one originally done by others. Three parallel studies of American physics have been added for comparative purposes. An example of the typical original social science study upon which our research is based is one featuring a random sample of members of the American Political Science Association designed to indicate the best, most read, or most prestigious journals in this discipline. We identified the nationality of the journals so chosen; envisaged each journal as an incoming channel of communications; and converted these original findings into nationality quotas. A similar reworking of the original findings was done in every case but two. Indeed, we are engaged in using social science to understand social science! We have made an effort to summarize the data presented here, so as not to try the reader's patience.

The data used for testing the competing models will feature the American professional journal, but an American edited social science encyclopedia, its biographic supplement, American college textbooks, and a sample of graduate reading lists of American universities have been included as well. These additions touch other aspects of academe, i.e., reach "below" the journal reader to the graduate and the undergraduate student, and give our analysis more credibility as a general study of social science communications. Certainly the professional journal has been awarded a crucial role in the communications systems of natural and social science. Its centrality in these enterprises has been attested to by, among others, Kuhn[12] and by Kaplan and Storer.[13] Before turning to the data, we first summarize the characteristics which we intend these data to expose. This is done in the form of the following questions or dimensions about proportionality and disproportionality. In the science model, proportionality will prevail on these dimensions. In the non-science model, disproportionality will prevail. In each case, the disproportionality associated with the non-science model is indicated. Obviously the fifth dimension cannot be addressed until we deal with the outgoing channels of American social science, the burden of the upcoming section. The dimensions are as follows (along with the disproportionality to be expected in the non-science model):

1. Domestic versus foreign channels or sources for channels: disproportion of the domestic;

2. Channels or sources for channels from the United Kingdom, Canada, Australia, and New Zealand

(white Commonwealth) versus other foreign channels:
disproportion in favor of the former named countries;
3.   Channels or sources from Western Continental
       Europe versus the Soviet Bloc and the Third World:
       disproportion in favor of the former;
4.   Disproportion of channels and sources for channels
       in the English language versus those in foreign
       languages: disproportion in favor of those in English;
5.   Disproportion between incoming and outgoing
       channels: disproportion in favor of the outgoing ones.

The terms "proportionate" and "disproportionate" have wide
currency in the above statements, and we provide three kinds of
guidelines below for coping with their meaning. But first we elaborate
upon the logic used here in assessing the incoming channels of
American social science. We start with the professional journal, the
usual publication used for our research. The assumption is that it is a
channel of professional messages which flows from the authors of the
articles in the publications to its readership. The flow of professional
messages is one-way without feedback, from the supply side to the
consumers, unless and until there occurs a reversal of roles, requiring
that the readers become authors themselves. The data of Table 1 is
crucial, because they suggest that the American professional journal is
the overwhelming favorite of American social science, completely
outranking foreign journals. The implication is that the American
journal (rather than the foreign journal) is the most widely read and
thus the major channel of incoming professional messages. These data
ground the journal on the consumer side with the American social
science organization and thus with American social science. This
grounding occurs because the journals were originally chosen by
random samples of nationwide American social science organizations.
Since the American journal was the overwhelming choice of these
samples (90.7 percent of the time as of Table 1), we can assume the
establishment of a link between these publications and the readership
of the national American professional association. The latter is
uniquely qualified to represent the membership of a discipline in the
United States.

Before turning to the problem of grounding our putative
channels on the supply side, we provide additional crucial information
on the data displayed in Table 1. The three associations sampled for
the original data were the American Psychological Association, the

Table 1

Nationality of Journals Rated as the Best or the Most
Prestigious by Random Samples of Members of the
American Social Science Associations[a]

Journals

Random Samples	American		British		Other[b] Anglophone		Continental European		UNESCO		Total
	#	%	#	%	#	%	#	%	#	%	#
Psychologists	89	92.7	4	4.2	3	3.1	0	0	0	0	96[c]
Political Scientists	54	85.7	5	7.9	2	3.2	1	1.6	1	1.6	63
Educators	31	93.4	1	3.3	1	3.3	0	0	0	0	33
Total	174	90.7	10	5.2	6	3.1	1	.5	1	.5	192

a. These associations are the American Psychological Association, the American Political Science Association, and the American Educational Research Association.

b. Refers to journals published in Australia, Canada, and New Zealand.

c. The nationality of 96 out of a total of 100 journals was identified. All 100 had titles written in English.

Source: David Koulack and H.J. Keselman, "Ratings of Psychology Journals by Members of the American Psychological Association," American Psychologist 30: 1050-1051; Michael Giles and Gerald C. Wright, Jr., 1975, "Political Scientists' Evaluation of Sixty-Three Journals," PS 8: 255-256; Terrence S. Luce and Dale M. Johnson, "Rating of Educational and Psychological Journals," Educational Researcher 1978, 8: 8-10; Frederick H. Gareau, "An Empirical Analysis of the International Structure of American Social Science," The Social Science Journal, 21 (1984), 2; Frederick H. Gareau, "The Multinational Version of Social Science," Current Sociology, 33 (1985), 84.

American Political Science Association, and the American Educational Research Association. These three studies were used, because the original research allowed the respondents to add journals not included on the lists of journals formulated by the researchers. This is crucial, because the journals summarized in this first table are visualized in our research design as channels of communications from the authors of articles to American social scientists. To fulfill this assumption, the respondents must be free to choose the journals themselves -- not have this choice dictated by the researchers. The original goal of the three studies was to designate the best or the most prestigious journals. We assume that this can be transformed to mean the most read journals. This transformation is justified by logic, i.e., what is considered to be the best or most prestigious will tend to be the most read. Further-more, the political scientists were told to rate only those journals with which they were familiar,[14] i.e., those with which they must have some reading acquaintance. "Best" was defined for the psychologists as those journals in which they would like to publish and/or "those journals in which you would expect material important to you as a psychologist to appear".[15] Presumably, the respondents would tend to read such publications. Nine of ten of the journals marked as the most read in a sample of the members of the American Political Science Association were found in another sample of the same association characterized as the best and most prestigious journals.[16] We identi-fied the nationality of the journals found in the original findings, and reduced the lists to the percentages displayed in Table 1.

The sum of the journals in the three samples displayed in Table 1 comes to 192 (counting duplicates). Of these, 174 or 90.7 percent are American published. On its face, this suggests a disproportionality, a bias of the American social scientist toward the American journal, and the data ground the journal on the consumers' or readers' side. Furthermore, this percentage suggests an affirmative answer to our first research question: that a disproportionate percentage of the incoming channels to American social science are domestic as contrasted with foreign. This conclusion is reinforced by the data displayed in Table 5. The data displayed there represent our first, and least persuasive, set of guidelines for judging the disproportionality of our data. The reader will find in this table three sets of percentages which purport to give a breakdown of the world's social science serials by region. A problem is that the percentages are based upon relative number of titles, not circulation or the number of articles or pages, thus undervaluing journals from the developed world. We have been informed that the first list, the World List of Social Science Periodicals (WLOSSP), is the best for comparative purposes.[17] Table 5 gives the percentage of "Anglo-American" journals at 16, 29, and 16. This category includes journals from the United States, the United Kingdom and other Anglophone countries such as Canada, Australia, and New Zealand. Whichever of these three percentages we accept as the standard for proportionality, the 90.7 percent of American titles in Table 1 is disproportionately national. Our data suggest that American social scientists receive a disproportionate amount of professional messages from domestic sources.

Of the 18 foreign journals identified in the three samples summarized in Table 1, 10 (5.2 percent of the total of the samples) are British; 6 (3.1 percent) are from the predominantly Anglophone countries of Canada, Australia, and New Zealand; one is from Western Europe; and the last one is published by UNESCO. These figures lead to the conclusion that insofar as the incoming channels of American social science are foreign they originate from white Anglophone countries. Sixteen of the eighteen foreign journals fall into this category. Again, these figures are disproportionate. Table 5 suggests that Western Continental Europe is the most fertile source of social science journals, representing 37, 56, or 53 percent of the world's total, depending upon which estimate we accept. Table 1 contains only one journal (of the total of 192), suggesting that this region is grossly under represented in the reading of American social scientists. So are the Soviet Bloc and the Third World, neither of which contributed to the 192 found in Table 1, despite the fact that they have substantial representation in Table 5. Our analysis so far supports the disproportionality referred to in the first four questions of our non-science model, disproportionality in favor of the domestic, but also in favor of the white commonwealth at the expense of continental Europe and, in a slightly more pronounced fashion, at the expense of the Soviet bloc and the Third World.

The data in Table 1 help to decide the issue whether American social scientists act out Storer's assertion that scientists learn foreign languages so as to understand the work of foreign colleagues. All together, 192 journals provide the data for the table. We thus "ask the data" how many are written in foreign languages, and the answer presumably should be a considerable number. This, because the most relevant data on the issue reveal that sixty percent of social science journals are published in languages other than English[18]. But the response is "none" -- every one of the 192 journals is published in English. Storer's dictum seems to have been ignored, and the data support the option of question five above, that a disproportionate number of incoming American channels are in English. So far all the evidence supports the second model, the non-science one.

The remainder of the data on incoming American channels, with the exception of those on graduate reading lists and possibly those on textbooks, speak to the "supply" side of the incoming channels. We turn next to the evidence presented in Tables 2 and 3, because this evidence most clearly grounds our channels on the supply side, suggests that the inputs to the incoming channels are overwhelmingly American. If we can establish the latter connection, then we can complete the communication loop by concluding that the channels, already shown to be received by American social scientists, are American authored and/or the sources on which they rely are American. Table 2 is persuasive in this regard. It suggests that the great preponderance of the authors of the most prestigious American journal for political science, the American Political Science Review, are indigenous. The American percentages for authors are 90.7 for the period 1970-1975 and 93 percent for the period 1974-1976. This tends to ground the professional journal on the supply side as a channel of professional communications by showing that the senders of the messages are overwhelmingly from the homeland as well. The American professional social science journal is, therefore, interpreted here essentially as a channel of professional communications in which American senders dispatch messages to their fellow countrymen as receivers. American social scientists are communicating essentially with other American social scientists.

Other data in Table 2 help answer the question where these American authors receive their professional messages. The answer has been given above by the data in Table 1 which has suggested that American journals are the predominant favorites of American social scientists and that, therefore, these journals are their major source of information. The data of Table 2 should be seen as being supplementary. They show that a sample which examined 10 articles of the American Political Science Association for each of the years 1974, 1975, 1976 found that 73 percent of the footnotes were from American scholars. This allows us to say with somewhat more

Table 2

Nationalities of the Authors and of the Footnotes in the American Political Science Review and Foreign Language Use in the American Sociological Review

American Political Science Review

Authors (1970-1974)[1]

U.S.	90.7%
Foreign	8.1%
Unclassified	1.2%P

Authors (1974-1976)[2]

U.S.	93%
Canadian	7%P

Footnotes (10 articles each 1974, 1975, 1976)[3]

U.S.	73%
United Kingdom	15%
Canada	1%
Western Continental Europe	9%
USSR	2%P

American Sociological Review

Language of Citations Quoted (1965)[4]

In English	91.9%
Not in English	8.1%P

1. Sami G. Hajjar et al., 1977. "The Literature of Political Science: Professional Journals in Four Nations," International Social Science Journal 29: 330.

2. J.A. Laponce, 1980. "Political Science: An Import-Export Analysis of Journals and Footnotes," Political Studies 28: 404.

3. Laponce, 1980: 410.

4. Robert N. Broadus, 1967. "A Citation Study for Sociology," American Sociologist 2: 20.P

authority that the sources used by the American authors of the American social science journals are American. In consequence, we assert that the evidence supports the thesis that in essence the American professional social science journal is a channel of professional communications in which American sending authors dispatch professional American messages to the American receiving social scientists. The American communications loop or circle is virtually an indigenous one, and the American journal has as its chief function the business of recycling domestically manufactured information. The incoming pattern of American social science communications thus parallels that of the larger American culture/society. Our conclusion is that the former is driven by the same ethnocentric values as those of the latter, or by the same structures. The ethnocentric bias cited above holds throughout our analysis, needing to be modified only to take account of a few foreign channels reaching American social science and to account for the fact that American social science periodicals have marginal foreign inputs. American foreign journals do have a substantial foreign audience; this point is developed in the next section.

The evidence above supports the first dimension of the non-science model detailed above, i.e., that American social science features a disproportionate number of incoming national channels. Table 2 also addresses the fifth dimension of the non-science model which looked for a disproportionate number of channels or their sources in English contrasted with foreign languages. This table indicates that 91.9 percent of the citations quoted in the American Sociological Review in 1965 were in English. The figure seems disproportionately Anglophone on its face. Such a conclusion is supported by a UNESCO study already referred to, which found that only 40 percent of social science periodicals are published in English, with 60 percent in other languages. The figures apply to number of titles, not to the amount of circulation.

The first three tables address other dimensions of the science, non-science models outlined at the outset of this section. Table 1 indicates that the great bulk of the foreign journals preferred by American social scientists were from white Commonwealth countries. The numbers come to 16 of the 18 foreign journals -- 9.3 percent of the total journals were foreign, and 8.3 percent of all journals were white Commonwealth. Only two foreign journals, the International Social Science Journal of UNESCO and another published in Norway in English were not from this group. We call this distribution bilateral, because its contents are almost exclusively American and white Commonwealth. Of course, the American share is predominant, with the white Commonwealth contribution being peripheral only. This distribution supports the first, the second, and the fourth dimensions of the non-science model, i.e., the disproportionality first in favor of the United States and then in favor of the white Commonwealth against all other foreign sources. We thus note that although the bulk of incoming channels of American social science are American, a small percentage are from white Commonwealth countries. The same bilateral configuration is found in Table 2, this time for the authors of the American Political Science Review (1974-1976), but this evidence is for the supply side. It shows that 93 percent of the authors were American and 7 percent Canadian. We call the next distribution found in Table 2 tripartite, because it adds a third party, Western Continental Europe. The specific data have been derived from the nationality of footnotes of ten articles of the American Political Science Review from each of the years 1974, 1975, and 1976. Seventy-three percent of the footnotes were of American nationality, 16 percent white Commonwealth, 9 percent Western Continental European, and only 2 percent Soviet Union. This tripartite distribution supports the first four dimensions of the non-science, i.e., those supported by the bilateral configuration with the addition that European continental sources account for a sizeable share of the foreign inputs, in this case footnotes, behind the white commonwealth, but substantially ahead of that of the Soviet bloc.

The distribution found in Table 3 is also tripartite and, like its immediate predecessor, its reference is to the supply side, in this case the authors of encyclopedia articles. We spend more time with this table because of the dimensions of the project involved. This study contrasts with the others in that its original purpose was to expose the increasing ethnocentrism of American social science. The method employed was to compute the nationality (by professional affiliation) of the contributors to the International Encyclopedia of the Social Sciences which was published in 1968 and its Bibliographic Supplement which appeared in 1979. The sponsoring organizations of the project included the blue ribbon social science organizations in the United States, and the editors who actually designated the contributors were all of American nationality. The total number of contributors to the encyclopedia was substantial, no less than 1505, and the number for

Table 3

Distribution of Contributors to the
International Encyclopedia of Social Science
and Its Biographic Supplement

	The Encyclopedia		The Biographic Supplement	
United States	1176	78.1	174	80.2
United Kingdom and Other White Commonwealth	159	10.6	29	13.4
Western Continental Europe	141	9.4	10	4.6
Soviet Bloc	4	.3	0	0
Third World	13	.8	2	.9
Israel-South Africa	11	.7	2	.9
Japan	1	.1	0	0
Total	1505	100%	217	100.0%

Source: Frederick H. Gareau, 1983. "The Increasing Ethnocentrism of American Social Science: An Empirical Study of Social Science Encyclopedias," International Journal of Comparative Sociology 24: 250.

the biographical supplement was 217. The encyclopedia gives the criteria used for the selection of the authors, namely to pick the most qualified and at the same time achieve as much "geographic" (read "international") representation as possible. The term "international" was deliberately attached to the title of the encyclopedia; the name of its predecessor published in the period 1930-1934 did not have this term attached.

Despite this universalist criterion and an international veneer, the distributions of the contributors for both the encyclopedia and its biographical supplement assume the tripartite form already encountered above (see Table 3). Americans represented 78.1 percent of the contributors to the encyclopedia and 80.2 percent to the biographic supplement. The white Commonwealth nations are responsible for respectively 10.6 and 13.4 percent of the total -- with the comparable figures for Western Continental Europe somewhat lower at 9.4 and 4.6 percent respectively. As is the case with the tripartite configuration, these three categories preempt the field, leaving only crumbs for the third world and for the Soviet bloc. The latter two traits characterize both distributions, but we refer specifically to that of the encyclopedia. This publication had only 13 contributors from the entire third world, of a total of 1505 contributors. All of Latin America had one; a scholar from a Sao Paulo museum contributed a 1-page biography on a German ethnographer. Only 4 contributors were chosen from the Soviet bloc. Each did a biography on an obscure social scientist, and the 4 articles totalled $7^1/4$ pages of an encyclopedia of almost 10,000 pages. Topical subjects such as communism or biographies of the giants of socialism were left in more familiar hands (Gareau, 1983: 253). Readers of the International Encyclopedia of Social Science are thus put on notice that the authors of the articles found there are not the international group that one might expect from the title. A reviewer of the encyclopedia confirmed our charge, finding ethnocentric bias both in the authorship and in the type of articles included.[19]

Table 4 also has a tripartite distribution. This time the table contains the summaries of the nationalities of professional journals, and again the intent of the original research was to identify the best journals. The journals were chosen by citation indexing, the most often footnoted in the literature of a discipline being regarded as its best. This technique features the "supply side" of the journal -- references which have aided the authors who have contributed to the journals.

Table 4

The Nationality of the Most Cited Psychology and Physics Journals: Derived from American Studies Using Citation Analysis (in percentages)

	Psychology Journals				Mean	Physics Journals			Mean
United States	83.3	89.1	89.1	81.8	85.8	41.6	42.0	42.6	42.1
United Kingdom	6.3	8.7	8.7	10.2	8.5	12.5	14.0	6.4	11.0
Other Anglophone	4.2	2.2	2.2	3.5	3.0	4.1	2.0	2.1	2.7
Western Continental Europe	4.2	0	0	4.5	2.2	29.2	16.0	21.3	22.1
USSR	0	0	0	0	0	8.5	-20.0	21.3	16.6
Eastern Europe	0	0	0	0	0	0	2.0	2.1	1.4
Japan	2.0	0	0	0	.5	4.1	4.0	4.2	4.1
Sample Size	48	45	46	88		24	50	47	

*   The first three of the summaries of psychology journals were based on data originally gathered in 1969, the fourth on 1977 data. The physics data are from 1969.

Source: Eugene Garfield, 1979, Citation Indexing: Its Theory and Application in Science Technology, and the Humanities (New York: Wiley); Louis C. Buffardi and Julia A. Nicholas, 1981, "Citation Impact, Acceptance Rate, and APA Journals," American Psychologist 36; Herbert Inhaber, 1974, "Is There a Pecking Order in Physics Journals," Physics Today 27: 40-41; Frederick H. Gareau, "An Empirical Analysis of the Interantional Structure of American Social Science," The Social Science Journal, 21 (1984), 29; Frederick H. Gareau, "The Multinational Version of Social Science," Current Sociology, 33 (1985), 89.

This contrasts with the data of Table 1, whose data was grounded on the consumer side, i.e., the journals were chosen by samples of the membership of social science organizations. Of course, in both cases the journal is regarded as an incoming channel for American social science. In this table, we contrapoise nationality summaries worked up from four studies of American psychology with similar summaries from three studies of American physics.

The three distributions consisting of nationality summaries of the journals most often cited in American physics will serve as our (natural) scientific standard. Therefore, these distributions can be looked upon as the "appropriate" ones as far as the first four introductory statements made above are concerned, as representing that part of the natural science model. We compare them by presenting the means of the four psychological studies first; next the means of the three physics studies. The figures from left to right represent the means for journals respectively from (1) the United States; (2) the United Kingdom and the other white Commonwealth countries; (3) Continental Western Europe; (4) the Soviet bloc, and (5) Japan:

| psychology | (1) 85.8 | (2) 11.5 | (3) 2.2 | (4) 0.0 | (5) .5 |
| physics | (1) 42.1 | (2) 13.7 | (3) 22.1 | (4) 18.0 | (5) 4.1 |

The distribution for psychology resembles the tripartite distribution, but the figure for Western Continental Europe being more modest than usual for this distribution. The evidence here thus supports the non-science model on all of its first four dimensions. The data serve a second purpose here by exposing the divergence between the distribution for psychology and that for physics, the latter serving as the standard for science. The overwhelming majority of the psychology journals chosen by citations (85.8 percent) were American. The comparable figure for American physics was only 42.1 percent. This suggests that American psychology journals, and by extension American incoming psychological channels, are much more ingrown and ethnocentric, dependent upon other American psychological journals or channels, much more so than American physics. We thus have reason to respond positively to the first query that American psychology depends upon a disproportionate number of national channels of communications when compared with American physics. Eleven and five-tenths percent of the mean of psychology journals in Table 4 were white Commonwealth ones. This number was such as virtually to preempt the foreign titles. Western Continental Europe accounted only for 2.2 percent and Japan for a mere .5 percent of the total. No journal from the Soviet bloc or from the third world made it to the lists. In the case of American physics, the most prolific source of foreign citations is Western Continental Europe (22.1 percent of the total) and the second such source is the Soviet bloc (18.0 percent). Each of these surpasses the white Commonwealth contribution, and the two combined almost equal the domestic one. American physics thus finds it easy to use Soviet and continental inputs for its journals, i.e., to cite journals from the regions. Divergent values or lack of complementarity do not block off such communications, nor do contrary structures. Neither these factors nor the complexity of the Japanese language shut off inputs from the Japanese physicists. Four and one-tenth percent of the physics journals designated in Table 4 are Japanese, but only .5 percent of the psychology journals. The uniqueness of the Japanese language has been given as a reason for the low level of foreign acceptance of Japanese social science.[20] The American physicist is so interested in the contribution of Japanese colleagues that their works are translated into English.

We judge the distribution of physics journals as presented in Table 4 to be the best example of the general science model, against which we can judge incoming social science communications. But Table 5 helps as well. The latter provides a basis for testing proportionality, not by providing a scientific distribution, but by showing the relative importance of regions for the production of social science periodicals. Our experimental distributions above should bear a rough proportionality to the regional breakdown, unless unscientific factors such as ethnocentrism or cultural/political factors interfere. Table 5 contains three regional distributions of social science periodicals. The three studies diverge considerably from each other, an indication of the non-consensual nature of social science, i.e., in this case what is a social science journal? This ultimately depends upon the identification of the social sciences -- a question which results in disagreement. The first distribution shown in the table, the World List of Social Science Periodicals, is said to be the most appropriate for comparative purposes. All three distributions point to Western Continental Europe as the prime source of social science periodicals. The Anglo-American world (the United States and the white Commonwealth) and the third world place second or third, their order depending upon which distribution is used. The Soviet bloc generally places fourth.

The distributions above which we impute to the incoming channels of American social science put Western Continental Europe in a poor third place, not in the first place which Table 5 awards this region. Another disproportion is the Anglo-American group which preempts our experimental groups, but which places second or third in Table 5. This table gives respectable places to the Soviet bloc and to the third world. Our experimental distributions relegate them to the periphery. We conclude that there exist disproportions between our experimental distributions and the regional production of social science periodicals. American social science shows bias, i.e., does not treat the regions in proportion to their production. The pattern of discrimination is basically that indicated above in Table 4 where we contrasted American psychology and American physics.

Table 5

Three Regional Distributions of Social Science Serials
(in percentages)

	WLOSSP[1]	CLOSSS[2]	UNESCO[3]
Western Continental Europe	37	56	53
Anglo-American	16	29	16
Third World	30	10	15
Soviet Bloc	15	5	16
Intergovernmental	2	—	—

Source: Maurice Line and Stephen Roberts, 1976. "The Size, Growth, and Composition of Social Science Literature," International Social Science Journal 28:135.

1. World List of Social Science Periodicals

2. Check List of Social Science Serials

3. UNESCO Statistical Yearbook

Table 6 presents reworked data on no less than ten studies, each of which deals with the discipline sociology. We thereby add this discipline to those already covered -- psychology, political science, and education. Physics, of course, is used in this chapter only for comparison. The data of this table go beyond the professional journal to add textbooks and graduate reading lists as channels of social science communication. Nine of the ten studies whose results are summarized in the table used citation indexing as their methodology -- the exception being data on the reading lists of American graduate students. The methodology in this last case was the sample, and this technique grounds the channel on the consumer side. The four studies on textbooks may be grounded on this side as well. If they are, the assumption is based on the notion that students ultimately will get around to reading the textbooks, thus grounding the channel in the discipline at this "low" level. The grounding may occur late, immediately before examinations, but this is grounding nonetheless. The emphasis of the remaining studies of the table is on the supply side, on the input side of the communications channels. In every instance the original findings consisted of the most cited or most listed scholars -- the intention being to identify the most important contributors in the field. We converted the lists into nationality summaries, excluding the old masters such as Durkheim.

The reader is asked to examine Table 6 where the impression is given that the total number of the most cited social scientists chosen in the ten studies of American sociology was 222. The correct number actually was 224, but we could not identify the nationality of two of them. Of the 222 identified, 220 (99.1 percent) were found to be American. The two exceptions are one Indian and one Swede (Gunnar Myrdal). The pattern is "all American," a label which suggests that virtually all of those chosen in each sample are American. The intensity of this inward focus is explained in part by the small size of the group of scholars indicated in each study, never exceeding 34. Nonetheless, the inward, ethnocentric focus is obvious.

The data analyzed in this section, with virtually complete consistency, support the non-science model presented above, i.e., the thesis that the pattern of incoming communications to American science is a non-scientific one. The term "virtually" was inserted in the last sentence only because of the slight variation in the findings of the studies, the variation among the three patterns -- all American, the bilateral, and the tripartite. But these are minor variations, considering

Table 6

Nationality of the Most Important or Most Cited Modern Scholars in American Sociology and Textbooks and of Reading Lists for American Sociology Graduate Students*

Primary Sources Used	Method Used for Choosing Sociologists	Dates of Primary Sources	Total Top Modern Social Scientists Chosen	Total of the Americans Chosen	Percentage American
Journals	Footnote Citations	1955	25	25	100.0
Textbooks	Footnote Citations	1955	22	22	100.0
Journals	Footnote Citations	1958-62	20	20	100.0
Textbooks	Footnote Citations	1958-62	20	20	100.0
Graduate Student Reading List	Polling of Amer. Grad. Depts.	1961	20	19	95.0
Journals	Footnote Citations	1967-68	21	21	100.0
Textbooks	Footnote Citations	1967-68	20	20	100.0
Journals	Footnote Citations	1970	34	34	100.0
Textbooks	Footnote Citations	1968-72	17	17	100.0
Journals	Footnote Citations	1970	23	22	95.7
TOTAL			222	220	99.1

* The old masters such as Durkheim have not been included in our enumeration.

Source: Mark Oromaner, 1980, "Influentials in Sociological Textbooks and Journals, 1955 and 1970," The American Sociologist 15: 169-174; Mark Oromaner, "The Audience as a Determinant of the Most Important Sociologists," The American Sociologist 3: 1968, 124-126; Mark Oromaner, "Comparisons of Influentials in Contemporary American and British Sociology: A Study in the Internationalization of Sociology," British Journal of Sociology 21: 1970, 324-332; William H. Swatos, Jr., and Priscilla L. Swatos, "Name Citations in Introductory Sociology Texts: A Note on Further Research," The American Sociologist 9, 1974, 225-228; Mark Oromaner, "The Structure of Influence in Contemporary Academic Sociology," The American Sociologist 7, 1972: 11-15.

the nature of social science, and that none of the 24 studies contradicts the first five propositions cited above as constituting the parts of the non-science model for incoming communications. Similarly, the data of none of the studies supported the competing science model. The reader will recall that the data used in this section were derived from 24 separate social science studies, done at various times and focused upon American sociology, psychology, political science, and education. The patterns of communications derived from this substantial data base were found to contrast with the patterns of communications of American physics and with the social science importance of the various regions of the world as measured by their production of social science periodicals.

Our findings suggest that the incoming communications of American social science are overwhelmingly and disproportionately domestic in origin, much more so than is the case for American physics and much more so than is warranted by the relative world importance of American social science. Merton's general criterion universalism is violated, more specifically what applies here is the particularist criteria nationalism, which Merton argues is contrary to science. Bias in favor of national social science messages is so strong as virtually to eliminate foreign ones. This is the same bias, and in essentially the same strength, as found in the larger culture or in the global structures introduced above. The American communications industry can be regarded as part of these structures. We have quoted Rosenberg above that this industry is the largest in the world, a position which "effectively excludes foreign material." We have found that this assertion applies to social science as well. What does not apply is Ben-David's assurance that the scientific community is effectively insulated from the greater society, so much so that the influence of this society can be ignored for many intents and purposes, because the work of scientists is effectively determined by their own work traditions. Our data suggest that what is true of the larger American society/culture is also true of American social science. The latter is not insulated from the larger society/culture, but it is greatly affected by it. Similarly, the structuralist would conclude that American social science is not outside global structures, but inside them and very much related to them.

The same assertions apply to the other three parts of the non-scientific incoming communications model. Each was confirmed by the data, and all point to US social science as being imbedded in

American culture/society, and in global structures as well. These three parts are the following: an overall disproportion in favor of the white commonwealth over other foreign channels; a similar disproportion in favor of Western continental Europe over the Soviet bloc and the third world; and a disproportion of messages coded in English over those coded in other languages. The disproportionality in the first two instances was demonstrated by contrast with the relative social science importance of regions of the world and, with the exception of the third world, by contrast with the pattern of incoming international messages of American physics. Language bias was shown by the contrast with the linguistic distribution of social science periodicals, with only 40 percent of them being published in English. The pattern does not accord with the principle of fullness of scientific communications enunciated by Kaplan and Storer and by Kuhn. The biases shown among the incoming messages follow the general pattern of biases of American transactions with foreign countries, except for the special case of Japan. These biases favor the white Commonwealth, then Western Europe, and both of these over the third world and the Soviet bloc. Singer has found a similar pattern for American international transactions, and again the parallel of global structures with the social sciences is confirmed. The same general statement applies to language, but there the impact of the monolingualism of American culture becomes more obvious. Of the combined sample of 192 favorite journals tested for this trait all 192 were published in English. The prejudice against Soviet bloc social science, a marked ideological bias found in American society and also in the general pattern of American transactions, was also revealed by the data. Despite a sizeable Soviet bloc social science establishment and despite the keen interest of American physicists in the work of their Soviet colleagues, American social scientists accept few messages from this region, according to our data.

Our overall conclusion is that the pattern of incoming social science message suggested here is a non-scientific one, because of its obvious particularistic biases. This pattern seems more a product of the idiosyncratic traits of American society or of global structures than of Merton's institutional imperatives and values, of Ben-David's glorious isolationism, or any version of the fullness of communications. Our data suggest that American social scientists are monolingual, ethnocentric, with bias in favor of the white Anglo-Saxon world and bias against Western Europe and even more so against the Soviet bloc and against the third world. A basic reason that social science messages from foreign centers are not widely accepted in the United States is the absence of a common professional culture shared by the social science disciplines of the world. United States centers socialize their members one way, with their own pattern of values, a pattern closely linked to American society. Soviet social science uses a very different process, with a pattern of values even more closely meshed with their society, many of the values taught directly contradicting the American set. Another basic reason for the U.S. acceptance of few foreign incoming messages is the U.S. superior position -- quite different from that of the third world. Little wonder that American social scientists generally spare themselves the pain of decoding Soviet messages, or that when Soviet and American social scientists do interact the result often looks like the dialogue of the deaf or a cold war confrontation. American social science culture has more in common with that of the white Commonwealth, just as the two larger Anglo-Saxon cultures resemble each other. For this reason, American social scientists take an interest in the messages from the white Commonwealth. Less commonality obtains with continental Europe and messages from there are less frequent as well. Even fewer come from the Soviet Union and from the third world -- and American culture has even less in common with theirs. The structuralist explanation puts more emphasis upon power than upon a commonality of culture. The two explanations will be counterposed in the next section.

Outgoing Messages of American Social Science: The Triumph of Structuralism

Our preoccupation in this short section is essentially that of establishing the pattern of communications sent out by centers of United States social science and to ascertain what light this pattern casts upon the characteristics of social science. We will see if this pattern can be explained in the same way as the incoming flow, i.e., by both the similarity between the culture of the United States and that of the receiving culture and also by the structures that bind them. This section will make us choose between these alternate explanations. A further goal is to establish the relationship between the quantity of imports and the quantity of exports -- to determine what has been called the "balance of communications." The reader will recall that the fifth question of those which formed the general non-science model sketched above was the disproportion of exports of communications over incoming ones, an "export" balance. We will relate the balance which we find with educational and other cultural balances and see how these findings can help us to answer two central questions of our research: the scientific/non-scientific nature of social science and the usefulness of structures in exploring our discipline.

The postwar spread of American social science and, therefore, of its communications as well, has followed the general postwar extension of the United States -- military, political, economic, cultural, informational, and educational. This spread has been dramatic, and it has occurred despite the contrasting cultures and values of the receiving countries, differing from that of the United States and from those of each other. This leads to the hypothesis that the global structures are a more accurate index of the spread of our disciplines and of their outgoing communications than any concordance of American culture with those of the receiving countries. These latter do have impact as we hope to show below, but it is essentially potential and delayed. In the last section, we learned that no matter how the data were gathered or what specific social science discipline was being investigated, the great preponderance of social science messages received by American social science seem to be domestic in origin. In this section we shall see that this is not the case for the countries of the first world and those of the third world examined here -- all of which are subject to American structures. We quoted above (Table 2) a study by Laponce of the nationality of the footnotes used by the official journals of the national political science associations of five countries. The study found that the preponderance of footnotes in the American journal are from domestic sources. It revealed, furthermore, that the US journal had an export balance with every one of the other countries involved. The contrast between the percentage of footnotes which American sources provided for the foreign journals and the percentage which foreign sources supplied for the American publication will serve as the gauge of the balance. The figures were as follows, the percentages in parentheses being in the order given above (American footnotes for foreign journals; foreign footnotes for the American journals): with the British journal (47, 15); the French journal (39, 1); the Canadian journal (49, 1); and the Indian journal (54, 0). These figures clearly suggest an export balance -- indeed, only British sources provide any real input for the American journal. Furthermore, in every case, American sources provided more footnotes for the four foreign journals than did domestic sources. This is indicated by the following figures, again US footnotes are listed first, the percentage of domestic footnotes second, and the countries are in the order as found above: (47, 42); (39, 37); (49, 29); and (54, 18).[21] The extent of the imbalance is illustrated by both sets of figures, the second set clearer in this respect than the first. In the first set only one of the two developed countries, the United Kingdom, offers competition to American imports, and this is the country closest to the United States culturally. This second set of figures better suggests that the extent of the imbalance correlates better with the underdevelopment or the dependence of a country than with any similarity with American culture. Development allows "resistance" to the global structures, the United Kingdom and France being in a better position in this respect than Canada or India. The first three countries listed have cultures quite similar to that of the United States, certainly when compared with the former, yet the fourth, India, is the most dependent on American sources , i.e., the greatest importer of these sources in relation to exports and also in relation to indigenous ones. India seems not to be able to resist these global structures, despite the gulf which separates her culture from that of the United States.

That social science centers in the American orbit are subject to her structures is suggested again by an analysis of footnote citations in the American Sociological Review and the British Journal of Sociology. An analysis of these found contemporary American sociologists among the list of the most cited in the British journal, but no British (indeed, no foreign) sociologist was found on the most cited lists derived from the American journal.[22] A study of the citations of the contributions from Quebec to the Revue Canadienne de Science Politique in every one of the four periods tested between 1968 and 1980 found that the richest source of footnotes was American journals.[23] In the last three periods the latter outstripped French journals two to one; and they were far ahead of the others listed, Quebec itself, and Anglophone Canada. Bhambri speaks of the post war "penetration" of Indian political science by the American discipline, and of the preoccupation of Indian practitioners with two American exercises in systems building, structural-functionalism, and general systems theory.[24] These paradigms took the place of the British ones, dominant in the pre-independence period, which were institutional and descriptive. In the post-independence period, American structures took the place of the colonial ones, and the dominant social science paradigm made a similar transition.

American social science has thus been able to penetrate countries with cultures as different from its own as those of French Canada and India. Moreover, the data above and much of them below point to "favorable" balances of social science transactions in favor of American exports over imports. Japan and South Korea can be added to the list of countries penetrated by the United States, but in 1949 China had to be stricken from it. With the penetrations, of course, come communications. Since 1978 dramatic political changes have occurred in this Asian giant, however, so that Sino-US social science relations have become possible once again. A study of social science in Japan speaks of the postwar "flooding inflow" of American empiricism to that country especially in the fields of economics, political science, sociology, and psychology.[25] Previously, European paradigms had been in the ascendant. Joung-Sik asserts that "American political science" (behavioralism) was imported into South Korea after 1960 "without much criticism or reflection".[26] This followed the return home of South Korean scholars who had studied abroad, generally in the United States and with US aid. In the pre-independence period, most Korean intellectuals received their education in Japan, "thus subjecting themselves to the influence of the Japanese." Accordingly, political science in Korea began with a German import (the Japanese had imported it from Germany) and one which continued to receive support on into the early postwar period, until it was eclipsed by American behavioralism. Again, American social science came in the wake of American global structures.

The first conclusion that the data of this section allow us to make is that global structures are a better index for the presence of American social science and its messages than is American culture. This is evident from the diversity of the cultures penetrated by American social science -- all the way from the United Kingdom, France, and Quebec, to India, Japan, and Korea. Chinese education and social science could be included before 1949, and its day may come again but under circumstances different from before. Whether the culture is close to the United States or not seems not to matter. In fact, cultures with little in common with that of the United States can be more penetrated, if the country is less developed. A case in point is Indian political science penetrated (as measured by footnotes) to a greater extent than British political science. Certainly American culture is closer to that of the United Kingdom. If culture were the cause or the index of penetration, then Indian social science would not be penetrated very much, certainly not more than that of the United Kingdom. But culture proved to be, as we saw in the previous section, a valuable index for the reception of social science communications by the United States. This points to the favored position of US social science. She accepts mostly messages in accordance with her culture and in her language, but her messages are accepted abroad without such accommodation. Her relations are vertical, and she has the advantage, as our structural approach alleges. The inequality is most noticeable in the case of the developing countries (see India above). Again this points to the importance of our structures.

The Monologue: a Vertical Relationship

A second conclusion from the data presented above is that United States social science enjoys an export balance of communications. Her social scientists send out large quantities of messages, but accept few in return. In effect, they talk, but they do not listen. This is the position of those in authority or those with the power -- the officer over the enlisted men or the patron over the maid. Again, the relationship is vertical, and it points to the presence of vertical structures. Specific evidence for this export balance is found in the research on footnotes cited above, but the general thrust of this section in contrast to that of the preceding one supports the same thesis. We are thus in a position to answer in the affirmative the sixth and last question of our general scientific-non-scientific model. We find a disproportion in favor of outgoing American social science messages over incoming ones. Scientific communities are characterized by dialogue, by the exchange of ideas -- not by a monologue in which one side talks and the other side merely listens. The disproportion in favor of American exports amounts to this kind of monologue or lecture.

This monologue, this refusal to listen to what would be Soviet and continental colleagues if the discipline were natural science, corresponds to a particularistic, ideological enterprise. The American physicist sees Soviet and continental counterparts as colleagues engaged in a common effort to discover the laws of nature, and, therefore, what they have discovered and what they say or write is of the utmost importance. No wonder that they are listened to, that an effort is made to study Russian or German. In contrast, the American social scientist sees his counterparts in the Soviet Union, and often even on the continent, not as colleagues dedicated to the common pursuit of truth, but as ideologues whose outputs can safely be ignored, except that occasionally they are critically examined and analyzed as ideology. In the case of the Soviet Union, they are even seen as official propaganda. or the supposed discipline is held to be so hemmed in by government restrictions that it, in fact, is not really a discipline. Powell and Shoup, for example, argue that political science has not yet emerged in Eastern Europe (except for Poland and Yugoslavia), because the requisite freedom does not exist there.[27] Lipset sees Soviet sociology as one which rationalizes government policies and supports communist ideology, contrasted with the American version of the discipline which he holds to be critical and independent of the government.[28] The charge of rationalizing government policy is richly reciprocated by Soviet scholars. Thus Egorov pictures American political science as a rationalization for American capitalism.[29] Chertina charges that Western modernization theory offers capitalism as the model for development and that development is presented as the transition from the traditional to capitalism. Moreover, Western social scientists denigrate Soviet accomplishments in Soviet Central Asia.[30]

The one way monologue, the sending of messages without receiving feedback -- this practice of American social science forms the same communications pattern as American television, news, films, and other cultural exports. The United States exports these "products," without importing them, in an essential one way outward flow with only insignificant feedback. The similarity of these patterns across category lines is no surprise to the structuralist -- for these cultural and social science flows are all the result of the same independent variables, and they are packaged together with their political, economic, social/cultural, communications, and social science aspects. A few examples from the general field of communications will show that social science fits nicely into what is a general structural pattern. Righter in her article on "the great information war" speaks of the "unrelenting one-way traffic" of ideas and values from the West to third world countries.[31] She asserts that most of these countries rely for their international and regional news coverage upon the four major Western news agencies -- Reuters, the Associated Press, United Press International, and Agence France Press. Third world critics argue that the preeminence of these (Tass can be added for some countries) results from historical accidents, imperialism, and technical preeminence, not from the quality of their services. These critics argue that much of the news sold by these multinational corporations is not truly "international," that it is selected to suit Western attitudes and interests, heavily biased against the third world, and that it is inaccurate and not objective. The same charges have been leveled against first world social science. Righter warns the West not to take this communications challenge lightly, and she points out that the third world uses UNESCO and the Non-Aligned Movement as the chief forums for lodging its grievances in this area. In 1976 at the Non-Aligned meeting in Tunis the provisions of the New World Information Order were spelled out. The latter calls for natural development of the media as an integral part of development programs; news exchange among the third world countries and the export of news from them to the developed world; and a challenge to the validity of Western news values.[32] In a later chapter, we will set forth the third world challenge to first world social science, a challenge which parallels this one.

Topuz argues that the notion of the free circulation of television programs applies in reality only to those wealthy countries which are in a position to produce such programs.[33] He adds, moreover, that the poor countries are dependent upon the rich countries for much of their programming. A big part of the reason revolves around the economics of the television industry, a high fixed cost enterprise. We discussed this concept in chapter II, but an example of it here should be welcome. In such an enterprise, the key to profit making is a large market, wide circulation. A TV program which costs $100,000 to make originally in the developed world will be offered for use to a small country for only $500, where the purchase price is based on the number of TV sets and obviously not on production costs. The original production costs were probably already covered in the developed country, and additional profit results as long as the charge to the developing country more than covers the variable costs, the cost of running off and distributing an additional copy. As we pointed out in Chapter II, social science is obviously the same kind of industry where the cost of creating paradigms can be considerable, e.g., support for libraries and universities and time off for research. But once the paradigm has been formulated, additional "copies" can be run off at a very reasonable rate. This is one economic reason that helps explain why television, news, and social science all tend to be a one-way traffic -- from the developed to the third world countries. Far and away the largest exporter is the United States -- a role this country enjoys in all these areas. Other important exporters in the TV industry are the United Kingdom, France, West Germany, and the Soviet Union --but the last named exports have been for the most part to other socialist countries. Thus the proper method of analysis is not the economic, but rather political economy or the structural. Topuz sees wealth as the major determinant of the TV independence of a given country, with the prior existence of a movie industry being the second factor. Dependency varies widely from China, Japan, and the United States, which are nearly self sufficient, to Saudi Arabia which is 100 percent dependent on imports, with America's close neighbors Canada and Mexico in between, respectively 46 percent and 39 percent dependent. Topuz concludes that the programs which dominate the international market are produced to entertain particular home markets and that their contents do not necessarily correspond to the needs of the society which imports them. He points to the dissatisfaction with the present lopsided system and notes that critics in the importing countries view it as a threat to their culture. Again, this points to the third world revolt.

Brief Summary and Discussion

This chapter undertook to test empirically whether social science has the characteristics of science or whether it is better viewed culturally or in the context of political economy and multidisciplinary structures. Advantage was taken of the fact that communications reveal much about the nature of enterprises, and the focus was put upon the international communications pattern of American social science to see if this pattern meets the scientific criteria set forth in the literature. The United States is so much the social science superpower that its characteristics cast light upon the whole social science enterprise. The literature provided the basis for the construction of two opposing models, a scientific one and a non-scientific one. They were tested against a quantity of empirical studies -- all but one done originally for other reason, but reworked here to further our objectives. Findings from twenty-three separate empirical studies were reworked to test the incoming communications pattern of American social science -- the studies being done at different times; focusing upon professional journals, textbooks, and graduate reading lists; and dealing with psychology, political science, sociology, and education. The data base for testing incoming communications was, therefore, extensive, that for the testing outgoing communications less so, but in our view, adequate.

The data gave overwhelming support to the non-scientific model. More specifically, our findings gave indication of bias or marked disproportionality in the pattern of incoming communications for American social science toward domestic sources and channels; white Commonwealth nations over all other foreign nations; continental Western European countries over those of the Soviet bloc and the third world; those in the English language over those in other languages; and outgoing contrasted with incoming sources and channels. The question of bias and disproportionality was established by contrasting the findings with the international communications pattern of American physics and with the relative social science importance of the countries measured by their journal publications in our disciplines. The evidence could be interpreted to mean that the American social sciences are ethnocentric, nationalistic, and ideological. We put them in the context of structural analysis which is a more valuable insight. They do not operate in accordance with the traits imputed to science by Merton, nor do they enjoy the insulation from the outside society as set forth by Ben David, nor the fullness of communication referred to by Kaplan, Storer, and Kuhn. Notable among the infractions was violation of the Mertonian institutional imperative universalism, which requires that truth claims be judged by impersonal criteria and that particularistic ones be avoided. Our data suggested that American social science has not succeeded in avoiding particularist bias in the receipt of communications. True, Merton's trait refers specifically to the judging of truth claims, but communications are viewed here as having such force that their impact upon judging truth claims is only a matter of time. The receipt of a predominance of communications from one sect or viewpoint will generally prejudice the judgment of truth claims in favor of that sect or viewpoint. The violations in the case of the imperatives set forth by Kuhn, Kaplan and Storer, and Ben-David are more clear cut and straightforward. Obviously, American social science does not enjoy "fullness of communications" or even "relative fullness of communications" -- incoming communications are described better by the terms partial, selective, and biased. Nor are these communications, or outgoing ones, isolated from the larger society. The pattern of incoming communications parallels American culture, whereas both the incoming and the outgoing ones are explainable in terms of global structures.

We found that the incoming pattern of social science could be explained in cultural terms, but also by reference to global structures.

In contrast, American outgoing communications were explained by global structures, the cultural dimension being helpless for this task. This provided evidence to justify the methodology adopted in this volume. American social science is part of the knowledge industry, and because of its development it enjoys the competitive international advantage of big business over small business, of the multinational over the local business enterprise. An obvious advantage is that incoming communications are in accord with American culture; American exports need not be in accord with the culture of the importing countries. This conclusion fits well with our use of political economy and global structures for explaining the postwar extension of the American social sciences. It does not accord with Storer's assumption that the modus operandi of social science is laissez-faire and that presumably the best will rise to the top or, at least, that this is the tendency.

A conclusion of this chapter is that the dominant sects in a big social science power such as the United States have a competitive edge in the dependencies -- an advantage over and above the intrinsic merits of the sects themselves. This helps explain the dramatic postwar spread of the dominant sects of American social science. These sects spread not merely to the third world, but also to the more developed countries of the capitalist world. The parallel between American social science and the American media and television was drawn, both, in our view, responding to the same independent variables and associated together in the same global structures. The pattern of their communications fits the same general mold -- messages flow from the American center to the peripheries with little counterflow.

The other remaining Mertonian traits -- communism, disinterestedness, and organized skepticism -- ill fit our findings. "Communism" means in the Mertonian sense the common ownership of the enterprise. Our findings see social science revealing more the traits of capitalist ownership, with the large and the powerful obviously in control. One set of "rules" exists for the United States, another for the third world. Incoming communications must match American culture, outgoing communications need not be adjusted to fit the cultures of the importing countries of the third (or the first) world. One is reminded of the unequal rules of the International Monetary Fund. Social science is revealed here as a sectarian undertaking, factionalism prevailing over common ownership and consensus. Disinterestedness also receives little support here, not that the existence of fraud or the conscious creation of pseudo sciences were found as a characteristic of the social sciences. What these sectarian enterprises lack -- and what natural science has -- is generally recognized tests which virtually eliminate the above and also the emergence of pseudo sciences. The social sciences contain no generally accepted methodology which can be used to eliminate what certain sects characterize as spurious claims and pseudo sciences. The last of the Mertonian traits, organized skepticism, falls victim as well to the sectarianism of social science. Members of the same sect are biased in favor of -- rather than skeptical of -- the outputs of their own sect. Their attitude toward the work of other sects is not so much that of skepticism as it is one of ideological rejection.

We offer this chapter as support for the efficacy of the approach to research which we adopted at the onset of the essay. It served this purpose quite well, and we feel good about what has been accomplished so far. It also helps us better to understand the young professor who introduced the volume, and it helps excuse us for constructing such an ethnocentric whipping boy. We are now located at a breakpoint in our analysis -- a breakpoint which divides the laying out of the foundation of the essay from a statement of the geography and the contents of social science. We have sketched the general characteristics of our disciplines. We next divide them into sects and site them. The reader will no doubt appreciate the difficulty which lies ahead: to summarize social sciences in a very limited number of chapters. We were torn between a topical approach which would divide the disciplines by types and a geographic division which would identify the dominant paradigms in the different countries and regions. Our way of dealing with this uncertainty will be noted in the next chapter -- it is to connect them.

NOTES

1.   Norman Kaplan and Norman W. Storer, "Science: Scientific Communications," International Encyclopedia of Social Science, 14 (1968), 112.

2.   Norbert Wiener, The Human Use of Human Beings" Cybernetics and Society, (Boston: Houghton Mifflin, 1950), 9.

3.   R.I. Tooze, "Communication Theory" in Approaches and Theory in International Relations, (London: Longman, 1978), 22.

4.   Karl W. Deutsch, The Nerves of Government: Models of Political Communication and Control, (New York: Free Press, 1966), 101.

5.   Joseph Ben-David, "Introduction," International Social Science Journal, 22 (1970), 17.

6.   Thomas S. Kuhn, "Second Thoughts on Paradigms," in Frederick Suppe (Ed.), The Structure of Scientific Theories, (Urbana: University of Illinois Press, 1974), 461.

7.   Norman W. Storer, "The Internationality of Science and the Nationality of Scientists," International Social Science Journal, 22, 1 (1970), 82.

8.   Victor Rosenberg, "Information Policies of Developing Countries: The Case of Brazil," Journal of the American Society for Information Science, 33, (1981), 206.

9.   Marshall R. Singer, "The Foreign Policies of Small Developing States," Chapter 12 of James N. Rosenau, et al., World Politics: An Introduction (New York: Free Press, 1976), 173.

10.   "Strength Through Wisdom: A Critique of U.S. Capability: A
       Report to the President," From the President"s Commission on
       Foreign Language and International Studies (U.S. Government
       Printing Office, Washington, D.C. 1979), 5.

11.   Paulo Freire, Pedagogy of the Oppressed, (New York:
       Seaburg, 1970), 77.

12.   Thomas S. Kuhn, The Essential Tension: Selected Studies in
       Scientific Tradition and Change, (Chicago: University of
       Chicago Press, 1977), 296.

13.   Kaplan and Storer, 112-116.

14.   Michael W. Giles and Gerald C. Wright, Jr., "Political
       Scientists' Evaluation of Sixty-Three Journals," P.S., 8, (1975),
       254.

15.   David Koulack and H.J. Kesselman, "Ratings of Psychological
       Journals by Members of the American Psychological
       Association," American Psychologist, 30 (1975), 1049.

16.   Thomas E. Mann, "Report on a Survey of the Membership of
       the American Political Science Association," P.S., (1974),
       382-385.

17.   Maurice Line and Stephen Roberts, "The Size, Growth, and
       Composition of Social Science Literature," International
       Social Science Journal, 28 (1976), 135.

18.   Ibid., 36.

19.   Gerhard Lenski, "Review Symposium," American
       Sociological Review, 33 (1968), 802-805.

20.   Joji Watanuki, "The Social Sciences in Japan," International
       Social Science Journal, 27 (1975), 189.

21.   J.A. Laponce, "Political Science: An Import-Export Analysis
       of Journals and Footnotes," Political Studies, 28 (1980), 410.

22. Mark Oromaner, "Comparisons of Influentials in Contemporary American and British Sociology: A Study in the Internationalization of Sociology," British Journal of Sociology, 21 (1970), 328.

23. Michel Leclerc, La Science Politique au Quebec: Essai sur le Developpement Institutional 1920-1980, (Montreal: Hexagone, 1982), 214.

24. C.P. Bhambri, "Political Science," in S.C. Dube (ed.), Social Sciences and Social Realities: Role of Social Sciences in Contemporary India, (Simla: Institute of Advanced Study, 1976), 166.

25. OECD, Social Science Policy, Japan. Organization for Economic Co-operation and Development, (Paris, 1977), 25.

26. Lee Joung-Sik, "Political Science in the Republic of Korea" M.S. Hsueh (ed.), Political Science in South and Southeast Asia (Maksati, Philippines: Asian Political Science Association, 1966), 163.

27. David E. Powell and Paul Shoup, "The Emergence of Political Science in Communist Countries," The American Political Science Review, 64, (1970), 572-588.

28. S.M. Lipset, "Commentary: Social Stratification, Research and Soviet Scholarship," International Journal of Sociology, 3 (1973), 355-401.

29. S.A. Egorov, "Principal Research. Directions in U.S. Political Science in the 1970's," Soviet Law and Government, 19 (1980), 61-77.

30. Z.S. Chertina, "The Bourgeois Theory of 'Modernization' and the Real Development of the Peoples of Soviet Central Asia," Soviet Law and Government, 19 (1980-1981), 3-20.

31. Rosemary Righter, "The Great Information War: Battle of the Bias," Foreign Policy 34 (1979), 124.

32. Ibid., 128.

33. Hifzi Topuz, "Television's One-Way Traffic," UNESCO Courier, 30 (1977), 16.

CHAPTER V

FUNCTIONALISM AND OTHER SCIENTIFIC AND NOT SO SCIENTIFIC PARADIGMS IN THE UNITED STATES

The four preceding chapters can be seen as attempts to give the general nature of our disciplines -- to estimate, as examples, their general modus operandi, their relations with government and society, their self-image, and their network of communications. Having made such estimates, we now turn to geographic location and to the paradigms themselves, our preoccupation for these next four chapters. The major purpose will be to indicate the multiparadigmatic nature of the enterprise and to mark the major characteristics and the locations of the paradigms. Of course, the reality of social science is much richer and vastly more complicated than anything which we can present here. Our task is heightened by the breadth of our declared subject -- our academic turf not confined to one social science, but dedicated to the enterprise in general. We are constrained, therefore, to continue to sample several disciplines. Our analysis must, therefore, include the multi-paradigmatic and the interdisciplinary -- to which we have added a third perspective, the geographic. This latter perspective reflects the fact that given areas have their favorite paradigms. What would seem to be reflected most in the geographic is the impact of dominant elites and dominant cultures, although other factors can have a bearing as well. In a given country or area, perhaps a majority of the social scientists in a discipline or a large plurality will subscribe to the same paradigm. The most obvious example was the Soviet bloc, and there the three perspectives tended to merge. Kremlin Marxism served as the meta-paradigm for all disciplines, as well as the vehicle for convergence at all levels -- the topical, the geographic, and the disciplinary. The convergence of the three perspectives in this chapter is more forced. Functionalism is the major paradigm in American sociology, and it has strong "scientific" sisters in other disciplines. But there is sizeable dissent against it in the

United States, plus support for it and kindred scientific approaches in other areas, especially in the free world. Nonetheless, we believe that our approach is defensible, if only because it includes the geographic, a perspective necessary for an understanding of our disciplines.

We start in this chapter with the presentation of the first of four meta-paradigms from the field of sociology. Constructions of Burrell and Morgan, they represent a first "cut," a thoughtful beginning for analyzing the topical aspects of sociological theory. They tend to be philosophical, and they thus serve well as an introduction for all the disciplines. They suggest that our disciplines express contradicting Weltanschauungen, like Kuhnian paradigms. The presentation of four meta-paradigms, this comparative procedure, tends to undercut the sectarianism of the young professor who was used to introduce this volume. Comparativism has a deflating effect upon dogmatism. The first of these meta-paradigms is called by its authors "functionalism," and it turns out to be in the same corner with positivism, in the corner with that ideology which would apply to our disciplines the assumptions and the methods of natural science. It is also in the same corner with the young professor. After noting its characteristics, we mark the widespread existence of similar paradigms in various other disciplines, besides sociology, in the United States in the post World War II period. In this way we combine the topical perspective with the geographic and the disciplinary. The present chapter is mostly on American functionalism and similar American paradigms from other disciplines, although something has been added on Chicano and black social science in the United States. The other three meta-paradigms for sociology have been reserved for subsequent chapters where they are matched up with their most likely areas and supplemented with similar local paradigms from other disciplines. This shifting and dancing back and forth among perspectives and regions should make the narrative more difficult to follow, but also much more interesting and profitable. Its main advantage is that it touches crucial aspects of our disciplines and with an economy of space.

This chapter deals with what were, or at least what became in the postwar period, the establishment American paradigms in the disciplines covered. These latter disciplines are sociology, international relations, political science, economics, and a composite labelled development theory. Our expectations, based on our analysis in Chapters II and III, should be that these paradigms will be conservative ones, as befits the leader of world capitalism, a country whose elites have interests all over the free world. We should expect a predominance of assumptions centering upon, and tendencies leading toward, the status quo, equilibrium, integration, and consensus. These are on the "regulation side" of the first dimension of Burrell and Morgan, as explained below. We do not expect dominant American paradigms habitually to cross the dimension to the "radical change" side -- there to countenance such unpleasant situations as conflict, coercion, deprivation, or even potentiality. These latter are the general preserve of the radical, "off limits" to the great status quo superpower. On the other hand, we should expect the paradigms to be "scientific." In terms used below, the paradigms should be on the deterministic side of the second dimension of Burrell and Morgan. The term "behavioral sciences" came into vogue in the 1950s to describe a new determined effort to study scientifically the subjects already studied by the social sciences. It all had the appearance of deja vu, and more than once before. Many of the issues had been covered before by Comte, as one example. By the middle of the 1960s the term "behavioral science" had been generally recognized, if not generally accepted. A key element was the decision of the Ford Foundation, which emerged as the largest private foundation in the world, to finance behavioral research.[1] Behaviorism thus became a significant part of the knowledge industry. The issue of "dirty money" did arise from time to time, but most establishment social scientists seemed more interested in being financed, rather than being concerned about such an "old fashioned" issue. The emphasis of this new "ism" is, of course, upon the scientific approach, but also upon basic, interdisciplinary research to include not just overt behavior, but also human beings as individuals. The chapter concludes with a section which suggests the main characteristics of Chicano and black social science.

The United States: Number One in Social Science

The chapter must be divided into two contradictory parts -- the larger establishment sphere which, of course, comes first in the front and the lesser part in the back which demands special paradigms for the study of the black and the Chicano. These parts do have two attributes in common. They are both social science, and they share a common home, the United States. This country became in the postwar period the great social science superpower. The structuralist would have anticipated as much. After all, after the shooting had stopped, the United States stood tall as the foremost power in many spheres, examples being the economic, the political, the scientific, the cultural, communications, and education. Social science was just part of a structure, with many other facets and with common causes. Social science has been merely a part of the general prosperity. As we have said, it is closest to education, to which we now turn for our analysis.

The American position in education stemmed from both domestic and external causes. Britain, France, and Germany experienced a general relative decline in all spheres, while the United States was in the ascendant. Post-secondary education in the United States witnessed a dramatic expansion, spurred on by the GI Bill of Rights which gave a scholarship to every veteran of the war. In 1949-1950 there were more than 1,800 institutions giving instructions on a higher than secondary level to an estimated combined enrollment of 2.6 million (30 percent of the population between 18 and 21 years old).[2] Approximately 800 of the institutions were universities and colleges -- slightly fewer than half being state supported. Some 250 were municipally supported. It is generally in departments of these institutions that social science is taught and where the research for the disciplines is performed. The figures for the institutions are somewhat misleading, because, as in so many other industries, a few of the enterprises set the pattern for the pack, in this case produce the paradigms and the research findings which are widely in use. Our disciplines in the United States and elsewhere tend to be elitist and oligopolistic.

The dominant American paradigms were distributed overseas as American structures expanded after the war. The United States became the world's greatest educator, taking the place of the United Kingdom and France. She became the center, not only for the third world, but the overseas center for first world countries as well. Only the second world seemed immune from her embrace, but even this was not completely true, as is exemplified by the case of Poland, which has maintained social science relations with the West. The United States became the center for seventy-four countries which modelled their educational systems after hers. At one time, USAID provided educational assistance to some 80 countries. But the motor force behind US extension was not exhausted at the official level. There were also the foundations, which played a crucial role both at the international and at the domestic levels. We met these institutions before in the third chapter, where Silva and

Slaughter alleged, based on exchange theory, that they gave their "dirty money" to American social scientists in exchange for ideological conformity and support. We remarked then that while agreeing with the results there was something too naive about such an obvious deal. No one needs to play the puta in social affairs; social science which we put in a social context comes in so many ideologies as to accommodate almost any policies and value systems. Just as dominant cultures manage to attract adherents, so do dominant paradigms.

We use Berman's study to gauge the present impact of the foundations upon our disciplines. He does not use exchange theory in his analysis, but money does play a crucial role. He finds the articulation between the federal government and the foundations at the highest level in Washington. There he would add one more stop for those who play musical chairs between the corporation and international bank board rooms in New York and cabinet level and sub-level posts in Washington. This additional stop is at one of the foundations -- preferably Ford, Rockefeller, or Carnegie. Three secretaries of state have done service with the Rockefeller Foundation -- Dulles, Vance, and Rusk. Paul Hoffmann, McGeorge Bundy, Robert McNamara, and John J. McCloy were "graduates" of the Ford Foundation. Such articulation -- and there are other examples -- builds more confidence than does the services of the academic manager. We suspect that this is not so much an improvement in a research design, as a shift in reality. Berman quotes a study which indicates that over half of the trustees of the thirteen largest foundations attended either Harvard, Yale, or Princeton.[3] Typically, foundation managers are white males, between the ages of 55 and 65, and Episcopalian or Presbyterian. These are the sound and prudent people who can be trusted with a business, a government, or a foundation. They are part of the establishment, but generally the liberal or progressive wing of it. Berman does not charge any conspiracy on their part. None is needed, for they are generally like minded in their defense of capitalism, its overseas expansion, and the fear of communism. American expansion overseas is for the mutual benefit of the United States and the host countries as well. But these fund folks are not a monolith, and occasionally they fund a radical social scientist. They are Democratic or Republican, more often liberal than conservative -- non-partisans dedicated to public service, not to partisanship.

Berman had access to the archives of the Carnegie Corporation and those of the Ford and Rockefeller foundations. His conclusion reached after years of research was that the foundations have had an influence on American foreign and domestic policies "as vital cogs in the ideological support system of state capitalism." They do this by encouraging certain ideas congruent with this system and with American policy in general. Most importantly for us, they encourage conservative social science paradigms which are also the dominant ones in the United States. Moreover, these foundation managers encourage elitism in American universities by subsidizing a few universities over the others, a policy they have applied to third world countries as well. Their funds helped create most of the foreign areas study programs of American universities. They have funded foreign scholars and concentrated their funding upon certain institutions overseas. They have helped train the indigenous leaders of the third world, financing favorite ideas over the competition. For the fiscal year 1955-1956, the Ford Foundation appropriated $557 million for grants, and in 1961 the Rockefeller Foundation established a $100 million fund for the development of third world universities. These represent prime, not representative, examples, and most of the American resources for the creation of social science knowledge are from elsewhere. The foundations actually supplement government resources and give added assurance that American social science will serve the interests of the dominant elites. Their impact is typical of the control of social science in the free world: encouragement through financing of favorite paradigms -- rather than the censorship of those not favored. This is a case of political economy.

Sociology
        Our intent is to discuss first the dominant American paradigms in sociology, international relations, political science, economics, and then development theory. We start with sociology, an appropriate beginning, because this "imperialist" discipline has the ambition to subject all aspects of society to its academic dominion. Our geographic turf in this chapter is equally expansive, the United States which in the post World War II period has been the social science superpower. We use the work of Burrell and Morgan, who construct two dimensions from which they derive their four meta-paradigms for sociology. They call the first dimension the subjective/objective and the second regulation/radical change. The first one is well named, i.e., the name

conveys its general contents, but they insist on giving an inventory of these contents. We believe this is valuable, and we start with the first dimension, the subjective/objective, by detailing its contents. This involves several facets, the first of which is the ontological. The issue here is whether the reality which the sociologist is investigating is of an objective nature, external to the researcher and thus imposing itself upon the observer from without. The alternative view is that reality is a product of the researcher's mind. The first position, that of the realist, posits a social world independent of the individual's appreciation of it. The contrary position, that of the nominalist, does not admit to any substantive structure in the real world. The structure must be imposed by the observer. Closely related to this issue is that of epistemology, a term which refers to the grounds of knowledge, i.e., how this world can be understood and how it can be communicated to others. The problem here is to separate what is true from what is false and to communicate this difference or knowledge to others. The positivist would transfer the epistemology of the natural sciences to social science. Anti-positivism takes many forms, but it is against the utility of a search for laws underlying regularities in the social world. It can, for example, give as the goal for social science mere understanding. We have discussed positivism, but not its competing intellectual tradition, German idealism, which is reserved for later.

The other dimension used in constructing the meta-paradigms is voluntarism-determinism. On one side of the issue is determinism, the sociological subject is assumed to be completely determined by the surrounding situation or the environment. The contrary assumption is voluntarism, the notion that the subject is completely autonomous and free to choose.[4] This latter notion is reflected in the assumption of consumer sovereignty in market economics or in the assertion that an election represents the "will" of the voters. The extreme position is that the choice of the individual is independent of advertising, ideology, and the other variables used in social science. When pressed, this position guts social science. Another relevant issue is the methodological debate between the ideographic and the nomothetic. The former connects understanding with first hand experience, getting close to the subject of research or viewing information from the inside. The inside view is called the emic, in contrast to the etic, the outside view. The nomothetic pattern is that of natural science, that of positivism, seeing matters from the outside and emphasizing the techniques of research. Certain procedures must be followed if the research is to be valid. Social scientists put together these procedures in "cookbooks" on the subject.

We follow Burrell and Morgan and bind these four strands together to form the subjective/objective dimension. The opposite poles of the strands are summarized below (the subjective on the left, the objective on the right):

nominalism - realism

anti-positivism - positivism

voluntarism - determinism

ideographic - nomothetic

Functionalism, the subject of this section, is located on the objective side of this scheme. But in order better to describe and locate it we present the second dimension, called regulation-radical change. Less complicated than the first, this dimension refers to the fact that sociological paradigms divide between those which concentrate upon positing and explaining social order and equilibrium (the conservative) and those which are concerned with change, conflict, and coercion (the radical). Burrell and Morgan assert that the former type paradigm greatly outnumbers the latter -- a statement which we accept for American sociology, but not necessarily for the rest of the world, and certainly not for some of it. This is suggested by the fact that much of argument they offer for the distinction in the dimension is the separation between Marxism and the likes of Durkheim, Weber, and Pareto. Again, we list in opposing columns key concepts, this time stressed in this dimension. Regulation is featured in the left column, radical change in the right.

the status quo - radical change

equilibrium, integration - conflict

consensus - coercion, domination

solidarity - emancipation

need satisfaction - deprivation

actuality - potentiality

Functionalism, as defined by Burrell and Morgan, belongs in the first column (we hesitate to repeat that it is the left column): it reflects these characteristics much better than those in the second column. It is a conservative, benign construction which tends to serve the status quo and which looks to equilibrium. Burrell and Morgan admit to variations in the concept which they have created, and they list four subgroups within this meta-paradigm. The first is social systems theory, which they present as a development of sociological positivism almost in its pure form. It uses mechanical and biological analogies for studying social affairs. The two paradigms discussed under this heading are structural functionalism and systems theory. We pass over the discussion of the former (the versions of Malinowski and Radcliffe-Brown) to offer these comments about systems theory. Of significance, as the reader will soon learn, they cite works from Parsons and from Easton, the latter on The Political System. The discussion of systems theory contains the usual: its supposed holistic view; the preference of open over closed systems; and the long, and some would say boring, list of concepts associated with the concept. Interesting is its emphasis upon equilibrium and the debt which it owes to biology.

The second subgroup under functionalism, as set forth by Burrell and Morgan, consists of interactionism and social action theory. We pass over them with the comment that they take the meta-paradigm to its limits by incorporating elements from German idealism. Parsons has journeyed across the functionalist meta-paradigm from a position consistent with Weber's theory of social action to positions well within the positivist framework. We pass over the other two categories lightly so as not to overtax the reader's patience. One such category is integration theory, and Merton's work receives much exposure here. Behaviorism receives high marks on one dimension -- its internal consistency.

Burrell and Morgan find a common core of meaning in functionalism, despite the heterogeneity which crept into the above narrative. They place the apparent diversity at the superficial level, the basic unity is underneath, especially at the level of assumptions. There, adherents share the common ontological view of the nature of society, and they observe and measure from the standpoint of the observer. They assume a continuing order and pattern in society. Their paradigm is geared to explaining what is and why the social fabric tends to hold together, even if they do allow for limited degrees of disorder. Their underlying conception is the emphasis upon the possibility of objectivity in explaining and predicting external reality. It assumes that scientific theories can be assessed objectively by reference to empirical evidence. The sociologist is seen as an observer who can act without affecting what is observed. The assumption is that there exists a scientifically objective formulary. Within the broad confines of these assumptions, variations do occur. The sociological theories within this meta-paradigm have been impacted by German idealism as we have seen and also by Marxism (as we have not seen).

Before leaving sociology behind, let us point to the continuing importance of functionalism to the American version of this discipline. To be sure, Burrell and Morgan attach a special quite broad meaning to the term, but this is a problem which we address below. There is evidence that functionalism achieved a near monopoly in American sociology in the 1950s and that its prominence continued into the 1960s. Oramaner examined copies of the <u>American Journal of Sociology</u> and the <u>American Sociological Review</u> for 1955 and 1970 to determine changes in the frequency of the authors cited. Any changes would be interpreted as changes in the popularity of paradigms. He was particularly interested in whether the citations of functionalists had declined between these two years. He found that they had, but that they still remained among the most often cited. Among the most popular authors cited in 1970 were Parsons and Merton,[5] both of whom were afforded prominent places in the presentation of functionalism by Burrell and Morgan. Thus we tie this latter version of the term to the general use of the term.

International Relations

We pass over other sociological paradigms inside and outside the United States to look at international relations theory in the United States. We return to competing sociological paradigms in the chapters which follow. International relations was put next, because of its similarity with our account of sociology. The discipline international relations witnessed a great expansion in the United States after World War II, a development congruent with her new position as a superpower. The discipline became international from the standpoint of the subject studied, but ethnocentric and inward looking from the standpoint of paradigms, communications, and her version of its history. We believe that our structures deal effectively with this apparent contradiction.

Like its colleagues, international relations is multiparadigmatic. Our principal task here is to present the "scientific" paradigm, which is the dominant one in the United States. Actually, we confine our remarks about it to those which will indicate the general direction which it has taken. The next section, devoted to American political science, a sister discipline, will give details which are applicable to international relations as well. Lijphart traces the emergence of this scientific paradigm, which he calls "behavioralism," to a "scientific revolution" which occurred in the 1950s.[6] This behavioral paradigm arose in the United States, and it can be contrasted with what Lijphart calls the traditional one, the latter having all the appearance of power politics or what we have described in a previous chapter as the balance of power. We cannot say that the behavioral one "took the place" of the traditional one in the sense of natural science. In social science, paradigms are not completely replaced, they only lose their rank in the multiparadigmatic setting. Like elephants, they tend to endure. And like rabbits, they tend to multiply. Behavioralism has become the predominant paradigm in the United States. Lijphart first gives a sketch of the traditional paradigm, which was dominant until the 1950s. We next devote a few sentences to it, space well spent for understanding the change to behavioralism. Lijphart pictures it as embracing the concept state sovereignty and international anarchy. It is state centric; it assumes that the actors in the international arena are states, not individuals or private groups, and certainly not classes. Each state is seen as being independent, except its prerogatives tend to be reduced by an inferior power position. International anarchy tends to be modified by a situation in which power is balanced, and by collective security. The traditional paradigm is realistic in the sense that a given state is seen as aggressive until its power is neutralized by countervailing power. When this occurs, international law can work. The question of world government may be viewed as part of the traditional paradigm or as part of a competing idealistic one. We take the latter view. Certainly the concept class struggle or imperialism is outside its parameters. These concepts belong to Marxism. The traditional paradigm generally used history and law as ways of approaching the subject.

Next we measure this traditional paradigm against the two dimensions of Burrell and Morgan, the better to compare it with the new behavioral paradigm. The traditional paradigm is compatible with the objective side of their subjective/objective dimension in three ways and incompatible in one. The concurrence is with realism (not nominalism) with determinism (not voluntarism) and with the nomothetic (not the ideographic). The traditional paradigm saw the subject matter of the discipline as being available to all and on the same essential terms. The symbolism of the balance of power, a big part of the traditional paradigm, suggests the determinism of this paradigm. The balance is the scale formerly used by a druggist, and it functions by the laws of gravity. The traditional paradigm sought to establish general covering type laws, applicable all around. One could object that it often used history, with its case studies, to accomplish this task. This use of history can disqualify the traditional paradigm from high points on the positivist scale, since that discipline was not recognized by Comte as a science.

The behavioralists set out in the 1950s to construct a scientific paradigm, in effect to move the discipline more to the objective side of the first dimension. As Lijphart says, many behavioralists say that their difference with the traditionalists is one of method, the substitution of the scientific method.[7] And they believe that they have done so -- an assertion hard to prove or disprove, since there is no generally accepted standard for the existence of "science" in social science. We do have available the first dimension of Burrell and Morgan, and the behavioralists in effect moved the discipline closer to its determinist pole. More interesting, they in effect moved the discipline closer to the regulation side of the second dimension. They moved it away from the side which contains conflict, coercion, and domination. They did this by such tactics as denying in their paradigm a clear cut distinction between the domestic and the foreign and between local violence and war. The same is found in the level of analysis problem in which distinctions between the domestic and the international are seen as matters of degree, not of kind.

Lijphart found that one of the first significant challenges to the traditional paradigm occurred in 1957 when Deutsch and his associates published a piece on the North Atlantic Treaty, in which they set forth the concept of the security community. If the traditionalists spoke of war and military alliances, Deutsch and his associates invented the concept the security community, an area where problems are resolved without resort to violence, where peace has broken out. These scholars helped spawn a whole peace industry, and as it grew, the paradigm was prodded in a benign direction, away from the focus on power and violence to a focus on peace and progress. If the traditional paradigm was useful for analyzing and rationalizing the policies of the European aristocracy, the new one was welcome to an expanding American capitalism -- indeed, an expanding American society. Peace research, social science dealing with violence and its absence, was praised for its ability to bring peace. The idea was at least as old as Comte, but it view, and its use was recommended at the international level.[8] But our main examples of this trend come from functionalism and integration.

It was Talcott Parsons himself who set forth the common values, upon which world order could be, in fact was being, built. Granting that trade often follows the flag, he denied that this was always the case. He found the existence of a certain amount of trade independent of government control, some order without this control. The same condition obtained for foreign travel, and he found proof for common values in the norms of international law covering both activities. He referred to other international relations and associations as evidence for the existence of an international moral order. Still other evidence he gave was the world acceptance of modernization.[9] This is the kind of reasoning that justified, and encouraged, if we use the examples above, trade, foreign travel, and public and private investments for modernization. If the classical economist saw foreign trade and investments as a way of increasing wealth and ultimately standards of living, those who followed Parsons saw them as a way of promoting world order and peace. One such school of thought grew up in the wake of Deutsch's scholarship. Putting its faith in the peaceful effect of almost all non-military transactions and with particular attention to communications, this group saw transactions as creating the security communities already alluded to. Deutsch was marching to the same tune as Cobden a century before. But his approach included all transactions, not just trade. Haas took a somewhat different view -- elitism, and he concentrated upon business, labor, and government elites as they worked together in the European Community to upgrade the common interest. He should be seen as a latter day St. Simon, but one loaded down with all the heavy jargon with which the new social science came equipped. Not only is capitalism not exploitative, but it upgrades the common interest and integrates the area involved. Capitalism is the liberator! The postwar American "science" of international relations provided a rationalization for the extension of things American overseas, not that this was necessarily the intention of its adherents.

Political Science

In this section we offer a brief look at political science, which in the American academic context is closely tied to international relations. The characteristics which we impute to political science can be applied in a general way to international relations as well. Certainly, the same general impact which international relations received at the hands of behavioralism was also experienced by political science. It became more "scientific," i.e. it veered closer to the determinist side of Burrell and Morgan's first dimension. Moreover, it has progressed quite far toward the regulative side of their second dimension, toward what we call benign social science to distinguish it from the malignant, radical side. This comes out in the new definitions of politics, in which the discipline is not framed in terms of a struggle for power as was the case formerly. The usual definition involves the notion that the discipline focuses upon the ultimate allocation of values.

In his 1966 presidential address to the assembled American Political Science Association, its president Gabriel Almond declared that "we are becoming a science".[10] The "we" referred to here was the American adherents to the discipline, a point made very clear in the remainder of the address. He argued quite openly that since the Americans make up the great preponderance of the world's political scientists, what they do the world of political science does. This kind of discourse has to be labelled "nationalist," but what concerns us most here are the components of the new American behavioral paradigm which allegedly had emerged. He saw it as the result of a Kuhnian revolution, and thus this was the scientific paradigm so long awaited. He identified it in the following way: the use of statistics; the use of probability theory; the differentiation and specification of variables; the use of systems analysis; and the use of a multi-linear theory of political development.

There is some discussion in the literature about what Kuhn meant by a paradigm (he obviously meant many things), but Almond's list certainly is not it. This list is really a conglomerate from which any number of faulted, "unscientific" paradigms can be -- actually have been -- created. Interesting is that virtually the whole list refers to the subjective/objective dimension of Burrell and Morgan -- the concern being what could be called the scientific interest. The first three of the list and the last one are concerned with this dimension. Statistics is used to quantify data and thus supposedly to set the stage for their more accurate use. Instead of giving information in a rough verbal order, we can present absolute sums or percentages, or at least rank orders. Probability theory is also touted as a great advance, because it allows for the exception -- which seems to be the rule in social science. We can thus have laws of social science, with exceptions built in better to accommodate exceptional human behavior. The "differentiation and specification" of variables refers to their careful use. One cannot argue with this principle. The last principle is an attempt to get away from one factor theories of development. Only one principle, the use of systems theory can be matched with the second dimension of Burrell and Morgan. It tends to the regulation side of the dimension -- to the side of equilibrium and status quo.

Somit and Tanenhaus and Easton have listed the characteristics of behavioralism and behavioral research in political science, and it is to these two lists that we now turn. We put them side by side, insofar as possible in a match up, in order to facilitate comparison. Easton's list is on the left, that of Somit and Tanenhaus on the right.

Easton	Somit and Tanenhaus
1. search for uniformities	1. emphasize observable phenomena
2. use of empirical tests	2. emphasize interdisciplinary research
3. use of greater theoretical	3. theory orientation sophistication
4. emphasis on basic research	4. emphasis on basic research
5. rigor in methods	5. rigor in methods
6. quantification	6. quantification
7. fact/value separation	7. fact/value separation
	8. the future as science

There is a striking similarity between the two lists -- four items are the same (numbers 4, 5, 6, and 7). In fact, the number threes, when explicated, have much in common. The other two on each side are compatible with each other, leaving #8 as the potential maverick. The emphasis in both lists is on the first dimension set forth by Burrell and Morgan. Behavioralism is, indeed, an attempt at being scientific. Its conservatism is unstated, implied. The first two of Easton -- the search for regularities and the use of empirical tests -- are well within the behavioral parameters. Somit and Tanenhaus set their first principle (emphasis on observable behavior) against the institutional approach.[11] They insist on studying the behavior of individuals or that of political aggregates. Their second point (the interdisciplinary approach) is buttressed with the argument that political behavior is only one kind of behavior, and its study could benefit from techniques developed in other disciplines. Numbers 3, 4, and 5 all address matters of great import to the faithful. Research should be more oriented to, or more sophisticatedly connected, with theory. Much of the theorizing has been at the middle range level, but systems analysis is available for those who want to try a larger view. Certainly, the behavioralist has tried to be rigorous (a famous word) in his application of science. He is so convinced of the need for the discipline to be scientific that he often embraces this goal at the expense of the discipline's historic role as an agent of social reform. Thus number 4, emphasizes basic research.

Evidence of quantification (#6) has been all too common in American political science in recent years. We are told that it allows greater accuracy, and, of course, it invites the use of sophisticated mathematical and statistical techniques. It is responsible for the creation of an industry, a highly capitalized one. And here it mirrors American business and the larger American society. Computers of increasing sophistication, together with loads of software and the latest statistical devices, all seem to be necessities for the quantifiers. Most behavioralists accept or accepted the fact-value separation (#7). The notion here is that social facts can be decided by social science, but values cannot be. Consequently, the social scientist should stick to the facts; or at least separate the two spheres, and give his professional opinion on the facts, separate from his personal value judgments. Easton himself did not make this separation.[12] Those who are status quo oriented have the tendency to revel in the facts, to cherish what exists as though it had moral value. Radicals are much less likely to do so. Despite what has just been said, the "post-behavioralists" have added values to what is sought. But they have the same scientific pretensions as the behavioralists. The last point of Somit and Tanenhaus is tribute paid to the social science myth. They allege that behavioralists believe that political science can ultimately become a science, but that it will be closer to biology than to either physics or chemistry. This prospect of maturity induces them to try harder in pushing political science along the road to this desired goal. We have treated this myth at some length in a previous chapter.

So far our analysis of American behavioralism in political science (and also in international relations) has placed these two disciplines in the same ideological setting with American functionalism. We do have a few additional traits to add to their characterization. Behavioralists are as famous for what they eschew as for what they embrace. They have rejected the institutional approach, as we have seen, but also the legal approach. International law and international organizations are held to be deficient as means to elucidate international relations. Another method to avoid is the historic method, which illuminates individual cases, but provides no laws. Behavioralism has a tendency to reduce social science to the psychological. It is not enough to divine how things are. The researcher must go beyond this to determine how the political actors think they are. This is a wholly different and much more complicated problem. Their research is full of references to images, attitudes, ideologies, and the like. Behavioralists have presented little persuasive evidence that they have solved the problem presented by these requirements. Certainly they have not in international relations. The focus of behavioralist research has been the middle range theory, the "small" theory presented in virtual isolation from the greater society. We believe that this is the case, despite the existence of systems analysis. The great holistic approaches are Marxism and traditional anthropology.

By now it is part of conventional wisdom to assert that behavioralism in American political science mutated to become postbehavioralism some time in the 1960s. This development represented a reawakening of values, the argument that science cannot be, or at least should not be, value free. But it has not led to the abandonment of the "scientific" commitment. Easton credits this development to the American cultural revolution, the effects of the Vietnam war, and the widespread influence of Kuhn's The Structure of Scientific Revolutions. He finds, moreover, that American political science is presently fragmented (he does not refer to the discipline overseas). Marxism has emerged, presenting various forms itself, and so has political economy, as the reader could imagine. American political science is thus doing its part to prevent the realization of the Millian dream. Easton believes that perhaps a majority of the American practitioners are still committed to behavioralism --actually postbehavioralism.

Economics

When we left American economics in the third chapter, it was recovering from the German onslaught of historicism -- a recovery which finally proved to be successful. It then returned to its own, inspired by British economics. Our first intention was to treat economics as if it were like any other social science. But then we discovered that it is special, i.e., that at least one economist had the courage openly to express its special attainments. It would be strange in an enterprise as human as social science if such ethnocentric feelings were not widespread and fervently held. Drucker is the pharisee referred to here, who stood in the back of the church and cried, "Father, we thank you that we economists are not like those other social scientists." Actually, he drew the distinction between the natural sciences and social science with respect to their ability to speak with authority. For example, a person trained in sociology, a discipline which has been around for almost two centuries, cannot speak with any more authority about society than anyone else. Drucker asked where this leaves economics "generally acknowledged to be the most 'scientific' of all the social sciences".[13] His reply was: certainly better than sociology, since economics does present a coherent body of theory which, when once mastered, provides an expertise which a non-economist does not possess. But he added that the body of undisputed economic theory is shrinking "before our very eyes." This countercurrent was registered because of the dissolution of the Keynesian consensus in the United States, an event discussed below. The reference to a coherent body of theory can be made only if one ignores Marxism, or pretends that it is not a social science. But pharisees are noted for their short vision.

Professor Lange sees the matter quite differently, perhaps because of his broad international experience. He found that for the more than the fifty years that preceded the bank crash of 1929 there were three paramount economic paradigms extent in Europe and the United States. They were the historical school, Marxism, and marginalism. The three schools "were so different in their views of the objects and the purposes of economics as almost to constitute different disciplines".[14] The historical school predominated in Germany, while the marginalist school emerged in the latter part of the nineteenth century to become the largest. Its predominance had been such (in Anglophone countries it had practically a monopoly) that certain economists identified it with then contemporary economic thought in general. Its approach is micro-economic, with a stress upon the individual's utilities and preferences. Value is based upon the act of exchange, undertaken by the parties for gain.[15] All parties benefit in terms of their subjective preferences from the exchange. This then generalizes into an optimal allocation of economic resources by means of the price mechanism. Production is incorporated into the theory as a special case of indirect exchange. Value arises from the interaction of individuals, based upon their psychological preferences. These individuals are presented as non-social beings, and how their preferences arise is a question outside the parameters of the theory. Its approach is thus "closed," ignoring as it does all of those techniques used, for example, in American society to influence the consumer.

We went into some detail with the marginalist approach, because it still is the dominant paradigm in the United States for micro-economics. It has served in this capacity for some one hundred years. After World War II, economics at the macro level in the United States, however, was taken over and all but monopolized by Keynesian analysis. Actually the two served side by side, each at its own level, until quite recently when the Keynesian dominance came unglued. Before turning to this, let us point out that marginal utility analysis leans way over toward the regulation side of the second dimension of Burrell and Morgan and away from the radical side. It is what we call a benign, conservative paradigm, not a malignant one. The common interest is served, everyone a party to trade benefits. And trade encompasses all economic activities: they all have the common blessing. Society, production, advertising all are dissolved into the safety of trade which upgrades the common interest. All society's problems -- strikes, racism, discrimination -- all these can be forgotten as we rivet our attention upon this jewel of the marketplace, the act of buying and selling. The obvious policy indicated is to let this marvelous mechanism of trade proceed, without the inefficiencies which government regulation introduces. Marginalism posits conservative assumptions; not surprisingly, the conclusions are of the same genre.

The reductionism of marginalism is the stuff which fuels economic conservatism, serving as the economic counterpart of the functionalism and integration described above. If the latter speaks of peace for all, the discourse of marginalism is the economic betterment of all. Kristol set forth its ideology in the form of a listing of "the bedrock truths about the human condition that were first comprehensively enunciated in the <u>Wealth of Nations</u>".[16] These included assertions of the widespread interest in material welfare; efforts to repress this "natural" interest lead to coercion; when allowed to flourish, this interest leads to economic growth; and everyone benefits, however unequally, from this growth; and the resulting expansion of the middle class leads to a liberal society and respect for human rights.

Lekachman, a critic, speaks of the conditioning which the recruit to American economics is likely to go through. Graduate programs so stress rationality, the maximization of benefits, and competition that graduate students are likely to forget that these are only heuristic devices, not portraits of business or consumer behavior. Lekachman wryly remarks that this is the point of an effective graduate program: "it enables the survivors to arise above the common sense with which no doubt they were endowed at birth".[17] Their training teaches them that tinkering with the economy, "artificial interferences," is likely to disturb its natural equilibrium, and ultimately interfere with human choice. Much as they dislike the enemies in wars on poverty and on racism, they are professionally wary of government actions in these areas, because these actions cannot be subjected to market tests. Lekachman lists the major parts of the ideology as faith in the dollar calculus, in human rationality, in value neutrality, and in equilibrium. All of these belong on the regulatory side of the second dimension of Burrell and Morgan.

Professor Lange argued that in the first decades of the twentieth century a divorce separated the economic theory of the universities from reality. This theory had nothing to offer, at least at the onset of the great depression, beyond the strange assertion that such a depression was impossible. What was needed was an economic theory, which if it could not explain reality, it would at least not contradict it. This was provided by Lord Keynes who formulated a macro-theory which set out to explain the depression, and in doing so, underwrote a whole new macro-economic industry. Micro-economics was left in the hands of the marginalists. The classical economist had ruled out a prolonged depression, because supply creates its own demand.[18] Wants were held to be insatiable, and through the circular flow of payments from suppliers to consumers and investors demand would create an equal supply, with, of course, the possibility of temporary gluts or shortfalls. But in the long run equilibrium would be re-established, and with no unemployment. Neoclassical economists refined and modified this explanation by using marginal analysis. Keynes' approach allowed that the deviations from equilibrium could persist for a long time, thus the depression. In a period of high unemployment, price levels would be "sticky" and nominal price levels would have a heavy impact. Keynes argued that the deviations from the supposed equilibrium could persist and that government intervention was necessary to provide full employment. Keynes' contribution lay in his drawing conclusions from this matter of "wage stickiness" and the problem of false signals given by the economy. He saw that the price of labor did not fall in the face of unemployment, as the neo-classicists had argued, and that this was a permanent feature of a modern economy. Keynes devised an explanation in macro terms, in such a way that "equilibrium" could be achieved at less than full employment.

Keynes thus introduced some dissonance into the dominant macro-economic model. Some persisting disequilibrium was possible -- thus it was "natural," and it required government action to correct. The Keynesian model pushed American economics away from the extreme right side, the regulatory side, of the second dimension of Burrell and Morgan. But what was called for was government reform, not government ownership -- enlightened regulation and liberalism, not socialism. Moreover, micro-economics was left untouched, wrapped up in its conservative cocoon. The Keynesian "revolution" was no revolution in the usual meaning of the term; it promoted state capitalism. It did make a growth industry of the discipline economics, if it was not one before. It is not that it pushed American economics farther toward the determinist side of the first dimension of Burrell and Morgan. Rather what it did was to spawn a highly capitalized, sophisticated national accounting system, devised for keeping track of national accounts and measuring the national output. After this caught on, the evening news in the United States would never be the same; it became highly quantified, and economists were in demand to explain the past and the future, as well as why what they had originally predicted did not occur. Administrations were given high marks when the national economy grew more (the g.n.p. grew more) than had been originally predicted.

The readers of this volume need not be told that national account figures are not hard facts, but that they are more in the nature of rough estimates, based upon somewhat logical assumptions. Their arbitrary nature is suggested by the fact that the capitalist world has one set of these concepts and measures, and the socialist world has a quite different set. Each is appropriate, if not "correct," because it reflects its respective ideology, which helps to establish its own brand of arbitrariness. The socialist accounting system does not count services in its total of production for the year, but only material production. This omission is profound, because in an advanced economy such as that of the United States, services account for the bulk of the "production." We next discuss only the capitalist accounting system and devote space only to gross national product (GNP), the most encompassing of the measures, from which most of the others can be derived. The gross national product is defined as the total market value of all final goods and services produced in a country in one year. To be counted, sales must pass through the market. It is as though the government added up the value of all the goods and services bought (or sold) in a year. The prices of everything are lumped together: food, rent, clothing, doctor bills -- but cigarettes, alcohol, and legal drugs as well. If the economist makes no judgement about the nature of the items, neither does he discount them because of their maldistribution. There are, however, other measures which deal with the distribution of income.

The national income accounts are basic for measuring the performance of economies. It is valuable to know if the GNP or the national income is increasing or not -- and federal administrations have been judged on this basis. While this is true, the measures are not absolute. Actually, a reduction in GNP may be judged beneficial under certain conditions. The measures are no substitute for judgement and what is good or bad ultimately is a philosophical issue. The measures must be seen in their ideological setting and within the context of their ultimately arbitrary definitions. This is only to say that there are instruments of social science. Like capitalism itself, GNP makes no value judgments about the moral worth of what is legally bought and sold. Business is business. Nor is there any option for the poor in the distribution of income. There are, however, arbitrary decisions -- more than those already aired, and strange results which arise from the characteristics mentioned and unmentioned. If Americans should spend more on cigarettes, the GNP would rise (unless they spend less on something else). Should marijuana be legalized, the GNP would go up.[19] Perhaps because these accounts are a male invention, the value of housework is not included in them. So when the American housewife left the nursery and the kitchen for the office, the American GNP went up. Perhaps the nation is better off, but perhaps it is not. The GNP does not provide the answer to this question.

We stand by what we said two paragraphs ago. Capitalist national accounting figures are useful, but they are ideological and somewhat, and necessarily, arbitrary. They must be used critically, with this in mind. The same precautions apply to socialist accounting measures. We seem to be reaching the same conclusion -- like a broken record -- but social science is like this. We do seem now to have something new to offer. It is that the Keynesian consensus among establishment economists in the United States is dissolving --and economics is in crisis (the record is stuck again if not broken). Drucker finds the reason for this in the inability of the Keynesian analysis to account for the productivity crisis in the United States and the United Kingdom, the "countries of the Keynesian true believers".[20] As we shall see below, Latin American scholars reject Keynes on other grounds. If we are to believe Drucker, the analysis which ostensibly was successful in explaining the depression had to be put to rest, because it could not explain the productivity crisis some forty years later. This hardly buttresses the claim, referred to earlier, of the special "scientific" status of economics. Lange would diminish this claim still further, his reference being to "academic economics." He claims that it not only failed to foretell the depression (it even held the depression to be impossible), but it also forecast the failure of the Soviet "experiment" and provided no viable plan for the development of the third world. We shall discuss soon the development plan which the first world did develop, and in an appropriate chapter its rejection by third world social scientists.

American economics thus seems currently to be in disarray, like American political science. Kristol finds that there are three surviving schools: the neo-Austrians, the post-Keynesians, and the radical humanists.[21] We shall not detail the beliefs of each. But we shall give a general view of the first two on the assumption that they probably have succeeded the Keynesians as the American establishment. They both reject the classic static macro-economic Keynesian model, but the post-Keynesians believe that such models, if made dynamic, are useful and could be used to plan and manage an economy. The neo-Austrians reject such models in any form, and strive to restrict economic meaning to what is taking place within an individual. The post-Keynesians argue that corporate monopolies and trade union oligopolies have destroyed free markets, and they, therefore, see the need for economic planning. The neo-Austrians tie their paradigm more to the entrepreneur than to the consumer. It seems that what we have here again is a paradigm for liberals and one for conservatives. Again, they are two faces to the American establishment. Both hold economics to be scientific. Even after the fall of Keynes from grace, American economics fits into the general mold we have been portraying.

The American Development Paradigm

This is the last of the dominant American paradigms which we will consider. The dominant development paradigm has been seen by American policy makers as having a direct bearing on the cold war. Arthur Schlesinger, Jr., remarked that both Washington and the American social scientist hoped to persuade developing countries to model their revolutions upon Locke, not Marx. W.W. Rostow, famous for his The Stages of Economic Growth: A Non-Communist Manifesto and for his contribution to the Vietnam War, considered one of the free world's greatest challenges to be to keep developing nations within its orbit. We have already seen that the dominant paradigms in American economics, political science, sociology, and international relations catered to the scientific as well as to a conservative or a liberal bias. These disciplines were the basis of American areas studies programs and its international relations programs as well. Not surprisingly, the same characteristics apply to the dominant American development paradigm, although we do not discuss its scientific pretensions. A study made of this paradigm for the period 1947 to 1968 concluded that it argued that modernization could be brought about by gradual change, administered by a well-educated elite, educated to democratic ideals.[22] A series of books at the time, directly or indirectly supported by the foundations, emphasized evolutionary change, political stability, institution building, and the mobilization of elites.

A group of American sociologists (Lerner, Levy, and Lipset) in their approach to development put emphasis upon those cultural and psychological factors which characterize modern man, i.e., which distinguish him from traditional man. They set up the polar notions of the traditional society and the modern society -- with the transitional in between. Their approach was essentially evolutionary -- traditional societies can eventually evolve into modern type societies, i.e., into the rational-legal developed Western types. They generally ignored the distorting influence of European colonialism or the present structural inequalities which interfere with development. Havighurst's study of Society and Education in Brazil overlooked the class inequalities which so characterize Brazilian society and which impede full development. The book concentrated upon exposing the shortcomings of the lower classes.[23] This reminds us of the cultural deficiency model to be discussed in the next section. This reminds us of the cultural deficiency model to be discussed in the next section. He pointed to the "passive fatalism" of these classes which seems to be the cause of their sorry condition. We will come across this notion again in our discussion of Chicano society. Paulo Freire, the famous Brazilian educator, also noted this trait among the deprived in his native land. But he put the blame for it on the myths which the upper classes propagate in order to maintain their position. His revolutionary pedagogy, as we shall see below, was designed to destroy this fatalism and to convince the deprived that they could control their destiny. But these revolutionary ideas were not a part of the American paradigm.

Rostow wrote his noted work <u>The Stages of Economic Growth: A Non-Communist Manifesto</u> during a "reflective year" away from his usual academic duties, made possible by a grant from the Carnegie Corporation. Latin American dependentistas love to contrast their approach with the three stages outlined in his work. They point out that the stages are ahistorical, and that development in this scheme is not impeded by international structures nor by the control and exigencies of central capitalism. They reject his benign approach, arguing that the role of the peripheral third world countries is assigned by the first world and for the latter's benefit, and so the peculiar historical situation and the concrete interests of the central capitalist states are all important in accounting for third world development and underdevelopment. Rostow also assumed the common interest -- the development of the third world served this interest. In terms of the second dimension of Burrell and Morgan, Rostow and his colleagues veer toward its regulatory side, the dependentistas toward the radical side.

If the American paradigm ignored the restraining and distorting influences of international structures, it was often charitable to the domestic social system as well. For example, in Latin America it played down or ignored the importance of class differences and the problem posed by stratified power relations. Dedicated to order and stability, it could hardly raise the issue of the controlling power of elites which obstruct development or which reserve almost all of its benefits for themselves. Revolution or dramatic social change was not a part of the paradigm. In fact, the theory tended to pander to domestic elite interests. The emphasis was put upon the training of high-level "professionals" who were to play key roles in the development process. This notion helped induce, or aided the rationalization of, higher allocations for the universities in India and other countries. Economists made the argument to fund these institutions at the cost of the "lower" grades and at the expense of equity and justice.[24] The paradigm thus tended to reinforce the existing unequal distribution of higher educational benefits.

A unique contribution by American economists to the paradigm under discussion was the theory of human capital and the related human resources theory of development. We referred to the first theory in our second chapter, but we develop the notion further here. The theory of human capital received wide currency after the Ashby Commission study of Nigerian manpower needs and their subsequent projection. The efforts of Schultz and his followers at Chicago University were widely publicized, and educational needs were touted as prerequisites for growth. They became a norm in the field of development. The campaign was orchestrated by the Ford Foundation and the Carnegie Corporation which convened a conference on the subject, and a publication of Harbison and Myers in 1964 sought to legitimize this component of development.[25] Again, this theory looks to the internal situation within third world countries for problems to correct in order to promote development. To develop requires more funds for the universities -- usually this means more subsidies for the higher education of the upper classes. The theory helps to forge links between these "professionals" in the third world and the United States, thus serving US policy interests and those of her dominant elites.

The emphasis in the above discussion is on the early postwar period, and much has happened since then. It is not too much to say that development theory by now is in crisis. It thus follows the lead of American economics and political science. The crisis goes beyond academe. Third world governments have espoused the cause against the American paradigm, and the United Nations and its agencies regularly play host to such complaints. We have more to say about this in our chapter on the third world (chapter 8).

Chicano and Black Social Science

This concludes the presentation of the dominant paradigms in several disciplines in the United States. These paradigms were pictured here as having both a topical interest and a geographic one as well. We classified them based upon two large dimensions, and we tied all of them geographically to the United States, although in reality they can be found elsewhere as well. This, the second part of the chapter, has a quite different tale to tell. Geographically, it still clings to the United States, but paradigmatically we now move over to the radical side of the second dimension, ideologically speaking close to the third world. We are also reminded of the early anthropology, which held European culture to be supreme and native cultures to be inferior. This spirit lives on in culture deficiency models -- the inferior cultures in this chapter being the Chicano and the black. The two centers of attention are black and Chicano social science; only a brief reference is made to female social science. The rationale for including these types of social science here is geographic, both types are found in the United States, and in a strange way they are quite home grown and authentically American. Neither the blacks nor the Chicanos have received much benefit from the great melting pot, which in a few generations seems to convert most immigrants into what looks and sounds like a common, standardized product. The Chicanos made their initial contact with American dominion, not by ship, but by virtue of conquest. The blacks came by ship, but not in search of freedom and money, rather in chains by virtue of slavery. What followed in both cases provides a fitting background for the social sciences depicted here. Also relevant was our discussion above of social Darwinism and of Burgess' view of the Indian. The reputed callousness of mainstream social science to the concerns, and even to the humanity, of the black and the Chicano have been major reasons for their desire to found their own social science, to create something really indigenous. The Trojan horse which would overturn establishment social science can be found in the third world, but also in the homeland.

This brings us to the definition of black or Chicano social science. Each can be given a minimum definition which means that existing social science will be called upon to use its present paradigms perhaps with some modification for the study of blacks or Chicanos. The maximum definition refers, however, to the creation of a new social science, the indigenization of the enterprise. A variation of this indigenization is research by the peoples involved, the emic rather than the etic. The emic/etic dichotomy here refers to race or ethnic group. Zinn gives a minimum definition in her valuable article on the possibility of constructing a sociological perspective better to study the Chicano. She argues that such a paradigm would include colonial theories and also micro theories which deal with oppression on a day-to-day level.[26] She quotes C. Wright Mills to the effect that the sociological imagination is needed for such a paradigm -- structure, history, and personality all can contribute to the new paradigm. She would use all the tools of sociology, and of the other social sciences, to illuminate the subject. But this is not enough to satisfy Mirande who calls this minimum approach of using existing sociological theories "the sociology of Chicanos." This he contrasts with his proposal, "Chicano sociology" which would be the implementation of what we call the maximum approach. He calls for a new construction, not a patchwork taken from what an existing sociology has to offer. In its own perverse way, this would be an American construction, something which arose as a reaction to American oppression. Mirande argues that the proposal to construct the sociology of Chicanos does not recognize the fundamental cleavage which separates the Chicano from Anglo society. By highlighting the political aspects of the disciplines, his arguments are very much within the spirit of the multinational version of social science. He argues for a partisan sociology, but, even more interesting, for one based on Chicano values. He wants created paradigms or theoretical frameworks consistent with the Chicano world view and responsive to the nuances of Chicano culture. His proposal is to develop a Chicano sociology with its own distinctive theories, methods, and paradigms.[27] He would not make the Chicano fit existing theories, but rather the theories would be created to fit the Chicano world view. These theories have not as yet been developed, but Mirande found some current research methods more in accord with this world view than others. Field research and participant observation appear consonant with this world view, but the methodology must not draw a distinction between participation and observation, nor between truth and feeling. The researcher must, of course, be allowed to be a partisan and an advocate of the Chicano cause.

There are thus these quite contrary views of what is Chicano and what is black social science. There are those who insist that a new social science must be created, whereas others, the minimalists, think that parts of existing social science can do the job. There is no airtight distinction between the two, some overlap necessarily exists between creation and the rearrangement of the existing, but the distinction is formidable. Watson has added to our understanding of the phenomenon with his definition of black sociology. He sets forth for it three characteristics: its primary focus is black social behavior; it is committed to the liberation of the blacks; and it is performed by black sociologists.[28] What is crucial in this definition is the last point. Black sociology must be performed by blacks. In his discussion, Watson does speak of the construction of new theories which will help to understand black behavior, but he makes explicit the personnel requirement. In this view, non-blacks cannot understand the black condition, nor can they do creditable research on the subject matter. Mirande did not explicitly restrict Chicano sociology to Chicano practitioners, but perhaps this restriction is implied in the requirement that the theory be based on the Chicano world view. In any case, to restrict research to practitioners of the minority group must be counted as part of the maximalist view of the paradigm as contrasted with a minimalist view. The same basic issues raised here emerge with the creation of third world social science as we shall see below.

Those who subscribe to the positivist position cannot accept the maximalist position as outlined above. Just as there cannot be a Chicano physics or a black chemistry, so there cannot be a female sociology or a black psychology. Positivists get fidgety even when a woman speaks of the feminine perspective in social science, for to them facts are available to all on the same terms and with the same outer wrappings. The black, the Chicano, or the feminist often start their analysis by complaining of the unfairness or the blindness of mainstream social scientists. Eisenstein took a similar tack in evaluating Matthews' view of feminism in sociology. Her point of criticism was Matthews unexamined assumption that sociology is a science, whereas feminism is an ideology.[29] The criticism rejected this view of sociology -- arguing that sociology has been biased in proceeding from a patriarchal point of view. Feminism owns up to its bias, and charges that insofar as sociology has proceeded from a patriarchal point of view, it is ideological as well. This candor is often found among third world social scientists, and it receives a warm welcome here.

The bill of particulars brought by these national aberrants against mainline American social science is a long and painful one. We suspect that the black list is as ugly as any, but we restrict our comments to two samples from it. The first is the neglect of W.E.B. Du Bois' empirical study of black living conditions in Philadelphia. This man, of course, is famous as the founder of the NAACP, and also as a black who actually did go back to Africa in his later years. He was a Ph.D. from Harvard, who had studied social science at the University of Berlin in the 1890s, the same time when many white Americans did the same. Before founding the NAACP, he went through an empirical phase whose high point was a fifteen month study of the black in Philadelphia.

He had decided "to put science into sociology through the study of the conditions and the problems of my own group." But he received no recognition from mainstream sociology for his efforts, and he was relegated to the periphery of the profession. "Except for reasons of racial prejudice, it is difficult to account for his being shunted aside".[30] He gave up on social science as a way of helping his people, and he turned to social action. Whether his neglect was racial prejudice is, of course, hard to determine, but the period referred to is one when racist social science and those who tilted in that direction were so popular. Perhaps the point which should be made is that the voguish racist platitudes of the then current stars gained currency at the expense of an admitted imperfect study, but one which was based on considerable research.

A more telling criticism is the black indictment of the research findings and recommendations of contemporary liberal social scientists. Theories which designate blacks as genetically inferior are no longer widely held. The more liberal view has gained currency that black people are culturally deprived and psychologically maladjusted and thus unable to compete in a white society. White describes the white researchers' encounter with a black situation and how they are likely to misread and to undervalue what they experience. Upon entering the black home, these researchers will notice a high noise level and Jet and Ebony scattered around rather than Harper's and The Atlantic Monthly. The non-standard English heard will be seen as bad grammar, not as a legitimate alternate dialect. The toughness of the children encountered, their ability to survive in an oftentimes hostile world of bill collectors, building superintendents, pimps, whores, sickness, and death will not be properly valued. The black family will be judged by white standards and thus misjudged and undervalued. If it is fatherless, the children, especially the boys, will be seen as nurturing psychological hangups. What may not be noticed is the extended nature of the family -- the comings and goings of uncles, aunts, brothers, sisters, deacons, etc.[31] A wide variety of adults and children participate in the childrearing process, so that the black child may avoid some of the problems of the more fortunate white children. Black children may emerge with a healthier psyche than whites who come from families with extremely rigid distinctions between male and female roles and duties. Another distinction, and one which could trouble the white researcher, is the hero model of the black child. The dominant white culture is steeped in the infallible hero, who scores his triumphs with godlike skill, and follows all the rules. In black culture, the hero is the brother who beats the system, never mind the rules, and gets away with it. Obviously, there are two contrary ways of interpreting black reality and opposite views here of the virtues of the system which produces the rules.

White used these examples to make his case that what is needed for a correct psychological analysis of black life styles is the framework of black experience. He found this need to be especially urgent for education, where the teacher's awareness of the strengths of black culture, rather than constant reminders of weakness, would aid the educational process. We leave the white researcher behind, perplexed though he must continue to be, to look in on his Anglo colleague, equally perplexed and also unduly critical, this time in the presence of Chicano culture. The negative evaluation of mainstream social science by those who would construct a Chicano social science is so similar to that of those who would construct a black social science that we can get on with the former while making comments applicable to the latter. The similarity exists despite the fact that black social science predates its Chicano counterpart by over 60 years -- the latter coming along only in the 1960s. Interesting is the fact that Latin American dependency theory emerged in this same decade as well. Cultural deficiency models were the common approaches used prior to 1960 to analyze Chicano behavior, the same approach used with such a devastating effect on the self-esteem of the black community. Culture can refer to the subjective dispositions which people hold in common, while social organization involves externalized, physical action regularly occurring among people. According to mainstream social scientists, Chicano behavior was caused by Chicano culture. It was held to be the consequence of deficiencies in Chicano values and lifestyle, rather than resulting from social organization, such things as structural discrimination. Just as the black family was singled out for special blame, so was the Chicano family. It was not faulted, because it is single headed and matriarchal, but rather because it is traditional and thus supposedly hinders modernization. The parallel in the two indictments should be obvious as we proceed. The problems experienced by both communities were held to arise from deficiencies in their respective cultures, not from the racism and the wage discrimination imposed by American society. The Chicano family did not serve as a refuge in an unfriendly world as Chicano sociology was to claim later, but was presented as an impediment to the adoption of an Anglo lifestyle, i.e., the latter serving as the vehicle for their equality and acceptance by the melting pot.

The mainstream portrait inspired by the cultural deficiency model in turn inspired the attempts to found a Chicano social science. The Chicanos were portrayed as somnolent, passive, and fatalistic, ahistorical or at best with a history not worth recounting. Their problems were held to be self-generated, due to their own culture. Their progress continues to be retarded by their large traditional families. Chicano sons are helpless victims of parental overindulgence. Chicanos were seen as a passive people, perhaps due to their religion, and they are often lazy. This was captured in those pictures of the Mexican or Chicano asleep, shaded by a tree or by his very large sombrero. Romano sarcastically refers to this social science portrait as a caricature of a world populated by vegetables, who are born, resign themselves to suffering, and then lay down to die quietly when their time comes.[32] Moreover, all the vegetables are seen as the same -- there is no variety amongst them. Romano asserts that the Chicano social scientist has found this portrait, i.e., mainstream literature on Chicanos, to be "sadly and uniformly wanting, on occasion spurious, and in other instances out-and-out distorted".[33] He judged the present situation to be unique in that those heretofore studied are now studying the studiers -- and he felt that this would introduce new perspectives for the discipline.

The situation is not unique as Romano imagined, a similar process based on a similar situation is unfolding in the third world. There, as we have seen, the first world blames the lack of development upon local cultures, not international structures, and third world social scientists are revolting against these structures. In one article Romano argued that the above portrait of the Chicano is false, in another that the portrait is not in accord with the Chicano self-image. Although ontologically separate, these two versions in practice come to the same thing for our purposes. Romano claims that Chicanos are pluralistic, and far from being ahistorical and docile, they have been active in the labor movement on a scale that has required the intervention of the US Army. They have created cooperatives, and they have their own dialect. For 50 years they have struggled for bilingual education, have published their own newspapers, and have worked to become bilingual. Romano concluded that the then contemporary (1968) mainline social scientists were perpetuating the very same opinions of Chicano culture current during the days of the American frontier and during the Mexican-

American War. These opinions obliterate the history and the historical significance of the Chicanos, as well as their claim to legitimacy in society.

The Chicano and the black social scientist reject any claim of mainstream social science to objectivity. It had its chance, and in their view it failed miserably. So what is needed is a new social science: (1) either the minimalist type, a collection of existing theories; or (2) the maximalist type, the creation of new paradigms based on contrary world views. Obviously, the first option is the easier one -- since Marxism and colonial theory are readily available for the task. Another variation is to confine research to the minority itself -- the center feature of Watson's proposal. We call this below indigenization of personnel to contrast it with the indigenization of paradigms, which is the maximalist position referred to above. There is no hiding the fact that forging new paradigms is a difficult task, time consuming and money consuming. Where is the government or the Ford Foundation to finance such a project? Minority paradigms should have a harder time of it than a third world paradigm, because they lack government support. It goes without saying that the multinational version recognizes their legitimacy as social science. But this is small consolation compared with the political opposition bound to be encountered, also that of mainstream social science.

Summary and Discussion

This ends the first of four chapters on social science as a multi-paradigmatic phenomenon. Actually in the interest of economy, we combine this aspect of social science with the geographic. The result in the main section of this chapter was a combination of the American and scientific/status quo constructions. This combination did little violence to reality, because it is those very paradigms which pretend to be the most scientific and which are best at protecting the essential status quo which is dominant in the United States. We sought to make this connection in the major section of this chapter, where we discussed functionalism in American sociology; behavioralism in American political science and international relations; Keynesianism and marginal utility analysis in American economics; and the American "technocratic" development paradigm. Each was measured against two dimensions -- the first called "subjective/objective" and the second "regulation/radical change." All paradigms were found to be on the objective side of the first dimension and on the regulation side of the second. We characterize such constructions scientific/status quo paradigms. Certainly, their characteristics are congruent with a science-loving superpower, whose reach has extended to the far corners of the free world. The paradigms tend to bless a myriad of relations by claiming that they serve a common global interest. The claim is legitimized as being "scientific," those disagreeing are condemned as being unscientific.

This chapter again looks to the foundations as the generous and continuing patrons of the dominant paradigms. We thus continued with a subject which had been broached in the second chapter. We suspect that by now the issue of "dirty money" is a non-issue, in a contemporary specialized, technocratic society where the fragmentation of responsibility is such as to have a marked cleansing effect upon almost everything and anything. The connection of the foundation with business and government elites seemed better established in this chapter, since its personnel cross up and back among the three types of service. We saw again that foundation support for dominant paradigms is definitely of the liberal sort -- the subsidization of favorite paradigms and their partisans is the modus operandi, not anything "undemocratic" like censorship. This modus operandi reminds us that we are practicing the political economy of social science, but government is also part of this liberal process. Functionalism, behavioralism, Keynesianism, and the American development paradigm all seem to be in crisis, i.e., their dominance is more and more diminishing. This parallels a decline in relative US power, and it bodes ill for the realization of the Millian dream.

The lesser half of this chapter stayed anchored in the United States, but it looked to those black and Chicano social scientists who are in rebellion against mainstream social science. They argue that it misrepresents and undervalues these minority communities. Far from being objective and scientific, it is biased, if not slanderous, and it has forfeited any right to investigate them further. What is needed is new social science, either radical ones based on the existing or new ones grounded in the world view of the minority being studied. In the lesser half of the chapter, the parallel between the geographic and the paradigmatic interest broke down, a fact which should remind us that these interests are only roughly parallel. They fit together better in the upcoming chapter. This last statement is vintage pre-1989 -- and it has diminishing meaning at this writing. The present chapter serves as an introduction to Chapter VIII where we encounter colonialism, but not the internal variety. It is the more dangerous external variety, which is more likely to attract the support of powerful dominant local elites, and thus it can have much more impact on the future of our subjects. The Chicano and black paradigms which we investigated veered toward the radical pole of the first dimension and toward the subjective side of the second. Both locations are logical, the latter because these dissidents must first break down the mainstream's exclusive scientific claim if they are to get a hearing. We refer the reader to the example above of the feminist attempt to do this. But social scientists, like the subjects they study, are a perverse bunch -- someone always escapes from the generalizations or categories which we would impose upon them. Thus Hayes argues that mainstream American psychology is not scientific, not an atypical statement, but wait for the rest. Its elite posture has given sanction to the use of pre- and non-scientific concepts in explaining the behavior of black people. It has moved from demonology to ids, egos, and superegos, to a variety of constructs such as personality and intelligence, which are no more observable or objective than the demons whose place they took.[34] The task of black psychology is to destroy the illusion of science "under which Western psychology presently hides its biases." Hayes would construct a "radical black behaviorism" in the traditions of empiricism, operationalism, and logical positivism. His approach is different in that he would arrogate to black psychology the hardest of the hard core "objectivist paradigms." Whereas most dissidents proclaim the need for a radical paradigm or one inspired by their Weltanschauung, Hayes would steal the "science" of social science from the establishment.

This chapter represents a breakpoint in our analysis -- from a discussion of the nature and chief characteristics of our disciplines to the more specific presentation of their different meta-paradigms. We used the work of Burrell and Morgan to establish these meta-paradigms, whose elucidation will continue on in the following two chapters. We found these meta-paradigms to be congenial to our analysis and congruent with the work of Kuhn. The divisions they represent tend to be ideological chasms, the separation being fundamental and philosophical. This should be obvious in the contrast between the dominant American paradigms in this chapter and the Soviet favorites in the next chapter. The dominant paradigms in this section tended to support the extension of the United States and her dominant elites. We shall soon see that Soviet paradigms play this same role for Soviet elites. Functionalism is an essentially conservative paradigm, and its use in the United States justifies the status quo. It was put to service in international relations theory to persuade that foreign transactions promote peace, e.g. form a security community. The dominant economics and development paradigms assured that these transactions would promote the common economic welfare, and functionalism enriched the arguments with promises of peace.

The chapter indicated that these promises were the reworked efforts of predecessors of the nineteenth century. Such bright hopes had already been set forth by Cobden, St. Simon, and Comte. The American behavioralist reworked these notions with the intent of making the methodology more scientific. American development theory centered its analysis upon local cultures -- traditional ones impeded progress, not international structures. Development was held to be for the common good, and could be attained without benefit of revolution. U.S. elites reached out to the rich and to the advantaged in the third world, and the theory of human capital, as presented, tended to rationalize support for these groups. Higher education, even study abroad, took precedence over basic literacy. The chapter contained a quote which argued that economics is more scientific than sociology. The skeptic might well question this when recalling the rise and the decline of the Keynesian analysis. We are told that this analysis arose because it explained the great depression, (the dominant paradigm held the depression to be impossible!), but it declined because it failed to explain the productivity crisis. Economics itself is now in crisis. Our analysis revealed that national capitalist account statistics are not hard facts, rather they are ideological, and they differ from those used in socialist countries. Both sets are ideological, useful, but also subject to criticism. Indeed, both are the products of social science.

NOTES

1.   Bernard Berelson, "Behavioral Sciences", The International
        Encyclopedia of Social Sciences, 2 (New York: Macmillan,
        1968), 41-45.

2.   Henry W. Ehrmann (Ed.), The Teaching of the Social Science
        in the United States, (Paris: UNESCO, 1954), 15.

3.   Edward H. Berman, The Influence of the Carnegie, Ford, and
        Rockefeller Foundations on American Foreign Policy: The
        Ideology of Philanthropy, (Albany: State University of New
        York Press, 1983), 32.

4.   Gibson Burrell and Gareth Morgan, Sociological Paradigms
        and Organizational Analysis: Elements of the Sociology of
        Corporate Life, (London: Heinemann, 1979), 6.

5.   Mark Oramaner, "Cognitive Consensus in Recent Mainstreet
        American Sociology: An Empirical Analysis" Scientometrics,
        3 (1981), 80.

6.   Arend Lijphart, "The Structure of the Theoretical Revolution
        in International Relations," International Studies Quarterly, 18
        (1974), 59.

7.   Ibid., 62.

8.   Jan Tinbergen, "The Need for an Ambitious Innovation of the
        World Order", Journal of International Affairs, 31, (1977),
        305.

9.   Talcott Parsons, "Order and Community in the International
        Social System", James N. Rosenau (ed.) International Politics

and Foreign Policy: A Reader in Research and Theory, (New York: Free Press, 1961), 127.

10.   Gabriel A. Almond, "Political Theory and Political Science", The American Political Science Review, 60 (1966), 869.

11.   Albert Somit and Joseph Tanenhaus, The Development of American Political Science: From Burgess to Behavioralism, (Boston: Allyn and Bacon, 1967), 178.

12.   David Easton, "Political Science in the United States: Past and Present," International Political Science Review, 6 (1985), 138.

13.   Peter F. Drucker, Toward the Next Economics, and Other Essays, (New York: Harper and Row, 1981), 202.

14.   Oscar Lange, "La Science Economique," Tendencies Principles de la Recherche dans les Sciences Sociales et Humaines, Premier Partie, Sciences Sociales (Paris: UNESCO, 1970), 293.

15.   Edeard J. Nell, "Value and Capital in Marxian Economics", The Crisis in Economic Theory, Daniel Bell and Irving Kristol (eds.), (New York: Basic Books, 1981), 174.

16.   Irving Kristol, "Rationalism in Economics", The Crisis in Economic Theory, Daniel Bell and Irving Kristol (eds.), (New York: Basic Books, 1981), 218.

17.   Robert Lekachman, Economists at Bay: Why the Experts will Never Solve Your Problems, (New York: McGraw Hill, 1976), 108.

18.   Daniel Bell, The Social Science Since the Second World War, (New Brunswick, NJ: Transaction Books, 1982), 66.

19.   Lekachman, 113.

20.   Drucker, 11.

21.   Kristol, 210.

22.   Berman, 112.

23.   Ibid., 118.

24.   Ibid., 122.

25.   Ibid., 116.

26.   Maxine Baca Zinn, "Sociological Theory in Emergent Chicago Perspectives", Pacific Sociological Review, 24 (1981), 168.

27.   Alfredo Mirande, "Sociology of Chicanos or Chicano Sociology", Pacific Sociological Review, 25 (1982), 503.

28.   Wilbur H. Watson, "The Idea of Black Sociology: Its Cultural and Political Significance", The American Sociologist," (1976), 121.

29.   Sarah H. Mattews, "Rethinking Sociology Through A Feminist Perspective", The American Sociologist, 17 (1982), 36.

30.   Elliott Rudwick, "Note on a Forgotten Black Sociologist: W.E.B. Du Bois and the Sociological Profession", American Sociologist, 4 (1969), 305.

31.   Joseph L. White, "Toward a Black Psychology", Black Psychology, Reginald L. Jones (ed.), (New York: Harper & Row, 1980), 7.

32.   Octavio I. Romano, "The Anthropology and Sociology of the Mexican-Americans: The Distortion of Mexican-American History," El Grito, 8 (1968), 23.

33.   Ibid., 12.

34. William A. Hayes, "Radical Black Behaviorism", Reginald L. Jones (ed.), <u>Black Psychology</u> (N.Y.: Harper and Row, 1980), 40.

CHAPTER VI

RADICAL MARXISM: THE SOCIAL SCIENCE
OF THE SECOND WORLD

This is the second chapter devoted to demonstrating the multi-paradigmatic nature of social science, while at the same time exposing its prime geographic locations. In the past, these strands fit together well, radical Marxism, being the dominant paradigm throughout the geographic domain of the second world. This statement refers to the immediate past, and it has less validity as time goes by. The regimes of Eastern Europe changed dramatically in 1989, and with the transformation social science has changed also. The disciplines in the Soviet Union are also changing. Radical humanism and interpretivism have been put aside for the upcoming chapter. Here we will meet the counterpart of the young American professor of the first chapter, equally dogmatic, but with a quite contrary ideology. While radical Marxism sat well in the second world, the paradigm has not been identical in every part of the domain, China since 1978 being an obvious divergent area. The other two parts of the domain, the Soviet Union and Eastern Europe, were more homogeneous, but since Gorbachev's rise to power social science is in flux in the Soviet Union, and it has undergone a revolution in Eastern Europe. We continue in this chapter to apply the typology of Burrell and Morgan. This provides continuity for our narrative, but it must be supplemented with more specific and detailed studies of the social science of the area. Moreover, the differences which separate first and second world social science are not confined to the paradigm. They extend also to the proper role of our subjects in society, a role which has been an issue between Western Marxism and mainline social science as well. This became obvious in our historical sketch in the third chapter. We have no right to pattern our view of the proper role of the social sciences after American practice, or any other national practice for that matter, and then impose this common role upon the second world. This would not be in the spirit of the multinational version of social science. Each area has the right to work out its own version of this role, subject, of course, to outside evaluation and criticism. This does not deny the fact that the second world deserves criticism for its often shoddy treatment of our subjects.

The second world is that area where the impact of the political and other dominant elites upon our disciplines has been the most obvious and the strongest. In the first world, these elites exercise impact mainly through their domination of education and their subsidization of favorite paradigms and research findings. This restrictive pattern is liberal, more like a pattern of encouragement -- the pampering and petting of what is favored more so than the prohibition of what is opposed. The liberal, first world approach is looser -- some radicals manage to slip through the net, and their status receives the basis for a measure of protection from the liberal myth of freedom. In the second world, the "liberal approach" is used, but especially in the past it has been supplemented by direct control, the prohibition of unwelcome paradigms. Unfortunately for our disciplines, there has been a longstanding antagonism between Marxism and mainstream social science, as we demonstrated in Chapter III. Sometimes mainstream social science has been equated with a narrow view of social science which excluded Marxist analysis. Our disciplines have had a doubly hard time in the second world. When they have been tolerated, they have been tightly controlled, but at times they have not even been tolerated. This was the case during most of the long, dreary Stalinist period and during the Cultural Revolution in China. Instances of some kind of practical research did occur at these times, but the social sciences as academic disciplines were gutted.

This chapter has two main parts and two lesser ones. The first of the former is our attempt to explicate radical Marxism, the second major part sketches the story of the disciplines in the Soviet Union and Eastern Europe. The most recent events in this last domain have not been taken into account. In order to accomplish our first purpose, however, we give a brief account of Marxism as it came from its founder. This serves as an introduction to both radical Marxism, developed in this chapter, and humanistic Marxism, the subject of part of the following chapter. Marx seems to have shifted from one to the other during his life. The chapter ends with a short account of Chinese social science and another which speaks of the social science cold war and the social science diplomacy of this war.

The Marxism of Karl Marx

In a real sense, we are correct in having saved the discussion of the historical Marx for this chapter, a non-historical one. Whereas there are no extant Comteans or Spencerians, currently there are a large number and many kinds of Marxists. The following short historical sketch is justified, if only because it should indicate that the Marxism of Marx was an open system, sometimes with key concepts left undefined. Moreover, the sketch will show that there is more than one Marxism which came from Marx himself. Two stand out: that of the young and that of the mature Marx. On both sides of his family, Karl Marx descended from illustrious rabbis, but his father converted to Lutheranism to save his job with the Prussian state. Karl later showed that he would not "sell out" so easily. He was baptized Lutheran, but became a notorious atheist. This was a hallmark of the group which he joined at the University of Berlin, the young Hegelians. Hegel had enshrined the Christian German state of Prussia as the highest point of human history to that time, but he had also presented a dialectic which sought to negate in order to bring about change and development toward greater rationality. The young Hegelian approach was to use the dialectic to criticize all social institutions, so that they would become more rational. Marx became an expert at criticism and invective, and later he would find a better source of change than rationality; namely, the proletariat. The young Hegelians looked to world revolution to establish the conditions such that mankind could live like the gods. In 1844 Marx wrote the Economic and Philosophical Manuscripts, a publication which was unknown until the 1930s, and not widely circulated until after World War II. The manuscripts reveal Marx as a humanist, who in one sense belongs in the next chapter, but he did advocate world revolution. The "young Marx" (he was 26 at the time) called for the moral regeneration of humanity through world revolution. He set forth the theme of the alienation and the loneliness of modern mankind, exhorted to authenticity, and appealed against the worship of money.[1] But the young Marx changed to become the "mature Marx," when two years later in 1846 he published the German Ideology. Beginning with this publication, Marx sets forth a new scenario of world history as class struggle, to be surpassed by a proletarian revolution and a classless society. The mature Marx preserved the humanistic goals, but added an analysis cast in the context of the impersonal concepts of labor, capital, modes of production, and inevitable scientific laws. His analysis thus shifted more to the objective pole of the subjective/objective dimension. Nonetheless, some of his followers interpret him in a humanistic manner.

The discovery of the Economic and Philosophic Manuscripts has given a whole new face to Marxism, parallel to what is called here humanistic Marxism. This equates roughly with Western Marxism as well. The manuscripts have provided social scientists with a precious source for studying alienation and its elimination, and they have facilitated postwar recruitment to Marxism. Interesting is that we can pin point the "maturing of Marx," an event which occurred some time between 1844 and 1846, i.e., between his 26th and his 28th year. We next turn to some elaboration of the difference, this to be followed by a statement of radical Marxism.

The year before the appearance of the manuscripts, Marx published the Jewish Question. In it he argued that Judaism is no longer a religion in the traditional sense of the term or even a racial group, but it has become a code of practical need, selfishness, and egotism. The modern commercial world is a world of money worship, and this worship of money he equated with Judaism. He found mankind to be living within the alien world of commerce, in which money had dethroned all other gods. Everything is expressed in its terms, and it has deprived all things of their intrinsic worth. It rules mankind, and he worships it. With Marx, it turns out that this worship is not confined to Jews, but Christianity has fallen into line as well. The only way to deal with the Jewish question, therefore, is to recognize Judaism as "a universal antisocial element of the present time".[2] A social revolution would make the Jew impossible, and would emancipate Christianity from the worship of money and thus from economic alienation.

In the Economic and Philosophical Manuscripts Marx spoke at great length of the alienation of mankind. This basic notion came from Hegel. If Marx had claimed to be a sociologist, he should have been quoting Comte, not Hegel. But Marx made no such claim, even if he took up those subjects with which the sociologist is concerned. Nor did he pretend to be an economist either. He referred to himself in Das Kapital as "a critic of political economy." His historical materialism was to be the science of society, but not sociology as distinct from philosophy, history, or political economy.[3] Hegel found the source of alienation in the separation of the spirit from its true essence, and the course of history was seen as being the process whereby spirit achieves its self-realization. Marx turned this around to center on humankind, the producer and creator of material and non-material objects, repossessing its own essence and achieving self-realization in the course of history. Marx also rejected Hegel's view of humankind as spirit, substituting for spirit a natural being within a world of natural and manufactured articles. Humankind is a creative being that accumulates material and cultural objects, who is actualized through human labor. But when the human species looks around it sees alien goods in a hostile world. This because humankind is forced to produce under the servitude of money, not in spontaneous self-determination. Capitalism is inhuman, because it deprives one of essence, the calling which consists in conscious and free activity. Marx associated with capitalism various forms of alienation -- the worker from the product, the forced nature of work, and the alienation of worker from worker. Capitalism reduces all human passions and activity to greed -- humans as producers have been estranged from their creative powers.

The cause of the "maturing" of Marx is a matter of speculation. Perhaps it was the influence of his new friend and supporter Engels, or his growing knowledge of economics. In any case, Marx held on to the themes of alienation from capitalism and freedom through revolution, but he added central concepts and themes so as to fashion a more "scientific" and objective product. He can thus claim his rightful place in this chapter. One such central concept is historical (or dialectic) materialism. This type materialism must be distinguished from mechanistic materialism which holds that reality consists exclusively of matter in motion.[4] The latter concept was rejected by Marx, in favor of historical materialism which sees humankind's consciousness and purposeful labor as creative and productive forces, which can change reality and ultimately human nature as well. Marx followed the Hegelians in viewing society as an intertwined totality, but he denied that its explanation lies in the spirit of its people. Marx was not concerned with society in general, but rather with specific societies, and he provided several types. He denied the Hegelian notion that the spirit of a people is at the base of every society. He seems to have put a specific mode of production in its place. This has led some to conclude that historical materialism is economic determinism, i.e., the doctrine that all social phenomena are unilaterally determined by the economic base.[5] Numerous passages in Marx and Engels favor this interpretation, but another is possible. It is that historical materialism assumes connections among various categories of social life, but none has absolute primacy. This ambiguity has led to two contrasting Marxist theories: the primacy of the economic base, and that of the interrelationship between the economic and other social facts.

Another central concept of Marxism is the division of labor, obviously tied in with the mode of production and possibly also to the issue of economic determinism. But this division is not the benign and mutually beneficial phenomenon found in Adam Smith. Rather it is dehumanizing, and it is ultimately tied to the class struggle. In mature Marxism, the class struggle takes the place of alienation as a principal concept. The relations of production are relations between classes, some of which possess producers goods and their subordinates who are not that fortunate. Marx and Engels provide no systematic exposition of classes, nor do they even bother to define them.[6] Their discourse on this subject is particularly difficult, because the meanings which they attach to the concept varies. Marx had only a minimal interest in the middle class -- his focus being on the proletariat. He adopted a polar model of classes, with the struggle under capitalism more and more assuming this configuration, and with the victory of the proletariat assured. Szacki uses Marx's emphasis upon the class struggle as a way of absolving Marxism from the charge of economic determinism. We return to this point soon. The Polish scholar admits that when discussing social development Marx and Engels often focused attention upon the mode of production, but this concept is a broad one which was meant not only to cover economic relations, but also a system of social, ideological, and political relations as well. The survival of a given mode of production is not guaranteed merely by its economic effectiveness, but the elites must dominate politically and ideologically as well.[7] So their reference to the mode of production must be interpreted in a broad sense to include aspects of society besides the economic. The reader need not be reminded that a contrary interpretation is possible -- and available.

Szacki applies this same brand of logic to Marx's view of the class struggle. Its starting point is economic, but it is so much more. It is also true that in the Marxist view the revolution will not come about if economic conditions are not mature, but the right configuration of political forces is necessary as well as a developed social consciousness.

Szacki argues that Marx and Engels put so much stress on the class struggle, which he sees in a much broader sense than the economic, and hence his emphasis is not narrowly economic. Lavine sees Marxism differently. In this view, the mode of production conditions or determines the general character of social, political, and spiritual life -- including philosophical and religious ideas. These latter are the superstructure, not determinant as with Hegel, but now determined by the mode of production. The humanistic Marxist of the next chapter thus has a choice among interpretations of Marx, or this scholar can return to Hegel. Ideology in Lavine's view of Marxism is part of the superstructure, but it has more specific traits as well. Specifically, it is the system of ideas in a society which is determined by the class structure and which reflects the thoughts and the interests of the dominant class. Ideologies present themselves as universal, but they are particularistic and they legitimize the power of a given class. These sets of rationalizations will stop with the victory of the proletariat. Szacki's view on this issue is "softer" as well. Marx and Engels, in his view, see ideology as false consciousness. What are to be avoided above all is the belief that thought is independent of other human activity, the ascribing to consciousness the role of efficient cause, and the identifying of social change with ways of thinking about it. The differences in these two ways of interpreting Marxism are typical.

Marxism is historicist -- economic modes of production cannot be understood abstractly, but they must be put in their historic context. Furthermore, Marxism is dynamic; and it proceeds not smoothly, but by revolutions. According to one view, Marxism traces the revolutions ultimately to contradictions in the mode of production, the growing forces of production come into conflict with the existing relations of production and the distribution of property. Marx sought to demonstrate this contradiction only in the case of the destruction of a static and restrictive feudalism by the expanding forces of capitalism. But he predicted the same basic contradiction and the same fate for capitalism. Despite its past achievements, it faces a fatal crisis of overproduction. An alternate Marxist position is to stress the class struggle as the road to revolution. This route argues that more and more of the work force under capitalism is being marginalized, dividing society into two opposing classes. The grave diggers of capitalism are the proletariat. Marx held a declining capitalism to be inevitable -- a prediction which has caused no end of difficulties for his followers. A currently highly productive capitalism has caused his entire formulation to be called into question. The non-occurrence of the revolution in so many parts of the world has rehabilitated the power of the superstructure among those who remain his partisans. These tend to be humanistic and Western Marxists who are generally non-deterministic. This general trait can be found also in Marxist dialectic logic and the notion of praxis. The dialectic allows for countercurrents, for shades of gray, and at best it escapes the rigid black/white divisions of positivism. Praxis is a kind of pragmatism, which holds that a theory is true if it works. It is a far cry from determinism and from the laws associated with science. These two aspects of Marxism tend to push the enterprise into the next chapter.

Marx was also an economist, and just as he turned Hegel upside down, so he did the same with Adam Smith and David Ricardo. No longer did the division of labor have the sweet smell of the common good and more for everyone. As we saw above, it alienates. As we soon shall see, under capitalism it is a form of organized, social theft. Marx defined capitalism as that mode of production in which the few own the means of production, and the many, the proletariat, who have only their labor to sell, work for these few. Marx borrowed from Smith and Ricardo the labor theory of value, i.e., the notion that the value of a product is equivalent to how much labor is required to produce it. He also set forth the companion concept, surplus value, to refer to the difference between the value of what is produced and the value of what is received by the worker. Surplus value is a form of exploitation, a kind of social theft -- the workers receiving enough for their subsistence and reproduction, but not the full value of the product which they produce. They are paid less, and the surplus is siphoned off by the capitalist in the form of surplus value. As a critic of neo-classical theory (marginal utility analysis) admitted, the Marxist labor theory of value "is a mare's nest of tangled issues and unresolved problems." But its competitor, marginal utility analysis, does little better, and both theories are prime examples of the opposing ideologies which fuel them. In terms of explanatory power, both are partial cripples, but with healthy parts as well. Each is a treasure, a precious resource for illustrating the difference between a functionalist paradigm dedicated to regulation and its opposite Marxist paradigm dedicated to radical change.

As we have seen above, neoclassical theory (marginal utility analysis) grounds value in exchange, which is supposedly undertaken by the parties (the traders) for gain.[8] Their gain, which is shared by both even if unequally, is ultimately subjective arising from individual preferences. Who these abstract persons are, how they are supported, what their preferences are based on, how their commodities are produced -- all these questions are outside the boundaries of the "science of economics." Neoclassical economics thus grounds value in individual preference and exchange -- but also in scarcity. This contrasts with Marxism which grounds value in the production and the reproduction of goods, the process which also maintains the social order. In this latter view, the production and the reproduction of goods are not a special kind of exchange -- but a key to value and to the social system itself. Marxism insists that economics be seen concretely, not abstractly as is the case with the neoclassicals. It must be viewed historically, in periods in which different and contrary social regulations obtain. Psychological preferences in the Marxist perspective are not determinant. They must be seen as dependent variables, or at least in relationship with the existing social system. For the neoclassicals, the law of diminishing utility is used to explain the consumer's preferences, and the whole social context of advertising, the distribution of income are outside the analysis.

A point not so obvious is that Marxism is anti-phenomenalistic, i.e., the assumption that the object of science is not what is immediately given in experience.[9] The social scientist does not try to analyze immediate states of affairs, rather the attempt is made to discover processes as if they were free of disturbances. Marx realized that the laboratory was not available for his use, so he used abstraction, or reference to the typical situation. For capitalism, this usually was the England of his day. The reconstruction of the course of events was not satisfactory, for Marx was looking for underlying laws. His approach is nomothetic. He was against the intuitive process of penetrating the essence of things and also against the ordering of immediate empirical data. He has been compared with Galileo in that he was searching out the laws which would explain surface data. He was not a functionalist, nor did he accept the ideal types of Weber. Some of his followers have strayed from this position. He understood cognitive activity to be historically conditioned, and he believed that his access to the working class movement gave him a clearer view of bourgeois society. His approach was in the spirit of the sociology of knowledge. Indeed, his work inspired Karl Mannheim. The latter hoped to escape the trap of relativism by relying upon unattached intellectuals; Marx depended upon the committed proletariat.

We point to one further trait in this brief general statement of Marxism. It is the state, and Marx's followers have certainly interpreted his view of this matter in contrary ways. For sure, he did not see the state in strictly legal terms, as did the traditionalists in the United States. His was more sociological -- the state being more of a class matter. One Marxist interpretation is that this institution is in essence directly controlled by the dominant economic class. Another finds the matter to be more complicated -- there being struggle within the dominant class or a state relatively removed from dominant class control. Szacki interprets Marxism in the latter way. The Polish scholar argues that Marx saw the state in two ways. One emphasized one class dominating the other (the theory of class domination) and the other saw the state as being practically "independent" of society (bureaucracy). The viewpoints are related, but they can be separated for analytical purposes. From the latter standpoint, the executive power constantly grows and maintains an immense mass of people in absolute dependence upon it. Marx actually (according to Szacki) saw the relative independence of the machinery of the state from class control. Thus again Marxism is an ambiguous legacy. Whichever Marxist approach is considered, however, it shows contrast with functionalism and its colleagues, the American sect detailed in the last chapter.

Radical Marxism

We begin this section on radical Marxism by recalling the two dimensions set forth by Burrell and Morgan from which these scholars derived four social science meta-paradigms, which we put to advantage in this study. The reader may remember that the first dimension was the subjective/objective, which put on the latter side realism, positivism, determinist, and the nomothetic respectively, and pitted these against nominalism, anti-positivism, voluntarism, and the idiographic. We found functionalism to be on the objective side in all four ways, and that is where radical Marxism belongs as well. Social laws can be discovered which explain and predict, but the determinism in Marxism can be modified by dialectic logic and the notion of praxis. In the radical Marxist view, humankind is the product of the environment, but we must add an environment created by humankind itself. Where radical Marxism really parts ways with functionalism is on the second dimension, that of regulation or radical change. Radical Marxism sees change, conflict, disintegration, and coercion in society rather than stability, integration, and coordination. We would modify this by adding that Marxism sees both sets of attributes, but recognizes them as being dialectically opposed to each other. It revels in contradictions, and stresses the malignant side of capitalist society -- the conflicts and the deprivation, and it looks forward to liberation and emancipation through revolution.

Let us elaborate upon this meta-paradigm. Radical Marxism is based upon an ontology which sees the social world as materialist, having an independent existence outside the minds of man. It is external to the viewers with its own proper structure. Its facticity is assumed, and it is material rather than spiritual. It imposes itself and its categories upon the researcher from its own position. This realistic metaphysics is supplemented by what can be called with some license a "positive" epistemology. Real laws can be discovered in the social world and communicated to others, just as in the world of natural science. Social science need not be content with providing mere insights, and one need not personally witness phenomena to understand them. The radical Marxist is a "scientist." In the radical Marxist view, the substructure is seen as dominant, as ultimately being determinant of the superstructure. This means that the means of production (roughly technology) and the relations of production determine the rest of social relations -- the state, religion, art, and so forth.[10] Radical Marxists are in the mold of the elder, mature Marx, and they are often correctly charged with being economic determinists. Humanistic Marxists put more emphasis upon the significance of the superstructure.

As economists, radical Marxists put emphasis upon surplus value and the crisis which they see as inherent in capitalism. Of course, their purpose is not merely to understand society, but to overturn the status quo, and economic crises provide the setting, and to a great extent, the vehicle, for the revolution. Capitalism is crisis ridden, thus providing the proper setting and propulsion. Their humanistic competitors favor dramatic change also, but more through acting upon the superstructure. The radical Marxist visualizes capitalism with its own time bomb ticking away, as its partisans revel in their excess wealth. The radicals emphasis contradictions, and of course they use the dialectic. They hold on to the charge by the "young" Marx that capitalism alienates, but this concept plays less a role in their analysis than it does with humanistic Marxists.

Burrell and Morgan divide radical Marxism (their term is "radical structuralism") into three subgroups. The first, obviously the most interesting for us, is the most objectivist region of the paradigm. These authors call it "Russian social theory," and we will equate it with the social science of the Soviet Union before recent modifications. The second subgroup is identified as contemporary Mediterranean Marxism, which features at the present time Althusser and Colletti. The third is conflict theory -- now in the hands of Rex and Dahrendorf. The last two subgroups lay outside the parameters of this chapter, but the first is our present concern. It focuses upon the mature Marx, Engels' interpretation, and those of Plekanov, Bukharin, and Kropotkin, to evolve into the official dogma of the Soviet Union. Engels survived Marx, and under his influence, the dialectic between the subjective and the objective worlds was left farther and farther behind, and the materialist view of history and society was firmly set. Partisans became convinced of historical necessity, as expounding Marxism was reduced to a science expounding the general laws which control society down to and including human thought. Plekanov bears the responsibility for steering Bolshevism along this path. Also responsible was Bukharin, a one-time colleague of Lenin, but cut down in the Stalinist purge in 1938. He has recently been rehabilitated in the Gorbachev era.

Bukharin occupies an extreme position of objectivism within the sociology of radical Marxism. It is sometimes called "vulgar" Marxism in the West, but it owes much to Engels. Bukharin's chief work Historical Materialism: A System of Sociology was obviously intended as sociology, not as economics. He viewed historical materialism as a general theory of society. Strangely enough, he did not use the dialectic, preferring equilibrium analysis. He was more at home with twentieth century physics than with nineteenth century German idealism. His system of sociology uses mechanics as its analogy, derived in an unmodified form from physics. His systems theory is Marxist, equilibrium with the environment being achieved through technology, which regulates the relationship between society and nature. Social change comes about through alterations in the balance, but the disequilibrium leads to crisis and revolutionary overturn. Change does not come through evolution as with most systems theory, but through cataclysmic crises and revolution. The Russian Revolution seems to be the inspiration. The model is committed to the revolutionary overthrow of capitalism, but it looks forward to a post-revolutionary harmony. Bukharin's exposition is a kind of early functionalism, but revolutionary, and definitely objectivist.

Ontologically realist, his approach follows natural science as the model for the epistemology of sociology and history and adopts a nomothetic methodology. He rejected free will, arguing that mankind's conduct is always conditioned. He was a friend of sociology, but unfortunately he equated this discipline with dialectic materialism. This notion was later taken up by Stalin, no friend of his, at the expense of sociology.

We confine our discussion to one more author before passing on to another section, social science in the second world. Our choice is Lenin, the undisputed leader of the Russian Revolution. He was also a sociologist, who criticized Bukharin for not using the dialectic. Like Bukharin, he was at first a partisan of sociology, but he later changed his opinion. He put great emphasis upon historicism, upon analyzing a given society in a given context. To him, the great contribution of Marx was to do just this, rather than to discuss society and progress in general.[11] His approach was holistic, with emphasis upon the dialectic, classes, and the class struggle. He argued that the concepts class and class struggle allow one to analyze society scientifically. He emphasized party organization, the significance of the communist party as the leader and the mobilizer of the proletariat. It bridged the gap between theory and practice. Lenin also wrote on the subject international relations, and he is given credit by Soviet writers for founding the "scientific" study of this field.

Social Science in the Soviet Bloc

One might have been tempted before 1989 to follow through with the logic of bipolarity, and to assign to the Soviet Union in its sphere the same privileges enjoyed by the United States in hers or to pretend that the Soviet Union as a social science power is on a par with the United States. This would have been a mistake as the events of that year indicated. Resistance to drawing this parallel is motivated by the realization that the Soviet Union's participation in postwar bipolarity has to a great extent been by courtesy appointment, a situation abundantly clear once we leave the military/strategic sphere. This was true even before the recent events in the Soviet bloc. There is but one capitalist system, and it engulfs most of the world. Its influence has shone through even to the inhabitants of the second world, especially in the cultural, communications, educational, and social science spheres. A phenomenon strange on its surface is that when Soviet and Chinese social scientists have sought enlightenment abroad, they have turned to the United States, the same direction to which other social scientist centers turn. We do admit, however, to some bipolarity in social science in the past, i.e., we see the Soviet Union as having played a dominant role in her sphere -- even if her global social science position is no match for that of the United States. Her dominion has been restricted, and the Americans themselves wield some influence in the smaller empire. Some consolation to the Soviets has arisen from their ability to decide upon the dominant paradigm to be used in their part of bipolarity.

The Soviet Union was so much the dominant military, political, economic, and educational power in the formerly unified Soviet bloc that the hypothesis logically followed that she was social science dominant as well. Our analysis refers to the immediate past -- it is not yet time to assess the impact of recent events. We intend to stress Soviet educational dominance: the reader will remember that we identified education as that sphere, that part of the structure, closest to our disciplines. The Soviet Union has been host to the great majority of students from the region who have studied abroad,[12] and young men of Eastern Europe bent on success study Russian. The latter also serves as the common language for the data bank for Eastern Europe.[13] When Volkov speaks of scholarly collaboration among the faculty from Moscow university and scholars in Warsaw, Sofia, Prague, Berlin, and Havana, we conclude that this interaction follows the pattern sketched in world system analysis. In fact, he maintains that Soviet higher educational establishments have trained "a large number of professors and lecturers for the chairs of the social sciences of socialist countries and regularly help to improve their qualifications".[14] We assume that this is essentially one-way traffic, with little counterflow. Volkov, however, did not mention the latter; he did not confirm our hypothesis. Soviet dominance was significant, but stress upon it must not blind us to the fact that it has not prevented public disagreements among colleagues in the region, nor has it dissolved the special ties which Polish sociology maintains with the first world.[15] In fact, Bauman argues that in the 1950s and 1960s Soviet sociology borrowed from the Polish discipline,[16] the center borrowed from the periphery.

Despite some variations and qualifications, the social science of the Soviet Union served as the center for the second world. This role put her at the apex of communications -- the source of professional messages and paradigms for the region. Second world paradigms featured dialectic materialism as the basis of social science.

Emphasis was upon a few select disciplines at the expense of others, with much practical, non-theoretical effort expended upon "the building of socialism." Paradigm similarity was much more pronounced in the second world than in the first. This similarity was illustrated by the discipline geography. James and Martin assert that although France and Germany influenced this discipline in Eastern Europe in the first two decades of the present century, "the geographical concepts and methods that prevail today have come from the Soviet influence".[17] The story is similar in all of Eastern Europe. After the communists proved victorious in China in 1949, the Soviet model was adopted there also. Economic geographers had a harder time adjusting to the new dispensation than their colleagues in physical geography. Scholars were made to accept Marxist Leninism, and the same practical aspect, already seen in the Soviet case, was introduced in China as well.

We concentrate upon education as the means to trace Soviet social science influence in the second world. It serves in our scheme of things as the indicator of social science extension and secondly of communication. We are eager also to discover whether the interaction is horizontal or vertical, the dependent relation we had encountered in the first world or those of colleagues and comrades. The place of Russian as the language of multinational interaction will serve as an additional indicator of the relationship.

The Western authors that we consulted had no difficulty sensing indoctrination as a prominent part of Soviet education and in detecting evidence of strong ideological orientation in the training of foreign students. In its structured form, this ideology is Marxism and translates as social science in the present essay. Mestenhauser pointed to Soviet ideology as mentioned above and then portrayed youth as being particularly vulnerable, because of their preoccupation with acquiring an education, any education, without much critical thought.[18] The Soviets seek such advantage, despite the fact that most of their foreign scholarships are in fields close to development -- science and technology. In the early postwar period, the Soviet program featured students from Eastern European and other socialist countries. After the death of Stalin, the program broadened to include countries of the third world. Mestenhauser offers as the major short term goal of this new extension the expansion of influence and the screening of students for intensive communist indoctrination. The long-range goal was identified as the creation of cadres sympathetic to communism and capable of running the institutions of their country.

Other motives included Soviet concern over, and the attempt to block, the spread of English as the world's medium of communication.

The educational exchange figures which we have seen support the thesis that the Soviet program has been politically motivated and that its relations with the second world (and the third world) are vertical, not horizontal. In our scheme of things, these characteristics are readily transferable to social science. Our conclusions for second world social science thus will duplicate those for first world social science; cross cultural communications "based upon equal partnership" do not exist there.

Most of the foreign students studying in the Soviet Union are from East European and other socialist countries. The countries of the third world which are the main participants in the Soviet program have "leftist" governments, and their connection with the Soviet Union is thus grounded in politics. Examples of these in 1962 were Cuba, Iraq, Indonesia, Algeria, Ghana, Guinea, and Somali. Although Eastern European countries have their own programs, these are much smaller than the Soviet effort -- their combined programs constituting perhaps one-third that of the Soviet Union. The latter serves as the principal foreign host for Eastern European students, but the flow of students in the other direction or from the Soviet Union to other socialist countries appears to be minuscule. The only direct data we have on this situation is that 50 Soviet students went to study in China early in 1957, and 70 entered Peking University in 1951.[19] This contrasts with 4,963 Chinese students who were studying in the Soviet Union in 1958.[20] A hint of this unequal exchange is contained in the account on social science of the Pro-Rector of Moscow University. It is true that he discussed joint authorship of books by Soviet authors with their comrades in Eastern Europe. But he ended his presentation with the assertion that Soviet higher educational establishments have trained a large number of social science professors for socialist countries and regularly help them to improve their qualifications.[21] Nothing was said about a reverse flow of academics -- an omission which we interpret to mean that no meaningful one exists.

Singer has made the observation that the fate of a language is tied to the power position -- present, but sometimes past -- of the principal countries which speak it. And the historical record generally bears this out. When French power was at its height, the French language was the language of diplomacy. The widespread current use of French and English respectively in most former French and English colonies is due to the imposition of these languages, with varying degrees of force and polite enticement. As American and Russian power has increased in the postwar period, so has the use of their languages. We should, therefore, expect Russian to be the social science language used for multinational discourse in the second world. Singer assures us that those young men of Eastern Europe who are bent on success study Russian. The best direct and explicit evidence which we could find which suggests the dominance of Russian in the socialist world was tucked away in a study by Vinogradov, a Soviet expert on social science information. He informs us that Russian is the language for AisMison, the automated social science information system and data bank of the socialist countries.[22] This organization was established in 1976 in Moscow by the academies of science of Bulgaria, Hungary, Vietnam, East Germany, Mongolia, Poland, the USSR, and Czechoslovakia. He went on to point out that most data banks in the West -- and, indeed, in the Western Europe -- use English as their language. At least at the level of data banks, these two languages (English and Russian) play their expected roles. In the context of our present analysis, this fact attests to the existence of vertical social science relations in the Soviet half of bipolarity. Viewed from a world perspective, however, Russian is no match for English.

As we have already noted, the notion of bipolarity must not be pressed too hard, i.e., the Soviet position in her sphere must not be assumed to have been identical with that of the United States in hers. Areas in which the Soviets had an advantage over the United States were in paradigm similarity and the degree of acceptability or non-acceptability of social science. The fit was so close that a description of the situation in the Soviet Union gave a generally reliable guide for the whole bloc. This was particularly evident in the long, dreary Stalinist era when social science was suppressed. We alluded above to the historic difficulties between Marxism and social science, and the dispute surfaced with a vengeance under Stalinism. The impact was not confined to the Soviet Union, empty social science chairs were discernible all around throughout the Soviet empire.

We next present a brief sketch of social science in the Soviet Union, a statement which until the immediate past served as the pattern for the entire second world. A word by way of an historical introduction is valuable, if only because it shows that Czarist Russia was social science dependent. The Imperial Academy of Sciences was established in St. Petersburg in 1724, and it served also as the first

Russian university. It included, among the subjects taught, law and history. Until 1733 its members were all foreigners. Struve counts the founding of the University of Moscow as the real beginning of the development of Russian social science. It included among its faculty many foreign professors, and foreign languages were used for instruction. In 1768 the empress decreed that Russian would henceforth be the principal language of instruction.[23] Later the works of Adam Smith and Jeremy Bentham became popular, and still later the works of Marx. In the nineteenth century the practice of sending students abroad was established, the favorite host institutions being German. Russian social science was influenced by the same intellectual currents which swayed the rest of Europe. These included those influenced by the works of Hegel, Comte, Spencer, John Stuart Mill, and Marx, to mention some of the major ones. The Russia of the Czars was certainly influenced by the West and dependent upon it in many ways, social science included.

The Russian Revolution represents a dramatic break in the history of Russian social science. Dialectic materialism became the base of the standard social science sects, and often it did service as social science itself. Political power shifted in the Soviet domain to the Marxists and away from the historic enemy which had supported bourgeois social science. This was to the detriment of the latter. Some disciplines had a relatively easy initial time of it, i.e., after having shifted to a Marxist paradigm. Reference here is to history, anthropology, and philology. In contrast, Soviet economists, in effect, had to start anew.[24] Marx had spent his time berating capitalism, not making plans or establishing blueprints for the socialist system. The Soviets had to forge an economy, not centered on the market nor upon the profit motive. Soviet social scientists became participants in the creation of a new system, rather than merely academic observers of the process. This is in accord with the practical bent in second world social science, which is often less evident in bourgeois versions, although the former is heavily laden with theory as well. The disciplines in Soviet hands did not undergo the heavy academic development witnessed in the West, nor does Soviet specialization match that attained in the United States. The favored Soviet disciplines seem to be economics, philosophy, history, and philology.[25] Brucan has reported that Marxism is new to international relations theory and that the academic status of the discipline is still in the making in socialist countries.[26]

Goormaghtigh feels that this discipline has not as yet arrived in the Soviet Union.[27]

A problem the new social scientists/planners faced was to fashion a system of national accounts. We have already referred critically to the Western, capitalist system of accounts, and the socialist one begs for criticism as well. This system is based upon the Marxist theory of value, according to which production or value is generated by productive labor expended in the sphere of material production. As Wilczynski reveals, the socialist system of accounts, both with respect to scope and valuation, is fundamentally different from the Western system.[28] We add that each is based upon a specific ideology, thus reducing what appears as "hard facts" to references to data filtered through and biased by ideologically based concepts. The socialist accounting system has six broad categories of material production, but more interesting are the eight groupings in the "unproductive sphere." Notable among these latter are health, social welfare, and "other services." Wilczynski informs us that though these eight groupings are classified as "unproductive," their usefulness is granted. A larger proportion of the work force in socialist countries is engaged in material production than in Western countries. The Polish scholar explains that the reason is partly because of different levels of development, but ideology plays its role as well. We can conclude that the socialist planners take their ideology seriously; they are not different in this respect from Western economists.

If the capitalist accounting system is faulted, so is its socialist rival. What is so special about material goods which puts them ahead of medical services, to take one example? A sick person needs medical services, probably more than a new chair in the living room. The socialist system has the advantage of eliminating much "fluff" found in the capitalist system, haircuts and beauty services for dogs and that California special, funeral services for, and now freeze drying of, favorite pets. But all services do not fit into these categories, which are still strange and exceptional. Services become a more important category as income increases, as it has in socialist countries. But their accounting system has a built in prejudice against this development. Conversions from one system to the other have been made, but the results are often in dispute. Neither accounting system measures the state of human welfare except in the grossest of terms, although each sheds some light upon the state. Both are very much in the spirit of social science.

Two authors previously mentioned, Lenin and Bukharin, contributed to the future fate of our disciplines in the Soviet Union. Both originally were proponents of sociology, but Lenin seems to have changed his mind. Bauman traces this to Lenin's reaction to a research report on divorce written by Pitrim Sorokin, which presented the new regime in an unfavorable light.[29] This broke the uneasy truce which had existed between the communist party and sociology. Bukharin in a sense contributed to the downfall of sociology as well. He equated the discipline with historical materialism, a position which was adopted by Stalin. This led Soviet scholars to state and restate the views of the mature Marx and other authorities rather than to do field research.[30] Soviet scholars became dogmatists, their work centered on the exegesis of the tenets of the Marxist masters, so as to discover the real meaning of historical materialism. All had to be tailored so as to support the Soviet regime. Radical Marxism thus became a status quo construction for the Soviet Union, but revolutionary for the capitalist world. Concrete social investigations were ignored. But anthropologists did carry on field research, because such knowledge of "primitive" peoples was thought to be necessary. So the Soviet Union presented the strange and sad picture of a country with field knowledge about its "primitives," but not about its developed ethnic groups. Stalin's policies reverberated throughout Eastern Europe, the countries there generally following suit. For example, Czechoslovakia, East Germany, and Poland abolished sociology courses in their universities as well as their sociological institutes. The Poles, however, managed to preserve the bulk of their sociological staff, East Germany and Czechoslovakia did not. Yugoslavia initially followed the Soviet lead, but after the rupture with the Soviet Union sociology was tolerated. After 1953, it was promoted by the Yugoslavian government as a way of obtaining knowledge to help manage the economy.

We rely mainly upon Shlapentokh's account of sociology in the Soviet Union to complete our account of social science there. An emigre, he was once a Soviet sociologist himself, and so his analysis is from the inside. He pictures Soviet sociology as the hostage, if not the prisoner, of the politics of the dominant elites. Sociology is at present benefitting from Gorbachev's new policy of glasnost (openness), but its future development depends upon whether this policy continues or not. Political control is such that "a Soviet social scientist is prevented from carrying out a study that is not supported by the state".[31] This is not the liberal control through the encouraging and pampering and petting of favorite paradigms and research findings, but the more direct Stalinist way. Furthermore, the Soviet regime is constantly concerned with those sensitive issues related directly to the power of the elites and to popular attitudes toward the Soviet system. Some revelations do occur during periods of liberalization, as at the present during the Gorbachev regime. Research on non-sensitive areas is allowed, e.g., the anthropological studies cited above. Almost all sociological publications have been centered on local restricted areas. Soviet sociologists have been allowed to conduct only one nationwide survey of the adult population.[32]

Shlapentokh names the period from 1958 to 1965 "the embryonic period" of Soviet sociology -- this because in his view an existing sociology had been effectively destroyed by the Stalinist system. During its reign, this discipline was considered to be bourgeois, and thus beyond the pale of socialist acceptability. Its condemnation was directly related to empirical research. When the discipline emerged anew in the post-Stalin period, the West served as the pattern for the emergence. Shlapentokh does not give the Poles credit for this process, as Bauman does. The Soviet Sociological Association was established in 1958, and a research facility was set up. Surveys were conducted during this period, usually rationalized as in furtherance of increased production. Shlapentokh calls the next period 1965 to 1972 "the golden years." Sociological research expanded into new areas, and the Institute for Concrete Social Research was founded. The pretense was dropped that the discipline's purpose was to enhance productivity. A number of conferences and seminars were held, and a bulletin was founded for the publication of research findings. Many contacts with the West were made, and beginning in 1966 Soviet sociologists regularly attended the annual meetings of the International Sociological Association.

The passing of the "golden years" was marked in the seventies by the gradual substitution of conservatives in important positions in the place of the "good guys." Ideologues began to play a much larger role in the Institute for Concrete Social Research. The work done during the golden years was denigrated. New publications were replete with official ideology with little in the way of supporting empirical research. Official approval for the Ph.D. in sociology was obtained during this sterile period, but the first undergraduate programs were not introduced until 1984. An article in Pravda in 1987 complained of the lack of sociologists in the country. The situation started to improve for the better in the middle seventies, as Soviet sociology found itself in its gray period, as party "moderates" pushed the "right wing extremists" aside. Progress was most noticeable in those areas of the discipline having a bearing on productivity. The Gorbachev era promises to provide more "golden years" for the discipline. A new star on the scene is Zaslavskaya, who in a paper published in 1984 identified bureaucracy as the major restraining force impeding Soviet progress. This theme has been taken up by Gorbachev, and her criticisms are of direct practical use to the new regime. She has openly charged that Soviet society is not socially homogeneous, approaching the communist ideal of a classless society. She finds that it is racked with deep contradictions and social animosity.[33] The regime has ignored the interests of the individual, and this in her view is the major cause of the Soviet dilemma. She has trained her sights on the discipline as well. In an article in Pravda (February 6, 1987), entitled "Restructuring of Sociology," she charged that sociology in the seventies had been persecuted. Soviet sociology lags behind the American version and because of its past neglect "Soviet sociology is sociology without sociologists." Such statements stand out, and seem strange, in view of the social science cold war which has been waged between the two superpowers. We refer to this war below.

Shlapentokh's analysis, while fascinating, is not without its problems and ironies. He tells us that Soviet sociologists are anti-Marxist, yet when abroad these scholars sense their differences with others who ply the trade, and they are made to realize their commitment to Marxism. They have gladly attacked Western Marxism, we are told, because they cannot imagine any scholar freely accepting Marxism. Of course, the Soviet elites approve of the attack, but for very different reasons. We are told that what galls the Soviet sociologist is the imposed official paradigm with its economic determinism and the neglect of the superstructure as causative agents.[34] But these are the very factors which have caused Western Marxists to reject Soviet Marxism and to make up their own paradigms. Soviet sociologists thus would seem to have more in common with Western Marxists than they do with American sociologists, at least the discussion to now supports this conclusion. Like the Western Marxist, they are Marxists. Moreover, like him or her, they wish to put more emphasis upon the superstructure. Logically, the Soviet sociologist should support Western Marxist colleagues, but instead he/she gladly attacks them. On the other hand, Soviet sociology has emerged deeply committed to mathematical analysis. Here the comparison has been made with the United States, and the Soviet sociologists have found their work wanting. One reason for the attachment to mathematics is that mathematicians have lent their support to sociology. Another is the great impact which the United States has had upon the Soviet Union and the rest of the world as well. The sociology of the United States is the standard upon which the Soviet scholars judge their trade. The structures featured in this volume have surfaced again. Soviet sociology thus has its ironies and its contradictions.

Almost any Western partisan of social science would be happy to receive the good news that sociologists have been in the forefront of the Soviet dissident movement. But this is not the message of Shlapentokh. Soviet sociologists have left the struggle in other hands, notably those of creative writers and even physicists. This development fits well with the predispositions of the multinational version of social science, which puts such stock in the impact of structures upon our disciplines. We will see below a parallel development in India. The social sciences there were so much the children of colonialism that they played little role in the independence movement. Most Italian professors, including social scientists, took the required oath of allegiance to Mussolini, and they kept their jobs. But sociology and other social sciences have a useful role to play in the Soviet Union, as our brief references to the work of Zaslavskaya suggest. Two general kinds of findings have resulted from Soviet empirical studies. One current finds the citizenry content and that they absorb the official propaganda. The other is critical, finding, for example, workers motivated not by collectivist values, but by individual gain or youth in search of professional status, not the role of the worker. This latter type finding fulfills the critical role which social science at its best plays.

Social Science in China

The fate of social science in China has also been intimately tied up with politics. Social science there fell on hard times soon after the revolution and what remained of it was gutted by the cultural revolution. But we are getting ahead of our story. Pre-revolutionary social science and education as well followed the patterns set in other third world countries -- the copying was of the West. Modern geography, for example, was introduced in China just before World War II. Indigenous ideas on the subject, of course, predate this event, these ideas being contemporaneous with classical Greece. The modern transfer occurred through a Chinese scholar trained in geology in Scotland and another, a Harvard graduate, trained in meteorology and climatology. The returnees passed on their knowledge and their enthusiasm to their students, several of whom traveled to the first world to complete their training. In the wake of the communist takeover, geography was restructured to fit the Soviet model. The discipline was divided into the physical and the economic. The former had a relatively easy time of adjusting to the new dispensation, because this discipline is a natural science. Many of the physical geographers of today are the students of the two itinerant geographers mentioned above. The economic geographers had a harder time of it, and those who replaced them did not have an academic connection with the past.

We have already looked to education as the carrier and the transporter of our paradigms, and it serves this function in our analysis of Chinese social science. Soon after the revolution, Peking eagerly embraced Soviet education -- its structures, methods, and textbooks. Politically, this period corresponds to the war by proxy in Korea with the United States. In the words of Fraser, the role that American ideas had played in China during much of the twentieth century were largely "usurped" by ideas imported from the Soviet Union.[35] The educational policies of the Koumintang and those of "Sino-Deweyism" were followed by a "spate of adoration" for the Soviet Union and her teaching methods. This was accomplished by a one-way flow of students, plus a counter flow of teachers, consultants, textbooks, and teaching equipment. There was some reciprocity, but it was not at the pedagogical level, and it was highlighted by such items as dancing teams, cultural groups, giant pandas, Manchurian tigers, and leopards of every kind. The Chinese school curriculum was revised, and the needed textbooks were translated from the Russian. The American model for the universities was replaced by a shrunken institution of nontechnical disciplines and the development of separate technical institutes. The population was urged to study Russian ideas and, of course, the Russian language. Fraser notes that a reaction to such copying followed the early enthusiasm, what he calls "adaptation" rather than mere imitation. Our preferred term is "indigenization," and we treat it as a broad concept which can affect all social science. There was a natural reaction in China against such devices as the "three-copy" teaching method. The process involved three copying steps without alteration: from Soviet teaching materials to the teacher's notes; from the latter to the blackboard; and from there to the students' notes. Objections to the procedure were met by the response that the teaching material originated in the Soviet Union. Those acquainted with colonial history and dependency theory will recognize this syndrome.

Chinese politics, internal and external, have witnessed more twists and turns since 1949 than we have information or space to disentangle. Relations with Moscow have been all but broken off, but Peking remains Marxist politically and so far as social science is concerned, but both of these kinds of relations have been established with the West. At present the favorite foreign educational site is the United States, where 27,000 of the total of 40,000 students (67.5 percent) are studying.[36] Peking seems determined to reduce both the total and also the percentage which goes to the United States. One acute and obvious problem is that most of the students who go to the United States do not return home. Our disciplines fell on hard times in the sixties and the seventies. Petzold argues that the ultra-leftists managed to abolish psychology in China from 1966 to 1976.[37] Note that the description in this section differs from that of the last. The term "ultra-leftist" now serves for the "rightists" of the last section. We have already witnessed this phenomenon of oppression in the Stalinist years, and there is little comfort in the fact that the chief abolitionist called for "proletarian psychology" as a substitute. This has some appeal to the comparative orientation of the multinational version, but not much. The remarks and the letter of three Chinese scholars who, in their words, "had studied anthropology" are instructive in understanding the situation of the time and Chinese social science in general. They pointed out that today (1972) sociology and cultural anthropology have been repudiated as disciplines in China, and they were grateful to their Western visitors for having stigmatized anthropology as the child of imperialism.[38] This did not prevent the

Chinese scholars "who had studied anthropology," an historical fact which they could not deny, from carrying on social investigations among national minorities. To be sure, this research was revolutionary work, implemented in accord with the principles of Marxist-Leninism, and whose purpose was to help in the building of socialism. The reader will recall that a similar situation existed in Stalin's Soviet Union.

The above is meant to emphasize what we have already seen above, that social science in socialist countries is often abolished, but also that it is assigned an eminently practical purpose, an aid in what is usually called the building of socialism. And this practical work seems to continue even during the suppression of our disciplines by a "Gang of Four" or a Stalin. Our comments are not intended to gloss over the extent to which social science was suppressed in China before its rehabilitation in 1977. Moreover, research seems to have been carried on regarding national minorities, not the majority Chinese. Psychology was abolished as a university discipline, as were the Institute of Psychology and the Chinese Psychological Society. Only after its rehabilitation were foreign psychologists invited in to lecture (starting in 1978), and only then did China join the International Union of Psychological Science (in 1980). The suppression and the rehabilitation were general, including other social sciences. A hallmark in their rehabilitation was the establishment in 1977 of the Chinese Academy of Sciences which now has 21 institutes under it, each specializing in what in the West are considered to be social sciences, but including also philosophy, history, and literature.[39] The inclusion of the former two subjects can be traced to a Marxist orientation, but the addition of the last seems distinctly Chinese.

The rehabilitation of social science is the result of political decisions, and it is part of a new orientation in development planning. The latter includes the rehabilitation of the expert, respect for teachers, and entrance examinations for universities. Cooperation with the first world is now encouraged. And English language programs are being developed throughout the country to facilitate the new interaction.[40] Ogden has asserted that although the Chinese are examining Western social science models, Marxist-Leninism is still relied upon to provide the fundamental substructure for the Chinese disciplines.[41] The basic Soviet university structure has been maintained and also the emphasis upon economics. The future suggests borrowing from first world social science, but we do not expect this process to assume any resemblance to the "three-copy" teaching method of the early post revolutionary period. The new Chinese product promises to be an indigenized amalgam, one which reflects, among other ingredients, Chinese culture. A distinctive Chinese view was affirmed by three senior social science cadres in Peking, who differentiated between the scope of Western and Chinese social science. They differentiated between natural and social science, arguing that the former is knowledge acquired in the struggle for production, knowledge of things related to nature. On the other hand, social science was understood to be knowledge acquired in social relations. They argued that literature, the fine arts, and the humanities are social sciences.[42]

Social Science Cold War and Diplomacy

We are so happy to report the last bit of information, because this view of social science parallels ours. Rather than savor the warm feeling which arises from support, however, we pass on to a subject which currently must appear inappropriate, if not mischievous. The subject is the social science cold war and the related problem of diplomacy, which we discuss in the present period of detente. But the current hugs of Gorbachev and the handshakes of Reagan or Bush cannot erase the secular history of strife between Marxism and opposing social science. Even the admission below by the Soviet sociologist Zaslavskaya that the American discipline is superior to the local version, should not make us forget this history. Furthermore, this history is a mixture, and the differences in social science are so fundamental as to all but guarantee the return to the storms of the past. Three main subjects constitute our discussion: the first two are the cold war as it has erupted in sociology and political science (including development theory) and the third is an analysis of the operation of the Vienna Center. The latter was intended to promote social science cooperation between Eastern and Western Europe, but instead of the free and open discussion its operations reflect a delicate and tightly controlled type of diplomacy exposing the fragility of such cooperation. The discussion of sociology below is a continuation of what has been said above, but different sources have been used. Furthermore, it is in the context of the cold war.

Shippee's charge that for many years before 1956 empirical sociology was a forbidden subject in all socialist countries except Yugoslavia[43] is a typical American charge. Note that above we agreed in general with this charge. Osipov and Rutkevich present the Soviet view when they deny that the discipline was terminated in the Stalinist era. They point to the "absurdity of the widely held view in the West" that Soviet sociology emerged in the 1950s or 1960s.[44] In reality, it witnessed extensive development in the 1920s, was somewhat held back after that "although never interrupted," and became especially active from the end of the 1950s. Shippee defined empirical sociology in a manner so as to include sociological research based upon quantitative or observed data. Characteristically, he found that such research has dangerous implications for the Marxist-Leninist belief system as officially set forth in Eastern bloc countries prior to 1956. In his somewhat dated analysis, he suggested that empirical sociology had recently been gaining there in comparison with historical materialism because of its instrumental use in national development; but sensitive political areas had been excluded from its jurisdiction.

More recent research from the Western side records a "setback" for Soviet sociology in the last decade. Though more recent, this research has in turn become dated by the arrival of the Gorbachov regime. The setback has been dated in the 1970s, with the discipline becoming more partisan and more subservient to its Marxist orientation. This contrasts with the discipline in the 1960s which was one of relative autonomy from speculative Marxism, a period which featured the creation of middle range theories. The change occurred, when research findings began to contradict Marxist ideology. The shift reinstated ideological purity and was associated with a change in the leadership of the Soviet Sociological Association. Zaslavsky agrees that such a forced retreat has occurred. In his view, the period of the semi-independent status of Soviet sociology ended in the mid-1970s. It succumbed, a victim of the consolidation of the victory of the new Stalinist group which has left its mark on other areas of Soviet spiritual and intellectual life as well.[45] Zaslavsky argues that the official attitude toward empirical sociology had always been ambivalent. On the one hand, the findings of the discipline were valued as a way of facilitating social control. But, on the other, the danger that Soviet sociology could not be cramped within the parameters of the ideology of the system was recognized as well. Zaslavsky predicts the following future trends for the discipline: an increase in secret studies, a broadening of the subjects declared off-limits to empirical research and more personnel changes in sociological institutions. In view of the changes which have occurred under Gorbachev, these predictions illustrate how fragile predictions about the Soviet Union can be. Perhaps we should say social science predictions in general.

Soviet sociologists, at least in the past, have not shrunk from the confrontation with their Western and American "colleagues." We refer to the assertion by Osipov and Rutkevich that Merton's admission that sociology is on the level with 17th century natural science applies to the West, but not to "Marxist scientific sociology." Kassof, in his analysis of the view held by Soviet sociologists of the American version of the discipline, concludes that they have declared "an ideological war" against it and against bourgeois sociology in general.[46] Their attacks have focused especially upon the United States, with the charge that because sociology there does not recognize the universal validity of Marxism-Leninism, it is politically reactionary and scientifically sterile. Bourgeois sociology is held to be incapable of formulating general theory and hopelessly mired down in insignificant and non-cumulative empirical studies. Furthermore, capitalism uses this sect as an ideological weapon to hide the exploitative nature of the system from the American masses. Bourgeois sociology is said to operate behind a scientific facade and to pretend to be objective. The American pantheon of the greats is taken to task, Merton for his unscientific middle-range theories and Parsons for his theory of social action. The latter is condemned as a banal, pro-capitalist theory, featuring psychologism and philosophical idealism. It misleads the masses into thinking that their condition results from subjective evaluations, not from the objective facts of economics. Only one prominent American sociologist escapes the criticism of being an all-out reactionary, C. Wright Mills. He is presented as a tragic hero, courageous enough to come out against the American ruling elite and perceptive enough to provide valuable insights into capitalist society. But he failed to yield sound Marxist conclusions. Konstantinov is quoted in this analysis as arguing that there exists only one scientific sociology, only one that produces objective truth. It is Marxist sociology: Marx discovered the laws and the forces of social development.

Political scientists and those engaged in modernization theory have also joined the struggle. Chertina in a study of bourgeois modernization theory and the development of Soviet Central Asia characterizes this theory as an attempt to conceal the differences between capitalist and socialist development.[47] It treats the present age ideologically and incorrectly as one of transition from the traditional to the modern, rather than as the transition from capitalism to socialism. The article charges that the partisans of this theory and of Western Sovietology attempt to discredit the progress made in Soviet Central Asia, going so far as to praise development under the Czars and charging the Soviets with a policy of Russification. Chertina's remarks are typical of the analysis of Western social science by Soviet Marxists and by some other Marxists as well. The former accept as legitimately scientific only those analyses based upon the ideology of their social science sect. All other analyses are held to be unscientific. Thus the polemic language is justified, for science is speaking of non-science. Truth has the right to talk down to falsehood and to be intolerant of it. The Marxist version of the social science myth assures its partisans that their analysis is scientific. Marxist ideology assures them that bourgeois social science is part of the superstructure of bourgeois societies, designed to support and to strengthen this society and to disparage the accomplishments of rival ones.

Theen's critique of a summary of the state of American political science by Kalenskii, a Soviet scholar, has the advantage that it allows us to present both sides in the ideological battle. Kalenskii's work emerges as one which accepts many of the methods of the American enterprise, but at the same time accuses it of being the obedient and flexible tool of American ruling circles, one of the avant-garde disciplines whose social purpose is to consolidate their position.[48] Too abstract, it betrays a conservative bias, and it has not developed an adequate theory of classes. Theen, for his part, finds the summary by the Soviet scholar to be selective and "too oversimplified and doctrinaire to be very enlightening." He presents the mirror image of Kalenskii's charge. He reminds us that the 1961 platform of the Soviet Communist party made it clear that the purpose of social science in the Soviet Union is to demonstrate the inevitable advance of communism, the deepening crisis of capitalism, and the disintegration of the colonial system. Theen argued that political science as an autonomous discipline has not as yet appeared in the Soviet Union. He assured his readership that if it does emerge, it will likely confine its research to purely descriptive studies of relatively powerless and insignificant institutions in Soviet society.

It remains for us to discuss the founding and the workings of the Vienna Center, set up by a vote of UNESCO in 1962. Our discussion is based upon the analysis of Adam Schaff, its president.

This discussion should be read in the general context of the claim that science enjoys open communications; indeed, that this is necessary for the existence of the enterprise. This was a problem discussed in Chapter IV, where the evidence did not support the thesis of open communications. Or the discussion can be centered, as it is here, specifically on the problem at hand, social science cooperation between Eastern and Western Europe. Obviously, the analysis is based upon the situation prevailing before the fall of communism in Eastern Europe. Schaff sees a need for the center if cooperation and communications are to be achieved there, because "the social sciences are ideological in nature." He informs us that the initiative for establishing the center had to await the proper political moment, detente and East-West rapprochement. Otherwise, this initiative would have been dismissed as being "utterly unrealistic."

The proper name of the "Vienna Center" is the European Coordination Center for Research and Documentation in Social Sciences. This name underlines the fact that the center merely coordinates research performed and paid for by others. It neither carries on research itself, nor does it pay for this activity. Its position in this respect is like that of the United Nations, which lacks the funds to carry on expensive medical and health research. The center's task is to stimulate, organize, and coordinate research carried on by national teams.[49] Moreover, the restrictions imposed upon the center in carrying on these coordinating efforts reveal that it is the weakest type of organization. The veto is available to every member, and thus not restricted as is the case with the Security Council of the United Nations. This weakness manifests itself as well in the provision of two heads for each project (one from Eastern Europe, the other from Western Europe). It also accepts research workers of inferior quality. The center rationalizes this by pointing to its function as a teaching institution, but this can also be imputed to weakness. Those technically less qualified must be accepted to fulfill delicate political requirements.

Concluding Remarks

As we have indicated above, the Chinese leadership is experiencing some second thoughts about their educational ties with the West, particularly with the United States. Changes in these ties would affect their social science ties as well. Chinese-American social science relations (also the political relations which are more their cause than their effect) follow a cyclical pattern, and we are not

entitled to allow the present amical relations to hide the cloudy side of
the cycle. The same comment applies to US-Soviet political and social
science relations as well. Underneath these cycles, however, there is an
underlying antagonism -- in the case of social science this is fueled by
the ideological distance which separates functionalism from radical
Marxism. The situation with respect to Eastern Europe promises to
be quite different because of the fall of Marxism there. The major
thrust of the chapter was not so much to catalogue this difference, but
rather to present one of four social science meta-paradigms and to site
it by placing it in the second world. The succeeding chapter follows the
same pattern, with two more meta-paradigms -- humanistic Marxism
and interpretive sociology. These will be sited in Western Europe.

The present chapter started with an account of the works of
Marx, "the Marxism of Karl Marx." Emphasis was upon the open-
endedness of his work and upon it as a source of various and
contradictory interpretations. A classic division is between the "young"
Marx (26 years old and younger) and the mature Marx (two years
older and more), the former being a humanistic, the latter, at least
according to some accounts, a hard core determinist. We followed this
with a statement of radical Marxism, and the latter in turn by the
disciplines in the second world. Our disciplines have received rough
treatment there. It is not much comfort to recall that they are engaged
in an historical "payback," i.e., for the exclusion of Marxism from
academe for so long. This knowledge gives insight into second world
exclusion, but it certainly does not excuse it. Our disciplines suffered
not just from exclusion, but, even when allowed, they are seriously
restricted. We have characterized the general type influence of the
dominant elites in the first world as "liberal." The emphasis in this
approach is upon the encouraging of favorite paradigms and research
findings, not the prohibition of unfavorable ones. The approach of the
second world goes beyond the liberal approach to prohibition.

This prohibition is illustrated by the Chinese experience. The
"Gang of Four" abolished the academic social sciences. They were
rehabilitated, with the more recent turn in Chinese policy, and now
social science cooperation is being carried on with the West,
particularly with the United States. Despite some second thoughts, this
cooperation persists. What form the Chinese construct will take should
be of great interest to the comparativist -- perhaps part Marxist, part
Chinese, with some additions from the West. The chapter ended with

the social science cold war, a subject of more than historical interest, despite the present detente.

We cannot leave this chapter behind without mentioning a few more of its highlights, i.e. without bragging a little more about it. The chasm which separates Marxism from functionalism stands out, and the reason for the dogmatist's "right" to excommunicate becomes clear. Economics can justify its scientific status, only if the sectarian making such a claim pretends that conflicting sects are not scientific. The sectarian could also, of course, just ignore the competition. Excommunication is the "right" and the claim both of the (Kremlin) radical Marxist and of the American functionalist. The assumptions and the methods of the radical Marxist when contrasted with those of the functionalist remind one of the disparity which divides Kuhn's paradigms. Based on conflicting world views, as though from different planets, what is a duck to one is a rabbit to the other. Specialization of production under capitalism to one leads to greater productivity and ultimately to more income for all, and even to peace. For the other sectarian, it is a form of theft, which produces alienation, and ultimately leads to revolution. The distinction was highlighted above in the contrary views of value, a fundamental concept in economic theory. The Marxist adheres to the labor theory of value, described above as "a mare's nest of tangled issues and unresolved problems." The neo-classical theory was faulted as well, but for its ahistorical, asocial assumptions. We must add also that each concept has explanatory value, i.e. gives insights. But they are ideological and contradictory. The political aspects of social science was emphasized in Shlapentokh's analysis of Soviet sociology and in the workings of the Vienna Center.

There is obviously much in this chapter which supports the structuralist perspective. Instead of the open communications and cooperation characteristic of natural science, the social science communications of Europe have betrayed all the fragility of those found in the United Nations. The diplomacy of the Vienna center is that of high politics, including a more extensive veto than found in the United Nations. This evidence helps support that already given in Chapter IV. Even the nature of the dissident movement of the Soviet Union gives aid and comfort to structuralism. The dissidents are not notoriously social scientists, but rather natural scientists and literary people. This evidence is similar to that provided below on colonial India and Fascist Italy. This is not to say that social science has no role to play in the second world. It stands ready to offer alternate, critical explanations based on logic and research findings -- not merely on ideology. That is, it will do so, if allowed to.

The multinational version accepts the social science of the Soviets as being legitimate, and at the same time it is critical of their excessive political and ideological restrictions. They have the right to their own paradigm, and to their distinctive manner of institutionalizing our disciplines and other practices. They favor the specialized social science institute, and they have developed the practical bent of the disciplines, but they have not gone far with specializing the disciplines. The limitation of the concept bipolarity became obvious above. The Soviet slice of the world was quite restricted, and the U.S. had penetrated and influenced it. This domain has recently diminished. As the leader of the capitalist world and of the larger bipolar sphere, the U.S. remains the number one social scientist. Thus when the Soviets and the Chinese turn to the West, they turn to the United States -- the very country they most malign at other times. Their present flattery must be balanced against their secular denigration, and their penchant for overstatement should be taken into account in interpreting both extreme positions.

The reader is encouraged to go on to the next chapter. What awaits there are the status quo social scientists and their radical opponents, but what they have in common is a skeptical attitude toward the "science" aspect of social science or its objectivity. The geographic locale is Western Europe, where these two currents fit best.

NOTES

1. T.Z. Lavine, From Socrates to Sartre: The Philosophical Quest, (New York: Bantam, 1984), 275.

2. Ibid., 277.

3. Jerzy Szacki, History of Sociological Thought, (Westport, Conn: Greenwood Press, 1979), 145.

4. Lavine, 289.

5. Szacki, 150.

6. Ibid., 153.

7. Ibid., 167.

8. Edward J. Nell, "Value and Capital in Marxian Economics," The Crisis in Economic Theory, Daniel Bell and Irving Kristol (eds.), (New York: Basic Books, 1981), 174.

9. Szacki, 169.

10. Gibson Burrell and Gareth Morgan, Sociological Paradigms and Organizational Analysis: Elements of the Sociology of Corporate Life, (London: Heinemann, 1979), 328.

11. Szacki, 384.

12. Marshall R. Singer, Weak States in a World of Powers: The Dynamics of International Relationships, (New York: The Free Press, 1972), 164.

13. V.A. Vinogradov et al., "Towards an International Information System," International Social Science Journal, 33 (1981), 41.

14. F.M. Volkov, "Higher Social Science Education in the USSR," International Social Science Journal, 31 (1979), 137.

15. La Mission Francaise, Revue Francaise de Sociologie, 14 (1973), 404.

16. Zygmunt Bauman, "East European and Social Science: A Case Study in Stimulus Diffusion," Roman Szporuk (ed.), The Influence of East Europe and the Soviet West on the USSR, (New York: Praeger, 1976), 107.

17. Preston E. James and Geoffrey J. Martin, All Possible Worlds: A History of Geographical Ideas, (New York: John Wiley and Son, 1972), 268.

18. Josef Mestenhauser, "Foreign Students in the Soviet Union and Eastern European Countries," Steward Fraser (ed.), Governmental Policy and international Education, (New York: John Wiley, 1965), 146. For what follows see also Frederick H. Gareau, "The Multinational Version of Social Science," Current Sociology 33 (1985), 96-98.

19. Theodore H. Chen, "Government Encouragement and Control of International Education in Communist China," Stewart Fraser (ed.), Government Policy and International Education, (New York: John Wiley, 1965), 115.

20. Mestenhauser, 149.

21. Volkov, 137.

22. Vinogradov, 41.

23. Peter Struve, "Russia," Encyclopedia of the Social Sciences, 1 (New York: Macmillan, 1957), 280.

24. J.D. Bernal, Science in History, the Social Science: Conclusion, IV, (Cambridge: MIT Press, 1971), 1179.

25.   M. Gapotchka and S. Smirnov, "Social Science in the U.S.S.R.: Status Policy, Structures and Achievements," International Social Science Journal, 28 (1976), 83, 85, 95.

26.   Silviu Brucan, The Dialectics of World Politics, (New York: Free Press, 1978), 9.

27.   John Goormaghtigh, "International Relations as a Field of Study in the Soviet Union," The Year Book of World Affairs, (1974), 250-261.

28.   J. Wilczynski, The Economics of Socialism: Principles Governing the Operation of the Centrally Planned Economics Under the New System, (London: Allen and Unwin, 1982), 42.

29.   Bauman, 99.

30.   Oleg Mandic, "The Marxist School of Sociology: What is Sociology in a Marxist Sense," Social Research 34 (1967), 448-449.

31.   Vladimir Shlapentokh, The Politics of Sociology in the Soviet Union, (Boulder: Westview, 1987), 2.

32.   Vladimir Shlapentokh, "The Sociologist: There and Here," The American Sociologist, 17 (1982), 139.

33.   Ibid., The Politics of Sociology, 260-261.

34.   Ibid., 92.

35.   Stewart Fraser (ed.), Chinese Communist Education: Records of the First Decade, (Nashville: Vanderbilt, 1965), 189. For what follows see also Frederick H. Gareau, "The Multinational Version of Social Science," Current Sociology, 33 (1985), 99-101.

36.   New York Times, March 24, 1988.

37.   Matthias Petzold, "Psychology in Contemporary China,"
        Chinese Sociology and Anthropology, 12 (1980), 6.

38.   Gene Cooper, "An Interview with Chinese Anthropologists,"
        Current Anthropology, 14, (1972), 480-481.

39.   Yang Cheng-Fang, "The Social Sciences in China,"
        International Social Science Journal, 32, (1980): 567.

40.   John J. Cogan, "China's Fifth Modernization: Education," Phi
        Delta Kappa, 72 (1980), 271.

41.   Suzanne Ogden, "China's Social Science: Prospects for
        Teaching and Research in the 1980's," Asian Survey, 22,
        (1982), 588.

42.   F. Braybrooke, "Recent Developments in Chinese Social
        Sciences," China Quarterly, 79 (1979), 594.

43.   John S. Shippee, "Empirical Sociology in the Eastern
        European Communist Party States," Jan F. Triska (ed.),
        Communist Party States, (New York: Bobbs-Merrill, 1967),
        282.

44.   G.Y. Osipov and M.N. Rutkevich, "Sociology in the USSR,
        1965-1975, Current Sociology, 26, (1978), 3.

45.   V. Zaslavsky, "Sociology in the Contemporary Soviet Union,"
        Social Research, 44, (1977), 351.

46.   Allen Kassof, "American Sociology Through Soviet Eyes,"
        American Sociological Review, 30 (1965), 114.

47.   Z.S. Chertina, "The Bourgeois Theory of 'Modernization' and
        the Real Development of the Peoples of Soviet Central Asia,"
        Soviet Law and Government, 19 (1980-1981), 5.

48.   Rolf H. Theen, "Political Science in the USSR: 'To Be or Not
        To Be,'" World Politics, 22 (1971), 687-688.

49.   Adam Schaff, "Social Science Cooperation in Europe," Inter-Regional Cooperation in the Social Sciences, 36, (Paris: UNESCO, 1977), 49.

CHAPTER VII

HUMANISM: SOCIAL SCIENCE IN WESTERN EUROPE, CANADA, AND JAPAN

This is the third chapter in a row whose mission is the dual one of describing a meta-paradigm and at the same time siting it. In the instant case, there are two meta-paradigms: humanistic Marxism, plus interpretive sociology and the latter's counterparts in other disciplines. We place the paradigms in Western Europe, but they exist in other areas; and other meta-paradigms exist in Western Europe as well. We briefly discuss Canada and Japan. Classifying Canada was not easy, but she did not seem to fit well in either of the two previous chapters, nor does she fit in the ensuing one. The latter is devoted to the third world, and Canada is too developed for that.

We have in the two previous chapters described the objective meta-paradigms, functionalism (in sociology) and radical Marxism. We sited them respectively in the United States and the second world. What remain are the two subjective meta-paradigms, which, of course, agree on this dimension, but disagree on the other dimension of Burrell and Morgan, the one which distinguishes between regulation and dramatic change. The dominant Soviet and American paradigms are in the view of their adherents objective, even scientific in a natural science sense. This commitment makes their ideological battle more intense, as the two sectarian orthodoxies perform mutual excommunication rites against their "unscientific" adversaries. Their agreement on one of the dimensions of Burrell and Morgan thus fortifies each for academic battle against the other. The present chapter is devoted to two subjective constructions which take a less dogmatic view of their scientific pretensions, but which disagree on ideology. In actuality, there are all shades and grades of distinction between those committed scholars who to the outsider appear to be overbearing sectarians who exercise full powers of excommunications for the unscientific, to those who will admit to being "scientific," but who do not belabor the point or excommunicate the opposition; to the humanistic Marxists, the phenomenologists; and finally the solipsists. This chapter deals with the last three mentioned. Explications of them are followed by illustrations from Western Europe, particularly from the big four of the region -- France, the United Kingdom, Italy, and West Germany. But Scandinavia will not be ignored. Sociology plus political science and the latter's colleague international relations serve as our featured disciplines for this purpose. These three sections of the chapter are of unequal length, with the sections on interpretive sociology and humanistic Marxism being quite brief.

Several issues, besides the basic multiparadigmatic trend, receive attention in this chapter. The social sciences not only survived during the long Fascist winter in Italy, but they prospered. Moreover, the last years of Franco's regime saw the importation of American sociology. Social science thus is compatible with Fascism, Spanish Falangism, and, of course, with colonialism, and some other forms of dictatorship. "Freedom" is not a prerequisite for the existence or even for the prosperity of our disciplines, as is sometimes alleged. The myth that freedom is a necessary condition for our disciplines thus does not seem to hold up under critical examination. On the other hand, they fared badly under Nazism; and, as we have already seen, under Stalinism; and the rule of the Gang of Four. The migration of social scientists during the Hitler years was extensive, and many went to the United States where they bore witness to the differences which divide the continental from the American versions of the disciplines. Our approach posits unequal, vertical relations among social science centers, a phenomenon already observed in our chapter on communications, and one which becomes most obvious in the next chapter. In this chapter, vertical relations become particularly obvious in the case of Iceland and that of Canada.

Western and Humanistic Marxism (Radical Humanism)

The reader is thus assured that there is enough substance in what follows to make it worthwhile to push forward with our essay. We start with humanistic Marxism, what Burrell and Morgan call "radical humanism." The reader will recognize that it is this meta-paradigm which inspires this volume. These authors argue that this meta-paradigm finds ultimate reality to be spiritual, not material. This view is shared with the interpretive paradigm, but these two approaches part ways on the issue that man is essentially alienated. Humanistic Marxism is subjectivist, perhaps in the sense in which Fichte was, or more probably in a Hegelian sense. Fichte avoided solipsism by acknowledging the existence of the external world, but he allowed access to it only through an understanding of the nature, structure, and functioning of the conscious mind. This is subjective idealism, which contrasts with the objective idealism of Hegel. In this latter view, there is a constant interplay between individual consciousness and its objectification in the external world.[1] Consciousness and the external world are locked in a dialectic relationship in which each defines and influences the other. This dialectic process generates progress toward a state of absolute knowledge in which the distinction between subject and object will be overcome and human consciousness will become aware of its location within "absolute spirit."

In his later years, Hegel increasingly saw Prussia as the embodiment of absolute spirit, and his analysis has often served conservative causes. Soon after his death, Hegelians split between a rightist faction which kept his teachings essentially intact and the "young Hegelians," leftists who used some of his methodology, but who changed the basic assumptions and the conclusions of the approach. The most famous adherent of this latter orientation was Marx himself, who employed Hegelian historical and dialectical methods, but who inverted the analysis so as to subvert, not to support, the status quo. The "young Marx" started from the premise of alienation; he had not yet moved to a hard determinist stand, oftentimes seen as economic determinism. Humanistic Marxism or Western Marxism turns for inspiration to the young Marx or to Hegel. These two forms of Marxism run parallel or actually fuse -- the disciplinary and the geographic come together, as the name of this chapter indicates.

Merquior gives a capsule account of the tenets of Western Marxism, a summary which serves equally for Marxist humanism as well. He finds that Western Marxism was born in the twenties as a challenge to Soviet doctrine. Its principal founders were Georg Lukacs, Ernst Block, Karl Korsch, and Antonio Gramsci. The group stood up, each member in his own way, to oppose historical materialism as set forth by Lenin and Bukharin.[2] The Western version challenged the central position accorded to objective economic laws by Soviet scholars. In the Western view, these laws did not serve as the motor force of history. In their stead, the Westerners looked to the superstructure, to culture and to ideology. Instead of analyzing the process of accumulation of capital, the Westerners, for the most part, wrote about problems of alienation and reification under capitalist conditions. Merquior asserts that it is not an exaggeration to call the Western version a Marxism of the superstructure, one in which culture takes precedence over the economy. Moreover, the discipline is seen more in critical terms than in scientific ones. This latter assertion of Merquior supports the thesis set forth in this essay. Western Marxists thus reject the "naturalism" of the mature Marx and of Engels. A final characteristic set forth by Merquior for Western Marxism is its eclecticism. This is more a permit to hunt, to shop, and to incorporate, than reference to a specific set of traits. This indulgence allows all manner of differences to creep in.

The identity of Western Marxism with radical humanism is evident in the identity of those chosen as the founders and the famous adherents of both groups. Pride of place in both instances goes to Georg Lukacs, who published his landmark <u>History and Class Consciousness</u> in 1923. This work was based upon Hegel's objective idealism, and it emphasizes the humanistic, more subjective aspects of Marxism. It appeared ten years before the discovery of <u>Marx's Economic and Philosophical Manuscripts</u>, a work of the "young" Marx. Suppressed during the Stalinist period, Lukacs' work has resurfaced. He pictured consciousness, ideology, literature, and art as being epiphenomenal to the relations of production, but central to any understanding of capitalism. His emphasis is obviously upon the superstructure, not upon the base. He attempted to reconstruct Marxism as a dialectic method and as a philosophy of history, free from the influence of positivism or evolutionism.[3] He tied scientism to capitalism, and opposed the notion that there can be anything like an objective Marxist sociology or that this discipline can separate facts from values. He reduced all social knowledge to that of social classes, thus opposing the positivist image of an objective researcher in the social sciences. But he avoided solipsism -- it is the proletariat which has the unique ability and the mission of seeing social matters as they really are.

In Lukacs' formulation, the charge is made that capitalism promotes the positivist notion that the laws of society are unalterable. Naturalism in social science is a product of reified consciousness, and also an ideological weapon of the bourgeoisie. This reified social world is ahistorical, atomized, and reduced to quantitative and abstract relations. Bourgeois thought is incapable of viewing society in its totality, the correct perspective and that of the proletariat. Lukacs saw the essential difference between bourgeois and Marxist social science to be method, not the various theoretical statements such as those which stress the primacy of economic motives. Most important distinctions are holism or totality and anti-phenomenology, which go beyond superficial and observable facts and which interpret the latter in terms of its concrete historical totality.[4]

Our second choice of a Western Marxist humanist is Antonio Gramsci, former head of the Italian Communist Party and even today a great inspiration for this party. Jailed during the Mussolini years, and sick on top of this, he wrote under these burdensome conditions. His works have become influential in the postwar period, especially in Western Europe. He was influenced by the Hegelianism of Benedetto Croce, and he argued that contemporary Marxism has lost its revolutionary zeal by incorporating positivist ideas at the expense of the voluntarism of the working class.[5] He identified determinism with fatalism, because it eliminates human activity from the vision of the world and tries to cram all facts into a single scheme. Fatalism, for him, is a relic of religious thought. He argued for a dialectic theory to transcend the classical determinism/materialism idealism/voluntarism debate. This would be a philosophy of praxis, constructed so as to give a total and integral conception. He rejected the naturalist position that the social sciences should follow the methodology of natural science -- each discipline should have its own proper and appropriate method and constructs.

A concept made famous by Gramsci is hegemony, which he applied to capitalism and which refers to elements outside the economy and extra to state coercive power. The bourgeoisie thus maintains its hegemony, not only through control of the economy and through the use of coercive political force, but also through cultural means. Here is an obvious reference to the crucial importance of the superstructure; and proletarian revolutions, if they are to be successful, must attend to it. He found superstructural elements to be particularly robust in the West, in contrast to their weakness in Imperial Russia. The latter was held together by an all powerful state. Consequently, the revolutionary struggle in the West cannot adopt the Soviet strategy. The Leninist frontal attack must be avoided in favor of a war of attrition, one of position, more complex and more subtle. The strategy of the Western workers and their allies must be first to acquire hegemony, i.e. dominance in the social arena, and then proceed to political dominance.[6]

Although Lukacs and Gramsci come within the contours of a non-determinist, humanist position, they were committed to revolution. Central foci of their analysis were the promotion of revolution, class consciousness, party organization, praxis, and a dislike for static positivism. We next turn to the Frankfurt, critical school, which has been characterized as "armchair Marxism" and "Marxism without a proletariat".[7] This school has shied away from political practice and has never identified itself with any political party. Its adherents are theoreticians, not activists, as they have moved toward intellectual criticism, not revolutionary practice. Moreover, this school has been notoriously eclectic, strongly seasoned not only with Hegelianism, but even with psychoanalysis and cybernetics. The school was founded in Frankfurt in 1923 (its official name is the Institute of Social Research), but it was forced by the Nazi regime to move -- first to Paris, then to New York. After the war, several members stayed on in the United States; others returned to Germany. Habermas, the most famous contemporary representative, disassociated himself from the German student movement of the seventies, left Frankfurt for over a decade, and coined the term "fascism of the left" to describe some aspects of that movement. The school has been characterized as Marxist, non-Marxist, and even as anti-Marxist. Szacki argues sarcastically that when in America it appeared to be Marxist. Perhaps the term "critical" is more descriptive, in that the school seems to hold all systems at arms length. Another justification for this name is the commitment of its adherents to change. This commitment contrasts with the positivist assumption of value freedom. This school has undergone dramatic changes in its over six decades of existence. One of its major earlier works published in 1936 (Critical Theory and Traditional Theory) was orthodox, relative to what occurred later. It pinned its hopes upon the working class.[8] The revolutionary fervor of the school has suffered one setback after another, a "down hill" march away from orthodoxy.

Though not tied to orthodox Marxism, the Frankfurt school has built upon foundations used before in the work of the young Hegelians, particularly Marx, a wide-ranging critical perspective designed to expose the shortcomings of capitalism.[9] Its adherents have sought to bring about dramatic change through a revolution of consciousness. The school developed as a reaction against orthodox Marxism, but particularly against positivism. It subjects functionalism to critical examination, and also the phenomenological school and interpretive sociology. In his One-Dimensional Man, Herbert Marcuse saw technology at work in advanced capitalism preventing change and obstructing liberation. In his view, technology does not necessarily represent a progressive force, used solely to control nature for the betterment of humankind. On the contrary, its function in advanced capitalist countries is to control and to enslave humankind. Advanced industrial society has succeeded in stopping dramatic social change. The consumer society, with its affluence and the creation of false needs, impedes the development of radical protest against the established order. The media do their bit by molding and controlling consciousness. A "happy" work force is maintained by the establishment of the welfare and the warfare state. In modern technological society, the logic of rationality pervades modes of thought and the organization of the material world. It is the task of critical theory to make this exposure and to explore alternatives, not to offer the bright prospect of a paradise of the proletariat.

Habermas has emerged as the leading contemporary exponent of critical theory. He argues that positivism serves the interests of those who wish to control, and he favors the critical which he insists is emancipatory, the dialectic (meaning transcending the subject/object dichotomy) and the hermeneutic in its attempt to understand the social-cultural world.[10] He too would shift the emphasis of Marxism away from the economic. But the direction of his shift is to the structure of language, its nature and use, not to a criticism of technical rationality as was the case with Marcuse. In Habermas' view, the problem of language has displaced the problem of consciousness. He posits two kinds of speech interactions, one a work situation and the other a general one. The first is dominated by purposive rationality, the usual form in capitalist industrialized societies, and a form characterized by domination and exploitation. It stresses means/ends relationships, and the capitalist system which it serves is rationalized by increased production and technical control. This situation contrasts with that of general interaction, more characteristic of pre-industrialized society. Interaction subsumes labor as a cohesive and an integral part of social life, and the system assumes reciprocal expectations about behavior. Interaction is seen as based upon speech situations emancipated from domination. Emancipation depends upon the extension of communications free of domination, free of the ends-means constructions which reduce mankind to the level of things. One is reminded of the distinction of Tonnies between Gemeinschaft and Gesellschaft, only Habermas insists upon casting this dichotomy in a linguistic framework, and he argues that <u>Gemeinschaft</u> relations are possible in advanced societies. Obviously, radical humanism is more intricate and complicated than what is presented here, but our purpose has been to make out its general nature and merely to suggest its general traits.

Interpretive Social Science

This section is patterned after the previous one, and its general purpose is also to suggest the general thrust of a meta-paradigm, not to present details. Here we give a capsule analysis of the meta-paradigm interpretive sociology, holding off on specific examples and illustrative material until the next section. We present the philosophical background for this construction, together with an indication of its subjectivity -- to suggest its scope. Like the previous section, it is brief. This, the last of the meta-paradigms treated in our analysis, shares the same basic subjective elements referred to in the previous section, but it is not committed to dramatic social change. It seeks to understand the world as it is, but within the realms of individual consciousness and subjectivity, within the framework of the participant, not that of the researcher.[11] The approach, when viewed as a general type, is nominalist, anti-positivist, voluntarist, and ideographic. The assumption of those who subscribe to it is that the world of human affairs is cohesive, ordered, and integrated. Problems of conflict, domination, contradiction, and potentiality are not part of its theoretical framework. Its ideology is conservative/liberal, not radical.

The history of this meta-paradigm is rooted in the German idealist tradition, at least this is considered to be the case by Western observers. Kant is seen as its predecessor, or at least as a key contributor to the basic approach of the tradition, because he argued that humankind possesses inherent, in-born organizing principles which are necessary for the structuring, arranging, and thus for the understanding of sense data. These organizing principles are held to be in the mind, a matter of intuition. They are <u>a priori</u>, and thus independent of external reality and of sense data. Granted that the world is a complex mix, an interrelation between <u>a priori</u> knowledge and empirical reality, the point of departure for Kant is in the mind, in the spirit. This assumption forms the basis of the whole German idealistic tradition. Idealism was eclipsed by positivism for a time, only to blossom forth again in the late nineteenth century as the neo-idealistic or neo-Kantian movement.

This movement in social science became identified with Dilthey and Husserl, and to a lesser extent, with Weber, as this movement returned to the problems of epistemology identified by Kant. The argument was made that mankind could not be studied through the methods of natural science, because humans are not things, but creatures each with a mind and a free will. In this view, to comprehend social life requires the speculative methods of philosophy and the study of social wholes. Dilthey drew a sharp distinction between natural science and our disciplines. The former investigates external processes in the material world, whereas our disciplines are concerned essentially with the internal process of the human mind.[12] These later can be understood only by conducting an internal investigation, in the context of the minds which generate the process and the inner experiences which the process reflects. The social sciences require a new methodology, verstehen (understanding), by which the investigator seeks to understand human beings, primarily by investigating their inner feelings and secondarily by observing the way the latter are outwardly expressed. Outward manifestations of inner feelings are to be understood through the methods of verstehen, the inward focus.

Actually it is Weber who has had the greatest impact upon sociology, and he has emerged as a bridge builder between idealism and positivism. But his construct is more positivist than idealist. He sought on one hand to understand the subjective meaning of social action, and to reduce this meaning to the level of the individual. On the other hand, his method looks to the objective, and it would provide causal explanations of social phenomena. He sought to build an objective sociology upon the foundation of subjective meanings and individual action. To do this, Weber used the construct the ideal type. It incorporates the spirit and the assumptions which characterize individual phenomena, but packages them into a larger, generalized category. The dispute rages on whether Weber should be classified as an idealist or as a positivist; he appears here as a bridge-maker who would join the two, but his tilt is in the direction of positivism. His emphasis upon verstehen is a methodological tool for overcoming obvious deficiencies in positivism. Through it all, he continued on to pursue his central purpose, which was to construct a causal theory, rather than following through on the full implications of idealism. He appears to be idealist only in terms of methodology, not in ontology, epistemology, and in his view of human nature. There is with little doubt that Weber is a partisan of regulation, not a proponent of dramatic social change.

Weber's contribution is a point of departure for those who would produce a really serious subjectivist version of our disciplines, but he did not go beyond methodology. The notion of verstehen in other hands has gone beyond Weber's focus, a methodological convenience designed to smooth out some of the grosser assumptions of positivism. In the hands of the partisans of phenomenology, it has assumed a central ontological position. This philosophical movement holds consciousness to be the matrix of all phenomena and sees them as the objects of intentional acts. It demands its own method. Its recognized founder, Edmund Husserl, came down hard on the subjectivist side of the subjectivist/objectivist dimension, which we described elsewhere. The external world cannot be assumed to be that unexamined common sense construction, usually taken for granted. It is revealed to be the artefact of consciousness, the latter plus human will being the creator of the external world. The subjective is the source of the objective. Ontologically, the world consists of a stream of consciousness, more accurately of a plurality of streams of consciousness. The task of epistemology is to investigate these streams, in order to reveal and to analyze the essential types and structures of experience. It uses intuition and insight as the means of accomplishing its task. Weber made a limited excursion into the realm of the subjective, and this excursion went little beyond attributing an element of voluntarism to the individual's interpretation of the world. In contrast, Husserl subjected the fundamental problems of the social sciences to criticism -- their problems of ontological, epistemology, and methodology.

Like other meta-paradigms, interpretive sociology has a broad reach, this time from solipsism to hermeneutics. We will pursue this subject briefly to suggest its scope. Perhaps the first mentioned parameter is a misplaced guidepost, because solipsism is more a philosophical position than a social science construct. In any case, it results in complete relativism and skepticism, and it marks the most subjective limit of the meta-paradigm. Ontologically, solipsism sees the world as having no existence beyond the sensations which are perceived by humans. In this view, there is no external point of reference, and so knowledge must be confined to individual experience. Knowledge is entirely individual and personal: there is nothing outside oneself and one's ideas. Solipsism is inward looking and self-sustaining, but it offers no prospect for the shared development of social science. In fact, it is a potential danger to our disciplines, to be sure no reason to dismiss it.

Transcendental phenomenology is a step away from solipsism, a notch closer to the objective pole of the subjective/objective dimension. It is a kind of phenomenology, and we distinguish here between the transcendental and the existential varieties. Phenomenology is not an investigation of external facts, a process so prized by the functionalist. Rather it leaves aside any question of objective reality to concentrate solely and only upon the reality of consciousness. It proceeds to describe consciousness as this latter phenomenon presents itself to the individual. The world of Husserl is thus a world of phenomena, of meanings, not one of objects. His world of transcendental phenomenology brushes aside the work-a-day assumptions of an objective reality in favor of pure subjectivity, the intentionality of which is a source of meaning. Consciousness is always required for revealing reality, which is not available to the observer any other way. On the other hand reality is not constructed by consciousness -- reality is revealed through it. Burrell and Morgan argue that Husserl came quite close, "dangerously close," to solipsism.[13] Husserl in his later years strove to assure objectivity for his approach with the concept intersubjectivity. Transcendental egos constitute others as equal partners, a partnership which becomes a basis for community. This concept laid the basis for the less subjective existential phenomenology.

We conclude this section with the existential phenomenology of Schutz, who sought to square phenomenology with social science. This is as far as we go with interpretive sociology, as this section is intended to be suggestive, not exhaustive. He put emphasis upon the phenomenology of the social world, thus "lowering" the problem from the realm of philosophy and the isolated individual to that of sociology, and in doing so he moved his analysis closer to the objective. Nonetheless, he attempted to broaden the problems originally raised for sociology by Weber, but in analyzing meaning he seems to have abandoned the strict phenomenological approach in favor of accepting the social world as it is commonly constructed. This allowed him to use the concept intersubjectivity as originally set forth by Husserl. He argued that the way we give meaning to our lives is through social interaction. This meaning is provided retrospectively, and the typing of meanings comes biographically, but in a social context. His typification resembles Weber's ideal types, but it would interpret what people do from their perspective. His typification is not only a methodological device, but it marks features of everyday life, seen in a social context. Throughout, he argued that the central task of social science is to understand the social world from the point of view of those inhabiting it, using concepts and explanations intelligible in the everyday world. Schutz's grand design is to link Husserl's phenomenology with sociology -- using Weber, but delving more deeply into the implications of the Weberian approach by moving beyond methodology. To make the connection, however, he moved away from many significant "subjective" assumptions of Husserlian phenomenology to embrace the objection, the outer social world.

We stop here with the discussion of interpretive sociology, the examples from this discipline serving for others as well. Our discussion has been abstract, sometimes pitched at the philosophical level. Hopefully, it did suggest the general thrust of the meta-paradigm as well as its breadth. The two dimensions of Burrell and Morgan used in our analysis in these last three chapters help in understanding the complexity and the contradictions existing in social science, which in great part stem from contrary philosophical positions. Like all typologies, the one which results from these dimensions has a hard time classifying given paradigms. This is the case once we leave aside extreme cases -- hard core Kremlin Marxism, the almost equally dogmatic, but conservative or liberal, American functionalism, or paradigms based upon transcendental phenomenology. One example of the shades of gray which exist once we leave the extreme end points is found in the usual American textbooks on international organizations. These present the material against a traditional, institutional background, one which often betrays a legal focus. Recognizable are several "add-ons" as well, from functionalism or from American development theory. The functionalist (more accurately identified as a "behavioralist" in political science) deplores the institutional/legalistic setting, and also the all around eclecticism. Those committed to this eclecticism would probably admit to being "scientific" if pressed to say so. Our criticism is a generic one for all social science typologies. Their value lies more in mapping out extreme limits and boundaries, but problems arise in classifying at the midpoints. Concrete examples of the positions suggested in this section and its predecessor will be found in the upcoming one.

Social Science in Western Europe

This section features the social sciences in Western Europe, their birthplace in modern times. Emphasis is upon the "big four," the United Kingdom, France, West Germany, and Italy, and upon the disciplines sociology, political science, and international relations. The central position of Western Europe in the social sciences has switched to match the overall secular decline in the hegemony of the region and the rise to power of the United States. A major purpose of the section is to fill out the previous one, by providing illustrations of interpretive social science. Western Europe is characterized by this type social science and also by Marxist humanism, but individual differences among the countries exist. This is not to say that American functionalism is not present, an import which accompanied the general American extension. Western Marxism should suffer somewhat from the recent events in Eastern Europe. This not reflected in what follows, based as it is on sources written before these events occurred. We add something also on the history of the disciplines, despite the fact that an entire chapter was previously devoted to this subject. We return in order to explore the general relationship between totalitarian regimes and the existence and the prosperity of social science. We do this by looking at Fascist Italy and, to a lesser extent, at Falangist Spain and Nazi Germany.

One of our first tasks is to point to the differences which divide American and continental social science. Proof for this distinction is found in a study which compared the articles contained in three American and two West German political science journals for six years in the sixties.[14] The German articles generally employed an historical, legal, philosophical, or institutional approach -- all amenable to the interpretive approach or radical humanism. American political scientists were found to be attached to other methods, and particularly toward the end of the sixties to those involving statistics. This latter is a central feature of American behavioralism. Another such comparative study analyzed all of the full length articles which appeared from 1970 to the end of 1975 in the official journals of the national political science association of the United States, Canada, India, and the United Kingdom. Empirical orientation was judged by the relative amount of graphic illustrations included in the articles. The American journal had far and away the most graphic material and was thus judged to be the most empirical.[15] The Canadian journal was further down the line, but not as far as the Indian and the British.

These findings suggest that political science in the United States is more empirically oriented than that in West Germany and also more so than in Canada, India, and the United Kingdom. The findings confirm a widely held impression, but they offer another type of evidence to support it. Schweigler considers 1965 as the take-off point for international relations in the German Federal Republic. This was the very first year in which political scientists outstripped their nearest competitors, the historians, in the teaching of international relations courses. In 1967/1968, the last academic year for which Schweigler gives figures, political scientists retained their premier position, the historians held on to second place. German youth turned to American innovations -- systems theory, quantitative methods, and other "scientific techniques". Many of these Jungen had spent time at American universities. This is of special historic interest, because young Americans who studied Staatswissenschaft in Germany in the 1870s and 1880s were stimulated to go back home to found what later became the American version of political science.[16] But American influence has not proved to be enduring. Toward the end of the 1960s, German youth in international relations and in social science generally began to turn away from the handiwork of the American establishment. An emotional anti-Americanism, was fueled by the Vietnam War. American social science seemed to have failed dismally. The "post-behavioral" revolution in Germany was a turn to critical concepts -- to those of Adorno, Horkheimer, and Habermas of the Frankfurter Schule. "Thus the social sciences in West Germany have become polarized between the traditional approaches (read interpretive) and the critical (read Marxist humanist) theories (with very little functionalist work in between)".[17] Many international relations scholars have forsaken their American behavioralist mentors, whose work began to be perceived as an instance, or a rationalization, of American imperialism.[18] In the late sixties the international section of the German Political Science Association launched a major project to analyze critically American behavioral projects and at the same time go back to the social-critical and structural-historical approaches of the European sociological tradition, a return to Marxist humanism.

Our next choice for analysis among Western European countries is the United Kingdom. The reader has already been put on notice that a comparative study of political science journals exposed this country as falling well down on the quantitative scale of the discipline -- below that of the United States, Canada, and even India. This discipline has had until quite recently a hard time gaining recognition in Britain -- a problem which had to be faced also in Western Germany. True, Political Studies, the periodical of the United Kingdom Political Science Association, has been appearing since 1953. But a year later Professor Robson could name only three British universities with flourishing political science programs -- those at Oxford, London, and Manchester.[19] Some ten years later, Dr. Nettl concluded that political studies had been institutionalized as one of the major social sciences in the country. The process occurred during the late fifties and the early sixties, the same period which saw the construction of the new red brick universities. Most of the departments existing in the mid-seventies had been created during this period of construction. Currently thirty-six of the fifty-three British universities offer a degree in political science.[20] The syllabi are given over mainly to the study of institutions and political theory.

International relations and political science are connected in the United Kingdom. At the undergraduate level, international relations in Britain is most often taught as a program in the latter discipline. Only eight universities have degree programs in international relations itself. The characteristics which we have imputed to political science are generally applicable to the other discipline as well. Johnston finds that despite the relationship between the two disciplines indicated above, the closest links remain between international relations and history and that this association continues to affect the direction of research. No matter what other differences may divide them, a majority of British scholars in the field agree that one of their major strengths is diplomatic history. The optimism which early on had existed about the potential contribution of behavioralism has by now dissipated -- with the discussion now centering upon whether this movement was detrimental to the discipline or not. Game theory and model building have lost their luster, and scholars have turned away from value free "science" in favor of the older British tradition of concern for values.

An advantage of the multi-national examination of our disciplines is the revelation that some of those cherished, parochial ideas and associations which are accepted as gospel in one country have little relevance to another. A case in point is the belief that political science is inevitably on the side of the angels of academe and that it thrives only in an atmosphere of freedom. Such faith is hard to reconcile with the story of this discipline in Italy, the next country to which we turn. The first departments of political science were created there in 1924, at a time when the Fascists were consolidating their power.[21] Silj regards this as happenstance, but some departments saw fit to serve the cause by offering such courses as the theory of Fascism and the demography of race. The tainted image resulting from collaboration was in part responsible for the slow growth of political science in the postwar period. Other causes of this phenomenon for political science and for all the social sciences were the tradition of idealism, the hold of the legal tradition on scholarship, and the power of the jurists in the university system.

We return below to the problem of Fascism and social science. First we take a glimpse at Italian sociology. Pinto finds Italian culture to be dominated by historicism and idealism, and thus always to have had an ambivalent attitude toward the social sciences. Crocean liberalism considered them as false, because they did not take into account individual action and freedom. Furthermore, the Weberian thesis of separating them from politics never took root in Italian sociology, as it has in America, for example. Pinto presents this discipline in the postwar period as evolving in five political-intellectual phases, each with its own special sociological approaches and themes, but each also closely tied to its own distinctive political and social context.[22] Her view is that sociology played one dominant role in each period, to be superceded by another in the succeeding period. Among those she identified were these three which are presented here in chronological order: (1) the sociologist as industrial and town planner, subsidized by the Olevetti industries in Northern Italy; (2) the sociologist as scientific expert, especially in development, using models imported from the United States; and (3) the sociologist as the leftist activist, rejecting American models and capitalism. The principal themes explored in the seventies were related to the hopes of the left -- studies of the working class and those related to transforming society. Italian sociology thus seems to follow what looks like a general continental pattern, or at least a trend, of veering to the left in the last sixties and early seventies. This trend should stop, or at least be attenuated, by fallout from the events of Eastern Europe in 1989. We have found this left leaning trend to have been present for sociology in West Germany and now Italy. France will soon be added to the list.

French political science has been found to fit into this same basic mold, at least this is the judgment of Macridis and Brown. The American scholars found in the early postwar period that this discipline in France was tied to politics and political activism.[23] The clear implication of these scholars is that this need not be the case or, at least, that these traits are overdrawn in the French case. They found a lack of political science in France, and argued that political speculation there has been associated with action. It often takes the form of a conflict of ideologies. In fact, French social science is often Marxist or interpretative -- denying any notion of value neutrality. In the view of these authors, French political literature reflects rather than analyzes ideological positions and attitudes, and it is more a call to action than an invitation to reflection and speculation. Argument rather than detached examination is the rule.

In the early eighties Lemert sketched a portrait of French sociology which is also "more intensively combative" than the American brand. He insisted that the term "champ" in the "champ of French sociology" (part of the title of his article) be interpreted as battlefield, and the academic battle takes place at close quarters in Paris, among combatants so well known to each other than footnoting is usually not required. The discipline in France is highly literary, lacking in specialization, intensely ingrown and ethnocentric, and, of course, elitist. The latter two characteristics are general in social science: the French seem only to have cultivated them better. The outsider is not completely cut off, but understanding the French text requires that one read from the entire field to the text in question. To talk of specialization in French sociology in the way in which one speaks of it in American sociology makes little sense. If one applies to it the standards of clarity of American functionalism, "the reading will go poorly".[24] The reader must suppress his own ethnocentrism and see the text as coded by the local field. French sociology, like Italian, is openly ideological; and its evolution, in Lemert's formulation, leads to an end point parallel to that where we left Italian sociology. The former went through its empirical period (1945-1954), and it has entered its critical one.

One must be careful when speaking of social science in Western Europe so as not to exaggerate its unity. Barents addressed this issue in a study of Western European political science, published under the auspices of the International Political Science Association. He found that the centers of European political science have a "strongly national outlook" and that one can speak of political science in Western Europe, but no such thing as a "Western European political science" is discernible.[25] The prohibition follows in part from the ethnocentric compartmentalization of the discipline. Other divisive influences mentioned by Barents are the communications problem caused by the more than half dozen languages in which political science in the area is expressed, and the disciplines varying relations with other disciplines. Thus the discipline is tied to law on the continent, but across the channel history and political theory serve as the associates. The varying identities of these associates contribute to the shape which each version takes.

We next turn to Scandinavia, an area which has two obvious lessons to teach. The first is that little social science consensus reigns there, despite the small area and a common journal, at least for political science. The second is social science dependence upon the great powers, a point which is most obvious in the case of Icelandic political science. The most notorious victims of dependent vertical relations are third world countries, but the first world has a quota as well. American functionalism has an outpost in the area, as is illustrated by political science in Norway. This discipline was introduced there in 1947, and the initial courses were taught by jurists and historians.[26] The first teaching position in the subject came ten years later, and the first chair in 1965. The big jump in political science enrollments in Norwegian universities came on the heels of this last event, and international politics became one of the two most popular specialties in political science. The Norwegian Professor Stein Rokkan took a leading role in data archivist work from the mid-fifties onward. This helped launch scientism in Norway, as political scientists and international relations scholars there abandoned history and jurisprudence in favor of the computer and all the other things which go with the behavioral versions of these disciplines. The Institute for Social Research in Oslo served as a bridgehead in Europe for a phalanx of visiting distinguished American social scientists.

The stories of the meandering of international relations are different enough in Finland and Denmark from those in Norway to merit a separate paragraph. As in Norway, the fate of this discipline in the latter countries has been bound closely to that of political science. Both disciplines went through their traditional phases and their behavioral periods, and both witnessed a great expansion. But both have also undergone post-behavioral revolutions. The latter in Finland seems mild, less so than that of Denmark. Anckar argues that behavioralism dominated Finnish research in the sixties, but by the mid-seventies this approach had been supplemented by an interest in the role of the state, societal needs, and the historical dimension.[27] However, behavioralism is still the preferred method in Finland, and "neo-positivism" is not a term of derision there. Events in Denmark took a more decided turn. At first the attack, launched mainly by students, was directed at value relativism, labelled as being in reality a transparent cover for conservatism.[28] "Objective" behavioral research was damned as being irrelevant. But the dissenters soon became Marxists, and Danish scholarship split into two competing groups with little interaction between them. The scientists make up middle range theories and do empirical things, while the Marxists seek to erect one overarching grand theory. Significantly, the latter have been influenced by their comrades across the border in West Germany.

Several facts about the situation in Sweden expose the danger of generalizing about our discipline, even in such a sparsely populated and culturally homogeneous area as Scandinavia. Despite the early establishment of political science in Sweden (a chair was established there in 1622), undergraduate enrollments since 1967 have witnessed what can only be described as a calamitous setback. Enrollments rose to 2,601 in 1967, only to tumble to 1,866 in 1969, to 561 in 1973, and to a mere 240 in 1975.[29] Furthermore, international politics has not proved to be a popular specialty within the covering discipline political science. These recent comments of Lewin and Nord seem particularly well taken: "international studies is still a marginal subject in Sweden -- more so than in many other comparable countries".[30]

The reader may well question our judgement, for the space which we now devote to Professor Grimsson's report on political science in Iceland. The reason for our extravagance is certainly not to be found in the productivity of the University of Iceland -- seventeen political science graduates in the years 1973-1976. The reason for our interest is the fact that Iceland is a developing country, and thus her problems in adopting or adapting political science (or international relations) are shared by a large part of the world. Her dilemma has been anticipated by the methodology of this volume. Professor Grimsson of the University of Iceland argues that political science at the present time is not a truly international discipline.[31] On one side, there are a small number of countries who dominate the discipline with their manpower, research, and language. On the other side, are the majority of nations, in which political science either does not exist or is in its early stages of development. The discipline in the latter countries is left in the busy hands of a few scholars. These harassed individuals must teach, translate, and keep up with all the divisions of the discipline. Grimsson predicted that if the two worlds of political science keep growing apart the discipline will most likely bifurcate permanently and remain divided by the cultural barriers imposed by this segregation. Note that our predictions deviate from this, but we are happy to receive collaborating testimony for this dependent relationship. One of the problems which

Professor Grimsson has found to be the most upsetting and time-consuming for his developing nation is the translation of the ever increasing volume of political science jargon into Icelandic. Iceland, of course, has its own distinctive language. The translation of key concepts, manufactured in such abundance by American scholarship, has been a major occupation of the Icelandic teaching staff. He says that the problem this raises for the developing world must be faced systematically if a truly international discipline is to emerge. Our prescription for the latter is given in the last chapter.

Canada and Japan

Our limited comments about Canadian and Japanese social science appear here in this chapter, their most logical location. Despite obvious and marked differences, the disciplines in both areas have manifested a dependency upon the world centers of our discipline. Moreover, both countries represent challenges to the methodology adopted by this volume. Canada has played host to the multinational for a long time without the adverse consequences often found in third world countries. Her distribution of income has been much more equal than that found in the third world. It is true that her culture has suffered from the American "invasion," and Canadianization has become an issue. Japan is a great capitalist country, dominant in world trade and global investments. But she has not matched this in social science and become a great social science power as well. The United States has been dominant along the various aspects of the domestic and international structures used in our analysis. This has not been the case for Japan.

Japan presents a fascinating spectacle, one of the great capitalist powers, but her social science export capability is limited by the distinctiveness of the Japanese language. This capability by no means matches that attained by the Toyota. It is estimated that Japanese social scientists publish some 1,000 books annually plus numerous articles, but almost all are in Japanese, and thus inaccessible to foreign scholars.[32] On the "import" side, Japanese scholars make use of social science materials written in English, French, German, and Russian. Japanese initiation to the mysteries of modern social science occurred after the historic Meiji Restoration of 1868, after the Japanese government had decided to open relations with the West.[33] Courses in law, economics, political science, and statistics were introduced in 1871 at the Tokyo Imperial University. Later sociology was added, that of Spencer and Comte. "In contrast to the United States -- to some extent to Western

Europe, Marxism remains extremely influential in Japanese academic circles, especially among social scientists".[34] This brand of social science made its appearance in the country after World War I. The social sciences blossomed after World War II, a phenomenon duplicated in many settings. Another such phenomenon was the postwar "flooding inflow" of American social science, especially in economics, political science, sociology, and psychology."

We saw above in chapter IV that Canadian social sciences are dependent upon those of the United States. The evidence supported overall Canadian dependence and that for Quebec as well. A distinction must be made between the English-speaking social sciences and those for Francophone Canada. That they must be treated separately is evidence to support the multinational version of our disciplines. Our emphasis below is upon sociology, with only an occasional reference to other disciplines.

Sociology as a discipline was introduced in Quebec in the 1930's. Its proponents rejected the versions of the discipline as formulated by Comte and Durkheim as being atheist.[35] Instead, they founded the discipline upon Christian doctrine, and used it in an effort to reform Quebec society. This Francophone version of sociology at first was influenced by the discipline as presented by LePlay in France, to be affected before and after World War II by minor impacts from the Chicago school and structural functionalism.[36] The Catholic Church was in large part responsible for promoting the original discipline as imported from France. In fact the discipline reflected not only the philosophy of this institution, but also its holistic vision of the world. It did not divide and parcel out the world into "middle range theories," but it insisted on a global view of society. It was dualistic, reserving one sphere for the moral, and a quite different one for the scientific. The two were not to be reduced to the material. Both spheres were part of the discipline, their methodologies were merely different. The fact/value separation did not occur, and it never became the issue that it did in American or Anglophone Canadian social science. The Francophone version is historical, and it is related to the movements for Quebec independence. It is also applied, not merely theoretical. Thus it became a means and an incentive for reforming Quebec society. It resembled European sociology more so than did the Anglophone Canadian discipline, but it has its own characteristics as well. It became a model for some of those Anglophones who in recent years would "Canadianize" their discipline.[37]

The development of sociology in Anglophone Canada was hampered by the traditional British definition of what are appropriate university subjects. This was part of the colonial inheritance of this part of Canada. Sociological analysis was introduced and utilized as an accessory in the disciplines Canadian history and political economy. The first separate department of sociology was established by McGill University in 1922, a second at the University of Toronto in the 1960's. The first followed the tradition of the University of Chicago, the second structural-functionalism. Thus American sociology gradually took its turn as the center to the periphery in Anglophone Canada.

Sociology in Anglophone Canada has been less holistic than in the French-speaking part. It has generally eschewed theoretical and methodological problems in favor of closing the societal information gap.[38] In the 1950's and 1960's it experienced rapid growth, so much so that many sociologists, notably those from the United States, were imported. In 1970-1971 only 40.3 percent of sociologists and anthropologists in Canadian universities were locals, whereas 38.5 per cent were Americans.[39] If one takes into account that Francophone universities hire few Americans, the conclusion emerges that nationals of that country outnumbered Canadians in the Anglophone institutions. By the late 1960's the impact of the American presence became apparent, as American dominated departments looked to old school ties to recruit south of the border. In the 1960's there emerged the "Canadianization" movement in sociology and in all the social sciences. It emerged as the same time when public opinion was becoming more restive because of American domination of the Canadian economy.

The drive for Canadianization took place mainly in Anglophone Canada, and as a reaction to United States domination. It was not confined to sociology, but included other disciplines as well. United States domination emerged after World War II, taking the place of the colonial domination of the British. Canadianization in the social sciences parallelled a similar general movement which strove to enhance national identity. The growth of the multinational corporation on Canadian soil helped fuel the new wave of national awareness and national consciousness. The early 1970's witnessed a spate of books which detailed American economic and cultural inroads. The movement itself pressed for Canadianization of university faculty, and strong pressures to hire Canadian academics emerged in the early and mid 1970's.[40] The American percentages have been diluted by voluntary programs to hire indigenes and by a law which gives preference to

Canadians. Moreover, the Canadian government decided to support the social sciences, and its largess took the place of that of American foundations which had been the previous source for subsides.[41] The Canadian government subsidized the discipline to the point that they could organize and became independent of institutions south of the border. The discipline is now less dependent upon American personnel, textbooks, and professional organizations. This has tended to relieve the discipline of foreign dependence, but it has promoted dependence upon the Canadian government.

A critical facet of Canadianization is to fashion disciplines which would emerge from, and thus reflect, the Canadian context. The Social Science Federation of Canada has affirmed that social science findings from other countries "cannot simply be imported and assumed to apply in Canada," nor can the assumption be made that such theories or methods are appropriate.[42] The federation added that what is needed is the study of Canadian social phenomena using appropriate theories and methods. To accomplish this goal, a macro-sociological framework has been advocated, one which would be appropriate for the nation. Moreover, this framework would have to be holistic and interdisciplinary -- and placed in an historical context. These latter requirements themselves distance the disciplines from those dominant in the United States. The historical context, of course, contributes to this distinctiveness, and it should be so tailored as to highlight the uniqueness of a Canadian prospective. These characteristics are those which we saw above described as applying to sociology in Francophone Canada. Political economy, neo-Marxism, and dependency theory have also been used. It is beyond the parameters and the competence of this essay to judge if these characteristics have been so fixed that they can with confidence be declared to be those of the newly emerging Canadian discipline. Our conclusion is that they have not as yet, and this estimate is shared by at least one expert observer.[43] Canadianization is the more difficult, given the free trade treaty recently concluded with the colossus to the south. Such a treaty tends economies, cultures, and social sciences to the detriment of the formation of independent disciplines in the periphery.

Social Science in Falangist Spain and Fascist Italy

We close the substantive part of this chapter by revisiting the relationship between the existence and the prosperity of our disciplines and totalitarian/authoritarian regimes. We have seen that Stalinism and sometimes other brands of Marxism are incompatible with their well-being. Here we examine the relationship in the context of Spanish Falangism and Italian Fascism. Five kinds of sociology have been identified in Spain,[44] three of which are important for our discussion. These latter are American structural functionalism, the critical, and the Marxist. The first emerged in the late 1950s, in a period of the partial liberalization of the Franco regime. American functionalism influenced the content and the methodology of this school, and it remained dominant in Spain for almost two decades. It flourished in the country during the sixties, during the so-called technocratic government of Carrero Blanco, a government dominated by members of the Opus Dei, the right wing "Holy Mafia" of the Catholic Church. Empirical research came into its own, and such techniques as survey research became very popular. There was little critical sociology to complete with the American import. The seventies witnessed criticism of structural functionalism, "mild" at first, but progressively more critical. The years after the death of Franco (in 1975) witnessed the triumph of the critical and the Marxist sects. The death of the general was a turning point for the whole of Spanish society, and for the discipline sociology as well. Communist and Marxist political parties were legalized, and sociology became more radical, more critical, and more Marxist. An increasing number of sociologists trained in Europe, not the United States. Radicalization grew apace under the influence of the Frankfurter school and dependency theory imported from Latin America. By 1976, critical sociology had become more extensive than empirical sociology, and functionalism was considered to be demode.

A reformed "fascism" of the Franco variety thus seems to be compatible with the existence and even the prosperity of social science, at least with American social science. We will see in the next chapter a similar compatibility between American social science and the dictatorships in the third world, notably in Brazil. Italian Fascism also seems to have been quite compatible with social science, this time its own brand. Our assertion is quite at odds with the allegation that Fascism is fatal to our disciplines. Indeed, an analysis of Italian sociology devotes less than six lines to the Fascist period, and these are intended to underline the "complete disappearance" of sociological analysis or its distortion.[45] Schneider has a contrary view of the matter. He asserts that even before the march on Rome, liberi docenti began to expound various aspects of Fascist doctrine in the universities. They offered courses in such subjects as recent Italian history, principles of national syndicalism, corporative law, and the theory of the state.[46] But so did those regular professors who had joined the Fascist party and who naturally became leaders in university circles. Notable among these was Giovanni Gentile. These scholars "applied their knowledge of the social sciences to the cause of Fascism." Efforts were made to change the curriculum in the universities and in the lower grades to accord with Fascist principles. Research bureaus were established and attached directly to the government. And an effort was made to concentrate in a few universities the teaching of social sciences according to the standards of the new dispensation. A notable effort in this respect was the creation of the Fascist Faculty of Political Science at Perugia in 1928, designed to train a new leadership. Lesser centers were established in other cities. Gentile himself founded the National Institute of Fascist Culture in Rome. Its official organ was Educazione Fasciste, and it enjoyed the cooperation of a number of reputable scholars.

It is hard to accept the thesis that Fascism almost exterminated social science in Italy, although the government did make efforts to redirect and to "reform" existing disciplines. Furthermore, two new disciplines emerged in Italy in 1924, at a time when the Fascists were consolidating their power.[47] The first Italian departments of political science were founded in that year. Sociology was also institutionalized at the time. Silj argues that the timing in the case of political science is happenstance, but still the coming of Fascism did not impede this new development. These departments saw fit to serve the cause by offering courses such as the theory of Fascism and the demography of race. The tainted image resulting from this cooperation was responsible in part for the slow growth of political science in postwar Italy. Italian professors in all fields were obliged to take a joint oath of loyalty not only to the king, but also to the Fascist regime. Of 1,200 professors only 11 refused, and this small group was dismissed.[48] This vote of confidence represented a propaganda bonanza for the regime, although many professors did this more for expediency than as an act of conviction. Vilfredo Pareto, the renowned sociologist, accepted a seat in the Senate, as did Pantaleoni, the dean of Italian economists. Lentini points out that Mosca, Pareto, and Michels have earned the right to be considered the founders of political sociology, and they and their collaborators and colleagues conducted relevant research during Fascist times.[49] This research centered on the social origin of university students, the aristocracy, and social mobility. Moreover, sociology was also institutionalized during Mussolini's time, again indicting that Italian

Fascism provided fertile soil for our disciplines. After collaborating with the regime, Croce broke with it to provide a rallying point for liberal opposition. But the only consistent organized opposition on a national scale was provided by the Italian Communist Party.[50] It went underground in 1926, and it provided a majority both of the martyrs and of the manpower for the underground which helped to liberate Italy. Its leader Antonio Gramsci spent many years in jail, and his publications from there have been, as we have already seen, a valuable contribution to Western Marxism.

That Fascist social science enjoyed a measure of international legitimacy, at least in the United States, is indicated by our own research whose central purpose was to measure increasing American ethnocentrism. It sought to do this by computing and by contrasting the percentages of American and foreign social scientists chosen by the American editors to contribute to the Encyclopedia of the Social Scientists and to the International Encyclopedia of the Social Sciences. Contributions to both works were controlled by American social scientists. They served as the gatekeepers, determining which experts were allowed to contribute articles. The first of these works was published in the period 1930-1934, after Mussolini had consolidated his power, and the latter in 1968 after Italy had become democratic. The study is the more relevant to our present argument, because nationality was operationalized by professional affiliation. This means that those social scientists designated as "Italian" were actually affiliated with institutions in that country, and not refugees residing abroad. Forty-nine contributors were so designated as contributors to the first encyclopedia (of the total of 2,223), which was published in the Fascist period. This contrasts with just four for the later encyclopedia published in 1968 (of a total of 1,505 contributors).[51] This seeming American preference for Fascist social science must be balanced against the fact that the American percentage of contributors was substantially greater in the latter work than in the earlier one. We, therefore, confine our comparison to this earlier work. The number of Italian contributors (49) was substantially less than the French (155), for example, but greater than that of Czechoslovakia (24), Poland (28), or that part of Germany which is now the German Democratic Republic (25). We believe that this gives a measure of legitimacy to Fascist social science. Our conclusion is that social science, not only survived in Fascist Italy, but that it expanded. Both sociology and political science were institutionalized at the time, and the disciplines in this Fascist domain received a measure of international recognition, notably from the United States. Distinguished American social scientists chose a substantial number of social scientists from this Fascist country to contribute to what became a standard reference for our disciplines. We shall see in the next chapter that the social sciences have prospered under some other forms of right wing dictatorships and under colonialism.

Conclusions

This concludes the chapter dedicated to humanistic Marxism, to the likes of interpretive sociology, and to the social sciences of Western Europe, Canada, and Japan. The two featured meta-paradigms were found to be "subjective" in contrast to the "objectivism" of Kremlin Marxism, American functionalism, and the latter's counterparts in other disciplines. The distinctions between the constructions were found to be fundamental, often philosophical -- for example issues of ontology and epistemology. But more specific social science issues were at stake as well, methodology and the issue of whether the disciplines can legitimately be modelled upon natural source or not. Each of the meta-paradigms had its own specific stimuli and content from which and in which the flight from objectivity to subjectivity took place. In the case of Western/humanistic Marxism, the stimulus and the content were provided by, or were reactions to, Soviet Marxism, that of Lenin and Bukharin. The stimulus was the attempt to escape economic determinism, the determinism of the base over the superstructure. The flight was away from economics to culture; away from the base to the superstructure; away from the accumulation of capital as a motive for capitalism to a concentration upon alienation. Dialectics and praxis were stressed rather than the economic. Humanistic Marxism can be as "revolutionary" as the Kremlin brand in its search for change. In fact as a practical matter, it may be more conducive to change. This because of its voluntarism -- its impatience with waiting for a cataclysmic economic crisis. It seeks to resuscitate Hegel or to return to the young Marx. Even this did not satisfy the revisionism and the extreme eclecticism of the Frankfurter school. It reformed Marxism ("deformed" might be more descriptive) to the point of adjuring the class struggle and even severing any connection with a political party. Perhaps this school should be called the "critical," without any reference to Marxism. Its presence here marks the extreme revisionist poll of Western Marxism. Western Marxists should continue to emphasize their differences with

Kremlin Marxism, but their cause should suffer by the publicity from Eastern Europe.

We found interpretive sociology to be a reaction to functionalism, and that its content has been sparked by German idealism. Society in this view must be seen from the inside, from the perspective of those analyzed, not imposed from the perspective of the investigator. Social beings are not so many material objects which can be legitimately treated as things, as the functionalist would. If Weber concentrated upon methodology, more typical adherents broadened the coverage of the meta-paradigm. The phenomenologists did just that by insisting that the primary source with which social science is forced to deal in our disciplines is human consciousness. Transcendental phenomenologists were sited toward the extreme subjectivist edge of this meta-paradigm. They insist that we must deal with the streams of consciousness of those investigated. Existential phenomenologists use the concept hermeneutics in order to socialize these streams of consciousness. They, therefore, push their approach in the direction of objectivism.

The last section of the chapter was devoted to our disciplines in West Europe. The big four there provided much of the subject matter, but Scandinavia was included, and even the outsiders Canada and Japan. This section provided a rich source of examples of Marxist humanism and of interpretive sociology and the latter's counterparts in political science and international relations. American functionalism has appeared in the region as well; it entered along with the general American "invasion." But this sect suffered a setback in the late 1960s and the early 1970s, and Marxist humanism was the chief beneficiary. The chapter explored further the relationship between totalitarian/authoritarian governments and our disciplines. Social science expanded in Mussolini's Italy, and the overwhelming percentage of Italian professors took the required oath of loyalty to him. His most consistent adversary was the Italian Communist Party, not the university or social science communities. The reader may recall from Chapter VI that the major source of dissent in the Soviet Union is not from social scientists, but from other intellectuals. This evidence tends to support the structural approach adopted in this volume.

Other on-going topical subjects explored in this chapter were dependency and vertical relations in general. Canada and Iceland provide paradigmatic examples of dependency. Canadian dependence upon the United States has expanded to include personnel dependency, a condition which inspired the government to enact corrective legislation. But Canadian dependency should continue and should expand with the new economic arrangement with the United States. Negative reactions to this and to the ever present "problem" of Quebec should enliven the future. Iceland's dependency reminds one of the situation in the third world, just as Professor Grimsson's complaint reminds us that social science is not really international. The upcoming chapter on the third world will explore these themes in greater detail.

NOTES

1. Gibson Burrell and Gareth Morgan, Sociological Paradigms and Organizational Analysis: Elements of the Sociology of Corporate Life, (London: Heinemann, 1979), 280.

2. Jose Guilherme Merquior, O Marxismo Ocidental (Rio de Janeiro: Nova Fronteira, 1986), 12.

3. Jerzy Szacki, History of Sociological Thought, (Westport Conn.: Greenwood Press, 1979), 386.

4. Ibid., 388.

5. Burrell and Morgan, Sociological Paradigms, 289.

6. Merquior, 145.

7. Szacki, 392.

8. Barbara Freitag, A Teoria Critica Ontem E Hoje, (Sao Paulo: Brasiliense, 1986), 150.

9. Burrell and Morgan, Sociological Paradigms, 291.

10. Ibid., 294.

11. Ibid., 28.

12.   Ibid., 229.

13.   Ibid., 242.

14.   David Pfotenhauer, "Conceptions of Political Science in West Germany and the United States, 1960-1969," Journal of Politics, 34 (1972), 554-591.

15.   Sami G. Hajjar et al., "The Literature of Political Science: Professional Journals in Four Nations," International Social Science Journal, 29 (1977), 327.

16.   Albert Somit and Joseph Tanenhaus, The Development of American Political Science: From Burgess to Behavioralism, (Boston: Allyn and Bacon, 1967), 7-9.

17.   Gebbard L. Schweigler, "Federal Republic of Germany," International Studies in Six European Countries - United Kingdom, France, Federal Republic of Germany, Sweden, Netherlands, Italy, (Ford Foundation, 1976), 71.

18.   Ibid., 97.

19.   Michael Hechter, "Notes on Marxism and Sociology in the USA," Theory and Society 8 (1979), 323.

20.   Larry Johnston, "United Kingdom," International Studies in Six European Countries -- United Kingdom, France, Federal Republic of Germany, Sweden, Netherlands, Italy, (Ford Foundation, 1976), 20-21.

21.   Allessandro Silj, "Italy" International Studies in Six European Countries -- United Kingdom, France, Federal Republic of Germany, Sweden, Netherlands, Italy, (Ford Foundation, 1976), 265.

22.   Diana Pinto, "Sociology, Politics, and Society in Postwar Italy 1950-1980," Theory and Society, 10 (1981), 672. For what follows see also Frederick H. Gareau, The Multinational

Version of Social Science, Current Sociology, 33 (1985), 23-27.

23.   Roy C. Macridis and Bernard E. Brown, "The Study of Politics in France Since the Liberation: A Critical Bibliography," The American Political Science Review, 51: (1957), 811-812.

24.   Charles Lemert, "Literary Politics and the Champ of French Sociology," Theory and Society, 10 (1981), 651.

25.   Jan Barents, Political Science in Western Europe: A Trend Report, (London: Stevens, 1961), 18, 76.

26.   Stein Kuhnle and Stein Rokkan, "The Growth of the Profession in Norway," Scandinavian Political Studies, 12 (1977), 65.

27.   Dag Anckar, "Political Science in Finland 1960-1975," Scandinavian Political Studies, 17 (1977), 124.

28.   Peter Nannestad, "Political Science in Denmark: Trends of Research 1960-1975," Scandinavian Political Studies, 12 (1977), 92-93.

29.   Elvander Nils Elvander, "The Growth of the Profession 1960-1975: Sweden," Scandinavian Political Studies, 12 (1977), 76.

30.   Leif Lewin and Lars Nord, "Sweden" International Studies in Six European Countries -- United Kingdom, France, Federal Republic of Germany, Sweden, Netherlands, Italy (Ford Foundation, 1976), 163.

31.   Olafur Ragnar Grimsson, "Pioneering Political Science: The Case of Iceland," Scandinavian Political Studies, 12(1977), 48.

32.   Jaji Watanuki, "The Social Science in Japan," International Social Science Journal, 27 (1975), 189.

33.   Teiza Toda, "Japan," Encyclopedia of Social Sciences, (New
        York: Macmillan, 1930), 321.

34.   OECD, Social Science Policy, Japan (Paris: Organization for
        Economic Co-operationa and Development, 1977), 25.

35.   Guy Rocher, "L'Avenir de la Sociologie au Canada" Jan. J.
        Loubser, ed., The Future of Sociology in Canada (Montreal:
        Canadian Sociology and Anthropology Association, 1970),
        16-17.

36.   Dan A. Chekki, American Sociological Hegemony:
        Transnational Explorations, (Lanham: University Press of
        America, 1987), 62.

37.   Harry H. Hiller, "Universality of Science and the Question of
        National Sociologies," The American Sociologist, 14 (1979),
        134.

38.   Chekki, American Sociology, 65-66.

39.   Paul Lamy, "The Globalization of American Sociology:
        Excellence or Imperialism" The American Sociologist, 11
        (1976), 110.

40.   Hiller, 131.

41.   Lamy, 9.

42.   Social Science Federation in Canada. Social Sciences in
        Canada. 6(1978), 2-22.

43.   Chekki, American Sociology, 76.

44.   Jesus M. De Miguel and Melissa G. Moyer, "Sociology in
        Spain," Current Sociology, 27 (1979), 55.

45.   Luciano Gallino and Edda Saceomani, "Two Generations of
        Sociology in Italy," Social Science Information, 10 (1971),
        135.

46. Herbert W. Schneider, "Italy," Encyclopedia of the Social Sciences, I, (N.Y.: Macmillan, 1957), 278.

47. Silj, Italy, 264.

48. Martin Clark, Modern Italy, (London: Longman 1984), 246.

49. Orlando Lentini, L'Analsi Sociale Durante Il Fascismo. (Napoli: Liguori, 1974), 181.

50. Christopher Seton-Watson, Italy from Liberalism to Fascism 1870-1925, (London: Methuen, 1967), 707.

51. Frederick H. Gareau, "The Increasing Ethnocentrism of American Social Science: An Empirical Study of Social Science Encyclopedias," International Journal of Comparative Sociology, 24 (1983), 154.

CHAPTER VIII

THIRD WORLD SOCIAL SCIENCE

If the preceding three chapters were accounts of the creators of social science, the current one presents the mirror of these creations. For so long, the third world has served as the inactive recipient, some would say the victim, of movements and activities whose origin is found elsewhere. This is a general phenomenon, and our structural approach puts social science in this context. Political economy has the same moral, the rich first world centers develop and establish vertical relations with the poor and the underdeveloped third world peripheries. But the story does not end here, for the inactive are becoming active -- in fact, the third world is revolting against first world domination. The revolt is many faceted, a general phenomenon, and it does include our disciplines. We put much stock in the revolt, arguing that it will prevent any social science consensus in the foreseeable future, a general requisite for maturity. The social science aspect of the revolt until now has generally been at the verbal level, or it has concentrated upon such matters as the indigenization of personnel. The big breakthrough in paradigmatic innovation has been dependency theory, a subject given much attention in this chapter. In fact, we have devoted a section to an analysis of it.

We start below with our disciplines in India, actually with Indian sociology. This is followed by education, cast in its role as the carrier of social sciences to the third world. Education is that part of the structures closest to our disciplines. Then we divide third world social scientists into the international clients, those who are tied to the center and the indigenizers or nationalists who are not so tied and who stress local paradigms. This division is necessary if we are to understand the connection between first and third world social science.

293

This is followed by two sections on the indigenization process -- our example being Latin American dependency theory.

Social Science in India

India provides an excellent example of the dilemma of our disciplines in the third world. The beneficiary of a long recorded history, India received the social sciences as a by product of colonialism. They were imposed, instead of emerging "naturally", i.e. in a milieu in which traditional values had been eclipsed by rational thought. They followed the British flag; first employed by the colonialists to promote the new dispensation. After World War II, the United States displaced the British as India's social science center, a transition which occurred for many third world countries. Like so many countries so situated, India has been restive in this peripheral role. Many social scientists in the Asian country have rejected or tried to revise their paradigmatic imports and to mark the disciplines with local characteristics. They have not been notably successful in this endeavor, as has been the case in other types of indigenization. The reader is asked to consider India's position and reaction as typical of the third world, but the parallel with Canada is also evident. As was the case with Canada, our featured discipline in what follows is sociology.

The social sciences were implanted in India, and in Asia in general, by the West, and they have grown in a transnational system of asymmetry and dependence. The conditions on the subcontinent did not meet Durkheim's stated conditions for the birth of sociology: the decline of traditionalism and the emergence of faith in reason, in what he called "science". Social science in India was "implanted" or "imposed" in British type universities, often to help in solving problems from the perspective of the colonial administration. Pieris argues that anthropology grew up as a discipline for studying the colonials, segregated from sociology which was reserved for the societies of the colonializers.[1] The distinction was the same as the medieval dichotomy separating Christian and heathen, and the modern one separating developed and underdeveloped. Anthropology in this view has been not so much the science of man, as the science of primitive man. It was a study in which the colonialists viewed the colonials as object. Whatever one thinks of these charges, the general view is that anthropology during the colonial era followed an evolutionary paradigm, with Europeans at the nadir of human development, and the rest of humankind located down the cultural scale. Hopefully, the lesser

breeds would in time close the gulf which separated them from the European, but a long period of evolution was required to close the gap.
India had traditional social science of a sort before the British imposition. In fact, there existed two traditions -- one Hindu with Sanskrit as its vehicle of communications, and the other Islamic expressed in Arabic and Persian. Islam makes little distinction between the religious and the mundane and Ibn Batuta, a Moroccan traveller, is often counted as an early social scientist in the Islamic tradition. Well known in the older Hindu tradition are the Karma Sutra (300-400 AD) and the Arthashastra (324-296 BC). The former is the best known of the Vedas in the Western world, famous for its explicit treatment of sexual positions and techniques. It also provides its readers with a portrait of life under the Gupta dynasty. In the Arthashastra, Kautilya wrote on public administration and international relations, providing his readers with an analysis preceding that of Machiavelli by many centuries.

The British impact was such that it dislodged, rather than combining with, these previous traditions. Colonialism reached through to the social sciences mainly via the school system, the social institution closest to our disciplines. Western sociological analysis appeared in the very early part of the present century, and the discipline itself was institutionalized somewhat later.[2] A separate department of sociology was established at the University of Bombay in 1919, to be followed at universities in Lucknow, Calcutta, and Mysore. It was not until after independence in 1947, however, that the discipline really found its place in Indian academe. An overwhelming majority of colleges and universities have come to offer the discipline as an autonomous study. Prior to independence, British influence was marked, and India followed the British academic tradition emphasizing social anthropology more so than sociology itself. The former was useful for its service to colonial administration, and its use helps account for the fact that rural India attracted more attention than city life. Since independence, it is American sociology which has become the dominant outside force, as empiricism and statistical analysis have come into their own.

The impact of United States sociology has been mediated through the exchange of scholars, the use of American textbooks, and subsidies from American foundations. In the 1950's and 1960's foreign degrees were prized -- the same reverence for things foreign usually

associated with colonialism. This was accompanied by the adoption of
structural functionalism, the favorite American paradigm. The reader
will note the similarity between the situation in India and that of
Canada, previously discussed in Chapter VII. Both former British
colonies, both countries were impacted as a result of this subservience.
After independence, the center position was assumed by the United
States, the new social science superpower. The Canadians were more
influenced by their southern neighbor, and they were slower to react
to American influence in social science. But both countries did react.

Roy, former secretary-general of the Association of Asian
Social Science Research Councils, finds that indigenization is a reaction
against the notion that social science paradigms generated in one
region necessarily have validity everywhere. This assurance is based
upon the naturalist assumption for physical science that nature is
uniform.[3] The problem is that the "universal" social science paradigms
are first world creations. Third world social science is reduced to the
position of accepting what is produced elsewhere. Roy finds that
indigenization is the trend in Asia. He argues for cooperation among
Asian centers of the disciplines, rather than interaction with the first
world. Such interaction at this time only leads to more dependence and
more borrowing of what is probably inappropriate.

The term "indigenization" when applied to social science has
several meanings. Its usual and "ultimate" meaning is a reference to the
creation of local paradigms. Our example of this is Latin American
dependency theory, and its analysis appears at the end of this chapter.
Sociology in India has some distinct characteristics but its
distinctiveness has not advanced to the point of indigenization. This
discipline has turned to macro-models and to an historical context --
directions which Canadian sociology has taken and which facilitate the
highlighting of national differences. Endogenous elements have been
added to the discipline as well.[4] The term indigenization can be used
to signify local control or administration of social science research or
to the substitution of local for Western languages used for teaching the
disciplines. This substitution has occurred in Indian universities, where
the many local languages are more and more taking the place of
English. As these institutions open their doors beyond the elites to
more and more students, the importance of English as the language of
instruction diminishes. We return to this issue later in the chapter.

The reader will recall the central position which education played in our accounting for the social sciences. It was that part of the structure closest to them, and its costs provided the most solid examples of their expense in our discussion of political economy. Education serves here as the indicator of social science extension, both in a colonial setting and in a milieu of non-colonial dependency, a situation sometimes called "informal empire." Of course, this chapter deals with both settings which resulted in the third world condition. We use education as the measure of US social science extension, despite the fact that its foreign "export" program is often in the hands of private foundations and despite the fact that its social science is less monolithic than that of the Soviet Union, as an example. We argued above that mainstream American social science has its peculiar characteristics, certainly to the extent that we can talk meaningfully about it. Furthermore, the multinational version need not assert that the foundations deliberately try to promote American foreign interests. Berman makes this assertion,[5] a "charge" which receives a measure of support from our discussion of nationalism in a previous chapter. But the support need not be deliberate. The heads of the foundation might merely be trying to promote and to propagate social science in general, without any particular version in mind. But the kind they support generally is the American brand. American culture would suggest this anyway. The probability that social scientists at this level believe in the dominant social science sects is great anyway.

A few additional comments in defense of this indicator, before we apply it to the problem at hand. The assumption that the American government uses its international aid program for other than disinterested reasons is suggested by a pro-American piece which offers, among other motivations for the program, promoting national objectives and withstanding "the extension of communism".[6] This assumption seems more plausible when we realize that most of the foreign effort by the American government is for the military education of members of foreign armed forces, and it seems illogical that part of the US defense budget would be deliberately "wasted" on disinterested foreign charity. The political motive, as well as the relations among the negotiators, comes to the surface for all to see in the public, or private, student exchange programs negotiated between the Soviet Union and the powers of the first world, especially the United States. Such exchanges are the only "true" student exchanges, where the principle of strict reciprocity is observed.[7] The relations among the negotiators here are basically horizontal, not obviously vertical or dependent, with neither of the parties so desperately needing, or feeling the need for, improved education that it is willing to accept the penetration by foreign political and cultural ideas. The elites involved tend to react horizontally, not in the typical vertical fashion of client to patron. Since desperation and dependency are absent or the need of local elites to ally with central elites, the upsetting prospect of foreign and ideological influence and subversion comes to the fore and becomes more salient in the negotiations. Mestenhauser speaks of the tense atmosphere which surrounds such negotiations and of a report by the State Department to the American public that such exchanges have been a two-way traffic.

The massive educational effort by France in general and particularly in her former African colonies is instructive in a study such as ours. France has emerged as the greatest exporter of teachers in the world, some 40,000 -- one out of every eleven in the profession.[8] Many of these are employed in Francophone Africa, where French paradigms are still important. The point is that this is a continuation, writ large, of the colonial situation -- it is even concentrated in former colonies. Thus the term "neo-colonialism." The enhanced influx of teachers is accompanied and reinforced by other forms of continuing penetration and dependency -- economic, political and communications. Singer points out that collectively the United States, France, West Germany, the United Kingdom, the Soviet Bloc, and Japan accounted for, i.e. served as the host countries for, 82.6 percent of the world's students studying abroad in 1963.[9] This group includes five of the first world's six publishers of social science journals, the index we use for assessing relative social science position. In that year, three times as many students were studying in the United States as in France, her nearest rival. Most of these students came from third world countries, but a substantial number were nationals of such developed countries as Canada, the United Kingdom, and Japan. It is easy to imagine that dominant American social science sects became part of the intellectual baggage of these sojourning students and that these sects returned to the homeland with them. The same essential transfer occurred as the United States poured millions of dollars into foreign educational systems after World War II, thus "helping to remold the educational systems of perhaps seventy-five countries in the American pattern".[10] The remolding process involved visiting professors, equipment, books, reading lists, syllabi, and American social science. Berman identifies the major social science sects exported by the American foundations as structural functionalism, behavioralism, and the theory of human capital --all "scientific" and technocratic theories, similar to the meta-paradigm identified as "functionalism" by Burrell and Morgan.

Social Science Communications in the Third World

Social science communications in the third world have been fixed by the vertical relations already discussed above, with their one-way flows notably from the United States, but also from other great social science powers. This can mean that a given third world country may be tied in a vertical relations to one of the great powers, perhaps the United States. Or it may have two centers, such as Indian political science -- the chief vertical relation is with the United States and a secondary one is with the United Kingdom. What is lacking is much return flow to the first world or much interaction among third world countries themselves. The parallel with the global structure of journalism and television interaction is obvious. An exception to the first assertion concerning social science is the use of dependency theory by Latin Americanists in the United States.[11] An exception to the second is the considerable cooperation among the social scientists of Latin America.

But the general pattern is well known, and in recent years, has come under increasing attack by third world scholars. Thus Bongoy speaks of the African vertical infrastructures -- economic, technical, and educational set up during colonial times -- articulated with the metropole -- and their continuance and even reinforcement to the present time.[12] He argues that colonial social science research was often aimed at probing for local weaknesses, so that they could be exploited and colonial domination perpetuated. Universities and research institutes were set up in a vertical fashion between colonized and the colonizer, but not among social scientists in what was French, British, and Belgian Africa. These structures have survived independence and have been accentuated by neo-colonialism and the hiring of large numbers of foreign social scientists. These scholars have their professional ties with their fellow countrymen, not with African practitioners. Bongoy offered a full portfolio of factors which he alleged impede social science communications in Africa -- among which we list language, differing professional backgrounds, neo-colonial relationships, and generally poor communications among African countries.

A similar situation exists in Asia, the result of the same basic factors. Despite efforts notably by UNESCO, regional cooperation there is very weak.[13] The following discussion, based on an article by the former secretary-general of the Association of Asian Social Science Research Councils, excludes China and other socialist countries in the area -- a fact which will become obvious as we proceed. Western colonial powers implanted their own educational systems and social sciences in Asia without regard to differing indigenous conditions. The disciplines have developed there in a milieu of asymmetry and dependence, without being articulated with their immediate environment and its characteristics. During colonial times, they were bound up with the interests of the rulers. The disciplines as taught in the universities have maintained, and carried over into the post-colonial period, their distance from Asian reality. This results in part from a routinized form of pedagogy and the divorce of the latter from research which is carried on in separate institutes. The postwar period witnessed Asian social science shift its dependence from Europe to the United States -- a development already suggested in our discussion of education.

Another shift noted by Roy, this one recent and qualitative, leads to indignation, but it has a bearing on communications as well. It is the self-assertion and the growing tendency of Asian social scientists to reject imported Western theories and methodologies. This has led to efforts to develop paradigms based on indigenous values and cultural orientations. Furthermore, this turning away from Western imports has made Asian scholars realize their common problems, which they share with other third world countries as well, and thus has lead them to look favorably upon regional cooperation. The new attitudes lead to questioning the ties which bind them with the center and induce them to try to forge regional ones. Roy went on to name several Asian organizations intended to promote regional communications, but their records hardly seem impressive, understandable given the strength of countervailing forces. Roy concluded that real international cooperation in the social sciences must await the strengthening of national and regional centers in the third world. And the strengthening must involve increasing independence from the first world. Otherwise, increased interaction, since it would be mainly with the first world, would only aggravate existing dependency relations. Such attitudes obviously can have an impact on the quantity and the direction of the flow of global social science interaction. Roy placed the changing attitudes of Asian social scientists in the comprehensive context of changing economic and political attitudes, a connection which we heartily endorse.

We agree with Oteiza, former secretary-general of the Latin American Social Science Council that social science is different there in that it enjoys high levels of collaboration, when compared with other regions of the third world.[14] This is readily apparent to even the half attentive reader of its literature. Such a reader usually confronts a situation in which the data and the illustration are of the region; the references are mostly to Latin American authors; and the analysis is often guided by dependency theory. At least this is the case for the literature of the "indigenizers," those Latin American social scientists who have broken with the center. The other group which maintains this connection can be called the "internationalists" or the "clients." Several common characteristics of Latin American countries help account for the relatively high level of social science interaction in the region. These factors include: two quite similar dominant languages; parallel histories and cultures; widespread poverty and underdevelopment; and the same "central" country, the United States, which often appears to be the capitalist oppressor if not the military aggressor.

Relatively high levels of regional interaction occur in Latin America, despite the concomitant existence of vertical relations, in social science and other fields, with the United States and other central countries. We will note the limitations of this cooperation below. It is symbolized by, and institutionalized in, the Latin American Social Science Council (CLASCO). The great regional expansion of our disciplines in the postwar period was accompanied by informal cooperation in the region. By 1960, it became obvious that more formal regional links were necessary, especially because of the strong institutional ties and "alma mater" relations between regional institutions and personnel with the United States and Western Europe. Five years of discussion led to the decision in favor of associating Latin American research institutions, which is the focus of collaboration of CLASCO. The establishment of the institution on this basis allowed the exclusion of purely teaching institutions or the more traditional juridically and philosophically inclined. CLASCO brings together 80 such research institutions, and it has added a graduate training program as well. Its procedures contain none of the diplomatic restrictions and roadblocks which we emphasized above in the

302   **The Political Economy of Social Science**

operations of the Vienna Center. Oteiza argues that CLASCO has helped move Latin American in the direction of regional collaboration. We would add that the organization is an institutionalized symbol of this collaboration. We endorse his statement that Latin American social science is far from having eliminated its unbalanced relationship with the United States and Europe and his further assertion that Latin American social science links with Asia and Africa are weak. The latter is an objective of CLASCO, and one of the nine areas it has earmarked for special research is "studies in dependency."

This is not yet the time to speak of dependency theory, but rather to summarize briefly what we have said to now about the global communications system of social science and comment upon it. The system has been exposed above and in chapter IV as one which features vertical relations: from the United States to the other Western social science powers and to most of the third world; formerly from the Soviet Union to the other socialist countries (except China) and to selected third world countries; and from the middle range social science powers, mostly in Western Europe and elsewhere as well, to their peripheries. The centers send out messages, but receive little inflow in return. The peripheries can have more than one center, but it seems that they have a chief center. A crucial feature of the system is the lack of communications among the peripheral states, their ties are with the center. This is notably the case among the third world states, an exception -- and this only to some extent -- is Latin America.

The reader is asked to recall the assertion above by Roy that Asia's priority must be the strengthening of its national centers and regional cooperation. These priorities must be attended to first, and only then can Asia increase her foreign interactions. If these priorities are not followed, the result can only be the strengthening of present vertical relations. The report of the 1976 UNESCO-sponsored conference on social science was more cautious, but its advice is in the same direction. The report called for the re-examination and the redefining of vertical relations, while at the same time adding that some benefit accrues to the dependent country from them.[15] This view parallels that of dependency theory, as set forth by Cardoso and Faletto. They argue that economic development requires, among other conditions, a period of relative economic isolation in which the domestic market is partially separated from foreign markets.[16] Since the focus of their book is Latin America, we can conclude that their advice is for the countries of this region to separate their economies partially and temporarily from the United States and Western Europe. This is the same advice of Roy for social science in Asia, except that he calls in addition for regional cooperation. Roy's advice contradicts that of Storer, just as that of Cardoso and Faletto contradict that of neo-classical economics. Storer sees science (and by extension, social science) operating according to the principles of laissez-faire.[17] Its development spreads by diffusion, especially when buttressed by foreign aid and notably after a nation possesses a certain critical mass of scientists (Rostow's take-off stage). Our analysis rejects this happy model, and it focuses upon the notion of the knowledge industry, an asymmetrical enterprise characterized by vertical relations.

The Internationalists/Clients and the Indigenizers

Our sketch so far of third world social science lacks one essential feature, and it is supplied by analogy with dependency theory. This approach recognizes two elements in the periphery, one tied to the center and benefiting from the connection, sometimes called the "center in the periphery." As we saw in chapter II, Galtung referred to it in these terms and as the center's bridgehead in the periphery. This element can be visualized in general terms as the well-off group, "generally no more than 20 percent" of the local population who have adopted the patterns of consumption of the center -- Coca-Cola, the automobiles, and the other products which the multinationals produce for them.[18] Classes or military and business elites are closer to the mark, for what our analogy is intended to point to is those social scientists in the periphery engaged in the vertical interaction with the center. Perhaps they studied there and maintain relations with their alma mater. Or perhaps they stayed home, but received the paradigms and research findings of the center from a local university. They could easily be the "technobureaucrats" of Latin America, perhaps neo-classical economists or acritical sociologists, who produce "technical" information for business or government. They could regard what they have learned as being scientific truth, or they might subscribe to interpretive sociology or to its counterpart in other disciplines. Besides, their beliefs correspond with their professional interests. They are called here "clients" or "internationalists" -- the reader can choose the name which is most pleasing ideologically.

The other element in dependency theory consists of those we named above "indigenizers." They represent the redemptive element in the theory that would cut or reduce ties with the center and increase them regionally, and develop their countries based upon an indigenized, local and more appropriate technology. The parallel to the latter in our scheme of things is an indigenized paradigm. The representatives of this persuasion, as it applies to social science, was found in our discussion of Africa, Asian, and Latin American interaction. Their analysis can be based upon theories derived from colonialism or Marxism, and they may be revolutionaries, nationalists, or both. The nationalists would limit changes to the international sphere, whereas the revolutionary insists on internal changes as well. The multinational version sees this element, without choosing among its variations, as the wave of the future. The tone of the discourse of the indigenizers should convince the most skeptical of their good faith. But we suspect that the realization of their ideological objectives are generally congruent with their professional interests.

We now use the testimonials of two "indigenizers" to illustrate the existence of these two elements. The complaints of the typical indigenizer are such as to leave no doubt of his/her existence, and these complaints are often aimed at the chief protagonist, the client/internationalist, thus testifying to the latter's existence as well. Alatas argues that the total experience of colonialism in Asia formed what he called the "captive mind." It is possessed by the university-trained Asian social scientists, educated locally or abroad, who have accepted uncritically the thought patterns of the West.[19] Uncreative, alienated from their own national traditions, they are unable to separate the particular from the universal. Alatas views this phenomenon as being distinctly Asian. Western observers, even when taken by Eastern culture, are selective in what they accept, but not Asians. We expand the concept to include the scholars of other colonialized peoples and also those living in dependent societies. Freire found them in Guinea-Bissau. Such scholars can follow the same general pattern -- those in penetrated society probably to a lesser extent. This type of social scientist imitates rather than adapts and domesticates. The notion that what is Western is universal Alatas calls "methodological imperialism". It assumes that what is valid in one place is valid in another, and we discussed this claim at some length in chapter I. This claim is one made by Western functionalists and Kremlin Marxists for their respective social science sects, but in the present context it is part of colonial oppression. Atalas charges that universities promote the "captive mind," and he would introduce courses there to expose this phenomenon. Akiwowo attests to the existence of this same phenomenon in his native Nigeria. He locates it among "certain well placed members of the Nigerian academic power elite".[20] They evince a strong belief in "the fictitious nature" of some supposed international standard. This elite demands that Nigerian scholars prove themselves by being accepted and recognized by European and American scholars. The phenomenon manifests itself in a general inability of Nigerian intellectuals to depart from the paradigms they absorbed in their universities.

The existence of these two elements in peripheral countries emphasizes a significant aspect of our social science model. The vertical interactions, which are so much a feature of the model, are mostly with the clients/internationalists in the periphery. This, because, in general, they adhere to the same social science sects as do the center. But this emphasis, in turn, requires its own modification, because social science is more Gothic than assumed above: it is a multiparadigmatic enterprise with many social science sects. Marxist paradigms from the center, for example, can receive a warm welcome from the indigenizers in the periphery, with Marxism providing the sectarian basis for communications. Indigenizers represent an ideological impediment to international interaction as well. They argue that the present structure of such interaction must be changed, certainly before such interaction is increased.

The Indigenization of Social Science

Indigenization of social science has come to mean many things -- and the indigenizers have been cast in the role of overturning many aspects of the status quo. Our emphasis is upon communications and social science sects. Atal, UNESCO regional director for social science in Asia and the Pacific, asserts that the struggle to indigenize social science has become worldwide.[21] But he explains that in Asia it has taken the form of teaching in indigenous languages with local materials, local research, and the determination of priorities locally, plus the attempt to create indigenous paradigms. He reported "progress" in all but the last field, notably in the substitution of Asian languages for Western colonial ones, with the result that the new generation of Asian social scientists is not able to communicate with what ideally would be Western colleagues. It should be emphasized that the conversion to local languages is part of the process of the democratization of the universities, instruction in Western languages being associated with the past emphasis upon elite education. The new generation has been reduced to a situation comparable to that of the monolingual American social scientists, except that English is an international language for the disciplines, whereas the Asian languages are not. Nonetheless, the "progress" already made, and that in the offing, bodes ill for the prospect of international communications.

An indigenized Indian sociology in all probability will come to terms with 4,000 years of history of that country, which has usually regarded intuition as the centerpiece of its epistemological system. One president of the All-Indian Sociological Conference affirmed that sociology in that country cannot be entirely objective. It must include "a little bit of obtuse philosophy" to provide a connection with the past.[22] Social science associations there have more than once questioned the appropriateness of foreign paradigms.[23]

Varma's analysis of Parsons' The Structure of Social Action illustrates the dilemma of a model, offered by a Western social scientist as a framework for studying a discipline around the world. It was rejected in the East as ethnocentric, as a view which reflects Western structures and values and rationalizes Western interests. The Indian scholar finds that this model reflects Parsons' perspectives on the structure and the functioning of American society.[24] The emphasis upon voluntarism and free will accords with American beliefs and ideology. But it is contrary to the teaching of most of the important Indian philosophical schools which accept the determinism of Karma. Furthermore, the Vedas would not attach much importance to the goal-oriented actions of Parsons, because they refer to the lower phenomenal sphere and neglect the higher realm. The kinds of goals posited in the model do not take proper account of man's moral and spiritual nature. The hedonistic ones reflect Western city life and are at variance with the Buddhist-Jain emphasis upon the rigorous control of the senses for the attainment of true happiness and spiritual bliss. Having attacked the model from the right, from that of traditional views and underlying values, Varma then rejected it from the perspective of the political left. The Indian social scientist characterized Parsons' model as a defender of monopoly capitalism and social conformity. It accentuates loyalty, integration, and, above all, adjustment to the system. Parsons may be a prophet for American sociologists, but his works "do not contain any program for action and concrete research work for the social scientists of the Third World."

The multinational version fully expects that when the Asian and African indigenizers, whether revolutionaries or nationalists, put their mark upon social science sects, the world will see a much less consensual social science. But the process of indigenization is just starting in those regions, and we turn to Latin American dependency theory for our example of the phenomenon as it has affected paradigms. The reader will note a strong parallel between the thinking of Latin American dependendistas and that of the indigenizers just considered from Asia and Africa. This is logical because one of the chief sources of this theory is the complex of ideas surrounding the doctrine of neo-colonialism, the other being critical Marxism.

The Emergence of Dependency Theory

Our third world example of the indigenization of paradigms is the creation of dependency theory in Latin America. We say "third world example" because indigenization is a general process which can affect any type of country or society. Thus the United States indigenized German psychology, preserving only the notion of experimentation, but changing the "soul" of the discipline.[25] Of course, dependency theory is not a theory in any strict sense, Cardoso preferring to call it an approach. Like the typical social science sect, it is an amorphous conglomerate of elements which have a general thrust, but nothing like the logical structure of science. Three of its characteristics invite comment. The first is its interdisciplinary nature. It is not confined to any one discipline, but has been accepted for many social sciences in Latin America. Included are economics, political science, international relations, sociology, and history. While it is an interdisciplinary approach, its focus is development -- normal since this is the major concern of the region. Secondly, it is regional; its proponents are from Latin American, not merely from one country in the region, and they have self-consciously set out to find an approach appropriate for the region. This case thus differs from the two previous cases of indigenization presented above, in that it is regional not national, and in that its creation appears to have been a more self-conscious process. The latter is the third characteristic of the approach, and this self-consciousness reminds us of the academic factor which we named as one of the causes of social science. The social scientists from the region have examined development theory from the first world, usually the structural functionalism of the United States, and found it wanting and have rejected it as not being applicable to Latin America. The analysis of Rigol differs from that of many of the colleagues of the region in that he refers specifically to social science in the Soviet Union, and does not confine his indictment to the first world. He characterizes as conformist both the functionalist sociology of the first world and the Soviet Marxist variety. Both posit a model of an existing society and look to development within the confines of respective existing institutions. He contrapoises to these the sociology of the third world, a sociology of liberation and revolution which looks forward to the transformation of social institutions.[26] Rigol exposes Latin American social science as usually being humanistic Marxism, not the Soviet variety. Although this author at times uses the term "third world," he indicates that his book is an attempt at summarizing the disciplines in Latin America. An examination of the book verifies that this is his focus.

Ignacio Sotelo characterizes the development theory imported from the United States by Latin Americans in the 1950s as structural-functionalism.[27] It was at first widely and uncritically accepted by social scientists in the importing countries, and greatly prized for its use of rigorous scientific methods. Empirical and pragmatic, it was a static theory biased in the direction of equilibrium and against revolutionary change. Sotelo made this charge, and then went on to argue that the imported paradigm was infused with the ideas that North American social scientists had borrowed from Max Weber. These included the intention of purifying the theory of any trace of philosophy or history. North American social scientists transformed Weber's notion of capitalism, which he had associated with rationalism, into the concept of modernity. Then they juxtaposed modernity with an opposite concept, namely "the traditional." Latin American society was then usually viewed as one in transition, with both its modern and its traditional spheres. The key to its development was said to be support for the modern section and the conversion of the traditional section to modernity. Often the transition was seen as being essentially a psychological one, a change in attitudes.

The theory of dependency resulted from more than the academic factor. It is an approach which stresses outside control and outside oppression. It resembles Chicano and black social science, just as the American development approach parallels cultural deficiency models. The center uses its control to oppress the peripheral countries and prevent them from developing. Hettne has called the approach the ideology of late-comers to development, and he argues that its roots go back to List. Cardoso believes that it is part of the constantly renewed effort to study structures of domination. Parkinson sees it as the continuation of the debate on imperialism where it left off in 1916, but this time from the standpoint of the developing countries. It takes a worm's eye view of imperialism. Its significance in the present analysis becomes evident only when we call to mind that it identifies the United States as the major center, and thus as the major exploiter and controller and that the peripheral countries of major concern are Latin American. This theory thus responds to the political beliefs and cultural predispositions of the region, especially those of the local intelligentsia. It is congruent with the suspicion with which local social scientists view the United States. The theory fits the Latin American situation in that it prides itself on being dynamic, a tool for radical change. As befits such an approach, history is a component of its essential methodology, and it is not antagonistic to philosophy or to ideology. It often borrows from humanistic Marxism, useful, as we have seen, for emphasizing and underlying domination and exploitation -- two characteristic features of the theory. The center develops at the expense of the periphery, and the latter does not develop because the center does. Or the development of the periphery is deformed because of the influence of the center.

A distinctive feature of the theory is the way that it uses history. Western economics, dominated as it has been by neo-classicism and the Keynesian approach, in a real sense ignored history. What was true for the United States was assumed to be true for Latin America as well. In fact, neo-classicism concentrated its analysis upon the isolated individual, so nations as such were ignored, as was any notion of historical context. This central notion was challenged and rejected by the scholars of the Economic Commission for Latin America, notably by Celso Furtado. These scholars rejected the then commonly held notion that underdevelopment was but one step in the linear process of capitalism by which the underdeveloped pass over to development. Rather their charge was that underdevelopment is an historical product of capitalism.[28] In this way, scholars šuch as Furtado "recovered" history and political economy and took at least part of the blame for underdevelopment away from the locals to place it at the doorstep of international capitalism. Since the time of mercantilism, the underdeveloped have been "inserted" into this capitalist system and controlled by it. Underdevelopment is thus a normal part of the system -- one part develops, the other suffers. Or the development of the periphery is distorted. This is the way the system works. Development of a given country must thus be put in a specific historic context, in the context of the international capitalism of the time. Abstract generalizations about traditional, modern, or transitional societies are no substitute for historical specificity.

A refreshing feature of dependency theory is that its proponents subscribe to an external view of social science. They have been self-reflective, conscious of the factors, external ones included, which shape social science. Graciarena and Franco in their analysis of the social sciences in Latin American reject the notion that these enterprises are "a mere unfolding of an idea, with its own internal logic".[29] They assure us that the disciplines in the region have been influenced by the surrounding societies, power structures, and political ideologies. An example of societal influence, already referred to, is the emphasis in Latin American social science on development, an emphasis also found in the larger culture. Salient events in the region have had their effect as well. Foremost among them is the Cuban Revolution, an event which helped to radicalize the Latin American academic world. It revitalized Marxist thinking in the region. This same external view of our subject has been taken by Ramos who is given much of the credit for introducing the idea of the indigenization of sociology in Brazil. In fact, Ramos himself accused his adversaries of not assuming a sociological position in their discussion of sociology. He obviously assumed this position when he posited a reciprocal relationship between social science and social reality. In accord with this thesis, he found "colonial sociology" existing in Brazil during its colonial period, and an attempt to formulate autonomous sociology at a time when Brazil was attempting to create an autonomous society.

An Analysis and an Explication of Dependency Theory

Dependency theory is the best example to date of third world paradigmatic indigenization, a process central to our general interpretation of the disciplines. Its crucial significance justifies the space which we now allot to the interpretation of it. The indigenization of paradigms is a generic process by which imported paradigms are modified so as better to reflect local conditions -- whether social, political, or situational. We have seen this process at work when American social scientists applied it to German brands of psychology and political science. The third world brand tends to be more revolutionary. Actually, it too can be merely nationalist/ethnocentric, i.e., the modification can be only in the direction of satisfying local cultures and the interests of existing local elites. Alternatively, its slant can be radical, disposed to serve opposing class/group interests.

Our analysis is pointed more in the latter direction, more in accord, therefore, with Latin American dependency theory. The region which spawned this theory has rightly been accused of possessing a mania for liberation, at least this has been the case for the left. Latin Americans on this side of issues have given us the theology of liberation and a revolutionary liberating pedagogy, in addition to dependency theory. The Vatican has demonstrated the same intolerance for the theology of liberation that the first and second worlds have shown for dependency theory. Father Leonardo Boff, a famous Brazilian adherent, was silenced for a year, and the Pope is using his powers to appoint more conservative hierarchies in Latin American countries. The two secular orthodoxies, Kremlin Marxism and American functionalism, have "excommunicated" the opposition as being unscientific, just as the Vatican has moved against the theology of liberation. Our focus in this section, however, is upon revolutionary pedagogy, specifically upon that of Paulo Freire, an educator of the illiterates. This Brazilian educator has made the Portuguese word conscientizacao famous in educational circles the world over. We use the process it connotes to analyze and to explicate indigenization, specifically the birth of dependency theory. This is done by way of analogy, a procedure which should give us insights into the birth of the theory and into the theory itself. The Portuguese word conscientizacao means the act or the effect of being conscious of, or of being aware of, something, for example, of an impending situation. It suggests more than casual or superficial knowledge, rather its reference is to the significant, even the dangerous, which one is advised to guard in one's consciousness and to give priority there. In Freire's hands, the word has grown to mean the process whereby illiterates, who are seen more as victims of an unjust society than merely as those who cannot read and write, are helped to become aware of their oppression, aided in unravelling and understanding the myths which hide this oppression. We draw the analogy between this term and the birth of dependency theory, a theory which exposes oppression and which sought to supercede the "myth", North American development theory. The connection of conscientizacao is not with technical education, the type adopted by the United States and given such wide currency by the American postwar extension. Literacy in Freire's view is not to be taught as a technical, abstract matter. What is at stake is no less than the illiterates' ability to express themselves authentically, stripped of the myths imposed by local and foreign elites. The goal of pedagogy is liberation, not reading and writing in a manner which reinforces these myths. Dependency theory does not pretend to be a technical construction so much as a liberating, authentic one, and its creators espoused this same goal.

Our analysis uses the liberation pedagogy developed by Latin American leftists to aid their illiterate countrymen better to understand a social science paradigm developed by other Latin American leftists. Two congruencies are evident, but a possible incongruity emerges as well. Our analysis once again assumes a close fit between education and the social sciences -- a congruence evident throughout the essay. Moreover, the authors of both are "co-conspirators" from the same region, conscious of each other, who quote each other and use Marxist humanism in their analysis. The possible incongruity arises from the intellectual and social distance which separates illiterates from social scientists. Freire's pedagogy was developed for the former, and the elitists found among the latter might find our comparisons not only fanciful and inaccurate, but distasteful as well. Such a coupling does not appear odd to us, because both the social scientist and the illiterate can before conscientizacao act in inauthentic ways, each the victim of structures and myths. Indeed, Freire himself found that the most alienated of the Africans in Guinea-Bissau were the assimilados, the educated elite that had accepted Portuguese culture. Portuguese colonial policy concentrated upon culture and education, and sought to de-Africanize the local students.[30] Everything African was denigrated, everything European was praised. Freire warned that unless dependent societies overcome their dependency and become things for themselves they will continue to experience the "culture of silence." Such a culture is one which is without its own authentic expression, using the one imposed upon it. The parallel, of course, is with social science. At first Latin American scholars used North American development theory, until they developed their own authentic expression, dependency theory. The culture referred to above before conscientizacao is not authentic: it is but an echo of the metropole. "The metropole talks and the dependent society listens".[31] The communications network is the vertical one sketched above for United States social science, with the latter cast in the role of the metropole.

Freire found that this vertical relationship exists not only for colonies and for dependency caused by colonialism, but for dependency in general, i.e. for that caused by informal empires as well. In both cases, the dominant myth serves the interests of the foreign elites and their local collaborators. The parallel of the dominant myth, of course, is the imported paradigm. The imposition of the language of the colonizer is a fundamental condition for colonial domination. In informal empires, the language of the center usually becomes a special language, one which locals are taught, and taught to revere and to cherish. American English currently serves that general purpose for social science. Liberation in any real or authentic sense can take place only if the people reconquer their own mode of expression, their way to designate their world.[32] In this volume, we call this process social science indigenization. This requires more than the use of local languages; it requires the destruction of the myths (the imported paradigms) which bind the indigenes. Fatalism, belief in the invulnerability of the masters, feelings of inferiority, and finally force also block liberation. But Freire's emphasis is upon justifying myths -- and, of course, their destruction through conscientizacao. Our emphasis is upon paradigms and liberation through indigenization. The oppressed are not accorded the courtesy of dialogue.[33] They receive slogans and myths foisted upon them by organized propaganda, and the oppressed cannot talk back. They receive the oppressor's view of the world (the imported paradigm), and this at the expense of their originality. The myths include the notions of the harmony of class interests, the benefits of foreign aid, that all can work who want to, and the charge that rebellion is a sin against God. The reader will note that these assumptions parallel those of the regulatory pole of the dimension set forth by Burrell and Morgan. Conscientizacao is found at the opposite pole, radical change.

The situation of the oppressed, more specifically, their manner of learning myths, resembles what Freire calls the "banking" approach to education. The reader will note the parallel with the social science communications of third world countries with center countries. The nature of this type education is suggested by the metaphor of the bank deposit, a deposit of knowledge by the educator into the head of a passive student. This type of pedagogy implies a teacher as narrator and patient, listening "objects" called students.[34] The educator sends out communications; the student receives them patiently, memorizes, catalogues, and stores them away. The student becomes an archivist. The process continues in a formal abstract manner, with no references to the existential experience of the student, and it is not related to praxis. The parallel is a paradigm which does not relate to the situation of third world countries. The process stifles creativity and any desire to transform. Education, in this view, is a gift from the teacher, self judged to be knowledgeable, to those judged not to know. In our analogy, the transfer of social science is from the developed first world to the underdeveloped third world. The teacher is the active element who educates, knows, thinks, speaks, etc. The student is the passive element, on the receiving side of these activities. The enterprise is paternalistic -- "help" with sympathy is given to the marginalized. This should remind us that the foreign aid of first world countries sometimes takes the form of aid to develop a social science infrastructure. Students get entangled in partial visions of reality, deal with one point or another, or with one problem or other.[35] They are taught to adjust to society, not to change it. The imported paradigms are not holistic, and they are conservative.

Freire's recommended pedagogy is dynamic and liberating, a process which resembles indigenization as practiced by Latin American social scientists when they rejected North American development theory and created their own authentic approach, dependency theory. This process involved the rejection of the "myths" suggested above in our reference to the regulatory, conservative side of a dimension of Burrell and Morgan. Perhaps a more difficult myth to overcome is that already referred to, the one set forth by the first world functionalists that theirs are the scientific paradigms, deviations are rejected as being "unscientific." Raul Prebisch gave evidence of the dimensions of this problem when he admitted that when he was young he felt "positive reverence for the economic theories of the centers," a reverence which began to diminish with the coming of the depression and which has continued to diminish ever since.[36] But such liberation is not easy. It is not a gift, but a process which results from struggle. The same can be said for indigenization, especially the rejection of "scientific" paradigms. In analyzing this process, we draw an analogy between Latin American social science communities and Freire's "cultural circles," his concept of an academic class. The give and take of his recommended pedagogical process for these circles resembles the give and take of these communities when cast in their best light. Conscientizacao emerges in the dialectic of these circles, just as dependency theory emerged from the dialectic of Latin American social science communities. Of special significance in this later respect is the fact that of third world social science communities the regional ones for Latin America are the most active. They reflect relatively developed disciplines as well as a high level of social/cultural, political, and linguistic commonality.

Freire's pedagogy starts with the "coordinator" (the teacher) carrying on a discussion or a debate with the students, the members of the cultural circle, in which the latter react by making contributions from their "concrete," existential experience. The "coordinator" is the teacher, the "cultural circle" the students. Emphasis is put upon the lives of the students. This is shown by the selection of the "generating words" which are used in the conscientizacao process. They must be in oral use by, and familiar to, the student, and they must fulfill certain technical criteria which do not concern us. That they are oriented to the work place is illustrated by several of the 17 words used in literacy campaigns in the Northeastern region of Brazil. These examples are the Portuguese words for plough, land, work, salary, profession, hoe, and tile.[37] The other words are tailored to the lifestyle of the illiterates as well -- Shantytown (Favela), the Batuque (an Afro-Brazilian dance), and the bicycle (for transportation). The discussion below shows that these words are linked to the social and political reality of the students and that they are designed to expose exploitation. Dependency theory has been tailored to the Latin American situation, and it has been designed to expose exploitation.

The coordinator leads the groups in the debate, challenges them -- using the "generating words" -- and from their reaction, designs or codes are constructed. Having done this ,the students are ready to reflect critically upon their own joint product. They can distance themselves from it, and criticize it, first in a superficial way and then in a profound manner. "Decodification" is the term Freire reserves for the analysis of the code, whereby the relationships among its elements are exposed, as well as those between the code and the facts of the real world. A situation is revealed which was not known before. Like humanistic Marxism, the process does not stop with surface events -- it goes to the heart of the matter. It is not merely phenomenonalistic. In this way, the myths which rationalize the structures of an oppressed and dependent society are unravelled and exposed. Freire argues that insofar as the student realizes the existence of exploitation, to that extent, his critical consciousness of realty is developed.[38] "Critical" thus comes to mean consciousness of exploitation. The student becomes conscious and critical of routine things which he accepted before as a matter of course. He is transformed into a subject reflecting on his own condition, not an object accepting, without thought, interpretations imposed upon him. The debates are intended to lead the student to the conclusion that humans use others as objects, and that their continuing bondage is affected through social structures. But these structures are human creations, and they can be modified or destroyed. The comparison is with the contents of dependency theory, indeed, with Marxist humanism in general.

An obvious point to this process of conscientizacao is that the reality which is revealed after the myths are stripped away is one of exploitation. This becomes obvious if we consider the instructions given the coordinator for the debate over the generating words mentioned above. In discussing the word "food," for example, questions of hunger and malnutrition are debated. The term "riches" is learned against the background of a debate over poverty versus riches and another in which the rich nations are pitted against the poor nations. Freire's debt to Marxism becomes obvious in his emphasis upon exploitation and, more specifically, in his pedagogical procedures -- the debt acknowledged in several footnotes.

Freire's concepts of codification and decodification suggest a pattern whereby Latin American social scientists unravelled and exposed the North American development paradigm and substituted dependency theory for it. The codification process was marked by contributions from the concrete existential experience of the members, especially from matters pertinent to their professional lives. A composite picture was struck, one that appeared less and less authentic, a badly integrated design inspired as it was by the paradigm from the North. Its fit with known concrete situations in Latin America became less and less convincing. This became more obvious as the Latin American scholars contemplated their composite creation -- first its surface appeared and next its underlying meaning. Its inauthenticity became more obvious during decodification -- the analysis of the parts of the composite picture, their relationship with each other and with the concrete situation in Latin America. This process allowed them to distance themselves from the North American myth (paradigm) and to understand it more clearly and deeply.

Freire equates a critical consciousness with one aware of exploitation, and his generating words and the recommended discussion accompanying them all point in this direction. The analogy is with Marxist humanism, which provides a key to Latin American indigenization, i.e. the switch from one paradigm to the other, as well as a prime source of the contents of the new paradigm. So far as the switch is concerned, Marxism argues that culture, education, and the social sciences can be, and are, used as methods to preserve and to promote oppressive structures. It thus provided a new prospective for understanding the North American promotion of its development theory, not as a way of spreading scientific information, but rather as a means of rationalizing capitalist expansion. Moreover, Marxism offered the emerging Latin American paradigm insights which better reflected the new mode: the notions of struggle and oppression rather than the common good of the American paradigm; the dialectic method and historical relevance rather than general abstractions; and commitment rather than objectivity. But the borrowing did not mean that Latin American social science traded one ready-made paradigm for another, the North American one for the competing Kremlin variety. A pliable, humanistic and Western Marxism featuring voluntarism, generally lacking economic reductionism was bent and adjusted to become part of a Latin American indigenized paradigm, a local creation which featured exploitation by foreign structures. It required the revision of the traditional Marxist version of Latin American history, and it was twisted to fit the local situation and fused with other indigenous elements. Its adherents have been authentic to the point that they have been accused (and with reason) of being nationalistic (regionalistic) and inward looking.

Conclusions

This chapter has a key role, we think not a contradictory one, in our analysis. At first glance and until recently, the third world was the great yang of social science, a reflector of action occurring elsewhere. The "elsewhere" was the first world which has fabricated paradigms and produced research findings, both to be exported so as to be adopted by the third world. This passivity is now ending -- the turbulent process which is bringing its termination is called here indigenization. Many aspects of the social sciences have already been touched by the process -- e.g., personnel and language. We saw that this was particularly the case in Asia. But the hardest part of the overturn is the paradigm, the latter's indigenization is the most difficult to accomplish and the most troublesome and upsetting for the development of a global consensus for our disciplines. It was for this reason that we devoted so much space in the chapter to the presentation and the explication of dependency theory, our example of paradigmatic indigenization. Quite appropriately, this construction emerged in Latin America, the third world's most advanced center for our disciplines, and that center with the best inter-regional communications.

Quite appropriately also, the chapter started with the Indian example of third world social science. This was followed by a section on the first world educational penetration of the third world. As indicated throughout the essay, education was visualized as that part of our structures closest to the social sciences. Education was presented as the vehicle of social science penetration. That section which detailed the shift in centers away from Western Europe to the United States was followed by another section which set out the structure of third world social science communications. This was revealed to be the other side of the U.S. communication system, already presented. The third world suffers from what Freire calls the culture of silence. It receives first world messages, but sends few in return. This is communications without feedback. Moreover, third world social science centers hardly communicate with each other -- another instance in which they reflect the larger global society. Latin America was set off as a partial exception to this lack of regional communication.

The birth of dependency theory is related to this partial exception. After all, it is a regional construction -- a joint Latin American effort by the social scientists of the region who obviously have communicated with each other before, during, and after its construction. We accounted for it in external terms, i.e. we saw it arising in response not merely to intellectual causes, internal to social science, but also as a reaction to external factors related to Latin American society. By the mid 1960s the imported North American paradigm seems to have been disconfirmed. Concentration inward upon this, however, fails to point to the ideological setting of the emerging construction -- its potential for anti-North Americanism, the impact of Castroism, and its focus upon development. These latter were presented above as requirements for understanding the emerging paradigm -- and they are part of our structural methodology. We attributed the creation of dependency theory to the radical social scientists in Latin America: these were distinguished from the internationalists/clients who are linked to the first world. We explicated the emergence of the paradigm with insights from the revolutionary pedagogy of Paulo Freire, another liberation construction from Latin America. The indigenization of social science can result from the revolt of local nationalists as well, i.e. those not committed to dramatic local change. This insight puts indigenization in proper perspective, an ominous one for those who are looking to the consensus which is part of social science maturity. We see more indigenization in the future, and little chance for the realization of the social science myth. This is a point developed in the upcoming chapter.

NOTES

1.   Ralph Pieris, The Implantation of Sociology in Asia,"
        International Social Science Journal, 21 (1969), 435.

2.   Dan A. Chekki, American Sociological Hegemony:
        Transnational Explorations (Lanham: University Press of
        America, 1987), 38.

3.   Ramasray Roy, "Social Science in Asia," Inter-Regional
        Cooperation in the Social Sciences, (Paris: UNESCO, 1977),
        21.

4.   Chekki, American Sociological Hegemony, 51.

5.   Edward H. Berman, "Foundations, United States Foreign
        Policy, and African Education, 1945-1975," Harvard
        Educational Review, 11 (1979), 145.

6.   Steward Fraser (ed.), Chinese Communist Education: Records
        of the First Decade, (Nashville: Vanderbilt, 1965), 218-219.

7.   Josef Mestenhauser, "Foreign Students in the Soviet Union
        and Eastern European Countries," Steward Fraser (ed.),
        Government Policy and International Education, (New York:
        John Wiley, 1965), 172.

8.   Jacques Poujol, "Foreign Students Exchange: France," Fraser
        (ed.), Governmental Policy and International Education, (New
        York: John Wiley, 1965), 237.

9.   Marshall R. Singer, Weak States in a World of Powers: The
        Dynamics of International Relations, (New York: Free Press,
        1972), 163.

10.   Ibid., 171.

11. Fernando Henrique Cardoso, "The Consumption of Dependency Theory in the United States," Latin American Research Review, 12 (1977), 7. For what follows see also Frederick H. Gareau, The Multinational Version of Social Science, Current Sociology, 33 (1985), 103-114.

12. Mpekesa Bongoy, "Social Science Cooperation in Africa" Inter-regional Cooperation in the Social Sciences, (Paris: UNESCO, 1977), 32.

13. Roy, Social Science in Asia, 13.

14. Enrique Oteiza, "The Latin American Experience and Inter-regional Cooperation in Social Sciences," Inter-regional Cooperations in Social Science, (Paris: UNESCO, 1977), 28.

15. UNESCO, Inter-regional Cooperation in the Social Sciences, Final Report of the Meeting, (Paris: UNESCO, 1977) 10.

16. Fernando Henrique Cardoso e Enzo Faletto, "Repensado Dependencia e Desenvolvimento na America Litina," Fernando Cardoso et al. Economia e Movementos Sociais na America Latina, (Sao Paulo: Brasilense, 1985), 129.

17. Norman W. Storer, "The Internationality of Science and the Nationality of Scientists," International Social Science Journal, 22 (1970), 93.

18. Fanny Tabak, Dependencia Tecnologica e Desenvolvimento Nacional, (Rio: Pallas, 1975), 153-155.

19. Syed Hussein Alatas, "The Captive Mind and Creative Development," International Social Science Journal, 26 (1974), 691.

20. Akinsola A. Akiwowo, "Sociology in Africa Today," Current Sociology, 27 (1980), 43.

21. Yogesh Atal, "The Call for Indigenization," International Social Science Journal, 32 (1981), 193.

22. B. Clinard Marshall and Joseph W. Elder, "Sociology in India: A Study in the Sociology of Knowledge," American Sociological Review, 30 (1965), 583.

23. Yogendra Singh, "Constrains, Contradictions, and Interdisciplinary Orientations: The India Context," International Social Science Journal, 31 (1979), 114.

24. V.P. Varma, "Talcott Parsons and the Behavioral Sciences," The Indian Journal of Political Science, 42 (1981), 2.

25. Edwin G. Boring, A History of Experimental Psychology, (New York: Appleton-Century-Crofts, 1950), 506.

26. Pedro Negre Rigol, Sociologia do Terceiro Mundo, (Petroplis: Vozes, 1977) 88-89.

27. Ignacio Sotelo, Sociologia de America Latina, (Rio de Janeiro: Colecao America, 1975), 18.

28. Francisco De Oliveira "Celso Furtado E O Pensamento Economico Brasileiro," Reginaldo Moraes (ed.), Inteligencia Brasileira (Sao Paulo: Brasilense, 1986), 153.

29. Jorge Graciarena and Rolando Franco, "Social Formations and Power Structure in Latin America," Current Sociology, 26 (1978), 85.

30. Paulo Freire, Cartas a Guine-Bissau: Registros de Uma Esperiencia Em Processo, (Sao Paulo: Paz e Terra, 1978), 20.

31. Paulo Freire, Conscientizacao: Teoria e Pratica da Libertacao: Uma Introducao Ao Pensamento de Paulo Friere, (Sao Paulo: Editoria Moraes, 1980), 65.

32. Freire, Cartas A Guine-Bissau, 145.

33. Paulo Freire, Pedagogia de Oprimido, (Sao Paulo: Paz e Terra, 1984), 56.

34. Frederick H. Gareau, "The Third World Revolt Against First World Social Science: An Explication Suggested by the Revolutionary Pedagogy of Paulo Freire," International Journal of Comparative Sociology 32 (1988), 175.

35. Freire, Pedagogia de Oprimido, 69.

36. Raul Prebisch, "A Historic Turning Point for the Latin American Periphery," CEPAL Review, 18 (1982), 23.

37. Paulo Freire, Educacao Como Pratica da Liberdade, (Sao Paulo: Paz e Terra, 1985), 145-149.

38. Freire, Conscientizacao, 32.

Chapter IX

SUMMARY, DISCUSSION OF THE VOLUME, AND THE FUTURE OF SOCIAL SCIENCE

Summary of the Volume

This, the final chapter, contains a brief summary of the volume, along with a forecast of the future of social science. Chapter III presented the social science myth, a mixture of history and futurology. Our view of this future is congruent with our analysis, and we believe reasonable and realistic. The volume features a permissive, yet an unvarnished, analysis of social science. The permissiveness arose in the acceptance of the major, often contradictory, paradigms as legitimate social science. The unvarnished presentation was evidenced in the attempt to expose myths and to include the bad along with the good. We saw that our disciplines offer valuable reasoned, experienced-based explanations of, and insights into, the social situation. They are valuable as such, and alternate to purely emotional, philosophical, or religious explanations. Such praise did not blind us to the fact that they are not "scientific" on any reading of what real, i.e. natural science, produces. Indeed, the social sciences have their philosophical, emotional, and cultural side. We devoted three chapters to the exposition of four major types of social science -- two Marxist varieties, plus the interpretive and functionalism. We found in our historical exposition of the disciplines that they have promoted reform, but that they have been on the other side of issues as well. All were accepted as legitimate social science, including social Darwinism, the Fascist variety, and the various brands of Marxism. We used the social sciences themselves, a kind of structuralism, to help rub the varnish from the myth-encrusted official versions of the disciplines.

Kuhn tied his "enlightenment" to his solution to the two related questions of whether to consider and how to dispose of findings, historically regarded as being scientific, but which currently appear to be more like errors, superstitions, or myths. His decision in both instances was affirmative -- first to consider them, and also to consider them as science. Our approach was similar, but contemporaneous, i.e. tailored to social science. We decided, at least in principle, to consider all historical, but more importantly, all contemporaneous social science paradigms and their findings and to accept them as being legitimate social science. Kuhn's permissiveness led him to tie scientific findings to the paradigm, discontinuous constructions. Findings have meaning only in relation to their respective paradigms, and the latter are based on contrary Weltanschauungen. Our analysis applied these notions to social science as well. The result for us was the recognition of a plurality of contemporary legitimate social science constructions, often discontinuous, based as they often are on contrary Weltanschauungen. The other side of the permissiveness is the foreswearing of the right to excommunicate "unscientific" paradigms as illegitimate. We saw that this was a practice of American functionalism and Kremlin Marxism. Research findings are not necessarily transferable from one paradigm to another. We found this to be true for the national accounting measures of the capitalist first world, which are not easily translated to make sense in the Soviet system. More and more, third world social scientists are casting doubt on the usefulness of first world measures. To paraphrase Kuhn: what appeared to be a live, virile capitalist duck now looks like a dead socialist rabbit. The increase in national income can mean merely that the American housewife is now neglecting her children, while aiding in the sale of useless products. The Soviet national accounting measures were found to be arbitrary and flawed as well, understandable only in ideological terms. Why denigrate medical services?

Our permissive approach implies logically that the social sciences are quite different from natural science. True, they resemble each other if natural science is viewed historically, social science contemporaneously. But they diverge if both are viewed contemporaneously. Natural science is that unique human enterprise with characteristics not shared by any other. Two traits stressed in our analysis were universalism and consensus. We found our disciplines with the tendency to be nationalistic and regional -- and to lack consensus. This tendency to national and regional bias is best expressed by structural analysis. We not only found our disciplines to be divided into four meta-paradigms, but we sited them, i.e. we indicated the predominate location of each. Such siting again contradicts the universalism of our disciplines, and points to the impact of various cultures and elites. As we have already asserted, structuralism provides the preferred approach for explaining the shape which our disciplines have assumed. It accounted for the preferred position of the United States -- both her export balance of communications and for the fact that her imports are in accord with her culture, but those of other countries need not be.

Our permissive approach to the "disposal" problem led quite logically to an external interpretation of social science, one which contributed greatly to an understanding of the shaping of the disciplines from factors external to the social scientists themselves and to their professional organizations. Our approach does reserve a voice for the latter, but it is a shared voice. The way we solved the disposal problem required us to look outside for explanations, but it did not determine the method for doing so. The groundwork for the choice was laid in Chapter II; the logic of the choice was confirmed in Chapter IV. Chapter II put the analysis of our disciplines in the contexts of political economy and international, interdisciplinary structures. The first context drew upon the fact that our disciplines have a decided economic aspect: indeed, they have industrialized to become part of the knowledge industry. We traced their evolution (in Chapter II) from their emergence at the hands of a few individual craftsmen to their expansion, capitalization, and concentration a century ago, but even more so in the post World War II era. Now "keeping up with the field" -- even more so adding new knowledge to the field, requires specialized libraries, expensive universities, and secretarial help. Researchers often have advanced degrees, often earned in developed countries, usually the Ph.D. The theory of human capital helped to highlight the economic aspects of our disciplines, especially their increasing capitalization.

Political economy contributed to our analysis by pointing also to the political connection of our disciplines. Education, so intertwined with our disciplines, is tied to, and dependent upon, government as well. Education, to a large extent even in societies with market economies, is subsidized by governments. Even if this were not the case, governmental elites can hardly be expected to sit idly and patiently by while the social scientist undermines their authority. We noted two paradigmatic ways that elites, government and otherwise, impact social science. The first is the liberal approach, characteristic of the free world. Its modus operandi is to encourage, perhaps to subsidize, favorite paradigms and their research findings, with the not coincidental result that opposing paradigms stagnate or even diminish or wither. The second is the totalitarian/authoritarian approach. It features heavy handed censorship, prohibitions by the Stalinists, the Nazis, or the Gang of Four. There are shades of gray between these two modal points, e.g. mandated high school courses in the United States which distort Marxism. The liberal approach is less traumatic -- some unwanted fish do slip through the net, but the system is in general effective. This is illustrated by our structural approach, which found dominant paradigms which serve the interests of local elites in the free world, a similar situation exists in the second world.

We used political economy, not as a terminal point which sets limits, but as an introduction, a bridge to widen perspectives. This discipline broke the ice for the more inclusive structural approach, which uses a collection of disciplines and their topical subjects as its method of analysis. Its adoption also makes unnecessary the staking out and the delineating of the various social science disciplines and their respective jurisdictions. Our analysis would have been very different had we not called upon what Gouldner has called the sociology of sociology or what could be called the political economy of education. We purposely obviated any of the jurisdictional quarrels of these and any other disciplines by looking to interdisciplinary, international structures. These were seen as many faceted, interacting with each other, but arising from past struggles among groups/elites. The various disciplinary segments of the structures were seen as interconnected, and as the usual companions of each other. Education was found to be particularly close to our disciplines, and economics was seen as a valuable method for smoking out the existence of the structures. Our structural analysis borrowed heavily from Galtung's version of world systems analysis and from Cardoso's dependency theory.

Our analysis was permissive and unvarnished, as already stated, but it was data based as well. This was shown especially in Chapter IV which used over 20 empirical studies to map out the communications network of American social science. It was demonstrated there that the incoming American network did not follow a pattern in accord with the canons of natural science. Rather this network proved to be ethnocentric, reserving most incoming channels for fellow countrymen -- the few foreign ones were from the white commonwealth or Western Europe at the expense of the second and the third worlds. The incoming social science network resembled the communications system of the larger American society, thus helping to justify our approach. Moreover, all of the channels in the sample were in English, suggesting that American social scientists are monolingual, like their fellow countrymen. This approach received further support from the pattern of U.S. social science communications. These latter formed the same pattern as those of the larger society in that exports greatly exceeded imports. Furthermore, U.S. imports of social science messages are more important for developing countries with cultures at odds with American culture than for developed countries with similar cultures. The social sciences of India and South Korea were found to be more dependent upon communications from the United States than those of France and Great Britain. U.S. communications imports were found to be predominantly from countries sharing similar cultures, but not so the imports of third world countries. This inequality is better explained by structuralism than by any cultural explanations. The same conclusion is warranted for the American export balance in social science communications and for the dominance of American English as the language for journals read.

A major conclusion drawn from Chapter IV was that U.S. social science communications do not adhere to the norms of natural science. Other evidence of the same persuasion was displayed -- to the effect that social science is ethnocentric and lacks consensus. Structural analysis bridges the gap and reconciles this ethnocentrism with the transnational nature of our disciplines. The ethnocentrism is generally that of the first world, and it is exported to, and imposed upon, the third world. But the third world, especially after it develops, veers toward the same trait. This was seen in our analysis of dependency theory, and, more generally, in our presentation of the indigenization process. Our structural approach seemed preferable to exchange theory, as used by Silva and Slaughter, to demonstrate how the social science establishment accepted the conservatism of a burgeoning American bourgeoisie in exchange for its financial support. This deal (as set forth in exchange theory) seemed too crass, without sensitivity, structuralism appearing to be more acceptable, a more logical explanation.

Chapter III, our historical sketch, placed the analysis in a dynamic framework. It pictured our disciplines as moving in modern times away from their founding homes in Western Europe to their new central office in the United States. An exception to this development was found to be the Soviet Union, the center of competing Marxist paradigms. The directing force in the transition was identified as the larger world structures. United States social science dominance was interpreted more as being the result of this overall dominance, rather than as that of the intrinsic worth of its disciplines. This same chapter also set forth the social science myth, well sited because this construction has its historic aspect. But the myth was not supported in our analysis -- indeed, we see the future of the disciplines in a contrary light. We see them as continuing on their non-consensual, non-scientific path in the foreseeable future, a forecast developed in the ultimate section of this chapter. Their future promises to be tied up with the third world, with its indigenization of these disciplines. True to the premises of our external approach, we argue that their long range, long term unification and consensus depend upon similar developments in world culture and politics, i.e. in global structures.

Our analysis thus puts the disciplines in a dynamic setting, a continuous changing process, not an iron box. The mantle of social science hegemon has passed from Western Europe -- from France, the United Kingdom, and Germany -- to the United States. This predominance has received enough competition from the Soviet bloc and from a resurgent Europe to the extent that the system can, with some exaggeration, be called a bipolar one or even a loose bipolar one. In any case, U.S. hegemony in social science is intimately tied to the overall hegemonic structures, and it is not solely or mostly a resultant of the superior intrinsic merits of American social science. This point cannot be emphasized too much, because U.S. establishment members are so tied to notions of the marketplace of ideas that success and "sales volume" indicate quality. They are tempted to conclude that we just might be witnessing the evolution of U.S. paradigms into the consensual international reference models of mature disciplines. Our argument is that U.S. hegemony is not the harbinger of social science consensus and maturity, but a temporary phenomenon due mainly to global structures, such matters as political and economic advantage. The end of social science history is not at hand, and U.S. dominance is not history's last act. Our view of the future has been spelled out in the last section of this chapter.

The central focus of our analysis was transnational as befits the study of science or disciplines often patterned after it. But we did not totally neglect the national level of analysis. There we found the national social science community, also elitist -- a case of oligopoly rather than the operation of perfect competition. Certain institutions and leaders dominate these national centers -- the resources referred to in Chapter II have much to do with the success of the elites. The leading centers tend to be the heavily capitalized, research oriented which produce the knowledge for the others. We saw that French social science elitism has its center in Paris. We described the French system as being paternalistic, a characteristic usually applicable in other social science centers as well, and in universities in general. The rise to the top is much easier if one goes to the correct institution, and becomes a client and a willing, even a cheerful and humble, collaborator of a member of the elite. Loyalty and collaboration in the United States can lead to entrance to the grant trail -- access to the funds of the government and private foundations -- an event which brightens the future prospects of the novice and lubricates the rise to the top.

Chapters V, VI, and VII attested to the non-consensual nature of social science and to its division into discontinuous sects. This statement is too extreme for all divisions, just as Kuhn's characterization is too extreme for all historic divisions in a natural science. But the potential for cosmic divisions in social science is there, such that, to use the Kuhnian expression, the transition from one paradigm to another is equivalent to cosmic travel, where what was learned on the previous planet does not apply to the present scene. What is learned within the framework of one paradigm is not necessarily transferable to another paradigmatic setting, because paradigms are separated by deep philosophical cleavages. These divisions can have their basis in discontinuous cleavages in, for example, ontology and epistemology. Chapter V developed this theme, before it went on to describe functionalism, the dominant American sociology, and other dominant paradigms in international relations, political science, economics, and development theory. This meta-paradigm has two faces: its dogmatic, scientifically pretentious side, and its basic conservatism.

These two characteristics have fit in well with the post war situation of the United States, i.e. major parts of the dominant paradigms have helped rationalize the interests of American elites and national extension. This extension has been pictured as promoting the global common good -- what benefits the United States and the first world benefits the third, and vice versa. The theory of human capital has been so presented that the higher education of third world elites (often at the expenses of the basic education of the masses) has been rationalized as a boon to development. Freer trade leads not only to efficiencies all around, but, if we are to believe the functionalist, peace as well. The same for the multinational, the first world export of culture, news, the cinema, TV, and on and on. All promotes the common good, all parties to the exchange benefit. The dogmatic part of the paradigm has its use also; it clinches the argument. The findings of the paradigms are claimed to be "scientific," with persuasive overtones in science-loving and science-respecting societies. Dissension is cast aside as being "unscientific," at best the expression of the values of ideologues.

The structural approach avoids, or at least ameliorates, the crass economism of exchange theory. In that approach, the elites get what they pay for, and pay for what they get, in what can be reduced to a commercial transaction, a kind of crass economism. Something like this occurs, but the results need not be conscious. Our reference centers upon results or functions, not intentions. Our discussion of the ideology and the myths of social science obviates the need for evil intentions and hopefully makes our position more tenable. Chapter V discussed paradigms other than the dominant ones, but they are sited in the United States. There are numerous minor species of this sort, but our choices were black and Chicano social science. Both are based on what their partisans see as the blindness and the prejudice of the partisans of the dominant paradigms. They thus part ways with the functionalist/positivist notion that the raw material of social science consists of "hard facts," available to all on equal terms. The charge of these dissenters was that partisans of the dominant paradigms do not understand what they see and that their paradigms are elite centered and biased against minorities. We met these same charges and arguments again in the discussion of third world social science.

Our other dogmatic meta-paradigm, Soviet Marxism, was set forth in Chapter VI. Its partisans fancy that it is scientific, but the paradigm is committed to dramatic social change, at least for societies outside the Soviet sphere. The paradigm has two faces -- one revolutionary, this one offered to the non-Soviet world and the other status quo, which buttresses the post-revolutionary Soviet system. But we are getting somewhat ahead of our story. First we must explain that the chapter had two major goals: to explain a dogmatic, "scientific" Marxism and secondly to site this Marxism. We sited it in the Soviet world, and it fits there very well if we remember that its revolutionary aspect is intended for the non-Soviet sphere. The discussion of it as a meta-paradigm put it in the context of a dogmatic, "scientific" Marxism, with an emphasis upon the economic base, at the expense of the superstructure. The chapter was introduced with a presentation of the ideas of the founder of the school. The "younger Marx" stressed alienation, and he serves as the inspiration for Western, humanistic Marxism. The "mature Marx" put more emphasis upon economics and economic determinism, and he serves to inspire Kremlin and dogmatic Marxism.

Chapter VI also provided a brief sketch of recent developments in China. There Marxism has opened up to the West -- the impact which this will have upon Chinese Marxism is difficult to assess at this time. We did make a preliminary assessment there, but in Eastern Europe dogmatic Marxism has suffered a severe blow, the victim of a sudden and what appears to be a popular revolution. The chapter also bore witness to the cold war, as bitter at the social science level as at any other. This promises to ameliorate if Gorbachev stays on at the top in the Soviet Union. The activities of the Vienna Center illustrate that social science diplomacy is as delicate and problematic as any other cold war negotiations. Despite current trends in the cold war, we stand by the claim that social science divisions can spawn bitter ideological battles. Certainly, the operation of the Vienna center attested to this.

Chapter VII sought to present the non-dogmatic, humanistic side of social science, both its conservative and its radical variations. This side is based upon several philosophical assumptions, which we shall not repeat here. Suffice it to say that the non-dogmatic humanist does not accept the natural sciences as the model for social science. This scholar does not look at their methods and to their laws as appropriate for our disciplines. The two meta-paradigms are interpretive social science (for sociology) and Western, Humanistic Marxism. The former is conservative, while the Marxist is revolutionary. The emphasis in the former is upon the world as seen by the subject researched, not the researcher. Western, humanistic Marxism is a Marxism of the super-structure, in contrast to the Kremlin type which stresses the base. The Western, humanist brand takes its inspiration from the younger Marx or from Hegel.

Chapter VII dealt also with Western Europe, the area where we sited the two paradigms referred to above. Examples were taken from sociology, political science, and international relations. Canada and Japan were given brief mention. The former in the past had been social science dependent upon Great Britain, but this dependence has shifted to the United States and with the new trade accord it should continue on into the future. Japan, after its opening to the West, also exhibited dependency, but the issue now is to what extent its economic extension will be accompanied by social science extension. An obvious inhibiting factor is the difficulty of the Japanese language. American social science has had the advantage of English, a language spread far and wide by previous British imperium. The last part of the chapter argued that social science flourished during the totalitarian rule of Mussolini. New disciplines were introduced, and Italian academe generally went along with Fascism. The general issue exposed there was what degree of freedom is necessary for the existence of our disciplines. Our conclusion is "not much" at least with totalitarianism of the right, and that the allegation that they only flourish in free societies is not borne out by the evidence. Totalitarianism of the left is another story: our disciplines have suffered under it. Perhaps this is related to the secular problems dividing the dominant paradigms from Marxism. Marxism triumphant seems to take its revenge. We suspect that the better explanation can be found in our structures. Social scientists were not in the forefront of the opposition to Mussolini, nor are they that noticeable for reform in the Soviet Union. Our structural approach seems justified again in generally tying them to dominant elites/classes. The same lack of political activism was seen in the independence movement in India, and social science often sided with the colonial master. A critical opposition by now has arisen in the third world.

Chapter VIII was devoted to social science in the third world. This conglomerate of regions on one hand is presented as the yan of social science, the large assortment of dependent, peripheral countries which import their disciplines, mainly from the first world. The chapter, however, stressed the active, revolutionary side of social science there. We found these two faces reflected in the membership of third world social science communities. One group, the internationalists or clients, are tied to the first world; while another, the nationalists or radicals, are in revolt against it. The impact of dependency was found present in third world communications, no surprise, because they constitute the other side of U.S. communications. Moreover, third world countries have few relations with each other. The network of third world social science communications was found to be parallel with that of their general communications pattern.

Much stress was put upon the third world indigenization of social science, especially upon dependency theory. This latter received pride of place, because it represents paradigmatic indigenization, not the usual third world form which deals with the indigenization of language or personnel. The Latin Americans have put together their own paradigm -- they have shown the way for the third world. And this paradigm is classic social science, deeply imprinted with the concerns and the ideology of the local scene, and, in this case, that of radical elites. Dependency theory, as an example, emphasizes development and caters to the anti-North American prejudice of local leftists. Our analysis of it in terms of the revolutionary pedagogy of Paulo Freire testified to its leftist orientation. It, indeed, has absorbed the ideology of the local left.

Other characteristics of the volume are expressed by the adjectives interdisciplinary, international, and critical. Of these, the most persistent has been the critical. The featured disciplines have been political science, sociology, psychology, economics, and international relations -- plus a sampling of others such that we claim that the resulting mix justifies our reference to the generic term social science." The international perspective at times complemented the critical by exposing nationalism and ethnocentrism. But this trait was justified in its own right, in that such perspective poses questions differently and teases out other responses than the narrow, local viewpoint. An ambitious goal of the volume was to present the dominant paradigms from several corners of the globe. This is a trying and taxing procedure, but one we hope the reader found worth the effort. Such a safari is necessary for social science, but not for natural science whose paradigms are the same the world over. The historical perspective also broadens, and it was employed as well.

Our criticisms were meant to be targeted solely at the intolerance and the exaggerated claims of social science, not at the disciplines themselves. There is no denying that the dominant paradigms in the first world bore the brunt of the criticism, a target made obvious in our opening remarks. These referred to an American functionalist, one committed to science, and not above denigrating other social science paradigms as being non-scientific. Our rationale for concentrating upon such first world targets is the global reach of its paradigms. It was singled out more for the extent of its geographic domain than for its unique "culpability". In fact the second world qualifies as being equally culpable, more so if we include the many prohibitions it has imposed upon our disciplines. We have deplored these prohibitions, and also the declared right of Kremlin Marxism to excommunicate the opposition. But most of our barbs were reserved for the larger domain of this bipolar world, for the capitalist elites who have so much more to say about the non-military subjects on the world agenda, including social science, than the Kremlin competition. Their "sins" are so much greater because of their greater range of opportunity. After all, it is the first world, still to some extent led by the United States, which is the larger, richer, more capitalized part of bipolarity. It is the part whose resources so outweigh those of the third world, but whose elites speak of equal opportunity, perfect competition, and horizontal relations all around, including those in social science. The evidence presented in this volume points to vertical social science relations and an overall lack of scientific traits for our disciplines. This did not prevent the obvious overstatement by a president of the American Political Science Association that American political science is becoming a real science. To make matters worse the reference was to American political science, not to the discipline as a global phenomenon. But the reference was understandable, in terms of our research, which suggested that the communications network of the social science of this country resembles the general American system -- essentially ingrown and ethnocentric. It lacks the openness of natural science communications. Another kind of ethnocentrism was the remark that economics was superior to sociology, because of the supposed higher level of agreement on concepts, "its coherent body of theory." Such assertions are possible only if competing paradigms are ignored or de-legitimized, in the instant case Marxist economics.

This volume takes its stand with the critical humanist brand of political economy and structuralism, and it is subject to the many criticism levelled in these directions. It takes its stand with the marginalized in the third world and with the American Chicano and with the American black. This choice is ultimately religious/philosophical, and it is difficult to imagine how such a commitment can be brokered and smoothed over, so as to appease extravagant super class interests. We appreciate the indigenization of the marginalized in both the first and the third world as the super class turns to a cultural deficiency model for the cause of their misery, without taking into account discriminatory structures.

The Future of Social Science

It is fitting that our last reference above was to third world indigenization, a subject of crucial importance to our estimate of the future of social science. Third world indigenization, as exemplified by dependency theory, seems destined to guarantee the non-consensual, non-scientific nature of social science for the foreseeable future. Its long run future can be different, depending upon the fate of the structures which we used here to chart its course. Quite logically, we tie this future to these structures. If they should point in the direction of horizontal relations, then we can expect communications and global transactions in general, including social science, to be more collegial and equal. Perhaps the world someday will reach such a happy state. Another development, which seems even more unlikely in the foreseeable future, which would greatly aid global consensus in the social sciences, would be world government. This assertion follows logically from the close fit which we find between our disciplines and politics. A world government could do much toward bringing more consensus to our disciplines. The same can be said for a world culture.

We believe that our prediction of the future of social science is more logical than the traditional one, i.e. that contained in the social science myth. This latter was set forth in chapter III. This latter notion assumes an essentially internal view of our disciplines -- maturity will arise somehow idiosyncratically from the hands of the practitioners. They are seen as being basically detached from society, operating on a plane which features pure logic and logical conclusions derived from research findings. True, government can affect the social sciences, but its activities are catalysts, which do not become part of them. The government's role is the idealized one found in "free enterprise" systems. This latter analysis appears not only illogical, but it provides no indicated method and path to follow in charting the future of our disciplines. Our approach provides an indicated method for such prediction. We speak to two future periods -- one when, and more importantly if, the structures change dramatically in the indicted direction and a second more immediate period, this side of such dramatic structural change. We focus upon the shorter time frame and upon two major issues of this period. The first is the question of which paradigms are likely to prosper and which are likely to recede. Conclusions reached on this question will then be used to estimate the overall trend toward "maturity" of our disciplines. Note that this term as used here is not meant to suggest a general likeness to natural science, e.g., the creation of strict laws of impeccable epistemic value. Rather the term has been diluted, relaxed to mean more a kind of openness and reasoned self reflexion, steps which should lead in the direction of the fraternity which we associate with the horizontal relations referred to above. In order to make this overall estimate, we must determine to what extent the competing paradigms serve maturity or retard it.

First we address the issue: which paradigms are most likely in the shorter time span to prosper and which are most likely to recede? We continue to use the four categories put forth by Burrell and Morgan for sociology, expanded to cover all social science. Two of them are deterministic with claims to be sciences. They are functionalism and Kremlin Marxism. These two contrast with the two voluntaristic mega-paradigms: humanistic Marxism and interpretive sociology. The second dimension, which measures regulation (conservatism) versus radical change (radicalism), divides the mega-paradigms differently. The two Marxisms are joined together on the radical side, whereas interpretive sociology and functionalism are placed together on the conservative side. A caveat is in order for Kremlin Marxism. It has been bifurcated -- status quo for the second world, but radical change for the rest of the world. This second dimension is the more useful for predicting, because it allows us to ground the prosperity of paradigms in their usefulness in rationalizing the position of elites/classes. We shall use the other dimension in our calculations, but we have less faith in the results thus obtained. Our prediction requires the following account of the evolution of postwar structures.

The immediate postwar period witnessed a global political system often called "bipolar". This term focuses on the fact that the predominance of power has been concentrated in the United States and the Soviet Union and that these two powers set the global agenda. Given the superior strength of the United States in almost every power category, the Soviet Union could be included in a "bipolar" designation only by courtesy, ignorance, or by including a number of caveats. The dominance of the United States has been so obvious both geographically and categorically. She has the most gross national product and the most allies, and she emerged as the world's premier movie producer, TV center, news gatherer, educator, and social scientist. She was the undisputed leader of world capitalism. Her dominant social science paradigms travelled far and wide -- to Western Europe, to Japan, to the Third World -- only the Soviet Bloc seemed immune from their grasp. In Western Europe, the import was forced to share billing with local paradigms, but in the third world it often emerged as number one. In many of the latter instances, the paradigms of the former colonial power were relegated to a secondary position. The rigors of Stalinism kept second world social science apart. But not completely so, impacts have been recorded there, notably in Poland and in China since 1978. Even the Soviets are not immune from American influence, as we have seen in a previous chapter.

The early structure of the postwar world has shifted to the extent that a newer dispensation has been re-baptized with such terms as "diffuse bloc system". The new structure continues to feature two superpowers, at least until recently, each with its set of allies, but the opposing blocs have decentralized and the allies are not as faithful as before. This is particularly the case of the Soviet bloc. The Western bloc has fallen out on many matters especially economic ones, but its members have managed until now to patch things over. Moreover, their relative power positions have shifted, particularly in the economic sphere, more in the direction of equality. Of great importance in this respect is the European Community, an organization which has been quite successful in promoting the economic unification of the major countries of Western Europe. Japan's burgeoning economic power is also partially responsible for the relative decline of the United States, and the continuing protectionist policies of the Asian nation have been a cause for friction. The Soviet bloc has witnessed a structural reversal with dramatic social science results. The Sino-Soviet split should have removed any doubts on this score. The changes in Eastern Europe in 1989 are even more impressive. Most Western observers grant that a basic assumption of our structural approach applies to the Soviet Union: that Soviet bloc social sciences serves the interests of local elites. In fact, their disciplines have been fashioned so as to serve the local status quo, but to inspire radical change abroad. Moreover, their health and prosperity depend upon current politics, improving with a Gorbachev, but declining with a Stalin. Chinese experience is, if anything, more dramatic. The "gang of four" all but killed our disciplines, but they have been rehabilitated by contrary policies since 1978.

World social science has generally followed these overall structural changes. When the Chinese elite decided that development required more relations with the West, her students started to study in the West, mainly in the United States, in order to absorb American ideas, including social science. At the time of the Vietnam War German youth turned its back on American behavioralism which it had embraced so avidly. As we saw above, it turned to the critical, to the Frankfurter school. Italian sociology made the same leftward turn at about the same time. Our argument is not for a one to one relationship between structural shifts and social science shifts; the argument claims a general tendency only. Japan's language presents a special barrier to social science expansion -- despite her economic expansion. Our disciplines are closely linked to education, and the Japanese language is unique and difficult. American English had a much easier time of it -- its path having been prepared by the British Empire and by British hegemony.

Central to our predictions are the policies and the fate of third world countries, specifically their revolt against the first world. We include China with them, even if she has shifted her policies since 1978. Moreover, we take this revolt seriously, even if it seems to be waged mostly at the verbal level, in the halls of the United Nations and in the conferences of the Non-Aligned Movement. Their revolt is against the first world -- starting in the postwar period in the political sphere, then the economic was added. By now, all of the categories in our structures have been included, notably the social sciences. The revolt with respect to our disciplines takes the form of "indigenization", efforts to fashion the disciplines more in accord with local situations, ideas, and presuppositions. This process is the logical reaction, the follow-up, to the imposition of our disciplines by our featured structures. When the locals have the power, they strive to make the required changes. We have already noted that UNESCO's regional director for social science in Asia and the Pacific has asserted that the struggle to indigenize social science has become worldwide.[1] He explained that in Asia the process has taken the form of teaching in indigenous languages with local materials, local research, and the determination of priorities locally, plus the attempt to create indigenous paradigms. He reported "progress in all but the last field", notably in the substitution of Asian languages for Western colonial ones, with the result that the new generation of Asian social scientists is not able to communicate with what ideally would be Western colleagues. It should be emphasized that the conversion to local languages is part of the process of the democratization of the universities, instruction in Western languages being associated with the past emphasis upon elite education.

The third world indigenization of social science should have two general impacts upon social science paradigms -- 1) radicalization and 2) penetration with local cultures. The first assures a future for Marxism, and we hereby take issue with those who argue that Marxism is dead -- all that remains is to wipe up after it. There is no denying that Kremlin Marxism has suffered dramatically in its own sphere and that this has repercussions upon Western Marxism, especially in the first world. More than one president of the All Indian Sociological Conference has insisted that Indian sociology must come to terms with its past, i.e. with Indian culture. It must include "a little bit of obtuse philosophy" to provide a connection with this past.[2] The above reference is to cultural impacts, but as we saw above, Professor Varma made reference to this impact as well as radicalization in his criticism of Parsons' The Structure of Social Action. The Indian scholar charged that the analysis reflects American city values at the expense of those set forth in Buddhist -- Jain philosophy and that it rationalizes monopoly capitalism. He charged that it contains no program for action and research for third world scholars.

Our example of paradigm indigenization by the third world is dependency theory, a subject explicated in the previous chapter. It used humanistic Marxism in its analysis, a meta paradigm which should see more service in furtherance of rationalizing the third world revolt. We see a busy and bright future for this meta paradigm in service of this revolt. Note that our reference here is to humanistic Marxism, not to the Kremlin variety. We expect more innovations in paradigm constructions in furtherance of this revolt, more indigenization, to cater to the radical and to the indigenous. To serve the revolt, the new paradigm can be radical, i.e. upsetting to the local status quo, or merely nationalistic, perhaps in support of the local status quo, so long as it upsets the international status quo. Enough should be of the former to assure the future prosperity of Marxism. We see Marxism, but a different brand of it, continuing on in China, despite the current connection with the West. The recent suppression of the student movement there should demonstrate that there are limits to the Western connection and to Western influence. The same can be said for Gorbachev's opening to the West, but not necessarily for the case of Eastern Europe.

The big loser in the third world revolt should be functionalism and parallel sects in disciplines outside of sociology. It is logical that this be so, just as it was the big winner in the great American postwar extension. It is the essential loser again as Western Europe reaffirms its identify, as this region shakes off the inferiority of the early postwar period. The winners in this region have been humanistic Marxism and conservative paradigms of the voluntaristic type. But humanistic Marxism should suffer from the decline of Kremlin Marxism in Eastern Europe. Humanistic Marxism and conservative paradigms of the voluntaristic type have been growing in the United States, probably for reasons closer to the disciplines than to the structures featured in this essay. We took pains to point out above that we do not regard the social scientist as a prisoner of our structures -- rather we picture the practitioner as interacting with them. And we believe that the claims of the functionalist and his colleagues outside sociology to special scientific consideration will more and more be subjected to criticism. Functionalist promises have so exceeded performance that incredulity has resulted and should grow apace. But humanistic Marxism in the United States should suffer some fallout from the events in Eastern Europe. A similar disparity and process cloud the future of that other "scientific paradigm", Kremlin Marxism. Our prediction is for its decline as well, but not for its demise. The decline of functionalism should be attenuated by current American ties with, and influence in, China, the Soviet Union, and Eastern Europe. In contrast, Kremlin Marxism should decline without any countercurrent -- the victim of structural reverses and false claims to being scientific.

Our analysis leads to the further conclusion that the social sciences are not in the foreseeable future headed in the direction of global consensus -- they are not following the path of natural science. Like the universe itself, they are expanding and diversifying, a process all but assured by the third world revolt. A necessary, but not a sufficient, requisite for their unity is a unified world and one in which transactions take a horizontal, not a vertical, course. Such a future seems distant -- so at odds with the present, but it can be imagined, and one should struggle and pray for it. In the meantime, we must affirm that the social sciences are not shifting so as to act like natural science -- they are not maturing in this sense.

Our prediction for the immediate future thus identifies one loser, one winner, and two paradigms in between. The loser is Kremlin Marxism, battered at both the paradigmatic and the structural levels. Its credibility is now open to question, given officially confessed failures when applied in the second world. Its structural support there has eroded as well. Humanistic Marxism suffers from this debacle, detractors tending to tie the two Marxisms together. But we place humanistic Marxism in a gray area, because of its continued use in the third world. Moreover, it has just recently found a place in American academe and one of its favorite centers, Western Europe, is increasing in importance. We put functionalism in a gray area also. It has declined in its favorite location, the United States, just as this country has declined relative to Western Europe and Japan. But it should recover some ground where Marxism has retreated. The victors in our scheme for the immediate future are conservative paradigms of the voluntarist type. Given the narrowness of their initial position, their victory, however, is a modest one.

The overall probable results of this should be more openness, more reasoned self reflexion, more "maturity" to use the term coined above. And now we come to our response to the second general question of this section. The decline of Kremlin Marxism and the stagnation of functionalism should increase reasoned self-reflexion and openness. Both excommunicate, a process which tends to stop communications. We concentrate upon functionalism, the more widespread paradigm. We find a large measure of truth in the charge of Habermas that this sect divorces epistemology from the perceiving and judging subject and reduces it to the study of the methodology or the philosophy of science.[3] It tends to turn away from any serious and critical consideration of social scientists and their communities and to focus upon what it assures us are the technical rules of a unique scientific method. It does not use the methods of social science as a means of investigating social science, and, therefore, it has a folk view of the subject. In this sense, it does not take our subjects seriously, i.e. seriously the way social science employs the term. Its energies are too often expended on writing "cookbooks" on how to do social science.

Not all functionalists fit this mold, but so many do that the above account is worth the telling. This situation is exacerbated in the

United States by an inner directed, ethnocentric communications network, in which American social scientists restrict their messages to a great extent to each other. This closed system was analyzed in chapter IV. It contrasts with third world communications, which usually have a large window to the first world in addition to the national communications network. Third world social scientists are forced to be comparativists. The growth of third world social science would seem thus to have an overall opening, broadening impact. So should the decline of functionalism associated with the increasing power of Western Europe and Japan, and its replacement with conservative, non dogmatic paradigms or humanistic Marxism. These are more likely to engage in serious self-reflexion and not focus exclusively upon the compilation of what are touted as the rules of the scientific method. The communications systems of social science in Western Europe and Japan are more outgoing than the American one, and the further development and expansion of their disciplines should aid openness.

The decline of Kremlin Marxism should also aid openness. The social science communications network of the second world seems to be essentially a closed one, although with Gorbachev its tendency is toward openness. This sect shares with functionalism the rite to excommunicate "unscientific", i.e., competing sects, -- a rite which serves as a hallmark of this sect. Let the record show also that the second world social science has never been completely shut off from the first world and that it sometimes turns westward for inspiration. But a cloud hangs over our disciplines in the second world. Historically, they have refused to recognize and to legitimize Marxism -- and the latter has often responded in kind. Marxist states have at times (too often) gone all the way and suppressed our disciplines -- at least as academic enterprises. Research for practical, specific goals has usually been allowed. This activity motivated by the desire "to build socialism" or whatever has been considered to be too valuable to give up. The main reason for this suppression of our disciplines, however, is not so much traceable to an historic vendetta, rather it is explained better by political economy or structural analysis. The Marxist elites involved have feared that social science analysis would not support their policies or their tenure. Our prediction must include the possibility, actually the probability, that future Soviet type regimes will suppress our disciplines, at least temporarily.

An apparent contradiction which we have faced throughout the preparation   of   this   volume   is   that   between   the nationalism/ethnocentrism and the internationalism of social science. We have "solved" the contradiction between first world nationalism/ethnocentrism and the evident transnational nature of the disciplines by the use of international structures. The first world imposes its nationalism upon its paradigms, which are then used domestically and exported to the third world. The nationalism is that of the first world, even when the export is located in the third world. We have said that the third world, when able, will reject this nationalism through the process of indigenization. But indigenization itself is a nationalistic/ethnocentric process whereby locals put their marks on social science -- insist on local languages or personnel, determine research projects locally, or create paradigms in accord with local conditions, interests, or presuppositions. Our example of paradigmatic indigenization was dependency theory, a construction well grounded in Latin American ethnocentrism.

How can we resolve this apparent contradiction between our prediction for third world indigenization and a more open, future social science? Obviously, the problem is unsolvable if indigenization is seen as the last step in the process. If the process stops there, the world of social science winds up with our centers pointed inward -- each focusing upon its peculiar conditions, interests, and presuppositions, and each carrying on in its own langauge. But the contradiction can be resolved if this nationalistic/ethnocentrism is seen as a necessary and transitory stage during which the third world countries regain their authenticity so as later voluntarily to cooperate internationally, to cooperate on a horizontal basis. One is reminded of the process of <u>conscientizacao</u>, whereby Freire's illiterates gain the ability to express themselves authentically. Once so equipped and thus situated, the newly transformed are able to engage in cooperation on a horizontal basis. In this sense, indigenization results in a transitional and necessary period on the way to real international cooperation. First nationalism and self assertion all around, then voluntary horizontal cooperation, not imposition on a vertical basis.

This is the way that third world indigenization and manifestations of this phenomenon can be squared with future maturity. Of course, there is no guarantee that indigenization will progress to this desirable stage, rather than being cut short at the ethnocentric/nationalist stage. And this stoppage could easily happen. Cultural impacts from the many third world countries can have a stark ethnocentric impact. These countries are a diverse lot, and their cultural impacts could have a separating impact. Reference above was made to the use of indigenous languages in India in place of English, a displacement made in the interests of opening up and democratizing the university. The immediate impact, however, is to close down international communications, which it is true are carried on in the imposed, colonial language. The world must create a truly international language, voluntarily and by horizontal "negotiations". Merely to refer to this problem is to underline the difficulty of attaining "maturity".

We hope that our use of this latter term will not confuse the reader into thinking that we have accepted the social science myth. We use the term to mean more openness, more reasoned self reflexion. The epistemic value of natural science is at a level qualitatively superior to that of our disciplines; and we insist that no evidence has been presented to show how they can attain a metamorphosis such that they can make this qualitative leap. None has ever made the transition, and social science teaches us to be wary of such prophecies under such conditions.

We hope also that the reader realizes that we admire and cherish social science. Our many criticisms in this volume are of those who exaggerate what it can do and who are intolerant of opposing sects. Our disciplines have been a boon to humankind by offering an additional type of analysis, one which is influenced by logic and the empirical/historical record, even if it is not deaf to ideology and emotion as well. Its value to mankind has been established, and it should continue to make its contribution.

NOTES

1. Yogesh Atal, "The Call for Indigenization," International Social Science Journal, 32 (1981), 193.

2. Marshall B. Clinard and Joseph W. Elder, "Sociology in India: A Study in the Sociology of Knowledge," American Sociological Review, 30 (1965), 583.

3. Jurgen Habermas, Knowledge and Human Interests, (Boston: Beacon, 1971), 73.

INDEX

349